ROUTLEDGE I
COLONIALISM

Volume 7

BRITISH IMPERIALISM
AND AUSTRALIA, 1783–1833

BRITISH IMPERIALISM AND AUSTRALIA, 1783–1833

An Economic History of Australasia

BRIAN FITZPATRICK

Routledge
Taylor & Francis Group
LONDON AND NEW YORK

First published in 1939 by George Allen & Unwin Ltd

This edition first published in 2023
by Routledge
4 Park Square, Milton Park, Abingdon, Oxon OX14 4RN

and by Routledge
605 Third Avenue, New York, NY 10158

Routledge is an imprint of the Taylor & Francis Group, an informa business

© 1939

All rights reserved. No part of this book may be reprinted or reproduced or utilised in any form or by any electronic, mechanical, or other means, now known or hereafter invented, including photocopying and recording, or in any information storage or retrieval system, without permission in writing from the publishers.

Trademark notice: Product or corporate names may be trademarks or registered trademarks, and are used only for identification and explanation without intent to infringe.

British Library Cataloguing in Publication Data
A catalogue record for this book is available from the British Library

ISBN: 978-1-032-41054-8 (Set)
ISBN: 978-1-032-41793-6 (Volume 7) (hbk)
ISBN: 978-1-032-41804-9 (Volume 7) (pbk)
ISBN: 978-1-003-35976-0 (Volume 7) (ebk)

DOI: 10.4324/9781003359760

Publisher's Note
The publisher has gone to great lengths to ensure the quality of this reprint but points out that some imperfections in the original copies may be apparent.

Disclaimer
The publisher has made every effort to trace copyright holders and would welcome correspondence from those they have been unable to trace.

BRITISH IMPERIALISM
AND AUSTRALIA
1783–1833

*An Economic History
of Australasia*

by

BRIAN FITZPATRICK
M.A.
University of Melbourne

With an Introduction by

THE HONOURABLE
HERBERT VERE EVATT
M.A., LL.D.
*Justice of the High Court
of Australia*

LONDON
GEORGE ALLEN & UNWIN LTD
MUSEUM STREET

FIRST PUBLISHED IN 1939

All rights reserved
PRINTED IN GREAT BRITAIN BY
UNWIN BROTHERS LTD., WOKING

Without a large proportion of poverty, there could be no riches, since riches are the offspring of labour, while labour can result only from a state of poverty. Poverty is that state and condition in society where the individual has no surplus labour in store, or, in other words, no property or means of subsistence but what is derived from the constant exercise of industry in the various occupations of life. Poverty is therefore a most necessary and indispensable ingredient in society, without which nations and communities could not exist in a state of civilization.

PATRICK COLQUHOUN

A Treatise on Indigence (1806)

INTRODUCTION

The one hundred and fiftieth anniversary of the foundation by Captain Phillip of the penal settlement of New South Wales falls in 1938. Such occasions are commemorated in Australia, and many interpretations of the story of the "infant colony" are advanced. Some are interesting, but they are not all consistent. Words are reissued from the old Mint; we are told how a "great Imperial design" was conceived by such statesmen as Pitt and Dundas, and how the Government of England took pains to "lay the foundations of a great self-governing Dominion." The truth is otherwise. It is very fitting that at a time of commemoration it should be revealed so lucidly by Mr. Brian Fitzpatrick.

Though some of the story requires direct and almost brutal telling, it is all of absorbing interest. The picture has been somewhat blurred and distorted by a romanticism which curiously enough seems to infect most economic historians. Thus Professor Shann's treatment of the quarrels which led to the armed overthrow of Governor Bligh in 1808 by John Macarthur and the New South Wales Corps, interprets the contest as between, on the one hand, the principles of Communism or Socialism as administered by Bligh and, on the other hand, the principle of freedom of exchange and adolescent Capitalism as represented by Macarthur and Co.!

Mr. Brian Fitzpatrick has given an economic interpretation of Australia's early history the substantial truth of which I think he proves practically to demonstration. As is so often the case, the interpretation derives, not so much from the discovery of fresh evidence as from a brilliant use of material already available, but insufficiently appreciated. It is a profound mistake to regard the penal settlement of Australia as a closed economic system. At all material times, it was subject to the control of the English Government of the day. During the fifty years between 1783 and 1833 the character of that Government altered a little, but it always sought to protect what it considered to be the economic interests of the governing classes of England. Of course, the pressure of Whitehall upon the economy of Australia was not uniform or constant. Attention was often diverted during the struggle against Napoleon, and particularly when there was a fear of revolution at home. But Mr. Fitzpatrick lucidly expounds the English policy of despatching "redundant poor" to Australia, so that the British Government might be supposed to have declared:

> And none can doubt but that *their* emigration
> Has proved most useful to the British nation.

Mr. Fitzpatrick brings out a point which has many implications, and is little understood. The so-called "colony" long remained little more than an extended prison farm. The absence of conscious Imperial design is sufficiently evidenced by the complete failure of the English Government to make clear legal provision for the civil government of the colony. As a result, many of the important orders and regulations of the early Governors were alleged to have been invalid. What is not sufficiently grasped is that, as was pointed out by the great English law reformer Jeremy Bentham, the colony, despite its already considerable area, was merely an "uninspectable Bastille." Upon that view, the Governor had all the powers of a head gaoler. The seven-years "transport", whose sentence had expired, had little hope of ever returning to England. Perforce, he became a permanent settler or labourer, and so he was doomed to accept all the directions of the gaoler. Indeed, it was nearly forty years *ab urbe condita* before the civil and constitutional law of the colony was placed upon a satisfactory footing. So much for the "grand Imperial design" of the English Government.

One aspect of Australia's history is of great importance. In the absence of a representative legislature, a free Press, or a general right of public meeting, the Courts became the only forum for ventilating grievances. The Criminal Court long consisted of six military officers out of a tribunal of seven, a fact which often accentuated the struggles between the peasant proprietors and the Governors on the one hand and the opposing class of military officers, rum traffickers, and large proprietors. Thus the overthrow of Bligh was the culminating point to a bitter series of law suits.

A close analysis of all the legal contests between 1788 and 1820 has not yet been made. But, in my opinion, the result will be to corroborate the essential truth of Mr. Fitzpatrick's thesis.

The author does not make the error of regarding the economic interpretation as the sole solvent even of the greater incidents in the history of the colony. He remembers the warning of Engels that "history makes itself in such a way that the final result always arises from conflicts between many individual wills, of which each again has been made what it is by a host of particular conditions of life. Thus there are innumerable intersecting forces, an infinite series of parallelograms of forces which give rise to one resultant— the historical event." But the economic interpretation of Australian history is of fundamental importance, especially in relation to the use and appropriation of the lands of the colony, every acre of which originally belonged to the Crown. The partial adoption of the Wakefield scheme discouraged the poorer settler, shattered the labourer's hopes of land ownership, and deliberately manufactured a proletariat for the purpose of supporting and extending capitalist technique. This led to vital social and political changes which no doubt Mr. Fitzpatrick will expound in his next volume as brilliantly as he has done in this.

I am permitted to incorporate in this Introduction the following opinion of the well-known American author, Mr. C. Hartley Grattan, who has read Mr. Fitzpatrick's manuscript:

"Glimpses of what early Australian history really means have been available in the works of such writers as Sir Timothy

Coghlan, Edward Shann, W. K. Hancock, and S. H. Roberts, but readers of them have necessarily itched to restate the significance of the data they presented, in more illuminating terms. Mr. Fitzpatrick has achieved in large measure the restatement that writers of a socio-economic bent would, in their individual ways, desire to make. He has shown how Australian development was conditioned by the trend of events in Great Britain, and has indicated how those events were in some measure patterned in accordance with happenings in the European-American world. He has shown in detail what other writers have hinted at: how Australia's beginnings were conditioned by three revolutions, the American, the French, and the Industrial, of which the last-named was unquestionably the most important. But he has not been misled into making Australia a blank tablet on which the Imperial authorities wrote what they pleased. He shows, indeed, how they lagged behind Australian developments, how they continued to try to force Australia into one pattern —peasant proprietorship, the peasants to be the convicts whose sentences had been completed or remitted—while Australia itself was moving towards a quite different system of exploitation. Unlike some of his predecessors, he avoids all *ex post facto* wisdom as to what that system was to be, and makes clear that the first distortion of the Imperial policy was simply a straight-out exploitative monopoly, engineered by a small group of military men, which made no dynamic contribution to Australia's development. Only gradually, and apparently in strictest accord with the evidence, does he show the opposition taking up a dynamic position to which it was inevitable that the Imperial authorities and the capitalists of Great Britain would alike conform: the exploitation of one of the most baffling of continents on a pastoral basis. Into this pattern he fits the story of convictism in a fashion which at long last makes that great Australian *bête noire* a phenomenon intelligible in economic and social terms, thus rescuing it once and for all from the hands of gloomy moralists who see it as a 'birthstain' and insipid sentimentalists who try to make it a somewhat macabre romance.

To tease such a convincing and illuminating story out of the welter of conflicting evidence and interpretation in which it has so long been embedded is a fine accomplishment, and Mr. Fitzpatrick thoroughly deserves all the kudos it will unquestionably bring him."

H. V. EVATT

SYDNEY
April 1938

PREFACE

THIS book describes the early economic history of Australia, which towards the close of the period under review became an important field of British Imperial development. The original settlement was made at the instance of the British Government upon a base so simple that we may fail to notice it in the maze of events. Yet the base remained for at least thirty years the chief reason for the colony in the judgment of official England. In fact, every British Ministry, from Pitt's in 1787 to Castlereagh's (nominally Liverpool's) in 1820, regarded New South Wales as a convenient, because remote, territory to which "redundant poor," whether convicted or not, might be despatched—there, on arrival, or expiry of sentence, or pardon, to be settled on peasant plots; so they would remain, not again to overburden the newer, capitalist-farmer economy of Great Britain and Ireland.

The instructions which Whitehall gave to every Governor, from Phillip (1787–92) to Macquarie (1809–21), were arranged uniformly after this conception of a use for New South Wales, and the Governors themselves were all conscious of the function their administration was to execute. Phillip had been less than two years with his thousand in the utterly unknown land when, "in order to know in what time a man might be able to cultivate a sufficient quantity of ground to support himself, I . . . ordered a hut to be built in a good situation, an acre of ground to be cleared, and once turned up it was put into the possession of a very industrious convict, who was told that if he behaved well he should have thirty acres. This man had said the time for which he had been sentenced had expired, and wished to settle." This first expiree made a beginning, of the designed peasant Australia, in November 1789, three months after the terms had been elaborated upon which "the disposition of many people to emigrate" might be satisfied in New South Wales. Before the first free immigrants entered the harbour of Port Jackson, James Ruse, the pioneer farmer, was independent of Government rations, and in March–August 1791 Phillip felt justified in establishing forty-four expirees at Parramatta, on plots of thirty to fifty acres apiece, with a guarantee of Government support for eighteen months. The Governor, instructed by the Secretary of State for Home Affairs, Lord Grenville, laid in this manner the foundations of what was intended to become, not a prison merely, but a community of peasant proprietors, a breed of men that enclosure and game laws were driving out of the home economy.

Further evidence that such a construction was the express intention of Government was forthcoming when a new Secretary of State, Henry Dundas, stepped into Grenville's shoes at Whitehall, and Major Francis Grose, as Lieutenant-Governor, into Phillip's at Sydney. "I take this opportunity of giving you directions upon such points as require more immediately to be attended to," Dundas wrote; Grose was to insert into all land grants the anchor-clause, "And it is hereby provided that the said (grantee) shall reside upon and cultivate the lands hereby granted for and during five years from the date hereof . . . and any sale or conveyance of the said lands before the expiration of the said five years shall be void. . . ." Similar assistance, upon similar conditions, had been available since 1789 to approved free emigrants, the earliest of whom, passages paid by Government, arrived at Port Jackson in January 1793.

The establishment of a peasant economy in New South Wales—or the establishment of the colony as a prison farm and a ground for small owners whom changed conditions at home had disinherited—was thus attempted with the utmost promptitude consistent with the difficulties of settlement on virgin soil half a world away from the imperial architects. Before Phillip left England he was empowered to settle ex-convicts; soon after his arrival he was empowered to settle poor freemen.

Then came the war with revolutionary France.

War broke out within a few weeks of the arrival at Port Jackson of five emigrant families in the *Bellona*, by which time about five thousand convicts had been removed to New South Wales from Britain. Few more assisted or other emigrants would make the long passage until the short spell of peace, in 1802–3, in a series of wars which engrossed the Secretaries of State from 1793 to 1815; and it would be twelve years from the outbreak of war before as many more convicts were landed in New South Wales as had been sent in half that time prior to 1793. So the war factor, accidental as far as the colonial scheme was concerned, made very early a serious modification of the scheme, and that unlooked-for circumstance of war was responsible for some developments, in the now neglected settlement, which altered the pattern from the original. For a small body of officers, holding little communication with Whitehall, and being scarcely subject to effective instruction from Ministers who were more concerned with coalitions than with convicts, was able to exploit Phillip's smallholders and persons under sentence so as to establish quickly a vested interest of large owners. Again, the intermittent flow of transported convicts in this war-time—in one year a single man, in the next year a thousand—made difficult the task of colonial administration after the set pattern, because the number of expirees due for land grants and other assistance, the number of convicts available for public undertakings, and the number of persons to be fed from the public store, alike varied widely from year to year, from Governor to Governor. In short, the administrative difficulty, coupled with the persistence of an officers' movement to "enclose" the new struggling peasantry, gave the colonial scene a character never contemplated when Pitt and Sydney, in thin times of peace, accepted New South Wales as an answer to the question, how to clear the British gaols and hulks of the thousands of "seven-years" men who had been sentenced under the most savage penal code in the civilized world, and how to clear the parishes of the poor.

The Imperial Government, however, ignored such complications as the war, and the peculiar twist it was giving to the line of development of New South Wales. When a Secretary of State or an under-secretary gave an hour's thought to the colony, he consulted the formula of 1787–89. An economy of monopoly was fashioned in New South Wales during the first years of war, later a beginning was made of a system of production with which a system of smallholding farmers would be incompatible; but Government clung to its original project, that must be resumed after the war. Accordingly Hunter, King, Bligh, or Macquarie, taking each his turn as Governor (respectively in 1795, 1799, 1806, 1809), would read a version of the instructions given Phillip long before, and find little inkling there of an appreciation that New South Wales might have changed in eight, twelve, twenty years of settlement. Brisbane's instructions of 1821 would still include the peasant formula. Whatever changes the wars had wrought in English society, the demand from England remained insistent that the colony should not cost much; should absorb shiploads of convicts sent as opportunity offered; be the scene of perfect administrative harmony, though the Governor have no executive assistants save those whose vested interest was opposed to Government's; create a public agriculture, though Whitehall omit to send ploughs or trained farm managers; settle effectively time-expired and pardoned convicts, though an officers' ring close to them the only colonial market, the store of the Commissary.

This strange insistence is the thread which joins Hunter's Administration, from 1795, and Macquarie's, until 1821. Officially nothing happened in New South Wales during the war: even the deposition of a Governor by his garrison made no great noise in Europe, where the guns spoke. A spasmodic irritability was almost all the Imperial Government vouchsafed in respect of the insignificant colony. It recalled Hunter for failure in his set task of establishing a peasantry while placating his rich officers who could not afford a peasantry; recalled King for accomplishing the establishment while alienating the officers; recalled Bligh for failure more spectacular than Hunter's; recalled Macquarie for repeating King's history on a grander scale after the war. Such an awful consistency, on the part of the British policy for New South Wales, during thirty-three years, is the lamp by which the economic as well as the political history of the times must be read. To examine the early period of New South Wales settlement—this first generation of Australian society—in the imagined light of "new economic policies," or in terms of this Governor who "favoured the emancipists," that Governor who "encouraged free settlers," can scarcely be more instructive than reading in the dark. What is really relevant is that every Governor was required to maintain a prison and plant a peasantry, and that this could not be done because of the development of a special local interest during the period of uncontrolled military rule 1793-95. There is the common economic contradiction of New South Wales administration from 1795 to 1821, when Governors with antediluvian commissions strove with a flood which was not provided for in the Estimates.

The creation of an officers' monopoly of trade and production was the principal internal factor of difficulty, as the uneven provision of transported convicts was the principal factor of difficulty from outside. Between four and five thousand transports were landed during Phillip's five years in office, only as many hundreds in nearly three years of officers' rule after him, between four and five thousand over Hunter's and King's terms totalling ten years, only a few more than a thousand during Bligh's administration and a second period of officers' rule: a total of four years. In sum, about ten thousand convicts survived the voyage, between 1787 and 1809. Then in Macquarie's dozen years nearly twenty-two thousand convicts were thrown upon a colony again unfitted for Whitehall's uses by two years of uncontrolled administration by the officer-monopolists. Of these transports, nineteen thousand, at the rate of two thousand five hundred a year, were landed between 1814, when the first peace with the Emperor Napoleon was made, and 1821.

An unparalleled responsibility was thrust in this way upon the Governor, who had to cope with a large convict population and a mounting expiree class in an environment which had been developed in scarcely any respect, at any rate for public purposes, since 1805. This fact, together with the lately augmented largeholder interest and the British Government's continuance of its original policy for New South Wales, was the ruling circumstance of Macquarie's much misunderstood policies. His success at the expense of the largeholders was enough to win his recall. But after him Brisbane, who would take the first steps (again under English instructions) towards a different place for the colony in the imperial scheme, was assisted by Whitehall's prudential stoppage of convict transportation; only seventeen hundred convicts arrived in 1822-23, at a rate one-third of the annual average of the previous eight years of Macquarie's government, and it was not until 1833 that the convict arrivals in any year exceeded Macquarie's total in 1820 of more than three thousand five hundred.

Enquiry as to why the Imperial Government departed in the early eighteen-twenties from its traditional prison-and-peasant policy for New South Wales, and what the new policy was, must be directed to the changed condition of England. New impulses were agitating British economy now: an industrial proletariat was rioting, and wrecking machinery; peace had involved the reduction of the volume of employment in farming and industry, and had cut the entrepreneur's profit so that he was disinclined to continue paying the heavy poor rate demanded for the support of hundreds of thousands of unemployed workers; at the same time a war-time accumulation of capital for investment sought fields overseas—and New South Wales was envisaged as a profitable field, now that John Macarthur had proved the adaptability of the country for sheep-raising with a view of producing fine wool. British statesmanship responded, with the advent of Canning, Huskisson, Peel, and Goderich to Liverpool's Ministry, to such radically altered needs of British and British Imperial economy; and policies for New South Wales of the emigration thither of persons of capital, the chartering of great enterprises for colonial development, and—in the colony—the sale in addition to the grant of land, and attempts to provide a stable currency, were some forms which the response took.

After that, the economic story of Australia for awhile gives an odd impression of the British Government's striving to preserve the old convenience of its "receptacle for offenders" simultaneously with the concession of colonial room for English capital and population expansion. Again the Governors were required to follow formulae; again local developments hindered the perfect performance of experiments in meeting English needs; and again Governors would in turn receive pained letters of recall—for overmuch zeal in the execution of their instructions.

The principal local development—the undeniability, by the eighteen-thirties, of the claim that great tracts in Australia were peculiarly valuable for pastoral use—displaced for a time in primacy immediate English needs as the determinant of the colonial economy, and led to further settlement in defiance of Government. Then, in the 'thirties and 'forties, English policy sought again, with a large measure of success, to assist the spontaneous colonial movement of expansion by providing at once the required capital, and, in the persons of tens of thousands of paupers, the necessary labour. Convict transportation to New South Wales was at length abandoned when, and only when, it had become clear that capital export and pauper emigration to Australia would be the most profitable form which English interest could take. (In after times, similarly, transportation was discontinued to all eastern Australia—and in England a Penal Servitude Act was passed to house felons at home—when, and only when, the discovery of gold in large quantities made uneconomic the further penal use of even Tasmania.)

The governing factor must not be lost sight of, that an imperial theory discarded since the American reverse was again in acceptation: again men believed that colonies might yield dividends, and the more flexible British policy towards Australia is simply an instance of a common-sense determination to make colonization pay. The history of the period shows that the British Government was seldom dilatory in grasping an opportunity of using its colony. At most stages, Government was prompt in taking the cue of need. For example, Addington's Ministry decided within a few months of the conclusion of peace with France in 1802 to establish with convicts and free emigrants sent direct from England a settlement at Port Phillip; and the only large parties of assisted emigrants to leave Britain between the original outbreak of war in 1793 and the final settlement of peace in 1814–15 left about the time of armistice 1802–3. Similarly with Castlereagh. By 1817 he had a quarter of a million discharged sailors and soldiers on his hands—and neglected New South Wales was recalled again, when the Liverpool Government advised the Governor of its wish that land be granted, on stated terms, to retired officers and discharged non-commissioned officers and men, who in the sequel were shipped in numbers to Sydney. Again, post-war reaction and the riotous protest of the distressed masses was approaching a culmination in the Peterloo massacre when J. T. Bigge was commissioned to enquire into the capacity of New South Wales as a convict receptacle. The peace of 1814–15 had at some points the immediate effect of cancelling wartime gains. Thus most of the occupied Dutch colonial territories had to be returned (which involved a restriction of the East India Company's field), and so attempts were made in 1824–27 to win back the Indies trade by colonizing in North Australia. After the peace, the French were free again to examine Australia with a view of colonization, and this realization spurred the British Government into sponsoring settlement of convicts and freemen on the southern and western coasts of the continent.

Such examples are not sifted from a mass of contrary evidence; it is safe to say that this epoch of British imperialism was distinguished no less than other imperial epochs by a constant effort to satisfy in the colonies domestic social and economic needs. At the beginning of November 1830, before Grey's Whig Ministry was formed, the Tory Secretary of State was instructing the New South Wales Government to make land grants to encourage the immigration of special classes of small freemen; but the Whigs, when they came to office later in the month, found the English agricultural counties in turmoil, and quickly, by the New Year, the incoming Secretary of State completed a plan for New South Wales by which masses of farm labourers would be received there as wage-earners bound by indenture or debt.

When we look farther into the eighteen-thirties, and into the 'forties, we find imperialism slower to adapt itself to the shift of emphasis from need to need. But those were years of the parturition of an Australian pastoral economy, and it is not surprising that Ministers faltered now in their task of reconciling the diverse interests of England in Australia—termini of convict transportation as some of the colonial settlements were; termini of emigration as they were becoming; fields for large investment as they were increasingly because of the rapid development of their industry of wool production.

Much of the economic history of Australia during the Crown Colonial period is however an account of sudden rapid adjustments of Australian economy attempted at Whitehall with scant or secondary reference to the colonies themselves. That persistent factor once understood, there need be little difficulty in following the details of this history of the first half-century of Australian economic evolution. What may be inferred easily from the sketch given is a necessity of taking stock periodically of contemporary conditions in

Great Britain, as an integral part of an economic assessment of Great Britain's Crown Colonies in Australia. For the British Isles were the starting-point of almost all of those who, voluntarily or involuntarily, reached an Australian destination at this period; few spontaneous local developments of economic significance went far without capital encouragement from Great Britain: step by step, far into the nineteenth century, British needs of expansion marched towards satisfaction with the advance of Australian economy—which in general they promoted.

Hence an arrangement of topics which may seem unusual, is made in the present study. Australia's Crown Colonial story, as indeed all its history, is utterly unintelligible in isolation, and no Australian history contemplates its fundamental subject-matter until the originating circumstances are well understood. It will be realized, then, that the present history of the interrelation of British and Australian economy took shape from researches into sources that, in many instances, had not been investigated by authors dealing with Australian economic history. Because of this, it seemed desirable to make numerous references, in footnotes to the text. However, the mass of material before the serious student of Australia is classifiable in simple terms. Two accomplished historians have, fortunately, made intelligible the situations in which the processes of Australian economic evolution were originated. The translated parts of the late Professor Élie Halévy's great work on nineteenth century society, *A History of the English People*, and *Histoire du peuple anglais au XIXe siècle, iii, de la crise du Reform Bill à l'avènement de Sir Robert Peel (1830–41)* (Paris, Hachette, 1923), and Professor D. G. Barnes's *A History of the English Corn Laws, 1660–1846* (London, Routledge, 1930) are scholarly analyses of the motives of British expansion. Much Australian history is a series of incidents of the imperial development to which those motives led; so that the task of the Australian historian is the less onerous for the guidance which Halévy and Barnes afford through the highways and byways of English society in the late eighteenth and early nineteenth centuries. The most valuable sources of information in the field itself are:

1. The *Annual Register* for the years 1783–1832, giving a panorama and some detailed descriptions of English life as seen by contemporary observers.
2. Hansard's *Parliamentary History* and the several series of *Parliamentary Debates* which succeeded it, over the same period.
3. *Sessional Papers of the House of Lords* and *Miscellaneous Parliamentary Papers*, containing reports from parliamentary select comittees and minutes of evidence given before them.
4. *Statutes of the United Kingdom of Great Britain and Ireland*, especially 1770–1834.
5. *Edinburgh Review* (published quarterly) for the period 1802–32: a useful guide to contemporary writings on social, political, and economic matters, and itself a well-reasoned commentary from a Whig point of view.
6. *Gentleman's Magazine* (published monthly) for 1783–1832: a useful record, with commentary from a Tory point of view.
7. *Weekly Political Register* of William Cobbett: comprising in 88 volumes from January 1802 to June 1835 a Radical criticism of "Condition of England" phenomena.

There is no such introduction to the Australian sources as Halévy and Barnes provide for the English sources. The indispensable material is to be found in:

8. *Historical Records of Australia*, series I, vol. i–xvi.
9. *Historical Records of Australia*, series III, vols. i–vi.
10. *Sydney Gazette*, 1803–32.
11. *Public Statutes of New South Wales*, 1824–37.
12. *The Acts of the Lieutenant-Governor and Council of Van Diemen's Land* (1840).

The introductory essays provided by the editor of the *Historical Records of Australia*, Frederick Watson, in each volume, are not as a rule concerned with documents that are likely to interest the student of economic history. But the two volumes of the *History of New South Wales from the Records*, especially Volume I by G. B. Barton (Sydney, Government Printer, 1889), are in general a reliable introduction to the first half dozen years of settlement. Dr. Eris O'Brien's interesting views in *The Foundations of Australia* (London, Sheed and Ward, 1937) could not be studied for the purposes of the present volume, which was completed before Dr. O'Brien's book appeared.

BRIAN FITZPATRICK

MELBOURNE
April 1938

ACKNOWLEDGMENTS

THE writer acknowledges a heavy debt to his friends for their help in his researches and revision. Kathleen Fitzpatrick, M.A. (Oxon), lecturer in modern history in the University of Melbourne, made available notes upon her research into questions of emigration to Australia. (After the completion of this work Dr. R. B. Madgwick's *Immigration into Eastern Australia, 1788–1851*, appeared.) The lecturer and tutor in economic history in the University of Melbourne, Herbert Burton, M.A. (Oxon), and Dorothy Davies, B.A., made many valuable suggestions when the MS. was being prepared and revised. Substantial changes were made in the treatment after Miss Davies had given the draft close critical examination. Patrick Martin Stanley drew attention to much of the fundamental stuff of this history, and the writer is appreciative of the various services generously given by C. Hartley Grattan, Mr. Justice Evatt, Professor R. M. Crawford, and Miss T. Lucas, B.A.

The University of Melbourne, through the Harbison-Higinbotham Trust and otherwise, helped to make publication possible, and the task of research was lightened by the co-operation of the staffs of the Public Library of Victoria, the Mitchell Library, Sydney, and the Public Library of New South Wales.

CONTENTS

CHAPTER	PAGE
INTRODUCTION *by The Honourable Herbert Vere Evatt,* M.A., LL.D.	7
PREFACE	13
ACKNOWLDGEMENTS	25

1. THE GENESIS OF AUSTRALIAN SETTLEMENT 29
    - (a) *Australia and the American Revolution*
    - (b) *The British Parliamentary System*
    - (c) *The Agricultural Revolution in England*
    - (d) *English Methods of Poor Relief*
    - (e) *Early Social Consequences of the Industrial Revolution. First Period of "Impaired Liberty"*
    - (f) *The English Population*
    - *Conclusion*

2. FIRST PHASE OF THE NEW SOUTH WALES PENAL SETTLEMENT 69
    - (a) *Crime and Punishment in Great Britain* circa *1788*
    - (b) *A Prison Farm Economy in New South Wales, 1788–92*

3. AN ECONOMY OF MONOPOLY IN NEW SOUTH WALES FROM 1793 92
    - (a) *Establishment of a Squirearchy, 1793–1800*
    - (b) *Re-establishment of a Peasantry, 1801–4*
    - (c) *Assisted and "Special" Emigration, 1793–1806*
    - *Appendices*
        - A. *Early Currency of New South Wales*
        - B. *Observed Resources of Early New South Wales*

4. THE DISTURBED ECONOMY OF POST-WAR ENGLAND 151
    - (a) *English Agriculture to 1817*
    - (b) *Contemporary British Manufactures, and Labour Conditions*
    - (c) *Contemporary British Public Finance and Banking*
    - (d) *Radicalism and Rioting, 1816–17*
    - (e) *Second Period of "Impaired Liberty," 1817*
    - (f) *British Foreign Policy and the Vienna Settlement of Europe, 1814–15*
    - (g) *Third Period of "Impaired Liberty," 1819*
    - *Conclusion*

CHAPTER	PAGE
5. TRANSITION TO A FREE ECONOMY IN NEW SOUTH WALES, TO 1821	189

   (a) Sheepbreeding for Fine Wool
   (b) Economic Consequences of Resumed Transportation
       Appendix
          Government Accounts

6. THE POST-WAR EXPANSION OF ENGLAND, AND FURTHER COLONIZATION IN AUSTRALIA	233

   (a) British Foreign Policy and European Constitutionalism, from 1823
   (b) British Trade and the Navigation Laws
   (c) The Penal Code and Transportation
   (d) "Combinations of Workmen"
   (e) Economic Crisis, 1825
   (f) Emigration, and Van Diemen's Land, North Australia, Western port, and the Swan River Settlement
   (g) Slavery in British Colonies
   (h) British Foreign Policy and British Trade, 1826

7. IMPORTATION OF CAPITAL INTO AUSTRALIA FROM circa 1822	293

   (a) Land and Emigration Policies, 1822–31
   (b) The Dollar System, 1822–5 and Economic Crisis, 1826
   (c) Reorganization on Sterling, from 1826

8. PAUPER EMIGRATION TO NEW SOUTH WALES FROM 1831	344

   (a) Parliamentary Representation, 1832
   (b) Condition of the Working Classes
   (c) The New Poor Law, 1834
   (d) Emigration

CONCLUSION. A PASTORAL ECONOMY IN NEW SOUTH WALES	368
TABLE A Some Acts of Parliament, 1707–1834	377
TABLE B Some Government Orders, etc., 1797–1834	380
BIBLIOGRAPHY	382
INDEX	387

Chapter 1

THE GENESIS OF AUSTRALIAN SETTLEMENT

(a) *Australia and the American Revolution*
(b) *The British Parliamentary System*
(c) *The Agricultural Revolution in England*
(d) *English Methods of Poor Relief*
(e) *Early Social Consequences of the Industrial Revolution. First Period of "Impaired Liberty"*
(f) *The English Population*
  Conclusion

AUSTRALIAN settlement began when Captain Arthur Phillip, Royal Navy, landed on the coast of New South Wales or New Holland, in January 1788, to establish a penal colony comprising, at first, more than 700 British male and female convicts and 200 marines. William Pitt led the Tory Government which gave Phillip his instructions under George III's commission, and Lord Sydney, as Home Secretary, was the minister immediately responsible for the trial of New South Wales, then inhabited by sparse nomad tribes, as a repository of British felons.

The venture was made at this particular time because the necessity had become urgent of disposing of a great accumulation of long-term prisoners (Edmund Burke said in 1785 that 100,000 lay in British gaols and prison-hulks under sentence of transportation). Until lately the disposal of these people would have presented no difficulty; but recently most of the British colonies in North America, including those which had received transported felons, had set up an independent United States Government. Of the neighbouring colonies which retained the British connection Quebec and desolate Nova Scotia were proved unsuitable by trial. Gambia in West Africa was surveyed for the purpose of the transportation system, but though the expenses of the voyage thither were less than those entailed by six or eight months' voyage to New South Wales, a humanitarian opinion abhorred the horrors of the African terminus and the Crown's investigators advised against its use. New South Wales, claimed for England by Captain James Cook in 1770 in the course of a voyage of discovery, was at last decided upon in the alternative to the Gambia jungle.

At the time of Phillip's initial settlement in Australia, the population of Great Britain was scarcely nine millions, and that of Ireland between four and five millions, and these small communities were already undergoing their early experience of a vast economic and social change. For the reign of George III, which had begun in 1760 and would persist until 1820, saw a transformation of English life. During his sixty years' reign the English peasantry was eliminated by enclosure of common lands and the application of large-farming; then much of the rural mass thus proletarianized was absorbed into machine industry made practicable by recent mechanical inventions. For example, in the England that Phillip left the first steampower cotton mill had lately been built (1785); within twenty years past the inventions of Richard Arkwright and Samuel Crompton had heralded the supersession of domestic manufacture by factory processes, and Arkwright had introduced on his own account the practice of employing child labour in quantity; Benjamin Huntsman and Henry Cort had elaborated during the last generation their formulae for casting and puddling iron.

Even without such means as these events portended, Britain was already great among European States. At this epoch those nations were most powerful which commanded the richest colonial fruits of native cultivation, or which controlled major territories in Europe; and Great Britain and France were settled competitors for leadership in the maritime race of the first group. Portugal, Spain, and Holland had been subordinated during the seventeenth and eighteenth centuries by the widely ranging colonizing and merchandising of these two. The chief Powers of the second group were Austria above all, Prussia, the most powerful and populous of the other German States, and the huge Russian Empire. The Ottoman Empire of the Turks was already losing grip on its great dominions in Europe under pressure from the Central Powers and Russia. Indeed, in these years immediately preceding the French Revolution of 1789–91 their rivalry for Eastern European prizes was the typical stamp of the contemporary international system—"if that can be called a system," writes the English historian of the French Revolution,[1] "which rested on no principle of action and set no limits to aggression on the weak except those dictated by the fears or jealousies of neighbours and rivals." The maritime Powers, for the rest, competed for the right to exploit backward areas beyond Europe—the West Indies and the East, America and India—continuing it seemed incessantly their struggle of more than two centuries' duration. But British power had set back the French in America and India. The old mercantile society of England was at the zenith of its wealth and influence, on the eve of the several revolutions which were going on while Australian settlement was projected or made.

Several revolutions, for additional changes, quite other than these readjustments within the domestic and imperial constitutions of England, were in train in Captain Phillip's world; and indeed not two revolutions—the American and Industrial Revolutions—but at least three, took place immediately before or during the colonization of Australia. The French Revolution is the third which we have to remark. "You, who have not exactly lived during the times of the French Revolution," a Scottish professor[2] would say to his students forty years later, "cannot imagine how long and how deeply it affected

---

[1] *The Revolutionary and Napoleonic Era, 1789-1815*, by J. H. Rose, p. 16; Cambridge University Press, 1894.

[2] Cit. *Essays on the Administration of Great Britain from 1783 to 1830*, by Sir George Lewis, p. 419; London, Longmans, 1864.

the thoughts, the feelings, and the interests of every human being, without any exception, that then existed in the civilized world." For while Phillip's convicts felled eucalyptus trees, far away in New Holland, heterodox claims were being propounded in France, where, as in England, landed property maintained the State for its protection. The French State was divesting itself of its ancient character, and radical philosophers of the mass were asserting:[1] "Every man has a right to the land . . . he gains it by labour, and his share ought to be limited by the rights of his equals. . . . All should have something, none too much."

In fact three far-reaching sets of circumstances, having origin or repercussion in England, might bring influence to bear upon the society of British outcasts which was being made in Australia: revolution in America, revolution in France, in England an agricultural and an industrial revolution.

The established power in England opposed all three. But all three would prove irresistible, and we may find that the truth of their incidence upon Australia is that settlement was only made there because of the success of the American Revolution, only perpetuated because of the accomplishment of a change of British economy, and only transmuted, at last, into a democratic society because the success of the French Revolution promoted eagerness among all European peoples for the institutions of a political philosophy which the British State rejected.

But first we need to consider those early circumstances which made an Australian community upon which those potent influences, the Agricultural-Industrial and French Revolutions, could operate: a community whose economy would be adapted to the requirements of the one, and whose political forms would be derived, if only in part and indirectly, from the inspiration of the other.

[1] *Cit. Select Documents Illustrative of the History of the French Revolution*, ed. L. G. Wickham Legg, vol. i, pp. 282, 283; Oxford, Clarendon Press, 1905.

THE GENESIS OF AUSTRALIAN SETTLEMENT

(a) *Australia and the American Revolution*

Before the British Government found serviceable Cook's survey of the eastern coast of the Australian continent, Britain's old colonial empire comprised India for economic exploitation and world trade, and North America for similar purposes and for the putting away of dissident minorities, political, religious, and criminal. The State had rarely founded a colony; most colonizing had been promoted by merchant adventurers. The Crown however had used the southern colonies of North America as a resort for transported criminals; felons had been shipped there for most of the period 1678–1775.[1] On the eve of the American Declaration of Independence five hundred "transports" a year were being sent.[2]

Now the system of expatriating convicted offenders had already the sanction of a considerable history. Portugal had used its colony of Brazil for the purpose from early in the sixteenth century; Jacques Cartier had taken French convicts to Canada in 1540; in 1638 the Swedish Government had colonized Delaware in North America with felons; late in the eighteenth century the dying power of Spain still troubled its dependencies in South America with offenders against the law; and England had sent scores of thousands and perhaps hundreds of thousands to the New World in prison-ships since a seventeenth century Act (18 Charles II, cap. 3) had "empowered the judges to exile for life the moss-troopers of Cumberland and Northumberland to any of His Majesty's possessions in America."[3] But though England had practised

---

[1] *Report of the Select Committee of the House of Commons on Transportation*, 1838, p. iii; *Sessional Papers of the House of Lords*, 1837–38, vol. xxxvi.

[2] Vide *A Short History of British Colonial Policy, 1606–1909*, by H. E. Egerton, p. 226; London, Methuen, 9th ed., revised by A. P. Newton, 1932. But parliamentary statistics of the period give a figure nearly double—an average of nine hundred and sixty transports a year, 1769–76; *House of Commons List, cit. Account of the Principal Lazarettos in Europe*, by John Howard, pp. 220, 246; London, Johnson, Dilly & Cadell, 1791.

[3] *Report of the Transportation Committee*, p. iii.

the system on a grand scale she had not practised it in freedom from criticism. In Elizabeth's time—an Act of 1597 made "exile" a punishment—Francis Bacon had written in his *Essay on Plantation*: "It is a shameful and unblessed thing to take the scum of people, and wicked, condemned men, to be the people with whom you plant." Nearly two centuries later a protest came from the convicts' wide gaolyard in America. A free colonist wrote in the *Independent Reflector*, a New York periodical:[1] "These very (transportation) laws, though otherwise designed, have turned out in the end the most effectual expedients which the art of man could have contrived, to prevent the settlement of these remote parts of the King's dominions. They have actually taken away almost every encouragment to so laudable a design."

As concerned America, however, questions of the morality or expediency of tranportation were emptied of content when the colonies there, except Canada, made war against the Crown from 1775 to 1783, to secure recognition as the independent United States of America, under the Treaty of Versailles 1783. At this date and for some time after, we are told, a general disillusionment repelled effective English opinion from all forms of colonial experiment. This disillusionment was deeper seated than any single objection to convict-colonization as immoral or impolitic or uneconomic; it gathered strength from such arguments and a wounded pride. India and the Spice Islands, administered by a great company, should continue to render profit to British shipowners and traders; the West Indian planters might by all means continue to use slaves for profitable sugar-production; but "in most Englishmen's minds the result of the (American) Revolution had produced a complex of ideas antagonistic to further colonial enterprise. Adam Smith and Lord Sheffield, from their different platforms, proclaimed that colonies did not pay. What then, asked the business man, could be the use of them? . . . Scarcely anybody

[1] Cit. *History of New South Wales from the Records*, by G. B. Barton, vol. i, pp. 556 *et seq.*; New South Wales Government Printer, 1889.

dreamed that new British colonies would ever replace the old."[1] And perhaps a distaste for further colonization was not confined to England, among the maritime Powers, during the generation of imperial standstill after the American Revolutionary War. For instance, a society founded in France in 1800 to promote exploitation of the natural riches of Africa soon broke up, though Denys de Montfort could paint in the *Philosophical Magazine* an attractive picture of Africa's accessible wealth and an eagerness in the natives to cull it for the European. "There exists," he wrote,[2] "no country in the world so susceptible of general cultivation. . . . The plants of India, Europe, America, and Australasia, or the fifth portion of the globe, will flower there in perpetual spring. . . . The Negroes, whose respect for the Whites is extreme, notwithstanding what they have suffered from them, will cheerfully give up their fields to be cultivated by us."

After the American loss the impulse of the old imperialism seemed dead, in England at any rate. It was only the urgency of the question of convict-accommodation which now induced a renewal of old-system imperialism, in the case of Australia, as the nineteenth century's new wind rose. Very soon after the convict-traffic with America was closed by the revolt of the colonies, an Act of 1776 (16 George III, cap. 43) empowered the British Government to confine sentenced persons in hulks. But humanitarians like Howard deplored the conditions of prisoners rotting experimentally in the marshes, and his *State of the Prisons in England and Wales*, which was published in 1777, the year after the enactment of the Hulks Act, had much to do with the preparation of a Penitentary Act (19 George III, cap. 74) requiring serious offenders to be confined in large institutions, in Great Britain itself, there to be kept at useful employment for their own redemption and society's gain. John Howard was one of the supervisors appointed to put the

---

[1] *The American Revolution and the British Empire*, by R. Coupland, pp. 251, 252; London, Longmans, 1930.

[2] *Cit. Annual Register*, 1815, pp. 539 *et seq.*

Act into effect; but no progress was made. In the event, English criminals would wait two-thirds of a century longer for their penitentiaries. For the time being, the old gaols and the hulks continued to receive sentenced persons—and liberal indignation mounted higher as the consequences became evident. "There is a house in London," Burke said terribly in the Commons,[1] "which consists at this time of just five hundred and fifty-eight members. I do not mean the House of Commons, though the number is alike in both, but the gaol of Newgate."

And if Newgate[2] was intolerably overcrowded, in that year of 1785, the alternative which threatened the inmates was no less fearful. Burke said (no doubt hyperbolically) that 100,000 persons awaited transportation to Gambia. "The gates of hell are there open day and night to receive the victims of the law." A Commons committee had enquired into the prison situation, and a man-o'-war's captain had been sent to the African coast, to seek a means of disposing of the condemned percentage of the British peoples. Two Orders in Council of December 6, 1786, announced the answer, and next year an Act (27 George III, c. 2) appointed "the eastern coast of New South Wales to be 'the place to which certain offenders . . . should be transported.'"

It came about in this wise that England's penal problem was solved tentatively (*vide* Chapter 2 (*a*) *infra*) after the despatch

---

[1] *Parliamentary History*, 1785, vol. xxv, col. 391.

[2] Newgate Gaol had a history of nearly seven hundred years before its demolition in 1902. The pressure on it and British gaols generally, after the American loss, was baldly stated in the King's Speech at the opening of Parliament in 1787 (*Parliamentary History*, xxvi, col. 211): "A plan has been formed by my directions for the transporting of a number of convicts, in order to remove the inconvenience which arose from the crowded state of the gaols in different parts of the kingdom." Professor Ernest Scott administers (*Cambridge History of the British Empire*, p. 91; Cambridge University Press, 1933) a sufficient rebuke to writers who "have expressed regret that some worthier motive did not inspire the settlement of Australia." He points out that, probably, only the actual motive could have transformed into "acquisitive desire" two centuries' indifference to Australia.

to New South Wales of Captain Phillip's first fleet, which sailed from Portsmouth in the spring of 1787. New South Wales would be another, larger Newgate.[1] Or, abuses which had troubled the conscience of 1785 would be removed along half the earth's circumference to a point too remote for the English imagination easily to compass. (It is not without interest that among those few members of the House of Commons who drew attention to the plight of prisoners in the hulks was Lord Beauchamp[2], for more than a century later another Lord Beauchamp, arriving in New South Wales as Governor, would affront contemporary Colonial opinion by reference to the community's "birthstain"—which that earlier nobleman had helped to impose.)

A cognate subject which agitated the Commons at this time was the policing of London, and in the debates[3] on the London and Westminster Police Bill which was introduced by the Solicitor-General, Archibald Macdonald, on June 23, 1785, we are given alike a vivid picture of the England in which the theft of five shillings from a till was punishable by death and, inferentially, a clear indication that many of those whose capital sentences were commuted (to life transportation) during the next few years were indeed "victims of the law" rather than "the scum of people." The judges themselves were generally reluctant to use their full powers under an excessively ferocious penal code which denominated two hundred capital offences.

---

[1] *Cf.* R. C. Mills's Introduction to the Everyman edition of Wakefield's *Letter from Sydney*, p. viii.

[2] *Parliamentary History*, xxv, cols. 430 *et seq.*

[3] *Ibid.*, cols. 888 *et seq.* Macdonald "drew the attention of the House to the crowds that every two or three months fell a sacrifice to the justice of their country"—in spite of which larceny was increasing. On the character of the convicts, note that Lieut.-Col. Collins, Judge-Advocate (*An Account of the English Colonies in New South Wales*, p. 26), Phillip, the Governor (to Dundas, October 2, 1792, *Historical Records of Australia*, I, i, p. 273), and Tench, Captain-Lieutenant of the Royal Marine garrison (*A Narrative of the Expedition to Botany Bay*, p. 133), all gave favourable accounts, 1789–1792, of the behaviour of the first convicts even in the arduous, wretched conditions of the early settlement.

The result was that executions in London were kept down to perhaps one a week while great crowds were sentenced to transportation for life, fourteen years or, usually, seven years.

The convict convoy of 1787 sailed, thus, in the practice of an expedient. The humaner system proved satisfactory, at least as far as Rio de Janeiro on the Teneriffe-Rio-Cape route of "5,021 leagues" from Portsmouth,[1] for up to that stage "only fifteen convicts . . . had died." Phillip's orders were not vitally influenced by any notion that Australian settlement might profit British industry or trade, although during the previous year or two such a notion of New South Wales had been projected by James Maria Matra in addresses to the Fox-North and Pitt Ministries. He suggested, with support from Sir Joseph Banks who had accompanied Cook, that colonization of New South Wales could solve the problem of the American loyalists, provide Britain with a base from which to open commerce with China and Japan, and a naval base, and a commercially profitable gaolyard, and a place for the reception of "redundant population." But the colonization of Australia was not made, though it would be pursued, after a

[1] *Vide* Barton, *op. cit.*, pp. 95, etc., for a summary of sources of information upon Phillip's voyage. The 11 ships of the first fleet were about 36 weeks in transit. One of the 212 marines died on the way, and (Barton) 24 of the 772 convicts. The total deathroll (wives and children were carried) was 32 according to Collins, *op. cit.*, cap. 1. Phillip sailed on May 13, 1787, and H.M.S. *Supply*, the armed tender in which he finished the voyage, arrived at Botany Bay on January 18, 1788. The fleet comprised H.M.SS. *Sirius* and *Supply*, 6 convict ships and 3 storeships.

There are several different accounts of the numbers carried, and casualties (*vide Historical Records of Australia*, 1, i, pp. 712, 729). The editor of the *Historical Records of Australia* concludes that 757 convicts sailed and 717 landed, including 529 males. Of the 717, 34 were under life sentence, 19 for 14 years, 600 for 7 years; sentences of others not in available records. Phillip wrote (to Sydney, Feb. 12, 1790, *ibid.*, p. 144) of "1,030 people who landed." Watson (*ibid.*, p. 727) corrects this figure to 1,024—10 staff, 209 marines, 31 marines' wives and 23 children, 717 convicts and 17 children, 17 men from the ships' crews and other civilians. Phillip wrote (*ibid.*, pp. 45 *et seq.*) that 48 persons died *en voyage* (including 40 convicts and five convicts' children), and 41 persons within 6 months of landing (including 28 convicts and 8 convicts' children).

view so wide and clear as Matra's. The twenty thousand "Tories" who had supported the Crown's cause in America during the Revolutionary Wars were in the issue accommodated in Canada. (The colonial population there was to find their presence almost as embarrassing as, at last, Australian free settlers would find that of the pioneer convicts.)[1]

Contemporary with the onset of profound economic change, the first colonization of Australia had nothing to do with any early realization of what the changes implied—a recasting of British imperialism.

(b) *The British Parliamentary System*

It has been said[2] of the British community of which New South Wales was a forced creation, "Politically speaking, Great Britain was one of the most corrupt oligarchies in Europe at the end of the eighteenth century. . . . About seventy inter-related families dominated the whole political scene." The description is fair. The "free institutions" which were often commended in the House of Commons which was one of them included a House of Lords in which 400 hereditary peers were entitled to sit with 30 bishops and with peers elected by the Scottish and Irish peerage to represent them at Westminster. Before Irish Union, the House of Commons comprised 558 members, of whom a majority (307 members) were said[3] to be "elected" by 154 persons directly or by influence;

---

[1] *Vide* Coupland, *op. cit.*, p. 259, and *Loyalists of the American Revolution*, by Lorenzo Sabine, *passim*; Boston, Little, Brown & Co., 1864.

[2] *A Political and Social History of England*, by Frederick C. Dietz, p. 462; N.Y., Macmillan, 1927.

[3] *Vide Petition of the Society of the Friends of the People*, presented by Charles Grey to the House of Commons, 1793; *Parliamentary History*, vol. xxx, col. 795. The Scottish boroughs and counties were a monumental example of the unrepresentative character of the British political system. There were in 1821 30 members of the House of Commons, for Scottish counties, and a Scottish county electorate of 2,987 voters in all. One borough member was returned by the City of Edinburgh, 14 others by 67 Royal Burghs of Scotland—in fact, by "67 self-elected town councils, each averaging 20 persons. In other words, in the year 1821, the 45 Scotch members,

81 of the 307 were the direct nominees of one or another of 40 peers; six peers controlled among them 45 seats in the Commons. Constitutionally, members of the House of Commons were elected to represent 40s. per annum freeholders of the county (82 members), or, by holders of a restricted franchise-right, to represent boroughs (403 members), or by a similar franchise in respect of Irish and Scottish counties and boroughs.

Alike in franchise qualification, nature of constituencies represented, and in the "management" of elections, the political system of England was antiquated as well as vicious. The county franchise remained—and would remain until the Reform Act 1832—as it had been laid down in the year 1430. No new boroughs had been denominated since the moss-troopers pestered Charles II in 1677 and a Transportation Act was passed, and naturally a huge proportion of the old boroughs were now but shells, surrounding nothing precious save the retained right of sending two members to Westminster. (There were four forms of qualification to vote in the borough —the voter must be a freeman of the borough, a member of a corporation borough, the holder of a burgage-tenure, or assessed for the payment of church and poor rates.) Even where the parliamentary borough was still a thriving town, its member was not necessarily representative of a wider electorate than was the member for Old Sarum, classic case of the decayed or rotten borough; thus the Tory leader of the House of Commons admitted,[1] as late as 1826, that there were but 33 electors for the borough of Edinburgh. In any case the changes of centuries in the distribution of population had engendered the wildest anomalies in the unchanging system of composing both county and borough representation in the House of Commons. Thus Lancashire, when its population

representing a population of more than two millions, were elected by 4,327 individuals" (*A Treatise on the Electoral Laws in Scotland*, by Arthur Connell; Edinburgh, Blackwood, 1830; reviewed in *Westminster Review*, January 1831, vol. xiv, pp. 137 *et seq.*)

[1] Speech of George Canning. *Vide Annual Register*, 1826, *History of Europe*, p. 101.

had mounted to 856,000 by the early effort of industrialism, sent but 22 members to the Commons to sit with 21 members from Cornwall, a county then with a population of 14,200. The ravages of time on mouldered boroughs left the Duke of Norfolk with the disposal of eleven seats in the Commons; another landed magnate controlled nine. These were "closed" or "nominated" boroughs. Where they were not controlled by members of the House of Lords, who by this convenience ensured that the lower House too should be a bulwark of landed property, they were in the hands of otherwise inoperative borough corporations or a handful of local landowners, who might be rich or poor. Such seats were customarily the subject of "treaty," i.e. they were open to purchase. A place in the Commons was found worth £5,000 or more, in recorded instances. This remarkable corruption still integral to the political fabric of England even forty years after Phillip sailed, is sufficiently epitomized in a casual reference by a chronicler in 1827:[1] "As is usual in the first session of a new Parliament, the reports of the electoral committees disclosed more than one scene of gross bribery, or badly managed treating."

At the very time of agitated discussion of the penal *impasse*, the Tory Prime Minister himself sought unavailingly to remedy some of the worst abuses of this infamous system of politics. "I know there is a sort of squeamish and maiden coyness about the House in talking on this subject (of bribery, etc.)"; William Pitt said in the Commons,[2] "They are not very ready to talk in this House on what at the same time it is pretty well understood out of doors they have no great objection to negotiate, the purchase and the sale of seats." In fact Pitt failed

[1] *Vide Annual Register*, 1827, p. 175.
[2] *Parliamentary History*, 1785, vol. xxv, cols. 442 *et seq.* Cf. *Parliamentary History*, 1795–97, vol. xxxii, much of which is occupied with debates on Pitt's Habeas Corpus Suspension, Treasonable Practices, and Seditious Meetings Bills. At this later epoch he is introducing legislation to procure the imprisonment of persons, like Horne Tooke, with whom the Prime Minister had sought parliamentary reform, only ten years before.

in each of three attempts of this, his liberal period, to secure a reform of Parliament by "establishing a rule, by which the representation should change with the changes of the country." His last Bill, of April 1785, was rejected on a 3.45 a.m. division of the House of Commons by 248 votes to 174.

In this intransigent England Tory politics was supreme from 1766 until 1830, a portentous period almost co-terminous with the reign of George III (1760–1820). The motive power of the industrial revolution was generated at this time in England, and in France the belated rise to power of a trading middle class of society, accomplished with the aid of the peasantry and the urban poor, convulsed every civilized community with liberal notions which those in authority stigmatized as "Jacobin." Whig ministries achieved office only twice, for periods of a few months, during the period, so that in British affairs the influence of great personalities like Charles James Fox and Edmund Burke was arrested in a parliamentary opposition usually futile. The landowners who constituted the House of Lords controlled, through the closed boroughs which they commanded, a substantial section of the House of Commons, and the small freeholding voters whose franchise they influenced or bought were a class politically privileged above the leaseholding farmers who in large undertakings were revising the system of British agricultural production. Professor Pollard writes:[1] "In the eighteenth century both Houses of Parliament were appanages of the highest class of society."

In this England at the time when "not one Englishman in fifty possessed a vote,"[2] the twin claims of the lower orders for "a vote in the laws they make, a home on the land I till," were made only as the land passed from the peasant's tillage and a whole large class of English society was made landless by State action through enclosure legislation. The distresses attendant upon the long wars with the French Republic,

[1] *The Evolution of Parliament*, by A. F. Pollard, p. 164; London, Longmans, 1920.   [2] *Ibid.*, p. 150.

Consulate, and Empire, did indeed, especially late in the period, stimulate a demand for popular representation; but whether forty years before the Reform Act, 1832, or years after it, democracy or demagogy was resisted savagely by most Whigs and Tories alike. Until much later in the nineteenth century the Commons of England were the chosen of a few. In the period of Tory dominance, at any rate, the millions of England stood outside and beneath Parliament. They were politically voiceless and without institutions except in so far as the State took cognizance of them as units to be governed, servants of hereditary owners, or—then the hulks, or New South Wales— enemies of property. Such were the free institutions of England as three revolutions shook the fabric of society from Paris to Pennsylvania.

(c) *The Agricultural Revolution in England*

If the world of the 1790's had seen already the crisis of two revolutions which were having effect beyond America and France where they originated, England itself was at this time in the throes of its double economic revolution. English economy was being revolutionized by an alteration of the method of agriculture (England's chief industry) from a tenant and peasant system to a system of large leasehold; and as the production of wheat and other cereals engaged the attention of capital more than the production of wool, a new mode of manufacture was being made possible by the development of the power loom, which, too, would for decades to come be concerned less with the old staple, wool:[1] cotton would bulk the larger in its scheme.

[1] *Cf.* the expressions of Defoe on the position during the first third of the eighteenth century and of Radcliffe on its last third. Defoe (1729): "The main article of the British trade (is) . . . the woollen manufacture" (*To the People of England*, p. 8; Hazlitt's *Works of Daniel Defoe*, vol. iii). Radcliffe (*re* 1770–88): The manufacture of "wool had disappeared altogether . . .; cotton, cotton, cotton was become the almost universal material for employment" (*cit. English Economic History: Select Documents*, edited by Bland, Brown and Tawney, p. 509; London, Bell, 1914.

Now social and political readjustments, consonant with these and similar economic changes, would be made during the period of Australia's incubation. Such readjustments would determine generally the nature of the later Australian community, the time of its birth, the rate of its growth and the human nutriment with which it would be provided from Britain. This lays upon us a necessity of close examination of the British economic and social laboratory in which much of Australia's subsequent experience was decided. And here we may find an expert guide in D. G. Barnes, the historian of the English Corn Laws.

Barnes writes:[1] "At the time of the American Revolution England was either exporting or importing a small quantity of grain"—the governing factor being simply the sufficiency, more or less, of the English harvest in any given year. "After the American Revolutionary War, England underwent a rapid development in industry and foreign trade, and as a consequence the export of grain became less, and the import more significant. . . . The city population . . . had increased so enormously that, in spite of the improved methods in agriculture, a considerable importation was necessary to offset the shortage. During the first war, 1793–1802 (i.e. Britain and her European allies *versus* the French Republic), the danger was due to the fact that no part of Europe was accustomed to produce wheat on the chance that there might be a shortage in England or some part of the continent. During the wars with Napoleon, especially from 1806 to 1813, this danger was increased by the Continental System (i.e. the French blockade of Britain-Europe trade)."

Thus a larger home consumption of foodstuffs, consequent on accelerated population increase accompanying the dawning industrial age—and there had been during the century an increase too in the use of wheaten bread—was contemporary with wartime, when importation to the measure of English

[1] *A History of the English Corn Laws from 1660–1846*, p. 69; London, Routledge, 1930.

demand was not easy. Still, British imports of grain reached more than £58,500,000 value during the twenty-one years to 1813.[1]

Consonant with this novel necessity, of an England which had as a rule been able to feed itself, was a rapid acceleration of a movement which for several centuries had been diminishing the peasant factor in English social economy. This was the enclosure movement. G. D. H. Cole gives[2] a summary of the last phase of this process, intensified because of the needs of the new large renting farmers: "A high return for the application of capital to the land, either in the form of drainage or clearance, or of stocking with extensive herds or flocks, could be got only when holdings were concentrated or enclosed. Enclosure of the open fields became the necessary completion of capitalist agriculture and of the high rents which the capitalist farmer could afford to pay. Hence the swift extension of the enclosure movement during the eighteenth century. Between 1700 and 1760 we have records of over 200 Enclosure Acts and over 300,000 acres enclosed; between 1761 and 1800 of 2,000 Acts and over 2,000,000 acres enclosed; and in the first fifty years of the nineteenth century, of 2,000,000 more acres and nearly 2,000 more Enclosure Acts." Barnes gives Slater's figures of enclosures during five periods between 1727–1845:[3]

	Acres enclosed	Acres enclosed per annum
1727–1760	74,518	2,192
1761–1792	478,259	14,946
1793–1801	273,891	30,432
1802–1815	739,743	52,838
1816–1845	199,300	6,643

So passed, during twenty-two years of war, more than a million acres of the traditional common pasture, fields and waste from the village communities and the little farmers of

[1] Barnes, op. cit., p. 118.
[2] *A Short History of the Working Class Movement, 1789–1925*, p. 28; Allen & Unwin, 1925. [3] *Op. cit.*, p. 106.

England. An effect was to make a sharp division between the interest of the great man and the small. "During the greater part of the eighteenth century, the landed gentry in Parliament could at least pose as the representatives of the great mass of the English population, the agrarian class; but after 1815 this was no longer possible. . . . By 1815 . . . agricultural society was . . . divided into three main classes: the landlord, the large farmer, and the agricultural labourer, who was subsisting in part on the poor rates."[1] In fact, the completion of enclosures proletarianized the mass of the rural population, within a few decades, by making smallholding unprofitable and reducing the expropriated smallholders to "the rounds," or to applying for Speenhamland dole-loaves, or to seeking work for wages in the growing industrial towns where the new machines were avid for hands to tend them. It could no longer be said of England of the late eighteenth century, as was truly said of England of the early part of the century:[2] "As yet there was no proletarian class, solely dependent on wages, and in particular on money wages, and expecting to leave its children in the same position." Indeed, whatever English policy for Australia might be half a century later, there was in this wartime no evident appreciation of the sociology which would strike Caroline Chisholm[3] with irresistible force: "To find employment for families that will enable them to rear a well-fed peasantry is a God-like undertaking." In Pitt's day and Liverpool's day of power the Divine purpose was rather given an opposite interpretation—"families" were better excluded from the land though the children might "find employment" in the factory; recipients of poor relief were scarcely "well-fed"; above all, the peasantry was being with great deliberation and efficiency obliterated from English earth.

The consequence, of enmity between classes, was inescap-

[1] Barnes, *op. cit.*, p. 113.

[2] *The History of the English Agricultural Labourer*, by Wilhelm Hasbach, p. 103; London, 1920.

[3] *Vide Caroline Chisholm, The Immigrant's Friend*, by Margaret Swann, p. 27.

THE GENESIS OF AUSTRALIAN SETTLEMENT

able as the mass of Englishmen were disinherited by laws made by the few. So Cole writes:[1] "The period of the Napoleonic Wars, and of the economic crises which succeeded it, is the blackest chapter in the whole history of the British working class. Driven from the land by enclosures; made redundant or exposed to the competition of child labour by the new machines; exposed to relentless persecution because of the fears engendered in the minds of the governing classes both by their misery and by the 'awful portent' of the Revolution in France; and enwalled in the hideous, stinking purlieus of the new factory towns, the workers underwent a long agony from which they emerged at length, exhausted and docile, into the Victorian era."

We shall see that this is a moderate expression upon the process by which England made superfluous a numerous class with which her Governments were at length able to extend British colonization in New South Wales and in Australia generally.

(d) English Methods of Poor Relief

How was the class used, in its desuetude, which more than a generation after the 1790's would chiefly people Australia? A social machinery was devised to maintain it, as the exigencies of war made its labour of temporary advantage to the agricultural interest of the country. This was the Speenhamland system which, philanthropic on the face of it,[2] was actually quite otherwise of intention. Soon to be used the length and breadth of agricultural England, the method was formulated at a meeting at the Pelican Inn, Speenhamland, near Reading, on Wednesday, May 6, 1795, when the assembled Berkshire magistrates posited:[3] "The present state of the poor does

---

[1] *Op. cit.*, p. 39.

[2] *Cf.* speech of the Prime Minister, William Pitt, December 9, 1795 (a few months after the institution of the Speenhamland system), on "the state of the labourer, relieved as it has been by a display of beneficence never surpassed at any period" (*Parliamentary History, 1795–97*, vol. xxxii, col. 705).

[3] *Cit. Select Documents* (Bland, Brown and Tawney), pp. 655, 656.

require further assistance than has generally been given them." The justices recommended farmers to pay agricultural labourers allowances, in kind, for their dependents, where the wages given were incommensurate with the increased cost of living.

This system of augmenting labourers' incomes in proportion to their fecundity was introduced at a period when wheat was 15s. a bushel and a labourer's wage from 7s. to 9s. a week.[1] Clearly the labourer could not work on the food he could afford to buy. So, now that prices were high, it was worth while for the parish, the local congregation of the landed, to subsidize the labourer so that he should have three loaves to eat every week, and his wife and each child perhaps half that quantity. The system "levied on the public as a whole part of the wages which the individual employer should have paid, and gave an excessive incentive to large families on the part of the agricultural labouring population."[2]

The historian who makes this comment points out, too, that the system was "a form of social insurance against rebellion" on the part of people whose lot without such assistance would have been intolerable. Another historian suggests[3] that the landed proprietor's view was the Government's view—"So long as the war continued, there was no need for emigration. The time when a statesman like Pitt preferred to promote a population of paupers rather than not to encourage population at all, was not a time for schemes of emigration."

The motive of Speenhamland relief was, then, substantially this: Now, when a full muster of agricultural labour, each unit at full strength, would be profitable, it would pay to keep the poor at home, and feed them, and encourage them to multiply.

---

[1] *Cf.* Lechmere, M.P., in 1795 debate on Whitbread's Bill to amend the Act of Elizabeth "to regulate the wages of labourers in husbandry": "No agricultural labourer can at present support himself and his family with comfort; for a barley loaf is at the enormous price of 12½d., while the whole of the labourer's daily wages amount to no more than one shilling" (*Parliamentary History, 1795–97*, xxxii, col. 712).

[2] *Vide* Dietz, *op. cit.*, pp. 467, 468.   [3] Egerton, *op. cit.*, p. 231.

Prior to the introduction of this system there was indeed statutory provision for the poor. An Act of 1601 (43 and 44 Elizabeth, cap. 2) had authorized "overseers of the poor" to "set to work" pauper children and adults, empowered the parish to levy rates with which to pay subsistence to the old and sick and buy "ware and stuff" for the employment of the hale; gaol was the alternative to parish-proffered employment. For nearly two hundred years, until the Speenhamland day dawned, workhouses after Elizabeth's pattern had been regulating the poor according to her Government's wisdom.

Again, a practice of "farming the poor" was commonplace in the society which Phillip's convicts had known. "The Contractor says that he shall lose £100 by his last bargain," wrote Eden,[1] "and will not take the poor this year under £700. Twenty-two poor persons are at present in the house, and 100 families receive weekly relief out of it. . . . The Poorhouse . . . is, like most others in the hands of contractors, in a dirty state." There, at Stanhope in Durham, the poor had been farmed in this way during many years; a contractor's bid in the early 1780's was £250. (We may note here that the right to profit from the poor by the sale of their work, upon acceptance of responsibility for their upkeep in consideration of a lump sum, is analogous to the principle of an early eighteenth-century Transportation Act (4 George I, cap. 2); this gave the person who contracted to transport convicted offenders to the Indies or America, at a time of "great want of labour in the colonies,"[2] property in their services during sentence. And now in 1795 there was still no great distance between poorhouse and prison-ship.)

While the poor were being knocked down at auction to speculators, Edmund Burke would be lamenting that the age of chivalry was past; the age of economists and calculators come. But evidently the conception of labour as a commodity

---

[1] *The State of the Poor*, 1797, vol. ii, pp. 168–69; cit. *Select Documents*, p. 657.

[2] *Report of the Transportation Committee*, 1838, p. iii.

was well understood before the age of economics. Well understood, too, even in that primitive age, was a technique of forcing labour, when labour was plentiful and therefore cheap, at rates below those ruling. So English parishes developed a system of "the rounds," which existed side by side with the bounty of Elizabeth, Speenhamland doles, and the Contractor. "This practice is not modern," it was recorded[1] in 1808. . . . "It is not supposed to be sanctioned by law. . . . When a labourer can obtain no employment he applies to the overseer (of the poor), from whom he passes on to different farmers all round the parish, being employed by each of them after the rate of one day for every £20 rent. The allowance to a labourer on the rounds is commonly twopence per day below the pay of other labourers, which is found to be a necessary check upon those who love liberty better than labour." In the old days poor relief by the various means cost perhaps £1,500,000 in the year, 1776, of the American Declaration of Independence, and perhaps £2,000,000 in the year before Phillip sailed.[2] Towards the close of the wars the annual cost would be about £5,000,000, and by 1818 as much as £7,870,801.[3]

Such were some of the circumstances which, Robert Owen said,[4] "inevitably formed such characters" as "comparatively a few individuals" afterwards deemed it "a duty and a right to punish even to death."

Truly the lot of the majority was miserable during the wars —though it would be worse after them. Between 1790 and 1822 the English harvest as a whole was a failure on eleven occasions.[5] Yet English trade and manufactures were flourish-

[1] *The Agriculture of Bedfordshire*, pp. 608, 609; cit. *Select Documents*, pp. 660, 661.

[2] *Vide The Economic History of England*, by E. Lipson, vol. iii, p. 485; Black, 1931. N.B.—Lipson points out, however, that the parish returns are dubious statistical material.

[3] *A History of the English Poor Law*, by Sir George Nicholls, ii, p. 466; London, Murray, 1854.

[4] *The Life of Robert Owen, Written by Himself*, i, pp. 267, 268; London, Effingham Wilson, 1837.

[5] The Prime Minister, Lord Liverpool, cit. *Annual Register*, 1826, p. 56.

ing. "The two opposing blockades," we are told[1] of the British and French policing of the seas, ". . . did little more than convert British commerce from a legitimate into a contraband traffic." It was not always even contraband; for instance, once during the wars Napoleon had to suspend the Berlin Decree of November 1806 in order to secure Yorkshire clothing for his troops *en marche* against England's Russian ally; similarly, Britain, with the enemy's permission, imported two million quarters of French grain in 1809–10. On this occasion the French Government issued export licences on its part, and the British Government, for its part, pushed through Parliament two Acts (49 George III, cap. 23, and 50 George III, cap. 19), to remove import duties which otherwise would have been levied on the enemy's bounty.[2]

(e) *Early Social Consequences of the Industrial Revolution; First Period of "Impaired Liberty."*

Even leaving the war and its enhanced demands out of account, British industry, still handicraft, found itself as the eighteenth century wore on in conditions favouring expansion. In 1754 Sir John Dalrymple had written:[3] "Among all the known countries on the surface of the globe, it was in Great Britain alone that the coal beds, the iron ore, and limestone, which constituted the three raw materials of the iron manufacture, were found together, and moreover in close proximity to the sea." A quarter of a century before Dalrymple, Daniel Defoe had said,[4] that of "lead, tin, and coal this island seems to have an exclusive grant . . .; besides these, iron, copper (etc.), which may be said to be in common to us and the rest of the world." Recognized by contemporary observers, then,

[1] *England in Transition, 1789–1832*, by William Law Mathieson, p. 145; London, Longmans, 1920.
[2] *Vide* for details Barnes, *op. cit.*, pp. 87 *et seq.*
[3] *Cit. A History of the English People in 1815*, by Élie Halévy, p. 227; translated by E. I. Watkin and D. A. Barker, London, Fisher Unwin, 1924.
[4] *To the People of England* (1729), p. 6; *The Works of Daniel Defoe*, edited by William Hazlitt, vol. iii; London, Clements, 1843.

was this essential condition of British industrial development, promising it a start in any race and an advantage in the race.

Again, England's island form now stood its entrepreneurs in good stead, for in the pre-industrial, mercantile age sea transport had been brought much farther in effectiveness than methods of land transport. Now England's large mercantile marine, with its coastwise auxiliary, was readily adaptable for carriage from English port to English port to foreign port of market—whereas in wide France, for instance, industry would have to face difficulties of land transport which had not pressed in the old days. Moreover, England got some of its raw goods, e.g. cotton, by sea.

Thirdly, the country's small area offered a favourable ground for the development of a canal system, which—approaching 4,000 miles of extent by 1830[1]—facilitated the distribution of coal at reasonable prices to industrial centres.

Cole suggests[2] a fourth factor of special significance, in England's "immunity from internal wars in the earlier eighteenth century."

For these and like reasons England took the lead in industrialism, incidentally complicating social issues which were already, as we have seen, vexatious enough as a result of the adjustments required to round off the enclosures policy. However, one section of the cottage manufacturers, the handweavers, experienced a brief prosperity even as the process gained momentum which was to displace agriculture and sea-carriage from their old primacy in English affairs. "From the year 1770 to 1788," said William Radcliffe, a contemporary manufacturer,[3] "a complete change had gradually been effected in the spinning of yarns. That of wool had disappeared altogether; and that of linen was also nearly gone; cotton, cotton,

[1] Porter's 1838 figures—2,200 miles of canals and 1,800 miles of navigable partly canalized rivers; cit. *An Economic History of Modern Britain*, by J. H. Clapham, i, p. 75; Cambridge University Press, 1926.

[2] *Op. cit.*, p. 18.

[3] *The Origin of Power Loom Weaving*, pp. 9, 10; cit. *Select Documents*, p. 509.

cotton was become the almost universal material for employment. The hand-wheels . . . were all thrown into lumber rooms, the yarn was all spun on common jennies, the carding (for the most part) . . . on carding engines. . . . In weaving no great alteration had taken place . . . save the introduction of the fly-shuttle, a change in the woollen looms to fustian and calico." That is, the cottager was losing his hold on the process of spinning yarns to be woven into cloth, as the mule-twist, the water-twist, and common jenny yarns came in increasing quantities from factories equipped with Crompton's mule or Arkwright's water-frame. But the cottager had this temporary consolation: that the great increase of the yarn output by these novel methods enhanced a demand for the services of the weaver, whose work no machine had yet been devised to do. The power loom was still round the corner.

But the advancing machine age was serving few so well. Arkwright found, for instance, as he set up his own spinning mills equipped with the water-frame of his invention, that "parish apprentices" (indigent children, the reponsibility of the parish) could fill his labour needs. He was the pioneer of this most inglorious traffic of English industry, at a time when the opportunities in life of a poor child of seven years were thus broadened to embrace the factory, where they had been limited to felonry.[1] Soon the first Factory Act (42 George III, cap. 87, 1802) would require magistrates to inspect mills in which such children were employed. They would neglect this duty.

So the industrialization of England began. And even before

[1] The condition of vagrant children at this time is revealed in a clear light by speeches in the Commons on the London and Westminster Police Bill, 1795, e.g. children of 7 or 8 years were picked up to be trained in crime; and "of the whole number hanged in the metropolis eighteen out of every twenty were under the age of 21" (*Parliamentary History*, xxxii, col. 705).

And note that the subject of the first execution at Sydney was a 17-year-old youth, James Bennett, a convict, convicted again of having robbed a tent, and executed immediately after sentence—May, 1788 (*vide An Account of the English Colony in New South Wales*, by David Collins, p. 27; ed. James Collier, London, Whitcombe & Tombs, 1910).

that "form of social insurance," the Speenhamland system, was introduced in 1795, the discontent of the masses, tumbled from their land and cottages, sent to day-labour in great men's fields or factories, found expression in a sustained agitation. As early as 1780 Major John Cartwright had organized a Society for Constitutional Information, a middle-class liberal body advocating parliamentary reform. This was revived in French Revolutionary times, to work side by side with the London Corresponding Society, a working-class political organization formed in 1792 chiefly at the instance of Thomas Hardy, a shoemaker. It maintained correspondence with revolutionists in France, before war began, and at home it was the model of many corresponding societies which were formed in the counties. Young Charles Grey, the future Prime Minister, founded his Society of the Friends of the People, which even after war broke out petitioned, as we saw, against parliamentary abuses. The Revolution Society, innocuously named after the Revolution of 1688 which it had been formed to commemorate, propagated French Revolutionary ideas now in the '90's.

The Prime Minister, William Pitt, and his Lord Chancellor, Eldon, launched thunderbolts by statutes and the courts against these movements. Aided by authority, John Reeves sought to neutralize the radical associations with his Society for Preserving Liberty and Property against Republicans and Levellers. (Liberty and labour were opposites, according to contemporary conservative thought, but liberty and property were of a kind.)

The first phase of the Government campaign against radicalism saw an attempt to use existing legislation and common law, especially that relating to treason, for the suppression of radical organizations by the indictment of their leaders. In 1794 proceedings were taken against Horne Tooke and others on charges of treason. Sympathetic London jurymen acquitted the accused, but Government had won the opening round of the contest. For all juries were not London juries, or radical, and New South Wales became a political, as well as a penal convenience when Thomas Muir, a Scottish barrister, and

THE GENESIS OF AUSTRALIAN SETTLEMENT

Thomas Palmer, a Scottish clergyman, were sentenced to fourteen and seven years' transportation for sedition. In the same year, 1793, three leaders of a Scottish convention of corresponding societies were sentenced to fourteen years' transportation for sedition. Reeves's group, Dietz relates,[1] "rounded up those suspected of desiring parliamentary reform, and judges and juries vied with each other in their zeal for convictions and atrocious sentences.... The Government, led by the Lord Chancellor and the law officers of the Crown, was not above inflaming the public with false reports, collected by its agents, of plots to overthrow the Government." Lord Eldon's simple political philosophy made him an admirable instrument of this reaction. "For forty years I have opposed all plans of reform," he said[2] in after times, "because I have seen no plan which, in my opinion, would improve the condition of the people." The parties of the other part were however less sure of their ground. While the London radicals "saw that the upper classes controlled the Government and profited themselves because they controlled Parliament," they "did not realize that Parliament was not an institution suitable to the working-class experience; and, above all, they failed to realize that the evils from which they were suffering were in the main

---

[1] *Op. cit.*, pp. 468, 469. The "Scottish martyrs" sent to New South Wales for sedition were Thomas Muir, Thomas Fyshe Palmer, Maurice Margarot, and William Skirving, who reached the colony on October 25, 1794, and Joseph Gerrald, arrived November 5, 1795 (vide *Historical Records of Australia*, I, i, p. 463, Under-Secretary King to Lieutenant-Governor Grose, February 14, 1794. Note 245, p. 771). A full account of the trial of these men, in addition to 22 others, is in *State Trials, 1793-94*, vol. xxiii, edited by Thomas Bayly Howell. Muir was accused (*op. cit.*, col. 118), that "having been present at a meeting . . . denominated 'A Society for Reform,' or bearing some such name . . . (he) did seditiously endeavour to represent the government of this country as oppressive and tyrannical, and the legislative body of the State as venal and corrupt, particularly by instituting a comparison between the pretended existing government of France and the constitution of Great Britain;" also of having advised persons to buy "seditious pamphlets" and to read Tom Paine's *Rights of Man*—"a most wicked and seditious publication."

[2] Cit. *Annual Register*, 1832, p. 136.

not political, nor caused by laws or statutes, but economic, caused by trade fluctuations, poor harvests, and war finance."[1]

But Pitt and Eldon harried the agitators none the less because they were not clear as to the origin of the working classes' distresses, and after the French Government declared war on Britain on February 1, 1793, it seemed a question which was the greater danger—the French abroad or the pauperized mass at home.

From 1795, Speenhamland year, the Pitt Government forged for itself, at the fire of Parliament, new implements with which opposition and dissent might be beaten down. The volumes of the *Parliamentary History* from 1795 to the end of the century are crowded with debates on repressive Bills which nevertheless were rushed through Parliament. Great Liberal lords lamented "this impaired state of English liberty"; but in spite of them and the radical organizations outside Parliament, Bill after Bill became law—a measure suspending the right of *habeas corpus* in order to facilitate the detention and confinement of agitating persons; a Treasonable Practices Act making unlawful the very discussion of political reform; the Corresponding Societies Act of 1799 to disperse the liberal leagues; Combination Laws to destroy the industrial workmen's trade unions in their infancy (39 George III, cap. 81; 39, and 40 George III, cap. 106, etc.).[2] The measures against the trade unions, which remained on the statute book for a quarter of a century—whereas the other repressive measures were re-enacted at crises but were usually dormant—were of a definitely class nature. "A single master," said Lord Jeffrey[3] of the legis-

[1] Dietz, *op. cit*, pp. 468, 469.

[2] *Vide* especially November-December, 1795, debates on the Habeas Corpus Suspension, Treasonable Practices and Seditious Meetings Bills; and King's Proclamations; and protests recorded in the *Journal* of the House of Lords by the Dukes of Bedford and Grafton, the Earls of Albemarle, Lauderdale, Derby, etc., against the measures and the manner in which they were hurried through the Houses (*Parliamentary History*, 1795-97, xxxii).

[3] *Cit.* Mathieson, *op. cit.*, p. 767. *Cf. The Wealth of Nations* (1776), by Adam Smith, Everyman edition, i, p. 59: "We have no Acts of parliament against combining to lower the price of work, but many against combining to raise it."

lation prohibiting "combinations, covins, and conspiracies of workmen"—"A single master was at liberty at any time to turn off the whole of his workmen at once . . . if they would not accept of the wages he chose to offer. But it was made an offence for the whole of the workmen to leave that master at once if he refused to give the wages they chose to require." The strike was offensive, the lock-out not. In quoting this passage Mathieson points out that the new laws forbade combinations of employers also; "but even if those of them who defied the law had been convicted," he comments, "—which they never were—the plight of their operatives could hardly have been less galling than it was," for the power of "direct action" was left with the employers while the workmen were deprived of it. Under the legislation of 1799–1800 even an act of an individual, which tended to "hamper" his employer, was punishable by three months' imprisonment.

Now it was during precisely this period of repression that the economic position of the masses became dire. The bad harvest of the first Speenhamland year was followed by a rise of the price of corn to more than 100s. a quarter, the highest level attained in 200 years.[1] (One quarter was, according to a contemporary estimate,[2] the average consumption of breadstuffs per capita per annum.) In their misery mobs rioted in London and the provinces; King George's carriage was attacked when he drove through London to open Parliament on October 29, 1795; a shot was fired. Pitt's reply to these demonstrations was the use of armed force against the rioters, the declaration of a ban on the export of foodstuffs, and the relaxation of the tariff and navigation laws to permit of the entry of foreign foodstuffs, duty-free, in any ship (under Act 36 George III, cap. 3, 1795). And the Commons carried his motion for the appointment of a select committee to enquire into the high price of corn.

In the closing years of the century the English mass was thus subjected to the stern and bitter influences of war, en-

[1] Barnes, *op. cit.*, p. 70. [2] *Vide ibid.*, p. 109.

closures, industrialization, and repression through the means of Parliament and the law courts. In the gaols or in New South Wales, when the century drew to an end, were many of those members of unlawful associations who had raised their voices against this *status quo*.

But violence, legal repression, and sops of momentarily freed trade could not serve more than an expedient purpose: the situation remained. One aspect, disturbing to the dominant sections, of that situation was the frightening rate of increase of the pauperized majority. The problems created by this increase in conjunction with the changes of British economy, could not be solved in Great Britain; accordingly the question of population in England has an important bearing on the development of the latest, and emptiest, of Britain's overseas territories, New South Wales.

(f) *The English Population*

In 1798 Malthus, a clergyman, believing that human life is a war between man's sex impulses and his material advantage, promulgated his notion that, sex being as a rule triumphant, population showed a geometrical rate of increase (i.e. 1, 2, 4, 16) while means of subsistence increased only in arithmetical ratio (i.e. 1, 2, 3, 4). Naturally this inharmony threatened overpopulation and consequent starvation. However, Sadler, consoling with a contrary dogma, postulated that "the law of population, by which the increase of mankind has been, and still is, in all cases, regulated, is simply this: The fecundity of human beings under similar circumstances varies inversely as their numbers on a given space." So all was and would continue to be for the best in a cunningly ordered world. But now Doubleday, a third theorist, found an unfortunate dispensation of Nature by which the poorest persons produced the *largest* families. "The great general law, then . . ." he explained, "is this, that whenever a species or genus is endangered, a corresponding effort is invariably made by Nature for its preservation or continuance, by an increase of fecundity or fertility; and that this especially takes place whenever such danger arises from a diminution of proper nourishment or food. . . . As applied to mankind this law acts thus: There is in all societies a constant increase going on amongst that portion of it which is the worst supplied with food; in short, amongst the poorest."[1] And from the Pelican Inn the call had gone forth for *more* poor!

These "natural" theorists all omitted to consider that growth of population varies in its rate according to the difference between birth-rate and death-rate, both of which are variables. So that a "law" that deals merely with reproductive capacity is not a law of population. Moreover, according to Clapham,[2] "Contrary to an opinion still widely held, the flood of life, which made Malthus and his generation speculate on the causes and cure of a redundant population, was due far more to life saving, since the mid-eighteenth century, than to reckless procreation since the great inventions." However, Malthus's generation was neither conversant with the theory of vital statistics, nor prone to ascribe to Cort and Crompton the increase of population which it remarked. It believed the human race to have declined in numbers since the brave days of classic antiquity;[3] it saw now a turn of the tide, heard the roar of the mobs at Westminster and the Tollgate; and as a rule it called out the militia. For authority was blind to the more "modern" understanding which Defoe, for instance, had displayed three generations before. He had grasped that, provided the available sources of primary and secondary produc-

---

[1] For a good account of these and contemporary population theories generally, *vide Population Problems*, by Warren S. Thompson, pp. 30 *et seq.*; N.Y., McGraw Hill, second edition, 1935.   [2] *Op. cit.*, p. 54.

[3] *Cf. Parliamentary History*, *1795–97*, xxxii, cols. 703, 704. Samuel Whitbread, a Whig, speaking upon his Bill for fixing a minimum wage for agricultural labourers, said in the Commons on December 9, 1795, that the poor rates had been increased to yield £3,000,000 at the end of the century as compared with £600,000 at the beginning of it: "nor is this prodigious increase of the poor to be ascribed to the advance of population, for it is doubtful whether any such increase has taken place." N.B. His Bill was rejected.

tion were not exhausted—and they were not exhausted in England—increase of population, even an additional increase by large immigration, was to be welcomed. "But if more foreigners came among us, if it were two millions, it could do us no harm," he wrote,[1] "because they would consume our provisions, and we have land enough to produce much more than we do; and they would consume our manufactures, and we have wool enough for any quantity." But from the windows of St. Stephen's, as the eighteenth century darkened or the nineteenth century dawned, ministers could not see beyond the angry mobs of London's poor and desperate.

What in fact was the contemporary position of population in England? Here our enquiry is limited by a lack of data. A medical statistician points out[2] that a regular record of births and deaths was not made in England and Wales until 1837 (though there was a decennial census from 1801), in Scotland until 1855, in Ireland, 1864. However, such a record was kept in Sweden from 1748, and we may use the state of population in that country at stages of the eighteenth century as a rough analogy with the English position, for purposes of comparison with later developments. We are told,[3] then, that in the decade in which Malthus published his first *Essay on Population* (published 1798) the Swedish birth-rate was 33·3, the death-rate 25·4 per 1,000 of population. Fifty years earlier the corresponding rates were more than 35 and 27. (*Cf.* the 1932 figures for Sweden: 14·5 births and 11·6 deaths per 1,000 of population.)

We have, then, these striking indices to the great change which was in progress as Malthus wrote of an unaccommodating world: that where a civilized society's rate of natural increase was about 8 per 1,000 at the middle and end of the

[1] *Giving Alms no Charity* (1704), p. 181; Shakespeare's Head edition of the *Works of Daniel Defoe, The Shortest Way with the Dissenters*, etc.; Oxford, Blackwell, 1927.

[2] *The Natural Increase of Mankind*, by J. S. Sweeney, p. 48; Baltimore, Williams & Wilkins, 1926.

[3] Thompson, *op. cit.*, p. 42.

eighteenth century, in modern times it is about 3 per 1,000; that the crude birth-rate has fallen to less than 44 per cent of the Swedish rate of Malthus's time, the death-rate to less than 42 per cent. It is probably true that a steep decline in the death-rate, in the late eighteenth and early nineteenth centuries, was the manner of most of the access of population which alarmed Malthus's England. Thus Thompson finds that in 1750 the London death-rate was evidently still as high as 50 per 1,000 and in 1800 as 30. (But the modern English death-rate is about 12 per 1,000.) We have, too, a twentieth century illustration of the salutary effect in lowering the death-rate, of the attack on the causes of disease which may be made by a society which is becoming economically more powerful through industrialization. The analogy, of Russia, with the condition of England during her so much earlier industrial revolution, is not perfect in its bearing on population. But the modern instance, like the older one, conveys some of the abruptness of the social changes which industrialization and the reinforcement of State resources make possible. Thus in Moscow of 1913, the last pre-war year, the death-rate was 23·1 per 1,000; in 1930 it was down to less than 13. The infant death-rate was 37 per 1,000 in 1913, 12 in 1930, after the years of rapid industrialization.[1]

So there are not wanting evidences and comparisons to support a contention that life saving on an enlarged scale contributed heavily to the increase of England's population during the early industrial era. Clapham's view of the prime importance of this factor, as against any remarkable rise of the birth-rate, is strengthened by the fact that there lacks evidence that the labouring population was more continent before the Speenhamland age than during it. He writes:[2] "That the industrial revolution, with the attendant changes in agriculture and transport, rendered the maintenance of a rapidly growing British population possible, without resort to the cabin-and-potato standard of life, is beyond question, but the sequence of

---

[1] *Vide A Scientist Among the Soviets*, by Julian Huxley, p. 67; London, Chatto & Windus, 1932.   [2] *Op. cit.*, pp. 54, 55.

events should not be misconstrued. First the death-rate fell, after 1740, in an age of growing comfort and improved medical knowledge . . . the age which ended, say, with the first application of steam to cotton spinning in 1790. Meanwhile the birth-rate rose, probably reaching its maximum—for England and Wales—in the decade 1780–90. The available statistics do point to a definite rise in the crude English birth-rate—the number of births per 1,000 living—between the first quarter of the eighteenth century and the beginning of its last decade.

"After 1790 the death-rate continued to fall rapidly until 1810–20. The evidence points to a slight rise during the following decade, but it never again got anywhere near the rates of the mid-eighteenth century. Had the birth-rate really risen during this, the Speenhamland, age, as is so constantly suggested by historians who neglect quantities, then there would indeed have been an 'avalanche of population.' There was something like an avalanche as it was, so effective had become the saving of life. . . . The conquest of small-pox, the curtailment of agueish disorders through drainage, the disappearance of scurvy as a disease of the land, improvements in obstetrics leading to a reduction in the losses both of infant and maternal life in childbed, the spreading of hospitals, dispensaries, and medical schools, all had helped to save life. . . . Now cheap cotton shirts and cleanliness were spreading slowly downwards through society."

Valuable as this epitome is, we ought to recognize that it may overstress some factors and understress others. And inasmuch as the "redundance" of English population, from early in the nineteenth century, was for long a persistent force in the development of Australia, we need to be as clear as possible upon what happened in this regard, and how. Thompson, for instance, believes, as he writes,[1] that "the great decline in the death-rate that has taken place during the last two centuries in the West is far more largely due to the improve-

[1] *Op. cit.*, pp. 43, 44.

THE GENESIS OF AUSTRALIAN SETTLEMENT

ment of sanitary and economic conditions than to the improvements in the practice of medicine.... As a consequence of these sanitary improvements and of the better economic status of a considerable part of the population it appears that probably for the first time in history it became possible, about the beginning of the nineteenth century, to have large towns and cities in which births exceeded deaths." That is, beginning late in the eighteenth century the industrial revolution did in its effects have this direct bearing on population increase: that it supplied the economic resources and engineering skill which were necessary if medical counsels of sanitation were to be realized. Similarly, Miss Buer writes:[1] "In endeavouring to elucidate the ultimate causes of the reduction of the death-rate, we may perhaps roughly classify them under the heads, 'increasing wealth' and 'increasing knowledge,' though obviously these two are most interdependent." Certainly it is true that the application of "increasing knowledge," e.g. in medicine, must have been more limited had it not been for the contribution of the "great inventions," making available funds and technique to carry out sanitation.

Such considerations perhaps brought Professor Carr-Saunders to stress the economic group of factors bearing on population increase. "Population growth," he says,[2] "is merely the response to increase in skill." Again, man strives to an optimum number; "this is the number which—taking into consideration the nature of the environment, the degree of skill employed, the habits and customs of the people concerned, and all other relevant facts—gives the highest average return per head." "As skill has tended to increase throughout history," he sums up, "so has the number economically desirable tended to increase." Robert Owen's observations, contemporary with the great English increase, led him to a sort

[1] *Health, Wealth and Population in the Early Days of the Industrial Revolution.* By M. C. Buer, p. 47; London, Routledge, 1926.
[2] *The Population Problem*, by A. M. Carr-Saunders, pp. 308, 55, 476; Oxford, Clarendon Press, 1922.

of anticipation of this mode of attack, and gave him a rod to beat Malthus with. Owen wrote:[1] "Mr. Malthus is, however, correct when he says that the population of the world is ever adapting itself to the quantity of food raised for its support; but he has not told us how much more food an intelligent and industrious people will create from the same soil, than will be produced by one ignorant and ill-governed."

Now these opinions seem to indicate that Clapham may underestimate a powerful economic factor. Moreover, as to the importance of medical and similar advance in saving life, at the early industrial period, we need to bear in mind that the great saving or prolongation of life achieved by medical and surgical advance has been brought about above all by the discovery of methods of antisepsis, asepsis, and anaesthesia, and to work on postulates like that of Pasteur's germ theory. But Lister, Pasteur, and their peers flourished long after the period of Clapham's and our reference. It was within the ten years before 1821, before the day of the great doctors, that the English population "was rising at a faster rate than ever before or since."[2] Nor was it until long after the first flood of industry, that enhanced knowledge of obstetrics found appreciable facilities. Nursing was not in general an occupation for trained persons until well on in the nineteenth century. Nor can the "spreading of hospitals, dispensaries, and medical schools" be shown easily as an aspect of life saving in 1790–1820. After all, cholera caused thousands of deaths as late as 1831, after some hospitals had installed water-flush sewerage systems—which gave into drains, some of them open, which ran into the Thames, the city population's chief water supply.[3] "In one

[1] *Op. cit.*, i, pp. 327, 328.
[2] *A History of England, 1815–1918*, by J. R. M. Butler, p. 26; *Home University Library*. We need not endorse the unverifiable part of his statement, i.e. "at a faster rate than ever before."   [3] *Vide* Buer, *op. cit.*, p. 105.
The statement quoted after this reference is cited by W. E. B. Lloyd, *100 Years of Medicine*, p. 35; London, Duckworth, 1936.
Cf. Account of the Principal Lazarettos in Europe, by John Howard (1791), p. 135, in which Howard mentions that water-closets were in installation in

THE GENESIS OF AUSTRALIAN SETTLEMENT 65

hospital," we are told of this time by a medical historian, "five out of every twelve patients who underwent amputation died, for the most part of sepsis: while outside, in private and country practice, only five out of forty-six succumbed. Women who were delivered out of hospital stood seven times the chance of coming safely through a confinement."

For these and other reasons it will not do to accept Clapham's account *in toto*.

But as to the application of knowledge to effect sanitary improvements, it is to be observed that significant measures in this field had been taken long before the industrial revolution arrived with funds. For instance, an Act "for the better paving and cleaning of the streets and sewers in and about the City of London" was passed in 1671, after the Great Fire. Two hundred and eleven Acts for paving, etc., were passed in the period 1785-1800, according to Chalmers' *Population* (1802),[1] and it is noteworthy that local authorities, including 300 Commissioners for paving, sewerage, "improvement," etc., "had done work not to be despised before 1835."[2] That is, we may fairly summarize, some measures of sanitation had been taken before the industrial revolution, but it was simultaneous with the enrichment of the community or portion of it, during the period under our review, that widespread improvement was undertaken. Again a contemporary judgment expresses much

the new wards of Guy's Hospital, London, in 1788; also, *ibid.*, p. 181, his reprint of the list of regulations which was displayed in the wards of the Royal (naval) Hospital at Haslar. Article X, an interesting commentary on circumstances, read: "That all nurses who disobey the matron's orders, get drunk, neglect their patients, quarrel or fight with any other nurses, or quarrel with the men, or do not prudently and cautiously reveal . . . all irregularities committed by the patients in their wards (such as drinking . . .) be immediately discharged."

Howard's accounts of English hospitals in general in the late eighteenth century does not wholly recommend them as agencies of life saving.

Cf. also *The Life of Florence Nightingale*, by E. Cook, p. 52; R. Nash's edition, 1925: "What was the use of praying to be delivered from plagues and pestilences, so long as the common sewers ran into the Thames?"

[1] *Cit.* Buer, p. 85.
[2] Clapham, *op. cit.*, p. 538.

of the truth of the matter. Thomas Bateman wrote in his *Diseases of London* (1819):[1]

"In comparing the catalogue of diseases, and the effect of the ravages occasioned by them . . . (in) our own times (with those of the seventeenth and eighteenth centuries) . . . we are naturally struck with the great diminution of the fatality, and with the total disappearance of some of the most formidable human maladies. . . . But the healthy condition of the metropolis seems to have been more particularly produced within the last fifty years, during which period it has most rapidly increased in extent and population. Until nearly the middle of the eighteenth century the mortality kept pace in some measure with the advancing population; the average number of deaths annually from the year 1720 to 1730 was 27,492 . . . (similarly to 1746).

"Now a large town is but an extensive camp, so constructed as to be destitute of the means of changing its situation, and therefore liable to be invested with the same diseases as are endemic in camps. Hence the necessity for the construction of privies, drains, and common sewers, and the advantages of a flowing stream . . . and of a hard and regular pavement preserved in a cleanly condition by proper scavengers. . . . We shall find the health of the inhabitants improving, *pari passu*, and exactly in proportion as these causes of their unhealthiness are removed, while the damps and colds of spring return as heretofore, and the rains and heats of autumn continue."

Bateman and Owen, then, these confident voices from the improving past, give us two conditions in which England experienced an "avalanche of population" while New South Wales lived through its penal period: increased production of the means of subsistence by the application of knowledge, and decreased mortality through the application of knowledge to means of safeguarding life. Modern retrospect, or what remains of its conclusions after test, appears to vouchsafe little more

[1] *Cit.* Buer, *op. cit.*, p. 89.

than these. At any rate Thompson, for instance, has reached a conclusion similar to those contemporary judgments:[1] "The industrial revolution largely removed the two great checks to population growth which had always been operative in greater or lesser degree until that time, namely, the lack of the necessaries of life, and the heavy incidence of disease due to the utter lack of sanitation, as we understand that term."

Conclusion

From these introductory discussions it may have appeared that the England from which Australia was being supplied with population in the last years of the eighteenth century, and the early years of the nineteenth, was a community which, in transition through multitudinous dolours to a new prosperity of new classes of men, was sloughing already many of its traditional forms. It was a community in which, nevertheless, political, social, and economic power was still chiefly reserved by those who for a century and a half since the civil wars had held it. The first generation of the new century would see their effort to retain the cherished basis on which their superiority had rested so long. The while, living conditions for the majority were still remarkably similar to those of medieval times; in all history until then there had been no change a tithe of that which was imminent or actually taking place. And this change connoted the settlement on new territories overseas of the surplus masses and the use of such territories by the agents of new enterprise, the capitalist-investor and the capitalist-industrialist.

But this expansion of England was only imminent when Phillip sailed, and even a generation later was scarcely perceptible. While a specific necessity dictated his sailing orders to Botany Bay, English notions of profitable expansion remained limited to "the Indies." With abundant cheap native and slave labour English enterprise gained the fruits of that rich earth, and with the premier fleets of the world distributed

[1] *Op. cit.*, p. 50.

them through the world's markets. For the most part and for most of the time, domestic production served the needs of the baker's dozen of millions in the British Isles, and England offered Europe the surplus of its hand weavers' work and its ironwork, and lately the work of its earliest machines. For the rest English interest was self-centred. Far from seeking colonies in remote regions, Britain's rulers were not seeking markets there. Its people were not of migrant habit. Government indeed gave some encouragement to free persons of respectability to go to New South Wales in order to grow food for the prisoners and their gaolers: so Australia's first immigrant ship, the *Bellona*, brought five settlers into Port Jackson on January 16, 1793, just five years after Phillip's first fleet. (The inducements were two years' provisions, free land, farming implements, and convict servants, made available by Government.) Now to consider the convict settlement itself, and the affairs of its members, of "those who were prosperous and those who were miserable, the drawers of prizes and the drawers of blanks in this strange lottery."[1]

[1] *Report of the Transportation Committee*, 1838, p. xix.

Chapter 2

FIRST PHASE OF THE NEW SOUTH WALES PENAL SETTLEMENT

(a) *Crime and Punishment in Great Britain* circa *1788.*
(b) *A Prison Farm Economy in New South Wales, 1788-92.*

(a) *Crime and Punishment in Great Britain* circa *1788*
IT seems that in "the age of growing comfort" (1740-90) of which Clapham speaks, prevalent serious crime in Britain took less of a bent towards the person and more towards property. Murders and other crimes of violence appear to have diminished in proportion and offences against property to have increased.[1] This character which English crime exhibited began to be noticed about the last quarter of the eighteenth century; towards the end of the first quarter of the nineteenth, authority found it especially disquieting.[2] The new direction of so much criminal enterprise should not have surprised, now that, for instance, stringent Game Laws accompanied Enclosure Laws and haled to the dock expropriated peasants who had snared a rabbit or a hare. The process of depressing a numerous class, by the increasing acquisitions of a numerically small class, had indeed been going forward steadily throughout the century, and this was mirrored in the protective devices of deterrent and punitive laws which became more numerous as a landholders' Parliament gathered fresh gains to conserve. Thus during the eighteenth century scores of offences were added to a capital list which had been fifty crimes long in James II's day. After the Revolution of 1688 which established the welfare of

[1] *Vide Three Criminal Law Reformers: Beccaria, Bentham, Romilly*, by Coleman Phillipson, pp. 164 *et seq.;* London, Dent, 1923. *Cf.* Chapter 6 (c) *infra.*
[2] *Vide* p. 239 *infra*, for Sir Robert Peel's statistics.

"the people"—the parliamentary term denoting the tiny proportion of voters—the criminal law manifested an emphasized savagery: sixty-three new capital offences were denominated in George II's reign; a parliamentary statement of 1770 gave one hundred and fifty-four as the total then, and Judge Blackstone said there were one hundred and sixty. Sixteen years later (i.e. in 1786, the year before Phillip sailed for New Holland or Australia) Sir Samuel Romilly said[1] there had been a considerable increase in the total since 1770. And in England where small thefts were now punishable by hanging the culprit, the range of more than a dozen contemporary forms of punishment still included such barbarous specifications as hanging, drawing, and quartering a man guilty of high treason (nominally the penalty until 1870), and burning alive a woman guilty of high treason. (Elizabeth Gaunt, sentenced by Judge Jeffreys a century before Phillip's sailing, was the last to undergo this punishment; but a woman was burnt after having been strangled, in 1773, another in 1799.)[2] The pillory,[3] the stocks, and the "cucking stool" were still used, though various mutilations which the law prescribed were not now practised.[4] As recently as 1745 some of the Young Pretender's followers had been half-strangled, disembowelled alive, and then quartered, in execution of the sentence passed upon them for their treason. Until 1783 murderers due for execution were taken in procession over the two-mile route from Newgate to Tyburn, there to be hanged publicly; and

[1] *Cit.* Phillipson, *ibid.*, p. 170.

[2] *Vide* Sir Stephen Janssen's statistics, *cit. Account of the Principal Lazarettos in Europe*, by John Howard, p. 256 (1791).

[3] The use of the pillory was abolished by 7 William IV and 1 Victoria, cap. 23 (1837).

[4] Mutilation was used in New South Wales, e.g. in October 1797, when, several persons having been convicted of murder, perjury, and forgery, "one of the criminals was condemned to suffer death; another to be burned in the hand and imprisoned twelve months . . .; and three to stand in the pillory, to which their ears were to be nailed. These last affording something like amusement to the mob, were sufficiently covered with dirt and rotten eggs" (Collins, *op. cit.*, p. 358).

FIRST PHASE OF THE PENAL SETTLEMENT 71

when legislation abolished the procession Dr. Samuel Johnson's indignation ran hot against the statute, which he said was "running mad after innovation." It was only in that year, also, that the moderate mercy of the drop was vouchsafed to persons being hanged; before that, slow strangling was the manner in which many passed, kicking from crude gallows by the highroads of England.

Imprisonment and transportation were other punitive methods used. Janssen computed[1] that in the twenty-three years 1749–71, 5,199 persons had been sentenced at the Old Bailey to transportation for terms of seven or fourteen years, and 401 "by the King's mercy" (i.e. for life, in commutation of death sentence). From 1769 to 1776, 6,720 were transported from all England—an average only half that of the previous seven years, because, we are told,[2] judges were growing reluctant to prescribe this form of punishment. Convicts sentenced to transportation were delivered by justice to contractors, who, vying for profit with those other contractors "for the poor," might sell them to a Maryland planter for the term of their sentences. (The transports of 1787 and thereafter would merely be "assigned" by the Transport Commissioners to the shipmaster conveying them, by him to the Governor, and, it might be, by him in turn to private service.)

The theory of the punishment of imprisonment contemplated two kinds of gaol—first, the county gaol, for the reception of accused persons before or during trial, of insolvent debtors, and of prisoners awaiting execution of some other sentence than imprisonment; second, the house of correction, or "bridewell," which was supposed to be reserved for criminals who had been sentenced to imprisonment. But the distinction was one of law rather than of fact: when John Howard made a tour of the gaols, in 1787–88, the common county gaols of England and Wales housed almost as many debtors as felons, and, just as in the hulk at Gosport was a heterogeneous company of some who were to be "transported for life, and

[1] *Cit.* Howard, *ibid.*, p. 255.   [2] *Ibid.*, p. 246.

some whose sentence was for a short term, among them . . . boys of only ten years of age," so in the gaols various classes of offenders were confined together. In Newgate, where in 1785, Edmund Burke had been aghast to find, as many as 558 prisoners were housed, Howard found 613 three years later. They comprised ten men and a woman awaiting execution of the death sentence, sixty-three men and nineteen women respited from execution, one hundred and eighty-three men and one hundred and three women awaiting transportation, fifty-seven men and nineteen women awaiting trial, forty men and four women imprisoned for non-payment of fines, and one hundred and fourteen persons imprisoned for debt.[1]

Yet this was after an era of "reform." After Howard's evidence before a select committee of 1774, Parliament had passed a series of relief Acts culminating in the Hulks Act, 1776 (16 George III, cap. 43); they included an Act (14 George III, cap. 20) to regulate cleanliness and ventilation in prisons, and another (14 George III, cap. 59) to make unlawful the holding for their "gaol fees" of persons who had been acquitted or who had not been indicted. Again, in 1779, after Howard's evidence before a select committee of 1778, Parliament had passed Judge Blackstone and William Eden's Penitentiary Act (19 George III, cap. 74), by which it was intended to establish two reformatory penitentiaries for sentenced prisoners. (This Act abolished the punishment of burning in the hand for felony.) None of these measures was effected except the Hulks Act, nor were later statutory provisions more effective. In 1788 liquor was still being sold to prisoners in Newgate and the Fleet, in spite of a 1784 Act (24 George III, cap. 54, section 22) which prohibited this practice. In Clerkenwell, prisoners were still in 1788 being detained for their fees (contrary to 14 George III, cap. 59). "In some county gaols," Howard wrote[2] of this last extraordinary abuse, "the salaries to the gaolers are in lieu of

[1] Howard, *ibid.*, p. 125. *Vide* his chapter on English gaols for description of a somewhat similar confusion throughout the country.
[2] *Ibid.*, p. 129.

all fees, whereby the hardship of forcing poor creatures to part with some of their scanty clothing, in order to purchase their discharge, is prevented." But such an arrangement was not universal. The rules of Hull Town and County Gaol, published in 1786 pursuant to Act 32 George II, cap. 28, stated as due from a prisoner 7s. a week for board and lodging, or 2s. if he provided his own food, or 6d. if he found his own bed as well, *plus* 13s. 4d. payment to the gaoler on discharge and 1s. 4d. to the turnkey. As for the requirement of cleanliness under 14 George III, cap. 20, even Flint Gaol, built in 1785, evoked Howard's adverse comment after a visit only a couple of years later. In Macclesfield of the silk weavers stood a gaol, the property of a peer, which comprised "four rooms at the back of the keeper's public house, quite out of repair, the staircase so ruinous that the prisoners ascend by a rope." Ninety-two army deserters lay in three 20 feet-square rooms of Westminster Prison; many of the men were "almost naked" and some were in heavy irons. Hertfordshire County Gaol had "no bath, though '—as Howard added, perhaps ironically— "though the surgeon observed the propriety of it in gaol fevers."

For convicts under sentence of transportation in Phillip's wake to New South Wales, the proper place before embarkation was none of these pesthouses, but one or another of seven hulks which lay moored in the Thames at Woolwich, and at the harbours of Plymouth, Gosport, and Langston. The hulk or galley was the means which had been devised to meet the emergency created by the cessation of the convict traffic with America. A month before Phillip's fleet made landfall at Botany Bay, the Plymouth hulk accommodated ninety-two men and a woman. Sixty-eight of the three hundred and sixty-six prisoners in the hulk *Dunkirk*, in August 1788, were confined in an area 57 feet by 18 feet, the room being only 6 feet high.

But the law had been merciful to great numbers of those who lay in the foul hulks and gaols of England. As we saw

(Chapter 1), the death sentence required in so many cases by the law was at last executed in only a small proportion of cases. True, out of 1,121 sentenced to death at the Old Bailey in 1749-71, 678 were executed—the offences ranging from "shoplifting, riot, and twelve other crimes" (by 240 persons) through housebreaking, highway robbery, and horse-stealing (660 in all) to murder (81). And in the next dozen years, 1772-83, the number of executions in London and Middlesex was 467, and in the four years 1784-87, 298. But, as Pitt's Solicitor-General of 1785 pointed out, wholesale strangling of youths, for any one of a plentitude of offences lately denominated capital crimes, did not deter others from hazarding their lives. Government policy at this time aimed a little nearer the root of the social evil, seeking rather to prevent crime, by improved police and detective methods, than to "declare new offences or punishments"[1]—though in debate in the Commons some members still protested that it was the failure to execute the death sentence as a rule that, depriving the law of its terror, encouraged the spread of crime. But as we may see from Janssen's figures the proportion of death sentences executed was comparatively high, in the period immediately before the establishment of the New South Wales penal settlement, and liberal opinion, revolted by the inescapable spectacle of public hangings, assisted in driving the Tory Government towards its refuge in the alternative of a new extended system of transportation. This was the King's mercy. A condition of the initiation of transportation to New South Wales was, indeed, the reluctance of many judges to insist upon execution of the death sentence upon small thieves, and a common habit of juries of finding that stolen guineas were in fact only shillings—so that an accused man who had stolen, for instance, twenty guineas from a dwelling or a till, would be found guilty of having stolen £1 19s. in the first case or 4s. 11d. in the second, in order to avert the death sentence from him. "In the early part of the nineteenth century," as a result of this sickened

[1] *Vide Parliamentary History*, vol. xxv, col. 888.

FIRST PHASE OF THE PENAL SETTLEMENT 75

social conscience, "the proportion of executions to the number of capital sentences passed varied from a fifth to a ninth."[1] Even earlier, the common expedient of juries, and the frequent exercise of the King's prerogative of mercy, had diminished greatly the number of executions after capital conviction. Voltaire had been provoked to write:[2] "It is singular that England, where the better classes are so enlightened, leaves on the statute book so great a mass of absurd laws. They are not executed, it is true; but they compel the nation to leave to the executive power the right of modifying or infringing the law."

This anomaly, with its background of a terroristic penal code and noisome, overcrowded places of confinement, attracted the shocked or irritated attention of philanthropists and the authorities alike. An upshot as far as parliamentary action was concerned was the enactment of the palliative legislation of the 1770's and 1780's. Even the first transports sent to New South Wales might share in the boons which were on offer. An Act (30 George III, cap. 47) gave the Governor power to pardon absolutely or conditionally.[3] For two pressing situations were exaggerating the difficulty of the problem of crime and punishment in Britain as the eighteenth century neared its end.

In the first place, offences against property, which kept pace with the proletarianization of great numbers by enclosures and

---

[1] *Progress of the Nation in its various social and economical relations from the beginning of the nineteenth century*, by G. R. Porter, p. 635; London, 1851. The proportion of capital sentences executed was lower in the 1830's on the eve of the abolition of transportation to New South Wales as uneconomic. In 1835, 34 were executed, of 523 capitally convicted; in 1836, 17 out of 494 = 1 execution out of 20 capital convictions; vide *Annual Register* (*History of Europe*), 1837, pp. 227 *et seq*: speech of Lord John Russell. After the recommendations of royal commissioners appointed in 1833, many crimes were taken off the capital list, in the late 'thirties.

[2] *Prix de la justice et de l'humanité*, article 11, 1777; cit. Phillipson, *op. cit.*, p. 169.

[3] *Vide* Grenville to Phillip, November 13, 1790, Enc., *Historical Records of Australia*, I, i, p. 208, for Phillip's authorization under this Act.

industrialism, were provoking at once a deepening of the penal code's horrors and a disinclination on the part of judges and juries to subject their fellow men to the code's worst rigours. In the second place, the cessation of convict transportation to the southern colonies of North America, almost complete by 1776,[1] was accentuating the pressure of convicted felons on Britain's penal accommodation. Authority strove by expedients to deal with the consequences of the crisis thus induced by two major sets of circumstances, while at the same time it responded to some extent to the demands of reformers for an alleviation of the condition of the chief sufferers—the "victims of the law" as Burke had justly called them. The acts of amelioration were not, as we saw, very effective. However, men like Bentham and Romilly were seeking, even before the extra aggravating circumstance of the closure of America to British transports, the reclamation for society of those who had offended against the laws. Bentham published in 1778 a pamphlet, *View of the Hard Labour Bill*, which advocated the author's views of the best reformatory system, as differing from those of Howard, Blackstone, Eden, and John Fothergill (a Quaker physician and philanthropist), which were embodied in the Penitentiary Act. Bentham offered, in March 1792, to accept responsibility for a thousand convicts under his Panopticon system. Parliament accepted the offer by Act of 1794

[1] It is to be noted, however (cf. *Annual Register*, 1788, *Chronicle*, p. 223), that although Phillip's first fleet had sailed for New South Wales on May 13, 1787, after Orders in Council had denominated New South Wales as the new convict terminus, apparently some convicts were being sent, even thereafter, to Canada.

According to the *Annual Register*, the Recorder of London and the Secretary of State for Home Affairs, Lord Sydney, discussed, in 1788, the ". . . delay of sending aboard those under sentence of transportation."

The report continued: "The season is over for sending them to Quebec or Nova Scotia; but assurances have been given that two ships . . . shall be ready by the latter end of March next, to convey convicts to America."

It would appear from this that the British Government, awaiting the issue of the penal settlement in Australia, still looked to such of America as still acknowledged the British authority, as being a possible transportation terminus.

(34 George III, cap. 84) and in 1799 Bentham bought the site of Millbank Penitentiary for £12,000. Old George III opposed Bentham's plan (*cf. History of the War between Jeremy Bentham and George the Third*, "by one of the belligerents"), and in 1811 a select committee of the House of Commons reported against the Bentham scheme. (Millbank Penitentiary was however established in 1816.) The Howard scheme did not come to anything. Fothergill, appointed with Howard and Whately (secretary of the Foundling Hospital) a "supervisor" of the execution of plans after the Penitentiary Act, died at the end of 1780, after which Howard resigned, because of differences with the third supervisor, and the project was allowed to lapse. Indeed it would not be for a generation that the penal code would be rationalized; and yet another generation would pass before a penitentiary system was much used in England. Reform had to wait upon the appropriate circumstance of necessity. The obduracy of the bad old system to reform, until necessity forced reform, is illustrated vividly enough by the inscription, revelatory of much that was characteristic of the age, which Howard found engraved in black and white marble at the front of the Flint Gaol, when he visited it in 1788. The inscription read:

In the twenty-fifth year of His Majesty George III . . . this prison was erected instead of the ancient loathsome place of confinement, in pity to the misery of even the most guilty, to alleviate the sufferings of lesser offenders or of the innocent themselves, whom the chances of human life may bring within these walls. Done at the expense of the county aided by the subscriptions of several of the Gentry, who, in the midst of most distressful days, voluntarily took on themselves part of the burden in compassion to such of their countrymen on whom Fortune had been less bounteous of her favours.

Karl Marx, the exponent of a materialist conception of history, could have enjoyed the implications of the inscription. John Howard said of the gaol behind it, simply, "It is not kept clean."

(b) A Prison Farm Economy in New South Wales, 1788-92

By a clearance of England's gaols and the transportation of long-term convicts to "Botany Bay," Pitt's Government might, it seemed, remove some accumulated consequences of the cruelty and ineptitude which had distinguished authority. Colonization, in an unexamined country, was connoted by this enterprise. And it must be impossible to approach understanding of the economic base which was to be laid now in Australia, or of the peculiar society which would be developed there, without constant reference to a principal controlling factor. That is the variation of the volume of the human and capital flow from Britain. This factor, in its application to the first thirty years of New South Wales settlement, is almost exclusively the item of transportation.

Now chiefly because of the wars the flow of convicts to Australia was intermittent; at times it was quite dammed from the colony; it varied as widely as the volume of an Australian river from season to season. But the original settlement was made for the reason, above all, that convict-settlers should fashion a reservoir into which later transports could follow them; the force of the flow itself, to be directed at the terminus, must gouge out a bed sufficient to contain a sustained stream from the prison-springs of England. Such was the theory.

We find that the main control of early Australian settlement was in practice a variable according to forces outside itself. If the variations were wide, lesser controls might well become greater, in which case the original plan must go awry. This is what happened in the first years. After three fleets had brought more than four thousand men, women, and children to Phillip's New South Wales in 1788-92, almost no convicts were sent until, after the turn of the century, a few hundreds were sent each year. The period of quiet, after Phillip's term, in the office of the Transport Commissioners, made possible as we shall see an irreparable breach in the Imperial Government's plan. Here we may notice simply that, the great majority of the first fleeters having served their sentences by

FIRST PHASE OF THE PENAL SETTLEMENT 79

1792, several administrations after Phillip's were dealing, not with a settlement which was almost absolutely a penal settlement, but with the raw material of a colony subject to local influences rather than to the influences which had determined Phillip's establishment and his proceedings in office, viz. the policies of Whitehall.

What this difference implies is of the greatest importance in any comparative study of early Australian epochs. Phillip was required to undertake, with meagre supplies of material except human material—and that of poor quality—a serious social and economic experiment. The first few administrators after him inherited his construction but were not forced, as he had been, to make room periodically, in his half-built colonial house, for unpredictable battalions for whom work and bread had to be found. In fact more than ten times as many convicts were sent to Phillip's charge during his five years as were sent during the three years' officers' administration of Grose and Paterson immediately after him. This circumstance, a vital one, is the weightier for the necessities, peculiar to Phillip's task, of establishing settlement; setting production in train on areas of which no geographical or economic survey had been made; caring, during the period of establishment, for a thousand people—with almost no means other than those supplied by Government in 1787. And, as we may now inform ourselves, Government's provision, human as well as material, was ill-selected.

Broken men and women from the gaols and hulks were much of Phillip's material for colonization. Few of them were atrocious criminals. On the contrary, the crimes for which six hundred out of his seven hundred convicts had been convicted were not indicative of depravity; by the standards of the time they were minor offences though felonies—for the six hundred were serving sentences of only seven years:[1] mild

[1] *Vide note 61, Historical Records of Australia*, 1, i, p. 729—83 per cent of the first fleet convicts who were landed were undergoing sentence of seven years' transportation.

punishment for lesser offenders, under a penal code ordaining death (which might be commuted to life transportation) for nearly two hundred offences. But, atrocious criminals as they were not, they were not the stuff for colonization. Too many of the people from the first six transport ships were tragically or ludicrously unfitted for the pioneering life and labour. "After a careful examination of the convicts," Phillip's surgeon said[1] some time after the landing, "I find upwards of one hundred who must ever be a burden to the settlement, not being able to do any kind of labour, from old age or chronical diseases of long standing. Amongst the females there is one who has lost the use of her limbs upwards of three years, and amongst the males two who are perfect idiots." (This report was made after the arrival of the second fleet in 1790.) "Such," the Governor commented, "are the people sent from the different gaols and from the hulks, where it is said the healthy and the artificers are retained. The sending out the disordered and helpless clears the gaols, and may ease the parishes from which they are sent; but, sir, it is obvious that this settlement, instead of being a colony which is to support itself, will, if the practice is continued, remain for years a burthen to the mother country." There is a mass of evidence to show the cogency of the first Governor's plea. His Judge-Advocate noted[2] the death, in October 1789, of a convict woman who had been sent out insane and had remained so. Hunter, who had sailed with the first fleet and would be Governor from 1795, recalled[3] before a select committee of 1812 that boys and girls of twelve years had been transported, and men and women of more than seventy years. Fifty-two of the original seven hundred and seventeen were found by the surgeon, six months after arrival, to be unfit for all labour, because of age or

[1] *Cit.* Phillip to Grenville, July 17, 1790; *ibid.*, p. 197; and *cf.* Collins, *op. cit.*, pp. 32, 41, 64, on the physical state of the convicts.

[2] Collins, *op. cit.*, p. 41.

[3] *Report from the Select Committee on Transportation*, ordered to be printed, July 12, 1812, *Minutes of Evidence*, p. 22.

infirmity.[1] The nominally able-bodied were in general a poor lot. John Palmer, purser of H.M.S. *Sirius* in the first fleet and later for years head of the Commissariat at Sydney, gave his opinion[2] that an average convict would do little more than half the day's labour of a free man.

These poorest of the poor types bred and spoiled in the slums and shires, and then imprisoned for years before being bundled aboard a convict ship, succumbed to disease with a remarkable readiness. Probably forty of the convicts, with five of their children, died on the trip out in 1787, and twenty-eight more, with eight children, died within the first six months of settlement.[3] So, less than fifteen months after sailing, only 637 of the original 757 embarked as prisoners, were available for work of any kind.

There was no early improvement of the position; by a count of July 1788, six months after settlement began sixteen per cent of the original transports were dead or useless; eighteen months later (before the second fleet arrived) the total loss since sailing day in May 1787 of convict personnel, by death, desertion, or original infirmity, amounted to nearly twenty-two per cent.[4] A death-rate of 47 per 1,000 per annum in the settlement in 1788–89 rivals the rates reached during the worst periods of the eighteenth century at home in England and (as only six of the seventy-two deaths in New South Wales during the first twenty-one months of settlement are attributable to the hangman) suggests an uncommonly high vulnerability among the pioneers of Australia. Unnatural vice was common where there was but one convict woman to four men, and where only one marine in seven had his wife. (In those circum-

---

[1] Phillip to Sydney, July 9, 1788, enclosure 3; *Historical Records of Australia*, 1, i, pp. 53, 54.

[2] 1812 Committee, *Minutes of Evidence*, p. 63.

[3] Phillip to Sydney, July 9, 1788, *cf.* footnote 1, p. 38 *supra*, for other accounts of mortality among the first fleet's people.

[4] For the figures on which this percentage is struck, *vide* Collins, *op. cit.*, p. 41, and Phillip to Sydney, February 12, 1790; *Historical Records of Australia*, 1, i, p. 144.

stances a birth-rate of 33 per 1,000 records a special response on the part of the settlement's few women.)

The colony was not better off for the reinforcement which the second fleet brought in mid-1790. "Of the 930 males sent out by the last ships," Phillip wrote,[1] "261 died on board, and 50 have died since landing." This was a death-rate of one in three, over a few months—and of the 619 survivors, 450 were on the sick list immediately after landing.

Yet Phillip's instructions[2] required him to found a colony which should maintain itself.

To add to the difficulties of forwarding this fantastic enterprise of the Crown, the Governor's garrison officers of the Royal Marines refused any duty other than military duty, and would not, for instance, assist in the management of the convicts in Phillip's attempt to have land cleared and cultivated. "Here are only convicts to attend to convicts," Phillip wrote,[3] "and who in general fear to exert any authority and very little labour is drawn from them in a country which requires the greatest exertions." And where were the practised agriculturalists who would help the settlement over its early stages? "Two people who were farmers," and the clerk of H.M.S. *Sirius* and a smith, were at the business of cultivation by May 1788. These were Henry Edward Dodd, who was Phillip's servant, William Broughton, Thomas Freeman, and Walter Brodie. Dodd worked hard and successfully on the land of Sydney from February 1788 until his last illness three years later; Phillip said of him that he was "the person who had been directing the convicts' labour at Rose Hill (n.b., modern Parramatta), and who was the only person in this settlement equal to the charge."[4] For of five superintendents sent out "to

---

[1] Collins, *op. cit.*, p. 197; elsewhere (*ibid.*, p. 189) Phillip gave the numbers who had sailed in the second fleet as 1,006 men and 89 women.

[2] Phillip's first and second commissions (October 12, 1786, April 2, 1787) and his instructions (April 25, 1787) are given in *Historical Records of Australia*, I, i, pp. 1–15.

[3] Phillip to Sydney, May 16, 1788; *ibid.*, p. 35.

[4] Phillip to Grenville, March 4, 1791, *ibid.*, pp. 247 *et seq.*

instruct the convicts in agriculture" only one was a farmer, though two of the others had been "used to farming" as youths.[1] However, one James Ruse, who had been sentenced in July 29, 1782, to seven years' transportation, settled down in November 1789 to be Australia's first independent farmer. Ruse told a sceptical Governor that he would be able to support himself, on his given acre, by January 1791, and indeed by February 25th of that year he "declined receiving any further support, being then able to maintain himself."[2] But Ruse was a rare bird of bright plumage, among those bedraggled, wing-clipped, ailing thousands. Most of them would be freed within a year or so[3] of Ruse's initial success; but how could they be fitted to fly?

The impediments were great. As if it were not enough to have saddled the enterprise with unskilled, inefficient, or disinclined labour, inept superintendents, a large invalid element, a crazy sex-balance, stiffbacked officers, and the responsibility of receiving more crowded, death-haunted convict ships, the Commissioners had omitted to provide Phillip with tools and

[1] Phillip to Grenville, June 20, 1790; *Historical Records of Australia*, 1, i, p. 185. [2] *Ibid.*, November 5, 1791.

[3] Many of the first fleeters had served a large portion of their sentences before sailing, and would have to be freed before, according to any commonsense expectation, a place as freedmen could be found for them in the new community; the authorities had made no provision for their return to England. Collins said in 1789 (*op. cit.*, p. 58, *et cf. Historical Records of Australia*, 1, i, p. 719), "Notwithstanding little more than two years had elapsed since the first fleet left England, some convicts claimed they had served their term"; but in any case they could not be freed, for Whitehall had omitted to send their papers with them (*ibid.*, pp. 179 *et seq.*).

At the time of the first fleet's arrival, in fact, the average period of sentence still to be served was four yearstwo months. As Phillip had hinted, the Government's policy was, incidentally at least, the deportation of the unfit; still in 1797 Hunter had to complain that many arrivals, having been sentenced to seven years, had but eighteen months or two years to serve (Hunter to Portland, June 10, 1797; *Historical Records of Australia*, 1, ii, p. 32). For several years of the new century many convicts were being sent without record of the sentence passed upon them, and forty years after settlement began Darling said that the transports arriving included some who were too young for labour.

seed and stock sufficient for the initial tasks of settlement. Phillip's instructions of April 1787 had indicated flax as a plant that should be grown—for "an ultimate article of export"—and the Secretary of State had anticipated an immediate efflux from England of free emigrants who should, without much cost to Government, solve promptly the problem of feeding the convicts on Government labour. Lord Grenville, finding "a disposition of many people to emigrate from this country," required Phillip to grant each such settler, on arrival, land, convict labour, tools, and seed grain as well as rations. Actually the first free emigrants arrived only after Phillip's departure from New South Wales; the ship *Bellona*, which brought them, carried nine female convicts (three under sentence of fourteen years) and thirteen free persons, including a family of seven. "I am sorry to add," wrote Grenville's successor, Henry Dundas, at the Home Office, "that the above settlers are all that have offered themselves." Major Francis Grose, Lieutenant-Governor after Phillip's retirement late in 1792 through ill-health, settled the five immigrant families on grants of 60–120 acres apiece at Liberty Plains (the Homebush-Strathfield suburban district of modern Sydney). However, during the first five years there was no immigrant to assist in the pioneering work. Convicts, discharged marines, and oddments from the first fleet were the pioneer colonists of Australia. Convicts who laboured on public works and then were set up as peasants—with afterwards some political offenders, whose services were not assigned to the Colonial Government, and some "gentlemanly convicts," who were liberated on tickets of leave as a matter of course—did the work of starting an Australian economy. For years there were very few farmers in Australia save "settlers from convicts" and "settlers from marines."[1]

[1] For the facts in this paragraph *vide Historical Records of Australia*, I, i, pp. 13, 125, 364 *et seq.*, 771; Howell's *State Trials*, vol. xxiii, note at the conclusion of the report of the trial of the Rev. T. F. Palmer, 1793; *Minutes of Evidence*, 1812, Transportation Committee, p. 29.

Phillip, in spite of difficulties, established nearly two hundred such before the first phase of New South Wales came to an end. His instructions had empowered him to grant freed convicts thirty acres each (fifty acres in the case of married men, with ten acres for each child). Such grants were to be free of quit-rents and taxes for ten years; a condition of residence and cultivation was specified; and the ex-convict was to be given working capital in kind, and Government-maintained labour. However, while all were still under sentence and ignorant of the land, public farming had to be got under way. In May 1788, four months after landing, Phillip reported that "the great labour in clearing the ground will not permit more than eight acres to be sown this year with wheat and barley. At the same time the immense number of ants and field mice will render our crops very uncertain." Again, it was necessary to detail some of the convicts for the officers' service, and Phillip had to seek instructions as to his power of assignment. "The not having the power of immediately granting lands" (i.e. receiving grants), he wrote, "the officers likewise feel as a hardship." In the meantime having power to make grants only to a projected convict-peasantry, the Governor set what hands he had to clearing and sowing. Dodd made the first sowing at the head of Farm Cove, and then superintended one hundred convicts put to cultivation on land at Rose Hill, a few miles inland. Bread was the first business, for none knew when fresh supplies of flour might be available from England. "Sheep do not thrive in this country at present," Phillip found in Australia's first year as a settlement of white men; and in any case the stock in hand was low, in spite of Phillip's purchases on his own and the public account, at the Cape of Good Hope *en route*. In May 1788 there were at the settlement seven horses, two bulls, five cows, twenty-nine sheep, nineteen goats, seventy-four pigs, five rabbits, and some poultry. A little later, three sheep died and (a serious matter) the cattle strayed.

By July the settlement on the western side of the Tank Stream (Pitt Street of modern Sydney), which was in the command of Major Ross, the Lieutenant-Governor, had about four acres prepared, and Phillip's main settlement on the eastern side had eight or ten acres. Dodd, "the only person cultivating for the public benefit," had by February 1790 advanced his Rose Hill enterprise so far as to have harvested 200 bushels of wheat, sixty of barley, and a little flax, maize, and oats, most of it being set aside for seed. The first Australian crop had been brought in during the previous November, "the Governor's farm" at Sydney having harvested about thirty-five bushels in addition.[1] Nevertheless the shadow of famine lay on the little company of a thousand, sent half-way round the world to this uninviting remoteness where they laboured uncheered by tidings from home.

The supplies in the Commissariat store began to look so meagre that in the autumn of 1790 Phillip sent to Norfolk Island, off the New South Wales coast, 65 military, with five dependents, and 183 convicts, with 27 children. Added to the party sent earlier to the island, the new arrivals made a total of 408 people, compared with 593 on the mainland, where the soil seemed less readily productive. During the year flour had to be sought by the despatch of a ship to the Cape of Good Hope, and from April 1st the settlers, already on short rations, were further reduced—officers, soldiers, officials, convicts alike—to a weekly allowance of 4 lb. of flour, 2½ lb. of pork, and 1½ lb. of rice per head. When a fortnight later, H.M.S. *Sirius* was wrecked on the reefs off Norfolk Island, only the small tender *Supply* was left to serve the settlement and bring it in touch with the far-off world of large, self-contained communities. (The transports and storeships of the original fleet had gone on to China.) After the loss of the *Sirius* the ration was reduced again, to 2½ lb. of flour, 2 lb. of pork, "1 pint pease" and 1 lb. of rice—"children under eighteen months

[1] Facts from—Phillip to Sydney, May 15, 1788, May 16, 1788; Phillip to Nepean, July 5, 1788; Philip to Sydney, July 9, 1788; Phillip to Nepean, July 9, 1788; Phillip to Sydney, February 2, 1799; *Historical Records of Australia*, 1, i, pp. 22, 35, 45, 52, 54, 146; Collins, *op. cit.*, p. 68.

excepted, who were to have only 1 lb. of salt meat." From long storage the pork, when boiled, shrank to "three or four morsels," and now the thousand had to tighten their belts and rest their hopes in the *Supply*, sent on April 17th to Batavia for stores. Undismayed, Phillip was at this time writing an account of his experiment with Ruse, "to know in what time a man might be able to cultivate a sufficient quantity of ground to support himself."

But such experiment must be limited, now, even more than hitherto, for, as Collins wrote in May, "Very little labour could be expected from men who had nothing to eat." What strength they had was devoted to preparing the cleared ground at Sydney and Rose Hill for sowings of wheat and barley. "The quantity of either article, however, to be now sown, fell far short of what their necessities required." Relief came from England two months after the *Supply's* departure, or three years and a month since the first fleet had left England.[1]

On June 20th the *Justinian* arrived with stores. A few days later the second fleet landed its hundreds of sick and dying convicts. On July 25th Phillip had 1,715 mouths to fill at Sydney, and 524 at Norfolk Island, a total of 2,239 in "New South Wales and its Dependencies"; 1,557 were convicts. Want was still a constant attendant. By March of 1791 Phillip had three brick stores built, a barracks for a hundred men in use at Rose Hill, and an officers' barracks almost ready at Sydney. (By June 1789 the colonial brickworks, which had "hitherto only made ten thousand bricks a month," had kilns in which thirty thousand "might be burnt off at the same time"; this was the source of supply of improved building material, where wattle and daub huts, and tents, had had to serve.) Later in the year, Phillip heard from Grenville that "systematic transportation" was to be pursued at a regular rate of two ships

---

[1] *Vide* Phillip to Sydney, April 11, 1790; *Historical Records of Australia*, 1, i, pp. 165 *et seq.*; Collins, *op. cit.*, p. 74; Phillip to Nepean, April 16, 1790, enclosure, *Historical Records of Australia*, 1, i, p. 175; Collins, p. 78; Phillip to Grenville, June 17, 1790; Collins, p. 82.

per annum. In fact systematic transportation would not be found possible for a quarter of a century to come, until after the wars; but at least Phillip had accomplished the beginnings of his peasant system of reception—of convicts who did not come, or who, if they had, would not have been welcomed as freedmen-farmers by the officers who would rule after Phillip. In November 1791 Phillip could advise Grenville that the first expirees had been settled on Parramatta grants, in accordance with the scheme of 1787. Forty-four expirees had been settled between March 30th and August 17th of this year, in addition to thirty-one time-expired marines who had elected to stay in the country rather than return to England (where the New South Wales Corps was being raised to relieve the garrison), and nine seamen and an ex-superintendent, a total of 85 settlers. (Two of the marines were from H.M.S. *Sirius*, the remainder from Ross's command.) The grants to these first colonists totalled 4,180 acres, the marines as a rule being granted sixty acres, the ex-convicts thirty or fifty acres each.[1] Phillip had power now to make grants to N.C.O.s and men of the military, but not to officers. In any case he could not have spared the labour for large farmers such as commissioned officers might expect to be. Phillip was "very far from wishing to throw the smallest obstacle in the way of officers obtaining grants of land; but in the present state of this colony the numbers employed on the public buildings . . . and in other

[1] N.C.O.s and men could be granted land under Phillip's additional instructions of August 1789. Grants to officers were authorized only by despatch of July 14, 1792, which was received by Phillip's successor, Major Grose. For the facts in the paragraph *vide* Phillip to Nepean, July 24, 1790, *Historical Records of Australia*, 1, i, p. 203, Collins, *op. cit.*, p. 57, Grenville to Phillip, February 19, 1791, Phillip to Grenville, November 5, 1791, *ibid.*, pp. 215, 278; *Return of land grants*, November 5, 1791, *ibid.*, pp. 279–282; note that Shann writes (*An Economic History of Australia*, p. 13; Cambridge University Press, 1930), "Phillip granted only 3,389 acres in all." Shann does not cite an authority, but apparently he got the figure from Rusden (*History of Australia*, by G. W. Rusden, vol. i, p. 183; Melbourne, Melville, Mullen & Slade, 1897). Actually Phillip's first batch of grants exceeded the figure given, and later grants brought his total to a good deal more than double the Rusden-Shann figure.

occupations equally necessary," left him few convicts for public farming, let alone farming experiments by unused persons from the mess.

Whaling, meanwhile, and sealing had been entered upon tentatively, and a few edible fish caught eked out the Commissary's thin ration issue. On the land Phillip's grantees numbered 147 by December—45 at Parramatta, 102 at Norfolk Island—including 73 ex-convicts, 62 ex-marines, 11 ex-seamen, and a former superintendent. About 400 bushels was harvested in 1791, but when sowing time came next year—"little labour is done at present, for the people are in general very weak," as in this season two years before. Weather conditions (which obstinately would *not* reproduce those of Sussex) changed to "a long drought"—there would be perpetual drought in Australia, according to the too English computations of the next forty years—but the 1792 maize crop was no less than 4,844½ bushels. Of this, 2,649½ bushels was issued as bread (as the 408 bushels of the previous crop had been), and 695 bushels kept for seed. The rest was stolen—for "from the time the corn began to ripen to the time it was housed, the convicts were pressed by hunger." Nevertheless public farming had progressed to a point at which a thousand acres was under maize, wheat, and barley at Parramatta and Toongabbe, a hundred acres was in gardens, and the "settlers from convicts," marines, etc., had 416 acres in cultivation, 1,516 acres in all. In October 1792, on the eve of Phillip's departure from the colony, there were 68 settlers at Parramatta, including 53 expirees, and one pardoned convict, and 104 at Norfolk Island, including 48 expirees, and 1,703½ acres was in cultivation.[1] But for years to come the settlement would have frequent spells on short rations.

[1] For these facts *vide* Phillip to Dundas, October 4, 1792, to Nepean, November 18, 1791, to Grenville, December 15, 1791, to Dundas, March 19, 1792, October 2, 1792, October 4, 1792, enclosure No. 1; *Historical Records of Australia*, 1, i, pp. 383 *et seq.*, 307, 324, 339, 373, 391.

It seems desirable to notice in a final comment on the subject matter of the foregoing chapter, the peculiar account and estimate of Phillip, and the early years of the New South Wales settlement, given by the only scholar to have published a complete outline economic history of Australia. Professor Edward Shann writes (*op. cit.*, p. 12) approvingly of Macquarie's saying, a generation after the first settlement, that Phillip "with slender resources accomplished much," but adds his own judgment which dismisses Phillip's achievement thus: "This ration system, based on a central commissariat store, was the economic last ditch, communism, but it sufficed to hold off wholesale death by famine." Again, Shann states his view that after Phillip's term, which on so abrupt a summary would be taken as having made a stopgap but seen no construction, two factors "opened the way in December 1792 to a new economic policy" (*ibid.*, p. 15). These two factors, Shann finds, were (1) the 1792 instructions from Henry Dundas, the Secretary of State, to Phillip (despatch received by Grose), empowering land grants to officers and the assignment of convicts' services to them; and (2) "the relaxation of control which occurs in every despotism at a change in rulers."

These conclusions are not well founded. In the first place, Dundas's instructions were not an amendment of Phillip's chosen economic policy, but they supplied an omission of the British policy as laid down for him; moreover, this course which legalized individual settlement by officers, was prompted by representations of Phillip himself. Phillip described the omission of officers from the scheme of land grants, for which others were eligible, in official letters to Lord Sydney, dated May 15 and May 16, 1788, and his despatch of October 4, 1792 to Dundas under this head crossed Dundas's instructions affirming the eligibility of officers for land and labour from the Crown. In one of his earliest despatches, dated May 15, 1788, indeed, Phillip reported, "It is necessary to permit a part of the convicts to work for the officers," to clear land for cultivation, and pointed out that under his instructions he was, strictly, without authority for the course he had taken. Further, on July 10, 1788, Phillip made it clear in a despatch to Lord Sydney that he realized the need for farmers, if the object was to be attained of colonial self-support. Again, the implication that the 1792 instructions "opened the way to a new economic policy" at variance from Phillip's—to a policy of settlement by individual rather than public enterprise—is in no wise justifiable by any comparison of the executive acts of Phillip, and of the military administrators, Grose and Paterson, who followed him. Phillip, in the circumstances of poor equipment, unaccustomed climatic and other local conditions, unskilled management and labour, officers' intransigence, almost complete severance from outside sources of supply, drought, and food shortage, established during his five years 172 settlers on land grants totalling about 12 square miles, of which about 3 square miles was being farmed at the time of Phillip's making his last return (October 1792). This was the measure of the individual settlement which he enabled from April 1791 to October 1792, eighteen months.

The grants which would be made under the "new economic policy" of the New South Wales Corps officers—a policy which therefore was by no means new—were in similar proportion; Grose granted 10,674 acres in his two years of office, Paterson 4,965 in his nine months. It might be, of course, that the

FIRST PHASE OF THE PENAL SETTLEMENT 91

"novelty" of the military men's economic policy consisted in their granting land to persons who could and would farm it, to the gain of the settlement, where Phillip's grantees could not and would not use the land. And indeed, Grose referred, in his first return of grants, to the officers as "at this time the only description of settlers on whom reliance can be placed" (Grose to Dundas, February 16, 1793; *Historical Records of Australia*, 1, i, pp. 415 *et seq.*, and May 30, 1793, enclosures, *ibid.*, 435, 438).

But Grose had been in the colony for no more than five months when thus he sweepingly characterized the community, and he could have known little of the planted settlers as farmers and nothing of his officers in this role; moreover, before his first year in Australia was out he was confessing to the Secretary of State, "I cannot but be alarmed at all I purchase, and everything I do, being unaccustomed to business, and fearful of acting so much from my own discretion" (September 3, 1793, *ibid.*, p. 447). Again, Grose's discretion failed at insistence on the requirement of residence and cultivation which Phillip had made a condition of grant, and which was impressed upon his successors by instructions from Whitehall. Thus Hunter found (Hunter to Portland, December 11, 1795, *ibid.*, p. 667), after Grose and Paterson, that his officer-predecessors had made grants without regard to the eligibility of recipients or to the prescribed forms; they had been in the habit of giving an order, "AB has my permission to settle," and, Hunter said, "this slip of paper served them as a sufficient authority to fix wherever they pleased." Assignment was made with such prodigality that, on Hunter's arrival, he "could scarcely call together twenty for any public purpose in New South Wales."

As to the other aspect of Phillip's "communism," rationing—which was, of course, not communism of any kind, but the inescapable procedure of a prison governor until he could make a gaol into a prison farm—Grose departed from it in the course of his "new economic policy" only so far as to make a discrimination in the scale of rationing: more to the soldiers, less to the convicts. And, in spite of his gratuitous assumption that officers of the N.S.W. Corps were the only reliable class of settlers available, Grose reported in September 1793 that Phillip's expiree-settlers were contributing to the colony's economy. "The settlers from convicts," he wrote, "have supplied the stores with some considerable quantity (of maize) from their farms, the which I have instructed may always be taken from them at 5s. per bushel, it being at the same time a cheap purchase for the Government and an accommodating market for the settler" (Grose to Dundas, September 3, 1793, *ibid.*, p. 447, *cf.* Shann's citation (*op. cit.*, *p.* 18) of this passage, "He (Grose) thought the 'settlers from convicts' an improvident crew, but he encouraged them to bring maize to the commissariat store by offering for it a fixed price of 5s. per bushel, 'it being, etc.' ").

It may be conceded, after this evidence, that it is a delusion to suppose that Phillip kept an unconstructive "shipboard communism" where farther-seeing military successors would, remedially, establish a new economic policy of private enteprrise.

Chapter 3

AN ECONOMY OF MONOPOLY IN NEW SOUTH WALES FROM 1793

(a) *Establishment of a Squirearchy, 1793–1800*
(b) *Re-establishment of a Peasantry, 1801–4*
(c) *Assisted and "Special" Emigration, 1793–1806.*
Appendices
    A. Early Currency of New South Wales
    B. Observed Resources of Early New South Wales

(a) *Establishment of a Squirearchy,* 1793–1800

MAJOR FRANCIS GROSE came to New South Wales in 1792 as Lieutenant-Governor and Commandant of the New South Wales Corps. This regiment had lately been raised to relieve the detachment of Royal Marines stationed at Sydney and to relieve, incidentally, the British military prisons of a proportion of the defaulters in them.[1] The relief of a garrison, and the advent of a new administrative head, would not ordinarily be worthy of special remark in a history of an economy. But Grose's coming with his regiment to New South Wales is in a special category. The captains and subalterns, surgeons and commissaries, in his command reversed within a few years the imperial policy for New South Wales, set up an economic system which was maintained in spite of the Crown during most of the long war-period, and, through the enterprise of

---

[1] The subsequent tumults of the New South Wales Corps detachment at Norfolk Island, during the administration of P. G. King as Lieutenant-Governor there, and the fact that some recruits for the Corps came under escort to the colony from English gaols, are less striking indicators of the character of the Corps personnel than the affair of the *Lady Shore* (*vide* Collins, *op. cit.*, p. 378). In 1798 this convict ship, *en route* to Sydney with a company of the Corps, was seized by the soldiers, who murdered the captain and delivered the ship to the Spanish authorities at Rio de la Plata.

one or two of them, forced at last the abandonment of the Imperial Government's plans for a peasant Australia. The pastoral occupation of the country by which they cancelled the official plans for an agricultural sub-division is, however, a story generally apart from that of their sabotage of the Government's settlement policy, during the years of unfettered military control in Sydney. It is with the story of their first enterprises that we are concerned first. We may have an impression of the results achieved by their peculiar brand of private enterprise when we have anticipated for a moment the narrative of seven years after Grose's advent to office, to consult some of the situations of the colony as the nineteenth century was about to begin.

When the year 1800 opened, ninety per cent of Australia's four hundred farmers knew that they, and most of the New South Wales population of five thousand, were economically in utter subjection to two dozen of their number. Seventy per cent of the people of the settlements (Sydney, Parramatta, the Hawkesbury, and Norfolk Island) drew rations from Government; but though officials fed them from the public store, it was not for the public they worked under the official's direction. Provisioning this majority was indeed almost the only essential function left to Government, in the colony which Government had set up for its purposes twelve years before. For the rest, those purposes had been subordinated to others. It was not that private enterprise had in the meantime succeeded communism: the plan of 1787–89 had looked forward to the evolution of private enterprise from a public enterprise necessarily initial. What had happened was that military rulers had diverted the evolutionary course: instead of pursuing as Phillip had the Imperial Government's arrangements for the settlement of ex-convicts and others as freeholding peasants in New South Wales, Phillip's two military successors had encouraged or allowed the settlement of a few persons on comparatively large holdings, and while not discontinuing the settlement of ex-convicts, had so perverted the official control of imports and the internal market as to make a fiction of the peasants' economic freedom. In sum, twenty-odd servants of the Crown had abused their authority to enlist the bond servants of the Crown in their private service at public cost, and to "enclose" the freed section of the community in a peculiar way.

The quickened enclosure movement of late eighteenth century England had already its parallel in infant Australia. In England the Crown gave legal form to the expulsion of cottagers by capitalist farmers; in New South Wales the operation was performed by an abuse of executive powers directly in the interest of the executive personnel.

Grose, under whose government an officers' system for New South Wales was substituted for the lately initiated Whitehall system, conducted his administration, from the early stages, in four circumstances of great importance. They were (1) the existence of Phillip's basis of an economy of production by public and small private farming; (2) the cessation of transportation because of the French Revolutionary War, in which Britain was engaged from early in 1793; (3) the distraction of Whitehall from the colony, and the impracticability of effective supervision of the Colonial Government, because of the war; (4) the long postponement of free emigration—that is of persons for whose settlement the New South Wales administration must be responsible to Whitehall—because of the war. Preoccupied even before Phillip's departure from Sydney with "the miseries of that precarious existence," aggravated by "the great drought,"[1] Grose soon was able to take action which, in the favourable circumstances mentioned, would render life in the colony less miserable for the regimental mess if not for the colonial majority.

Grose assumed control in mid-December 1792 of New South Wales and its four thousand people, including nearly two hundred farmers on about eight thousand acres of granted

[1] *Vide* Phillip to Dundas, October 2, 1792, enclosure, Grose to Phillip, and Grose to Dundas, January 9, 1793; *Historical Records of Australia*, I, i, pp. 381, 414.

land, of which a quarter was in cultivation. His abandonment of the imperial scheme was heralded when on Christmas Eve he bought the rum cargo of the American ship *Hope*. By the New Year, he had introduced a discrimination in the common ration scale, in the military's favour. By April, ten of his officers, including Lieutenant John Macarthur, were equipped with small grants of land. Before the year 1793 was out, convicts in large numbers had been withdrawn from public service and impressed into the service of the farmer-officers and Phillip's public farmlands had been allowed to go out of cultivation or had been alienated. Cargoes had been bought by officers from traders calling at the port, and soon officers would charter ships to fetch cargoes to Port Jackson, for sale at profits ranging from 500 to 1,000 per cent. The farmer-trader-officers were permitted to pay wages in spirits, and the Commissariat store fed the officers' bond labourers. Such was the stuff which was soon fashioned into a system highly profitable to perhaps one in two hundred of the colonial population and oppressive or ruinous to the one hundred and ninety-nine. Here was the beginning of a system of monopoly which contributed nothing to the development of a colonial economy, but which is of profound importance to the study of Australia because in frustrating colonial development after the Pitt-Phillip pattern it placed much economic power in the hands of a man, John Macarthur, who long subsequently was able to show the Imperial Government how to use profitably its Australian lands still mostly waste lands.

In May 1793 officer-settlers at Sydney and Parramatta had 452 acres of farmland; Grose's first return[1] of land grants (for the period December 31, 1792, to April 1, 1793) showed 400 acres granted to five *Bellona* immigrants, 190 acres to five expirees, and 160 acres to two ex-marines, and 725 acres to ten officers (including 100 acres to Macarthur), a total of 1,575 acres to 22 persons. So far, Grose followed Phillip's practice of grants, with that addition only which Phillip had sought

[1] Grose to Dundas, May 30, 1793, enclosure; *ibid.*, pp. 435 *et seq.*

power to make and which Whitehall had empowered in fresh instructions. Like Phillip, Grose had to meet a situation of food shortage; in January 1793 there was but five months' supply of flour and ten months' supply of salt meat in store. The *Bellona* brought flour, but it was "rotten, stinking, and maggotty," and the only useful items of her cargo were 79 gallons of rum and 198 gallons of wine. In June Grose was instructed by the Secretary of State to prevent "the secret and clandestine sale of spirits, by subjecting such sale to the view and inspection of proper persons directed by you to attend them." Macarthur had actually been appointed in February as inspector of public works, and Grose had noticed at once that "by the assistance of this officer we get a great deal more done than we used to do."[1] Certainly, as far as the sale of rum was concerned during the Corps regime there was nothing secret or clandestine about the traffic, which was so large a business still in 1811 that a Governor had to bargain with the rum-ring in order to finance the building of Sydney Hospital.

Now the Lieutenant-Governor permitted the officers of his regiment to enjoy a practically exclusive right of exploiting the limited avenues of exchange in the colony. The avenues comprised (1) the occasional availability of speculative cargoes on offer of sale at Port Jackson; (2) the occasional market, for grain and meat raised in the colony, when the New South Wales Commissariat store was opened to buy, and the Commissary's power to buy colonial produce, at a fixed price, from such individuals as he chose to single out from among the offering farmers; (3) the use of the labour supply furnished from the body of convicts in the colony. Two further manipulations enhanced the officers' privileged use of these avenues. The factors were (4) the discontinuing of public farming, and (5) Grose's distortion of his instructions limiting the importation and sale of liquor, by permitting officers only to retail rum in the colony and to use their credit for the ordering of rum

[1] *Vide* Dundas to Grose, June 31 (*sic*), Grose to Dundas, February 16, 1793; *ibid.*, pp. 441–2, 416.

cargoes from abroad. Add to these factors the situation that of the colonists only the officers, or some of them, had credit abroad, and the circumstance of Whitehall's long distraction; and the explanation of the firm establishment, within a very short time, of an officers' monopoly in New South Wales dealings is sufficiently clear. The unique circumstances in which an extraordinary transformation of Phillip's prison-and-peasant colony was made may now be detailed.

In alienating the Crown lands Grose, and after him Paterson, were not guilty of excess. We saw that Phillip's grants totalled (probably) 8,000 acres, Grose's rather more than 10,000, and Paterson's less than 5,000 acres. Granting in three years about 16,000 of the 24,000 acres granted in the six years of effective settlement 1790–95, the military administrators of 1793–95 did not dissipate the Crown's land. After sixteen months under Grose the officers had nearly 1,000 acres in cultivation, and three times that acreage was newly cleared. But although in announcing these achievements in late April 1794 Grose said somewhat precipitately that because of the officers' exertions enough grain would be available to tide the colony over till the next harvest, Grose's successor had to record, a few months after harvest, the arrival from India of the *Endeavour* with grain and cattle. Grose had ordered this shipment for the Commissariat in 1794. The commodities imported were paid for in Treasury bills for £13,430, an expenditure which is to be compared with £8,070 drawn on account of grain received from local farmers in the 1794 season In fact, therefore, the colony was still a long way from self-sufficiency in breadstuffs. During their terms Grose and Paterson added about one hundred to Phillip's list of more than one hundred and seventy farmers; the settlers were by late 1795 farming perhaps double the Phillip acreage of 1792. Evidently the few officers farmed much above their proportion of this not otherwise extraordinary increase; but in the circumstance that the score or so of farming officers had virtually eliminated as competitors the peasant farmers (who were a dozen times their number), the inference would be grotesquely inappropriate that the officer made a good farmer where the ex-convict made a poor one. The relevant deduction from the scanty economic records is that neither in an extension of agriculture or the productivity of the farms, nor in relieving the London victualling board of its liability of feeding the colonial population, did the three-years' period of officer-preference issue in a discernible advance of New South Wales economy. Even assuming the conditions in which Phillip's agencies had done the pioneering work in 1788–92 to have been no more onerous than those in which the officers applied themselves to the land in 1793–95, there was nothing to show at the close of the period that the one method, which eliminated both public and peasant enterprise, improved in results on the other, which was based on public and peasant enterprise. And of course the achievements of Phillips' system ought to be heavily "weighted" in any comparison.[1]

Grose had sailed from Sydney on December 17, 1794; Captain William Paterson, who assumed as administrator the command of the colony until a Governor should reach Sydney, resigned his charge to Captain Hunter, R.N., on September 11, 1795. Until in his turn he was succeeded by Captain King, R.N., in September 1800, Hunter was forced to maintain, in spite of a plenitude of his Government and General Orders to the contrary, the economic regime so firmly established under Paterson and Grose before him. He could do nothing for the

[1] For a suggestion that some revolution of production was made under Grose and Paterson, *vide* Shann, *op. ctt.*, pp. 17, 18. For the facts given in the paragraph *vide* Surveyor Alt to Grose, April 269 1794, Grose to Dundas, May 30, 1794, Paterson to Dundas, June 15, 1795, June 16, 1795, Hunter to Portland, October 25, 1795; *Historicdl Records of Australia*, 1, i, pp. 469, 470, 497–98, 530, 532 *et seq.*, *cf.* Hunter to Portland, August 20, 1796 (*ibid.*, p. 596), in which the Governor who succeeded to the Administration after Paterson reported that 246 settlers were farming 2,747 acres and (*ibid.*, p. 664) about 20 officers were farming 1,172 acres, a total of 3,919 acres in New South Wales. (It is to be noticed that most of the available information about the Grose-Paterson regime is from Collins's *Account* and the reports of Hunter and King. The military administrators wrote few despatches and did not make many or exhaustive returns.)

advancement of Australian production. True, from the figure of about 3,000 acres in cultivation when he came, the farmed area was increased to about 4,000 acres a year later, 5,000 acres by the end of 1797, 6,000 acres by the end of 1798, to nearly 8,000 acres by September 1800, when Phillip Gidley King became Acting Governor with instructions to do what Hunter had tried vainly to do: remove the officers' monopoly and guide the colony back to the lines laid down in 1787-89 and followed from 1788 to 1792. In the eight years before King, the cultivated area had been more than quadrupled; but because the unit of comparison is virtually the beginning of Australia as a farm, the increase is not impressive. This may have been the fault, not of Hunter's administration, but of the imperial authority which delegated to him its official powers in respect of the colony but not any proportion of the strength of its executive arm. The officers had discontinued, in the three years before him, a means of encouraging production which Phillip had tried, and had undertaken an experiment in another means—and that, chiefly, was devoted to nullifying such achievement as had been reached by Phillip's means of public farming and peasant settlement. If Hunter, instructed as he was to revert to Phillip's methods, had been supplied with executive assistance sufficient to restore those methods, and sufficient to put a stop to the officers' system of monopoly, he and his successors might have reinforced Phillip's basis and made an Australian agricultural economy early. But Hunter was sent as a lamb among the wolves.

Shann says[1] of Hunter's predicament, "Whitehall's injunctions to keep down expenses and maintain prison agriculture made an uneasy and divided duty." With the addition to "prison agriculture" of the phrase "and the effective settlement of time-expired and emancipated convicts," this statement meets the case. For Hunter found as he wrote[2] "two

[1] *Op. cit.*, p. 29.
[2] Hunter to Portland, May 25, 1798; *Historical Records of Australia*, 1, ii, pp. 148 *et seq.*

distinct interests in the colony—that of the public, and that of the private individual," and found himself alone in caring for the public interest. The Government gave him no effective assistance in the task it had set him. In 1798 he wrote[1] in commentary upon strictures represented to the Secretary of State, the Duke of Portland, by the officers' leader, John Macarthur: "He says he is no advocate for farming upon the public account. I have long held the same opinion; but my instructions having differed from such opinion, it has been my duty to attend as far as possible to them, and this adherence has been one source of discontent to many here." "This adherence," however, made no serious check of the system by which the officers continued, throughout Hunter's administration, to expropriate Phillip's unfortunate peasants. Instances of the use of the system are given[2] by one of the few honest men in the colony, the Judge-Advocate, Lieutenant-Colonel David Collins, later Lieutenant-Governor of Van Diemen's Land, in that portion of his *Account of the British Colony in New South Wales* which relates to the closing years of Hunter's term: "The delivery of grain into the public storehouses, when

[1] Hunter to Portland, July 25, 1798; *ibid.*, pp. 160 *et seq. Cf.* Hunter to Portland, March 3, 1796, *Historical Records of Australia*, 1, i, pp. 556 *et seq.*, in which despatch Hunter urged the encouragement of the emigration of free settlers who might take convicts off the Colonial Government's hands—to reduce costs and encourage private farming. Professor Roberts writes (*History of Australian Land Settlement*, 1788–1920, pp. 10–24; Melbourne, Macmillan and Melbourne University Press, 1924) erroneously that Hunter instituted "State aid" to farmers in the form of fixed Commissariat prices (the system had been instituted by Grose), that Hunter's "State Socialist" ideas aroused the opposition of the Secretary of State (the Duke of Portland's policy was more "Socialistic" than Hunter's inclination), and that "another consequence of the certainty of Government aid in the last resource was that the settlers plunged recklessly into debt." (The reasons for the small settlers' position are bound up with the process of the officers' monopoly. Settlers having no market at the Commissariat—which meant no market at all—and being forced to sell their produce at unremunerative rates to buy goods sold to them by the buyers of their grain—at 500 to 1,000 per cent profit—were doomed to debt, whether or not they were by disposition or through circumstances reckless plungers.)

[2] *Op. cit.*, pp. 376, 377, 443.

open for that purpose, was so completely monopolized that the settlers had but few opportunities of getting full value for their crops. . . . The settler found himself thrust out from the granary by a man whose greater opulence created greater influence. . . ." (Persons of "greater opulence" were almost all civil or military officers; and Collins goes on to say that the excluded settler had to sell his grain, at half the Commissariat price, to the settler who had ousted him, upon which the sharp practitioner resold the peasants' grain to the public store at the full fixed price. Collins relates that two or three men, out of scores of settlers in the Hawkesbury district, supplied the whole of 1,500 bushels for which a market was announced on the opening of the Commissary's store at the Hawkesbury in 1798). . . . "The poverty of the settlers, and the high price of labour, occasioned much land to have been unemployed in (1800). Many of the inferior farmers were nearly ruined by the high price that they were obliged to give for such necessaries as they required from those who had long been in the habit of monopolizing every article brought to the settlement for sale, a habit of which it was found impossible to get the better, without the positive and immediate interference of the Government at home."

The Government, preoccupied with matters larger than the state of New South Wales, did not interfere. The Secretary of State indeed found the officers' commercial practices "contrary, as you very properly observe," he told Hunter, "to the nature of their institution"; but his suggestion of a remedy was confined to pointing out that by a limitation of the assignment of convict labour to the officer-settlers their "corner" at the Commissariat market would be dispersed as public farming, encouraged with the labour withdrawn from the private farms, returned an increased production. Portland, under the delusion apparently that Hunter could discipline all his officers with some of them, commanded too that the ring should be prohibited from selling rum to peasants and convicts. But Hunter had no hands to stay the rum-sellers; still "the prices were raised by that (rum) monopoly to so high a degree that it was the ruin of many of those poor people"; and even though the peasant drank no rum he was ruined by the general monopoly. The Principal Chaplain and a surgeon reported in 1798 that many of the ruined peasantry were sober and industrious; "the falling landed interest" was falling because of the high prices of all goods; it was the general retail monopoly which had driven many from their farms.[1]

After Hunter, King summed up the administration's difficulty when he said,[2] "Where can I look to for support but to myself? For it can hardly be expected that those will promote plans of industry, when the success must prove the infamy of their own conduct." And King, having an honest Commissary, would be better equipped than Hunter to deal with the monopolists. In Hunter's time, the inspector of public works whom he inherited from Paterson, Captain John Macarthur, was foremost in opposing the enforcement of public policies— King would say[3] of the colony and Macarthur's place in it, "Half of it belongs to him already, and he very soon will get the other half"—the Commissary, James Williamson, was an accessory of the ring, the principal surgeon, William Balmain, was a leading member of the ring, and he and at least one of his assistants, D'Arcy Wentworth, were active like Macarthur in supplying the lowly with rum at extortionate prices. Such was the condition to which a score of officers of the New South Wales Corps and civil administration, aided by circumstances favourable to exploitation, had brought Phillip's promising community by the turn of the century. Settlers by scores had been ruined, crops were mortgaged to buy bread, bankrupts

---

[1] *Vide* for these references Portland to Hunter, September 18, 1798; *Historical Records of Australia*, I, ii, pp. 225 *et seq.*; Bligh's testimony upon the rum monopoly in *Minutes of Evidence*, 1812 Transportation Committee, p. 46; *Report of the Commissioners of Enquiry* (the Rev. Samuel Marsden and Thomas Arndell), *Historical Records of Australia*, I, ii, pp. 141 *et seq.*

[2] King to J. King (Under-Secretary of State for the Colonies), May 3, 1800, *Historical Records of Australia*, I, ii, p. 505.

[3] King to J. King, November 14, 1801; *ibid.*, vol. iii, p. 347.

were thrown back on Government rations, ground went out of cultivation. "Unless some mode is established for putting an effectual stop to the trading of the officers and others," Hunter had written urgently at the beginning of 1798, "and consequently to the immense prices . . . instead of our cultivation increasing I fear we shall raise less grain every year." And that farmers were leaving the land was clear from the report of the commissioners of enquiry later in the year; they found that debt had overcome four of the sixteen peasants at Parramatta—all who remained of Phillip's original settlers were the sixteen; in the six mainland districts only twenty-one held their holdings, of seventy-three whom Phillip had planted. No public farming had been done since 1792. Convicts from the old public farms had helped the monopolists to riches." Had those who have been so improperly disposed of been employed on Government's land already cleared," Hunter said, "and in clearing more for the benefit of the public, I do not hesitate to say there would not now have been the occasion to purchase so much grain as we find at this time unavoidable; but had that been the case, it would have ruined the expectation of officers and settlers whose interest appears to have been more considered."[1]

The futility of Hunter's unassisted attempt to break the monopoly is brought out by his disregarded orders which, repeated by him as if repetition could achieve what announcement had not, would be repeated again by King: in the last case to some effect. Half a dozen representative orders of the kind may be listed:[2]

---

[1] Hunter to J. King, June 1, 1797; *Historical Records of Australia*, vol. ii, pp. 9 *et seq.*

[2] For copies of these Government and General Orders *vide Historical Records of Australia*, 1, i, pp. 202, 212–13, 216, 216–17. They illustrate Hunter's ineffectiveness well enough, but not necessarily his "weakness" as a personality. For such a too simple account of Hunter's failure *cf.*, e.g. Rusden, *op. cit.*, vol. i, p. 236, with reference to an Order of 1799 forbidding local distillation of spirits: "As was his custom, Hunter shrank from giving effect to his order." King repeated the terms of the Order referred to, but only after he had been five years in the Administration, with executive assistance such as Hunter never had.

(1) September 18, 1797.—The Governor "finds it necessary to inform the settlers generally that, as they all know the terms on which they have been allowed to settle, he is surprised to find so many complain of their want of ability to provide for themselves and their families after having been victualled and clothed at the expense of Government for eighteen months, which is six months longer than was at first intended."

(2) April 21, 1798.—(After a farmers' petition that the Commissariat price for maize should not be reduced, in view of their high labour costs, the high prices which they must pay for necessaries, and other distresses.) The price would not be reduced at present by the Governor; "but as it is no less his duty to reduce the heavy expenses of this colony to Government than it is his wish to render the situation of the industrious farmer easy and comfortable, they must look forward to a reduciton of the price of grain of every kind before long."

(3) April 23, 1798.—"The settlers having at different times complained that the receiving of grain into the public stores when open for that purpose was so completely monopolized that they could have but few opportunities of getting the full value for their crops" (and must sell to others at half-price) . . . "and that they were thereby constantly involved in debt and distress"—the Order so often given that actual growers should have preference at the stores would be repeated. "Orders have but too frequently been frustrated by circumstances which have not been known to the Governor;" "the Commissary must act upon Orders, or the Governor would "take a more serious view."

(4) May 20, 1798.—(After Portland's instructions of August 31, 1797, received May 18, 1798.) Only two assigned servants are allowed to each officer, to be maintained by Government; other assignees must be maintained by their master who might pay in grain and meat for the requisite supplies from the Commissariat store. (This Order was to take effect from August 1st, a further Order of August 15th announced, and a return of surplus assignees must be

made to Major Johnston, commanding the New South Wales Corps.)

(5) June 11, 1798.—The ship *Hunter* having arrived from India with a cargo of articles of general utility, the Governor directed that her cargo should not be sold until the farmers had supplied their own agents to buy.

(6) June 25, 1798.—There was now no need for the farmers to nominate agents; the officers had agreed to buy in all the settlers' behalf.

Knowledge in London of this last order, so eloquent of Hunter's utter defeat by his officers, led to the Governor's recall by the Secretary of State. "I cannot but apprehend," Portland wrote,[1] "that the order of June 25, 1798, has been considered as a sanction to officers engaging in traffic, as an apology for the proceedings which I have but too much reason to fear may be found to have disgraced his Majesty's service in the persons of several of the officers of the New South Wales Corps." Portland should have realized the irony of his expressed "disappointment of the manner in which the government of the settlement has been administered."

[1] The despatch in which Portland made this comment, and by which he recalled the Governor, is reproduced in *Historical Records of Australia*, 1, p. 388; it was dated November 5, 1799. *Cf.* S. Macarthur Onslow's version of the reason for Hunter's recall (*Early Records of the Macarthurs of Camden*, p. 56; Sydney, Angus and Robertson, 1914). She suggests that Hunter, to encourage the farmers, had bought grain in excess of the quantity required to meet the needs of the convict establishment. The weevil and fly moth laid waste the surplus stacks, and "so severely was Governor Hunter censured for this by the Secretary of State that it led to his resignation." Miss Onslow evidently took for gospel John Macarthur's story of excessive Commissariat buying, in an interested letter to Portland complaining of Hunter (in *Historical Records of Australia*, 1, i, pp. 89 *et seq.*; Portland to Hunter, August 30, 1797, enclosing Macarthur to Portland, September 15, 1796).

It should be noted that much of Professor Shann's account and interpretation of this period and later Administrations, in the early chapters of his *Economic History of Australia*, is from Miss Macarthur Onslow's collection of documents and her accompanying commentary. The *Macarthur Records*, a valuable source of information, are at many points apt to mislead, or give an erroneous or partisan account. They should be used only in conjunction with the more extensive range of documents in the *Historical Records of Australia*.

The bald facts, of economic purport, are then, that without making any significant contribution to agriculture,[1] and without lending their special abilities to other service of public utility, an officers' cabal deliberately retarded the development of New South Wales, ran counter to the imperial policy, and debauched and expropriated the helpless colonial majority, with no other object than the enrichment of the few who had been able, as it were fortuitously, to seize the power. John Macarthur and his comrades of the Corps officers' mess did not demolish Phillip's economic construction because already in 1792–93 they, or any of them, looked forward to depasturing flocks of fine-wooled sheep on the plains. For, at the beginning of their system, none of them knew anything about either plains or sheep.

Their system was subjected to a more forthright supervision than Hunter's, when Phillip Gidley King, who too had been present at the settlement of 1788 and who had afterwards commanded at Norfolk Island, took over the administration from Hunter in 1800. Before consulting the measures by which he proceeded against the monopolists, it will be helpful to notice what the two chief classes of colonial society—peasants and officers—thought of the situation to which he came.

Now in 1800, 354 settlers—almost the whole body of mainland farmers except the two dozen officers—sought to draw Whitehall's attention to the lot to which they were reduced. One hundred and eighty-one Parramatta farmers set out in a memorial that Hunter, "from his peculiar situation," had not the power, though they credited him with the goodwill, to reform the colony. They told the story of forestalling, monopoly, and profiteering, and concluded that "if they continue to groan under this load of oppression, agriculture must soon be at an end, the colony in want of grain, and consequently the

[1] I.e. in a balance between their services in "greatly forwarding the clearing of land and raising grain," and their demoralization of the peasantry, destruction of peasant farming and public farming, cf. King to Portland, March 1, 1802, *Historical Records of Australia*, 1, ii, pp. 421 *et seq.*, for an interesting comparison of three types of settler: officer, immigrant, ex-convict.

expenses of Government increased, as many farmers will have no other means of support than the public store." A similar petition from one hundred and seventy-three Hawkesbury people was lodged with Hunter on New Year's Day 1800.[1] Hunter upbraided the farmers for being, many of them, improvident; but it is noteworthy that in a subsequent review of the situation he supported *post facto* the peasants' appeal to the self-interest of Government. He would tell a House of Commons select committee[2] that during his term it had not been necessary to import flour from England, but that, before he left, the Commissariat price for grain having been reduced (by King)—"I said, the farmers will be obliged to give up; it turned out so; and the Government of this country was obliged to send out flour to the cost of £70,000 sterling."

To set off against the peasants' petitions, the records[3] supply us with a revealing picture of the officers' New South Wales of 1794, as seen from the Macarthur homestead, a fine brick building, at Parramatta—Elizabeth Farm. John Macarthur's wife Elizabeth wrote to her friend Miss Kingdon:

"Some thousands of people are fed from the public stores, perhaps between three or four thousand, all of whom were formerly supplied with flour from England to meet the demand for bread. But since, so many individuals have cleared farms and have thereby been enabled to raise a great quantity of grain in the country, which at the present time is purchased by the Commissary at ten shillings a bushel, and issued for what are termed rations, or the proportionate quantity due to each person instead of flour. In payment for which the Commissary issues a receipt, approved of by the Government; and these receipts pass current here as coin, and are taken by

[1] Hunter to Portland, February 1, 1800, enclosures 2 and 4; *ibid.*, pp. 440 *et seq.*, and *cf.* four addresses, from 180 farmers at Kissing Point, Sydney, etc., to King three years later, expressing satisfaction at the breaking of the monopolies; King to Lord Hobart, March 1, 1804, *Historical Records of Australia*, vol. iv.
[2] The 1812 Transportation Committee, *Minutes of Evidence*, p. 24.
[3] S. M. Onslow, *op. cit.*, pp. 50, 51.

masters of ships and other adventurers. When any number of these have been accumulated in the hands of individuals they are returned to the Commissary, who gives a bill on the Treasury in England for them. These bills amount to £30,000 to £40,000 annually. How long the Government may continue so expensive a plan is difficult to see." The Macarthur farm servants, she explained, were expirees off rations. "They demand an enormous price, seldom less than four shillings or five shillings a day. For such as have many in their employment it becomes necessary to keep on hand large supplies of such articles as are most needed by these people, for shops there are none.

"The officers in the colony, with a few others possessed of money and credit in England, unite together and purchase the cargoes of such vessels as repair to this country from various quarters. Two or more are chosen from the number to bargain for the cargo offered for sale, which is then divided amongst them in proportion to the amount of their subscriptions. This arrangement prevents monopoly, and the impositions which would otherwise be practised by masters of ships."

An equally odd account was given by Macarthur himself in his analysis of the condition of the colony in 1796, after Hunter's appearance. Macarthur submitted to Portland that the colony could be self-supporting and relieve the Imperial Government of much expense. Farming, which was the means of self-sufficiency, ought not to be undertaken as a public enterprise. The individual farmer should be able after eighteen months to keep his assigned servants in bread, for a man required but twelve bushels a year for his consumption and here the worst harvest would return fifteen bushels per acre; the cultivation of a single acre, therefore, would ensure the satisfaction of one man's needs. But in New South Wales the farmers were either on poorly selected sites, or they were idle and dissolute. "Had these men," Macarthur wrote, "instead of being permitted to become settlers, been obliged to employ themselves in the service of an industrious and vigilant master," they would now be feeding themselves and providing a surplus.[1] As it was, the Commissariat bought grain in excessive quantities; there was waste in other ways: for instance, speculative cargoes from India, of sugar, would be available at 7d. per lb., but a dallying Government, buying its sugar supplies three months after the ship's arrival, would be paying double that price.

This was one way of describing the effects of a rigged market and forestalling.

Not less startling in effrontery was a document which Captain John Macarthur, Surgeon William Balmain, and Commissary James Williamson presented to Hunter early in 1800 (when the ruined farmers of Parramatta and the Hawkesbury, in their hundreds, were denouncing the officers' system). These officers had chartered the *Thynne*, arrived now from India with rum, tea, etc., and had sent an agent to buy a cargo for her in Bengal. The goods in her hold, they said, were intended for their own use; otherwise they would have had

---

[1] Macarthur's letter is reproduced in *Historical Records of Australia*, I, i, pp. 89 *et seq*. It is interesting to find (S. M. Onslow, *op. cit.*, pp. 349 *et seq.*; Macarthur to Bigge, February 7, 1821) that Macarthur a quarter of a century later was still representing to authority that men once convicted should be forever quelled.—Transported convicts ought to be handed over to large proprietors, "intelligent and honourable men." "The democratic multitude would look upon their large possessions with envy and the proprietors with hatred. As this democratic feeling has already taken deep root in the colony, in consequence of the absurd and mischievous policy pursued by Governor Macquarie, and as there is already a strong combination amongst that class of persons, it cannot too soon be opposed with vigour."

It is worth while, as a further means of assessing Macarthur's and his wife's accounts—artless no doubt in Elizabeth's case—to consult the evidence given by Maurice Margarot before the 1812 Committee (*Minutes of Evidence*, pp. 53, 54). Margarot was in the colony from 1794 until 1810. He arrived as a transport under sentence, but as a political offender was given his freedom within the colony. There is evidence (e.g. Howell's *State Trials*, vol. xxiii, and Rusden, *op. cit.*), that he was a famous liar concerning matters in which he had a substantial interest. In this matter, however, his testimony is supported by the record of facts, and it may be worth weighing as the observations of one of the very small contemporary group of educated, non-official free persons in New South Wales.

to pay excessive prices for goods bought of speculating shipmasters; now "the lower description of inhabitants" might bid for speculative cargoes among themselves; this happy arrangement would "effectually prevent a repetition of the unfounded charges that have been made against the officers of monopoly."[1]

Passing on to the Secretary of State this communication, Hunter commented merely by suggesting that he be empowered to declare a duty on rum imports. It was not ten days since he had written home, "I cannot wonder at the settlers . . . supposing that I have no real wish to relieve them, when time after time my endeavours for that end are frustrated by an inattention to the orders so often given out, and that by the very people to whom they are directed in the Commissary Department." Outside the Commissariat the poor farmer was no better off, nor his servant: "when the labouring man receives his hire in wheat he goes to the publican to obtain articles in exchange. It is then observed to him with a sneer, 'I don't want wheat, but I'll take yours at seven shillings and sixpence a bushel, and give you tobacco at fifteen shillings.' This is the only place where such an article can be had."[2]

There seemed nothing Hunter could do for the public weal except (a course obnoxious to him) revive public farming. If he were to reduce the Commissariat fixed price for grain—as the sense of his instructions required, as he sought himself to do, and as Macarthur cynically suggested he should do—the effect must be to diminish the small share of store receipt-currency which the officer-manipulated Commissariat still permitted the peasants, so to accelerate their approach to bankruptcy. Let the Governor seek to make available directly

---

[1] The letter referred to was presented on the day before a public meeting of small farmers drew attention to the high prices they were required to pay for commodities (*Historical Records of Australia*, 1, ii, p. 434). The officers' letter is reproduced in *ibid.*, pp. 436 *et seq.*

[2] Hunter's first cited statement is reproduced in Hunter to Portland, January 5, 1800; *ibid.*, and the second in Hunter to Portland, March 2, 1798, *ibid.*

to the small men cargoes in port; and his only executive agents, who were the monopolists, could make a public spectacle of him, without gain to the peasants, in their manner of June 1798. He toyed with regulation of the rum traffic and the officers laughed at him, asserting their importations were for their own consumption. Even the undertaking of public agriculture, which he at last decided upon after his instructions, must narrow the small settler's approach to the Commissariat market, for as things were, if the public farms augmented production, the Commissary must buy less officers' wheat, and the officers would buy less peasants' wheat for resale to him. But Portland was repeatedly demanding "attention to the reduction of the unwarrantable expenses which have been hitherto incurred in the settlement,"[1] and Hunter had to do what might be done in that direction, giving up the small men's problem as hopeless of solution.

By March 1797 the Governor had restored enough convicts to public service to be able to release a hundred of them to bring into cultivation the deserted fields at Toongabbe, untouched since Phillip's day. In 1799, seeking ground for Government, he had fenced a paltry thirty acres at Portland Place, below the junction of the Hawkesbury and Colo Rivers. The 1798 harvest had been a failure, "the whole colony were nearly naked," and each small extension of public farming increased the Governor's anxieties, because of his lack of competent managers. In fact Hunter made small rehabilitation of public farming: after King assumed the government he found that the original liquidation by the military of Phillip's farms had left but 300 acres to be sowed with wheat "on the public account"; this was in 1800. Hunter had failed to secure for the farmers freedom either to buy or to sell, and he had failed equally to re-establish public farming, which might be a backdoor means of breaking the officers' monopoly.[2]

[1] E.g. Portland to Hunter, August 31, 1796, *ibid.*, vol. i, pp. 649 *et seq.*
[2] *Vide* Hunter to Portland, May 1, 1799, January 10, 1798; Hunter to J. King, November 1, 1798, *ibid.*, vol. ii, pp. 351 *et seq.*, 118–19, 235.

(b) Re-establishment of a Peasantry, 1801–1804

King, sent to assail with stronger forces this bad business of the officers, arrived at Port Jackson on April 15, 1800, in the transport *Speedy*. He was Lieutenant-Governor under Hunter until September 28th—using this novitiate of nearly six months to make a close inspection of the state of things in the settlements—and, superseding Hunter then, he retained the administrative direction of New South Wales until August 12, 1806, when Bligh succeeded him.

King carried some bastions of the New South Wales Corps defences. Under him an energetic revival of public farming was made; he instituted at the Commissary's stores a system of buying grain direct from the growers, established a Government retail store to sell supplies at reasonable prices in grain; he regulated rum imports with some small success, and—in the short term, most effective stroke of all—he broke the officers' line by using every excuse to arrest a ringleader and ship him off to England to face the army authorities there. But under Grose, Paterson, and Hunter, the officers had entrenched themselves strongly in comparatively great landed possessions, and this fact King could not overcome—that about one per cent of landowners held about twenty per cent of colonial land, and six per cent of landowners (i.e. thirty-five civil and military officers) owned not far short of half the total of land alienated. A large interest had been vested in a very few persons, during nearly eight years; and the five or six hundred peasants whose small-holdings King fenced round with protective devices could never be the forerunners of a colonial landed majority. In spite of the Imperial Government a certain distribution of economic forces had been made, and the logic of that distribution could not be confuted by belated recollections at Whitehall that Pitt and Sydney had planned, and Phillip had begun to execute, a quite different arrangement.

However, King worried the lords of colonial manors. The first man on whom he pounced in his forays as Lieutenant-Governor was Hunter's aide-de-camp, Captain George Johnston.

King had found that no fewer than 1,500 convict labourers drew rations from the Commissary though their services were at the disposal of settlers. Before he had been a month in the colony, King made his first assault upon the officers' system that had brought about this convenient arrangement. He had Lieutenant-Colonel Paterson (administrator in 1795, now officer commanding the New South Wales Corps) arrest Johnston for having paid a sergeant of the Corps his military pay in the form of rum overvalued at 24s. a gallon (compared with 10s. a gallon at the ship). Johnston was a ripe subject for a reforming official. In an economic sense he was Macarthur's *aide* rather than Hunter's, for he occupied a key position in the monopolists' ring, running most of the Government stock on his own farm and habitually distributing the increase among the members of the ring.[1]

Next, King instructed Major Joseph Foveaux, Lieutenant-Governor at Norfolk Island, "to take especial care that no officer . . . or other person whatever, be allowed to receive provisions or clothing from the public stores for more than two convicts"—in execution of Portland's 1797 instructions, which Hunter's Orders of 1798 had failed to make effective. The Commissariat practice of giving the officers whatever they demanded was to cease; the "several officers" who had "entered into the most unwarrantable traffic with settlers and convicts for the sale of (rum)" were to note that henceforth no spirits might be landed without the Lieutenant-Governor's permit; the officer-forestallers must themselves be forestalled by the establishment of a Government store on the island. This was in June. In July King bought for the Government 53 head of cattle at £37 a head from Hunter, Foveaux, and Captain Kent of H.M.S. *Buffalo*, as a step towards the reassembly of a public herd.[2]

---

[1] King to J. King, May 3, 1800, *Historical Records of Australia*, 1, ii, pp. 505 *et seq*.
[2] King to Foveaux, June 26, 1800, and *Regulations*, *ibid*., pp. 512–520; *re* the cattle bought, King said that the price paid (£37 a head) compared with £80 a head which the owners could have got by slaughtering the cattle for sale to the Commissariat butchery (King to the Secretaries of the Treasury, July 7, 1800, *ibid*., pp. 524 *et seq*.).

At the time, Government held 300 to 400 acres of farm land compared with more than 7,000 acres in private hands; nearly 800 cattle and 400 sheep, compared with settlers' 300 cattle and 6,000 sheep. King sought without delay to weaken the economic power which the handful of officers exerted by their ownership of a great part of the colony's 5,000 acres of wheatlands. At the 1801 harvest, after his acceleration of Hunter's public farming enterprise, wheat was got in from nearly 500 acres (*cf.* 300 acres in 1800) of Government land, and maize from 300 acres (*cf.* 100 in 1800). To have almost doubled the effective public holding seemed a fair start, though the acreage would have to be doubled again to pass Phillip's total of nine years before. At the same time, convicts were being detached from private to public service, so that in December 1801 more than 25 per cent of those at work were on the public farms, and in March 1802 about the same percentage of an increased number of 1,212 convicts. By August 1802 the public farms aggregated more than 1,100 acres in wheat and maize (*cf.* settlers' 14,800 acres), and next year King acquired for Government another farm at Castle Hill, where 300 acres was sown with wheat. The new Secretary of State, Lord Hobart, gave King the odd instruction not to employ more convicts on public farming than remained at any given time on Government's hand; but King was able to quote some results, by this. Cornwallis Farm, which he had rented in 1801 at 15s. per acre per annum (£128 5s. for its 171 acres), had produced nearly 4,000 bushels of wheat which, at the reduced Commissariat valuation of 8s. a bushel, saved Government nearly £1,500 outlay, after rent had been paid. Now the Government runs had just three times the number of cattle owned by "a few individuals," and the Commissariat butcher's purchases could be reduced.[1]

[1] *Return*, July 7, 1800, King to Portland, November 14, 1801, enclosure No. 4, *Historical Records of Australia*, ii, p. 527, and iii, p. 340; *re* employment of convicts, note that at the general muster of July-August only 107 convicts were shown as in public employment, including 30 as farm labourers (King to Portland, March 1, 1802, *ibid.*, iii, p. 408); King to Hobart, May 9, 1803; Hobart to King, February 2, 1803, *ibid.*, vol. iv.

During these first years King had not been inactive on other fronts against the officers. He legislated for the mainland as he had instructed Foveaux to legislate for Norfolk Island, upon the rum traffic, etc. In September 1800, even before taking office as Acting Governor, he instructed Paterson to call a meeting of officers and inform them that no rum was to be landed on the mainland without permit. This Paterson did, and a few days later Balmain and Wentworth, admitting that they had imported 1,400 and 3,000 gallons respectively, for sale, humbly offered the rum to Government at £1 a gallon. King gave them permission to retail their stocks at that price, in return for their pledges not to engage in further speculation of the kind.[1]

Like Hunter he had bombarded the officers' positions with Government and General Orders, typical specimens of which may be given:[2]

(1) December 3, 1799.—No rum to be landed without permit.
(2) July 10, 1800.—In Commissariat purchases of wheat, the actual grower's offer to be preferred.
(3) October 1, 1800.—

> (*a*) No more than two assigned servants per officer would be maintained by Government; others might be employed on farms, but the master must feed and clothe them.
>
> (*b*) No forestalling in the purchase of cargoes of visiting ships; the Government to buy and retail; private retailers limited to 20 per cent profit.
>
> (*c*) After October 30, 1800, only approved persons to issue their promissory notes as currency (for discussion of currency, *vide* Chapter 3, Appendix A, *infra*).
>
> (*d*) No landing of rum, or retailing of rum without permit. Maximum price of £1 a gallon for spirits; 2s. lb. tobacco.

[1] King to Paterson, September 8, 1800; Paterson to King, September 12th; King to Paterson, September 18th, *ibid.*, ii, pp. 542-5.
[2] *Historical Records of Australia*, 1, ii, pp. 594, 595, 622.

(4) October 2, 1800.—List to be supplied by October 4th of assigned servants in each officer's employment, with the names of the two whom it was desired to retain.

Why should such orders, published by King, have more effect than the similar orders published by Hunter? The answer is, that as in the case of their similar efforts to revive public farming King succeeded in comparison with Hunter, so in other fields King's greater measure of success is attributable largely to the fact that he had effective instruments and agents, where Hunter had not. Lieutenant-Colonel Paterson and Major Foveaux, field-officers in rank, bethought themselves of their hopes of army preferment, when King made it clear that he was not to be diverted from his own instructions; and soon King had the inestimable advantage of a Commissary (John Palmer, formerly purser of H.M.S. *Sirius* in the first fleet) who was not an officers' creature. Hunter could not have done much with Captain Johnston, too long an integral part of the ring, nor with the venal James Williamson of the Commissariat.

In fact the first of the monopolists to be got rid of for the nonce were Johnston (under arrest)[1] and Williamson, who left the colony in H.M.S. *Buffalo* in September, when King entered into his full powers as Acting Governor (his appointment was not, however, confirmed until some years later). "Should he return to this country," King wrote of the civil functionary, "I hope he will not be allowed to bring a pedlar's pack with him." Johnston was "the wealthy man of this colony," but, the Acting Governor conceded ruefully, there remained rich officers in New South Wales. He egged on the officer commanding to worry those who remained. Balmain and Wentworth had been disciplined and had promised reform, Williamson had been replaced and Johnston arrested for irregular practice as an officer; but Captain John Macarthur

[1] Johnston returned to the colony about two years later in the *Minorca* (*vide* Major-General Brownrigg to Under-Secretary J. King, June 12, 1801, *ibid*., iii, p. 107). He and Paterson were reconciled at Government House (*vide* King to Hobart, November 9, 1802, *ibid*., p. 564).

MONOPOLY IN NEW SOUTH WALES

remained, of whom the Duke of Portland wrote ruminatively: "Considering Captain Macarthur as an officer on duty with his regiment, I can by no means account for his being a farmer to the extent he appears to be, and I must highly disapprove of the commanding officer of the Corps to which he belongs, allowing him or any other officer to continue in such contradictory situations and characters." King had to put down Macarthur, if Macarthur was not to set the reformation at naught. But Paterson, who tried to do it for him by *force majeure*, after Macarthur had provoked him into issuing a challenge to fight (on Paterson's refusal to join in the officers' boycott of Government House), came off worst in the encounter at arms. Earlier, when King was dealing with the Commissary, the two surgeons and Hunter's *aide*, Macarthur had determined to make the voyage to England. He had therefore offered to sell to Government Elizabeth Farm and its stock, for £4,000—a low figure for 1,000 acres of grass (100 cleared), 300 acres of land cleared and fenced, 10 horses, 50 cattle, 600 sheep (some of them pure merinos), a brick house, and farm buildings. But the duel, which occurred while King awaited Portland's permission to buy Macarthur out, gave him grounds for arresting Macarthur, whom he sent under arrest to England at the end of 1801.[1]

The next to go of the large owners among the officers was William Cox, paymaster of the New South Wales Corps. He was suspended from duty in 1803 for defalcations. In November 1802 he owned 1,440 acres, the whole of which he had bought, and Government sequestrated to trustees his farms, stock, and

[1] For the facts in the paragraph *vide* King to J. King, September 28,1800, ii, pp. 669 *et seq.*; Portland to King, June 19, 1801, iii, p. 101; Macarthur to King, September 30, 1800, ii, p. 538.

Elizabeth Farm originated in Grose's 100-acre grant to Macarthur in February 1793. Grose granted him a further 100 acres in April 1794, Hunter made two additional grants, bringing the farm acreage up to 320, and Macarthur bought the balance, 780 acres, from Parramatta small farmers.

When Macarthur returned to the colony in 1805, it was in the smile of a new Secretary of State, Earl Camden, and with an order in his pocket for a large grant of land (*vide* Chapter 5 (*a*) *infra*).

£4,000 of other property. Individuals, as well as the military chest, had suffered through his peculation. Early in 1804 the trustees of Cox's estate (Marsden, Wentworth, Robert Campbell, and Captain William Rowley) reported that of Cox's debts nearly £8,000 was due to the army agents; they had £1,500 worth of his 3 per cent stock against that debt, and secured King's permission to make up several thousands of pounds of the balance with wheat from his farms to be bought by the Commissariat store, making 10s. in £1 of his obligations.[1]

Such successes did not, however, lull King into a belief that he had made a permanent breach of the officers' position. Probably he realized that conditions must be changed, as well as personnel, before the inducements of public service in Australia would be other than the opportunity which public service offered "to impose on the public and to join in sharing the immense profits that have been made of the shameful monopolies that have so long existed here, and which have been uniformly applied to the misery and ruin of the labouring settlers." The Colonial Office sought to help him towards fulfilment of his task by, for example, permitting ships' officers to bring out goods to New South Wales, for sale at prices up to a maximum fixed by the Governor. And King himself used a device of encouraging competition with the Sydney traders' ring. Robert Campbell, of the firm of Campbell, Clark and Company, of Calcutta, was at hand to further his project. (He had arrived in Sydney from India in Hunter's time (1798) to buy and sell.) In March 1801 King contracted with him to buy for Government stock which Campbell would import from India, and in April 1803 the firm's ship reached Port Jackson with a cargo of cattle and—contrary to the prohibition by Lord Wellesley, Viceroy of India, of the export of spirits, and King's prohibition of its import into New South Wales—

---

[1] For the misadventures of William Cox, *vide* King to Hobart, November 9, 1802, enclosure No. 13, iii, pp. 613–14; King to Hobart, May 9, 1803, and Memorial of the Trustees, iv, pp. 159 *et seq.*, and 542.

14,000 gallons of rum. When that contract was made, New South Wales had 5,500 inhabitants, half of whom drew rations from the Commissary, all could, however, buy provisions (paying in grain) at the new Government store, which was open on Mondays; of the 420 farmers, 17 per cent were in gaol for debt or contemplating farms which were under execution for debt. The position within a year after the arrival of Campbell's cows for Government was substantially different. Thirty-two military officers held 10,000 acres; and, in addition, Macarthur and Balmain owned nearly 5,000 acres; but there were now 553 settlers on 25,000 acres. Three of them held from 350 to 1,028 acres each. Placing them with the favoured group, we find, then, that early in 1804, 37 persons held 17,000 acres and 550 held 23,000 acres: averages per farmer of 404 and 42 acres. More than half of the 550 worked farms of 30 acres or less, and nearly one-third, farms of from 30 to 100 acres. Macarthur with 3,400 acres was the largest landowner, and four others had more than 1,000 acres each: five men owned one-fifth of the 40,000 acres that had been alienated in New South Wales[1]—but there *were* 550 peasants. Their situation

[1] *Vide* on the inducements to public service King to Portland, September 28, 1800, ii, p. 60; on the regulations for ship's officers' trading, J. King to the Transport Commissioners, August 1, 1800, *ibid.*, p. 551; on the contract with Campbell (approved by Portland, January 30, 1802), King to Hobart, May 9, 1803, iv, pp. 73 *et seq.*; on the Government store (October 1, 1800, to August 7, 1802, references), ii, p. 622, iii, pp. 40, 45, 249, 253, 133, 256, 462, 465, 623, 632; on the land position, King to Hobart, March 1, 1804, Nov. 9, 1802, August 7, 1803; iv, p. 498; iii, pp. 613–14; iv, pp. 314–15.

As to land grants, which King made extensively, it is to be noticed that a confident statement of the precise acreage granted by any early Governor ought not to be made. The records are incomplete, and the incorporation in some official returns of re-grants or confirmations of grants discounts the totals. Professor Roberts errs in stating (*op. cit.*, p. 10) that Hunter during his five years' Governorship made grants totalling 28,279 acres— "nearly twice the area granted by all his predecessors." Hunter's return, on which apparently this statement is based (Hunter to Portland, February 6, 1800, ii, pp. 454 *et seq.*), includes grants which had been made originally by Phillip, Paterson, or Grose, dating back to Ruse, Phillip's pioneer. In any case, probably the grants made by Hunter's predecessors totalled about 24,000 acres (*vide* p. 97 *supra*).

was improved to a noticeable degree. Thus, where 70 per cent of the population were on rations in 1798, when the officers' system was at its most obdurate, about 50 per cent were so situated in 1801 and only 37 per cent in 1804—although more than 3,000 convicts had arrived between 1798 and 1804. Fewer persons drew subsistence from the store in 1803, when the population was 7,000, than in 1798, when it was 5,000; the numbers on rations were 2,595 and 3,535. So at this time when a new Secretary of State began a term of office which would inaugurate officially a wider economic curriculum for New South Wales,[1] the second of a series of attempts to draw a "small man's frontier" on the map of Australia achieved relative success—but with the considerable limitation that little more had been won for the small men than the gaps between large holdings.

But King after 1800, like Macquarie after 1817 and the Premiers Robertson and Gavan Duffy in the 'sixties, worked in a hindering circumstance—not then very pressing but already in being—which exerted a more or less stultifying effect on the execution of a policy of small-settlement; that is, though some contemporary imperial needs seemed to demand a peasant use of Australia, the paramount demands of Australian conditions must lead to a different conclusion. This factor, ultimately the determinant, was the adaptability of much Australian land to pastoral uses, requiring large capital but sparse settlement—rather than the closer settlement of numerous small farmers without capital. In the first years of the nineteenth century, John Macarthur's experiments in breeding sheep for fine wool (*vide* Chapter 5 (*a*) *infra*) were advanced far enough to gain recognition in England, first on the part of the woollens manufacture, then (in 1804) on the part of Government. However, the chief impediment to King's task of re-establishing

---

[1] Lord Hobart wrote to King on May 17, 1804, advising him that Earl Camden was now Secretary of State.

On the proportion of population on rations, *vide* ii, pp. 222–23; iii, pp. 4 *et seq.*; iv, p. 628.

in New South Wales a peasantry from convicts and poor immigrants was not a claim of the sheep-capitalist for wide lands; that was scarcely made: it was, as in Hunter's time, the very different and separate circumstance of the officers' policies of monopoly and enclosure. It was Macarthur, the trader-farmer-monopolist, who exploited the peasant colonizing of New South Wales after 1792, not Macarthur the sheepbreeder, and it was his monopoly that King fought, not his vision.

The thread of the original English policy for Australia, which King, and later Macquarie, took up after Phillip, is seen clearly as connecting these administrations, when their common policy of expediting peasant settlement by emancipating convicts for the land is realized. Up to 1800 about 300 convicts had been pardoned, absolutely or conditionally.[1] In the three years up to 1800, too, 1,200 persons (mostly convicts whose sentences had expired) went off the victualling list of Government: a number as great as that of all the transports who were landed from the beginning of Grose's administration to 1800, seven years. By mid-1797, even, 700 convicts had been freed on the expiration of their sentences.[2] Although Grose had inaugurated[3] a system of permitting the return to Britain of those expirees who could buy or work a passage thither—a course which the British Government had not contemplated: no provision was made for the return of expirees—a large proportion of ex-convicts stayed in the colony as Pitt and Sydney had anticipated, and these had to be settled. But the officer-capitalists having won their pre-eminence in the mean-

[1] *Vide* the editor's introduction to *Historical Records of Australia*, 1, iv, pp. xi, xii, for figures of emancipations.

A conditional pardon, as distinct from an absolute pardon, allowed the convict his freedom only as long as he remained in the colony. "Returning from transportation," i.e. returning to Britain except after expiry or absolute pardon, was punishable by death. The great majority of pardons granted were of the conditional order.

[2] Hunter to Portland, June 10, 1797, ii, pp. 24, 563–64.

[3] *Cf.* Grose to Nepean, October 12, 1793, i, p. 455, notifying that several expirees had been allowed to leave in the *Boddingtons* (or *Boddington*) and *Sugar Cane*.

time, it behoved King to reinforce his peasants as well as to protect them. He provided the safeguards which have been noticed; in addition, he pursued a strategy of reinforcing the peasantry by emancipating convicts in large numbers. Thus the average annual number of pardons which he granted was seventy-eight, so that within four years he might have exceeded the total of emancipations (300) made in the twelve years before him.

Such a policy was the more urgently needed, to assist his general policy, by reason of the comparatively large number of convicts landed in 1801–3 inclusive—more than 2,000. As many as possible of "old hands" had to be got off the store; and almost the only means to that end, in view of the strictly limited wage-labour market, was their emancipation to possible self-support on farms. This is the setting of the achievement mentioned earlier: King's reduction by 1804 of the percentage of the population on rations to 37, compared with 70 in 1798. It was too, of course, another aspect of King's part-solution of the problem which Hunter's means had failed to solve: the re-establishment of the dispersed peasantry, though in a territory still for the most part held unshakably by the rum squirearchy of Macarthur.

Whitehall was, however, not more pleased with King for his tentative success than it had been with Hunter for his failure. As Secretary of State Lord Hobart had consistently supported King's execution of the State policy for the colony; but now at the moment of comparative success the inevitable local reaction, the estrangement from the Governor of the owner-officers of the garrison, brought the order for King's recall. Lord Hobart was gratified by the settled state of the colony, he wrote on November 30, 1803, excepting "the unfortunate differences which have so long subsisted between you and the military officers of the colony." King was therefore to return home as soon as a successor, who would be "free from the opinion of party," could be found. It might have been some consolation for the Governor to re-read four grateful addresses which one hundred and eighty settlers had sent him earlier that year, thanking him for having, "by the extirpation of that great evil" of monopoly, made "our circumstances easy, our families happy, and given a prospect to our children of being useful members of society."[1] (Hunter, too, had read farmers' addresses—of another purport—when *his* letter of recall was on its way.) The fact is that every Governor from Hunter to Darling, over a period of thirty-five years, would be recalled for one of two basic reasons: either he had tried, and failed, to execute Whitehall's policy, or he had executed it but too successfully, in the sense that his success had inevitably antagonized vested interests in the colony.[2]

[1] From the address of 27 farmers at Kissing Point. For this and reference to three similar memorials, *vide Historical Records of Australia*, 1, iv; the addresses were dated March 1–29, 1803.

[2] If we omit to regard the several administrations during the economic infancy of New South Wales chiefly as more or less effective executors of the Whitehall policy for the colony, we must fall into misunderstanding of contemporary events. Thus Roberts properly dissents (*op. cit.*, p. 17, *footnote* commenting on Frederick Watson's editorial notes to *Historical Records of Australia*, iii–iv) from Watson's extraordinary conclusion upon King: "It is difficult to trace any direct influence of the Governor in improvements of the conditions of life in the colony." However, some of Roberts's own more painstaking analysis is equally invalid, for the reason that he evidently fails to understand the simple, persistent basis that the Imperial Government wished its convicts settled in the colony on expiry or pardon, sent them thither in numbers varying widely from year to year, administration to administration, and yet had to pay heed to the large economic interest vested in the colony since the regime of unfettered monopoly-trading in 1793–95.

Roberts writes (*op. cit.*, p. 13), ". . . Hobart, the Secretary of State in 1804, ordered the curtailment of public agriculture and dispersion of the Government herds.

"At the close of King's regime, therefore, came many changes in land policy, the whole amounting to a complete *volte-face*. Since the past had shown that to guarantee a price was wasteful, and that public farming was retrogressive, the stress was now on settlers, and it was the cardinal feature of the new ecomomic policy of 1804 to aid them as much as possible. More bond labour was to be allowed, premiums of stock were to be given to deserving settlers, and the Government was to advance loans in kind."

Ignoring minor mistakes in this account, we should notice the more serious mistakes, in order to keep King's economic significance in a proper light. ". . . Hobart, the Secretary of State in 1804."—But Hobart concluded his

(c) Assisted and "Special" Emigration, 1793–1806

King seemed to have made a road along which the poor Australian colonist might travel unmolested, with his passport term as Secretary of State early in 1804, having been in that office since August 6, 1801, or throughout the period of King's effective administration of New South Wales as a prison-and-peasant colony.

". . . more bondlabour . . ."—More bondlabour was not allowed to settlers. Hobart's predecessor, Portland, had instructed King in June 1801 to recall excess assignees from officers, to use them in public farming, and had authorized him to buy Macarthur's sheep and cattle for the Government (iii, pp. 99 et seq.), and Hobart had required a further withdrawal of convicts from settlers (Hobart to King, April 5, 1803, iv, p. 519), so that where the officers (comprising most of the larger farmers) had had 276 convicts at their service in August 1800, the average between September 1800 and the end of 1800 was 128, and at the New Year the number out was only 58, including a dozen in the service of the Governor and Lieutenant-Governor. There was no *volte-face* in 1804. Certainly, when King had, as it seemed, consolidated the position of the small farmers he released some convicts to their service from the public farms (King to Hobart, March 1, 1804, iv, p. 519), and stated his intention of continuing this course; but this was no more than an act of his (and Whitehall's) policy from 1800, by which public farming was to save the Government money and break the monopoly of the large farmers at the Commissariat. "More bondlabour" was made available to large farmers only after Macarthur's successful representations to Camden; this policy took effect from 1805.

" . . . premiums of stock and loans in kind. . ."—To assist the earlier established policy of encouraging small farmers, Hobart had recommended as early as August 1801—a fortnight after his appointment as Secretary of State—the hiring by Government of oxen to peasants who were able to secure ploughs or carts (*cf.* King's Government and General Order of February 6, 1804, iv, p. 499). King had been providing loans in kind, i.e., sheep, cows, etc., since his restoration of the Government flocks and herds, 1800–1803. Prizes for farmers adjudged to have raised the best stock, kept their farms best, etc., were introduced by King in each of the six mainland districts in May 1803 (*cf.* Government and General Order of May 9, 1803, iv, p. 123).

"The stress" has, as we have seen, been "on settlers," i.e. small settlers, since King's return to New South Wales in 1800. Hunter's failure effectively to lay such stress had indeed provided the reason for King's appointment. Some stress was laid on large settlers, i.e. pastoralists, after Camden became Secretary of State, but this was another and a later affair.

"The second element of the new policy," Roberts continues, "was the disposal of produce by the operation of supply and demand, to further which King tried to adopt a system of tender, with safeguards against the monopolists (1804)." However, in May 1803 King had recommended to Hobart

of servitude or emancipation or Whitehall approval, towards a plot of ground which should be his own and capable of giving him and his family sustenance. But it was to turn out that the land would not tolerate the imperial disposition of it. It would graze great flocks on unfenced uncultivated plains, more readily than it would yield, season by season without let of flood or drought, a few hundred bushels to each of a few hundred peasants on 30-acre blocks. The enforced realization of this was already in 1804-5 modifying somewhat the official view of Australia, but it would be nearly thirty years before the pastoral claim quite superseded the other in the interest of England.

But the pastoral idea was large in only a colonial head or two, as King approached the apex of his brief-lived peasant structure, and it was a more immediate power that cancelled much of his laborious achievement—he had broken the officers' monopoly of importing and retailing, but, as we saw, he had not broken their landhold. When Macarthur came back in triumph to Sydney in 1805, half of one per cent of the colonial population owned half the acreage which had been given away in New South Wales, and a power was entrenched which King could

(iv, p. 123) that the existing Commissariat fixed price of 8s. a bushel for wheat and 4s. for maize (King had reduced the price of wheat from 10s. to 8s. in 1800) should be continued "until the industrious part of the settlers are able to work the plough with effect." Next March he did reduce the price of wheat to 7s. 6d. for the Sydney and Parramatta districts and 7s. for the Hawkesbury, having first called for tenders (iv, p. 518). He had received no tenders under the ruling price of 8s. except from persons whom he deemed to be angling for a revival of the old monopoly of supplying the Commissariat, which King had broken early in his term. The New South Wales farmer's produce was not, in practice, disposed of to Governmnet "by the operation of supply and demand," i.e. in an open market, until nearly twenty years after 1804, when Brisbane, on instructions, abolished the fixed price system. Thus the average price a bushel given at the Commissariat store for wheat was: 10s. bushel, 1792-1801; 9s. 6d. bushel, 1802-11; 8s. 10d. bushel, 1812-21 (*vide* Colonial Secretary to the directors of the Bank of New South Wales, May 16, 1822, *Historical Records of Australia*, I, x, p. 734). Until 1822, "supply and demand" operated merely to the extent of causing large fluctuations in the "fixed" price, e.g. in early 1814 from 10s. to 8s., from 15s. to 10s. (Macquarie to Bathurst, April 28, 1814, viii, p. 144).

not dislodge: the power of wealth. New South Wales was a land of large proprietors, now for awhile dragooned into tolerating five or six hundred small fry as neighbours. King in his battle for a free peasantry clamoured for immigrants who should have been trained to hold their own on the land. The immigrants were not forthcoming; and Macarthur with his tale of rich pastures had the ear of Whitehall. In this breathing space before the whole battle must be fought over again on a larger scale, when the world war should be over, King faced defeat at home and abroad, as Macquarie would face it in 1821.

The character of immigration into New South Wales at this early period reflects faithfully that essential opposition—colonial proprietors *versus* peasants, the nature of the land *versus* the original wish of Government—and its inescapable outcome. At home in the colony the great proprietors held their acres: which interest or which policy was being assisted effectively from Britain?

In the first instance the Imperial Government tried to forward the old policy for the colony, by encouraging the emigration from the British Isles of small persons; but this halfheartedly, for "so long as the war continued there was no need for emigration" to solve English domestic problems. The *Bellona* arrived at Port Jackson on January 16, 1793, two days short of five years after Phillip's landfall at Botany Bay, and, as we saw, instructions had been promulgated before this by which assisted free immigrants, as well as officers, ex-soldiers, and sailors, and ex-convicts in the colony, were to be afforded land, working capital, and sustenance. But that was before the war.

The conditions proffered in the pre-war period had been attractive enough—50 to 100 acres at a nominal quit rent, two years' provisions, convict servants, grain for seed, a supply of farming implements (but these last were few in the colony in the 1790's), after free passage for the expectant settler and his family in a convict ship. Yet there had been no rush for places. In the years after 1792, when the *Bellona* sailed for Australia, war brought its profits, Speenhamland provided bread enough in the shires, and free Englishmen had not yet resigned themselves to their "redundancy" in their enclosed homeland.

However the *Bellona's* thirteen free persons, who arrived to find the colony on short rations, added a new class to the colonial population; they brought the number of farmers up to nearly two hundred, including ten officers of the garrison, 107 ex-convicts, 66 seamen or marines, and three functionaries or ex-functionaries of the civil establishment. These were an odd lot with which to build a commonwealth. Most of the marines who had stayed to settle, when their comrades went home in 1791–92, had stayed because, their officer, Captain Watkin Tench believed, they were infatuated with various of the female convicts. Indeed, the exhausted, broken men from the hulks, the lovesick Royal Marines, and the handful of unaccustomed free people, who made up so large a proportion of the first farming community in Australia, must have been ineffectual enough, even encouraged by the full rations which often they did not get. Grubbing on their little grants at Parramatta, The Ponds, Prospect Hill, and Liberty Plains, they seemed poor material to Major Grose's officers.

Few assisted emigrants left for New South Wales during the remaining years of the eighteenth century. The French Republic declared war on England in February 1793; soon the maritime roads were barred with brigs and frigates, and, three convict fleets and some lesser convoys having landed the survivors of perhaps five thousand convicts sent in 1787–92, only eight convict ships, carrying perhaps 1,250 transports, reached Sydney, after the *Bellona*, before New Year's Day 1800.[1]

---

[1] The reference in the previous paragraph to Tench is derived from his *A Complete Account of the Settlement at Port Jackson*, pp. 39, 40; London, 1793.

The transportation figure for 1787–92 is, roundly, from Coghlan's figures, *cit.* Barton, *op. cit.*, p. 463, and the figure for 1793–1800 is from the estimate in Hunter's return of January 1800, in *Historical Records of Australia*, I, ii, pp. 563, 364. But it should be noted that the comparison of Hunter's figure with Coghlan's is a doubtful one. Coghlan gives statistics of arrivals, except for 1787–94, and 1811–23, for which years his statistics are of departures

There were few conveyances available, then, for free emigrants, who if assisted must make the passage in a convict ship. Half-a-dozen persons found their way to New South Wales, however. A single emigrant arrived in October 1794; in February 1798 the Secretary of State advised the Governor that five more were sailing; they were to have 100 acres each on the mainland or 50 at Norfolk Island, their passages had been paid, and they were to be allowed twelve months' rations two convict servants each, and seed and implements.

The plans had gone awry, then, by which according to the Whitehall notion of 1789 surplus free persons were to be assisted *en masse* to the ends of the earth, and by which according to the notion of 1787 convicted persons were to be exiled likewise; the project of a regular supply of transports, at the rate of two shiploads a year, was never realized. Whether in the case of the free people the chief cause of breakdown was the difficulty of transport in war conditions, or the war-time

from England. The departure figures of any year cannot simply be taken to represent the arrival figures for that year or the next. For (1) sailings were not restricted to any particular season of the year; (2) the voyage occupied anything from four months to eight months (*cf.* the first fleet's eight months passage in 1787–88, with the *Mary Anne's* passage of four months twelve days in 1791; *vide* Tench, *op. cit.*, pp 133–34); (3) deaths *en voyage* were a large, and widely varying, factor of difference between numbers of convicts to leave and numbers to arrive (*cf.* e.g. Tench on the *Mary Anne*—"To demonstrate the effect of humanity and justice, of a hundred and forty-four female convicts embarked, only three had died" (*en route*), i.e. a death-rate of 2 per cent—with more comprehensive figures). Thus, of 3,833 transported 1795–1801, 385 died on board: 10 per cent; of 2,398 transported 1801–12, 52 died on board: 2 per cent (1812 transportation committee *report*, p. 101). Phillip reported that of 930 men in the Second Fleet, 261 had died on board: 28 per cent (*Historical Records of Australia*, 1, i, p. 197).

Coghlan's figures, which are stated to be from official sources, do not agree with some given by, e.g. Hunter and Darling during their terms.

The single emigrant to arrive in 1794 was John Boston (in the *Surprize*, October 25th). He came with a project of curing fish, and Hunter was instructed to give him favourable treatment (Dundas to Hunter, July 1, 1794, *Historical Records of Australia*, 1, i, pp. 603 *et seq.*).

The five intending emigrants of 1798 were mentioned in Portland to Hunter, February 6, 1798, enclosure No. 3, *ibid.*, vol. ii.

coldness of Government towards emigration, or a failure in the labouring classes of that "disposition to emigrate" of which Pitt's minister had spoken somewhat precipitately, there was virtually no emigration to Australia during the first war period, the period of England's struggle with Revolutionary France.

The next reinforcement of the tiny immigrant body at the settlements was made about the time of the short peace in Europe, from March 1802 to May 1803, before England's resumption of war with Imperial France.

Here a rather puzzling situation presents itself. Now that the seas were free there would be, in the normal course, more clearances per annum of convict ships from Britain and an increase per annum of both convict and immigrant arrivals at Port Jackson. After the war with Napoleon broke out, there would be cessation. But the case is not so simple. Actually the number of convict arrivals (1,128) seems to have been greater in 1801, the last year of the first war, than in the three years 1802–1804 (no convicts arrived in 1804, as the enquirer would anticipate finding); more transports arrived during 1801 than in any year between 1791 (the year before the allies attacked France) and 1815 (the year of the final overthrow of Napoleon). Before considering the contrasting fact that the period of peace was, as we should have expected statistics to show, a period of temporary revival of small-man emigration, we shall do well to examine this apparent anomaly of convict transportation: intimately connected with the sort of emigration that had been contemplated, that is the emigration of the poor.

In the first place, it was not punitive measures against the Irish rebels of 'ninety-eight and thereafter that accounted for the peak level of convict transportation in 1801. Certainly some United Irishmen (and persons who had been so rash as to appear in Dublin streets between dark and dawn) arrived in that year. The *Ann* from Cork brought to Sydney on February 21st "137 of the most desperate and diabolical characters . . . together with a Catholic priest (n.b. the Reverend Peter O'Neil) of most notorious, seditious, and rebellious principles,"[1] and during the year the courts were busy with that proportion of the Irish ultimately transported, to whom a trial was vouchsafed, so that in August the Home Department was notified[2] that 350 convicts from Ireland were to be sent in the *Atlas* and *Hercules*. But these ships did not arrive until July 7, 1802, and June 26, 1802, respectively. (Of 320 who actually sailed, 127 died on board, and "the survivors," King wrote,[3] "were in a dreadfully emaciated and dying state.") Four hundred more Irish, "mostly rebels," arrived towards the end of the year 1802.

The facts are that most of those transported in the years of peace 1802–3 were Irish (about 600 in three ships, out of a total of about 1,000 transported from Great Britain) but that few of the 1801 transports were Irish. This seems to deepen the anomaly. But probably an explanation of the exceptionally great English convict traffic of 1801, and the exceptionally small traffic of the peace-years, is to be found in contemporary English social history. Examining this field, we notice that periods of high prices for breadstuffs were periods of heightened civil commotions: periods, consequently, of unusual activity in the criminal courts, gaols, and prison ships. Now a period of "severe privations and sufferings (for) the lower orders" was remarked[4] early in 1800, when English wheat prices rose above 100s. a quarter, to reach 154s. 2d. in March 1801. From this month, the price of the food-staple of the poor fell steadily, to below 50s. a quarter in the winter of 1804. There was rioting in the winters of 1799 and (especially) 1800, sometimes so serious that the militia were called out.

Here, probably, in the extraordinarily depressed condition of the English poor at the beginning of the century, is the source

---

[1] King to Portland, March 10, 1801, *Historical Records of Australia*, I, iii, p. 9.

[2] Transport Commissioners to J. King, August 26, 1801, *ibid.*, iii, p. 269. Many had not been convicted; most had no papers to show the term of sentence.

[3] King to Hobart, July 23, 1802, iii, p. 531; November 9th, p. 654.

[4] *Vide Annual Register*, 1801, p. 1, and Chapter 4 (a) *infra*.

of the heavy transportation of 1800 to early 1801. During nearly four years, from the spring of 1801 to the winter of 1804, on the other hand, foodstuffs prices were falling or low; during that period few convicts were sent to New South Wales from England, so that it is reasonable to infer that the contemporary state of comparative plenty brought about the condition of an actual decrease of transportation at those seasons when natural and political conditions alike were favourable to a large transportation.

It should follow that the improved economic position of the English poor offset, equally, the opportunities which peace offered of emigrant sailings. But, as prices fell in mid-1801, 21 emigrants left for New South Wales in the *Minorca*, *Canada*, and *Nile*. Six months later, Lord Hobart announced his endorsement of two others, and they, with 47 men, women, and children, sailed in the *Perseus* and *Coromandel* in February 1802. Thirty-four emigrants, including Bedell, a farmer specially recommended to King, received permits to sail in the *Glatton*, later in the year. Two batches set out in 1803: 46 men, women, and children in the spring, in H.M.S. *Calcutta* and the *Ocean* convict ship, bound for Port Phillip which Lieutenant-Colonel David Collins was to settle, and 59 at the end of the year.[1]

The total numbers advertised to sail were thus 21 in 1801,

---

[1] For these statistics *vide* J. King to P. G. King, June 19, 1801, ii, pp. 108-9; Sullivan (under secretary) to King, January 30, 1802, ii, pp. 365, 377, August 5, 1802, pp. 533-34 (but Bedell, Twistleton, a clergyman, and Sergeant Peate did not sail in the *Glatton*: King to Sullivan, May 9, 1803, iv, p. 245); Sullivan to King, April 5, 1803, Hobart to King, April 5, 1803; Sullivan to King, November 30, 1803, iv, pp. 66, 63, 429. Other figures of the free settlers who accompanied Collins to Port Phillip are in Collins to King, February 29, 1804, *Historical Records of Australia*, III, i, pp. 221 *et seq.*

Note that John Dunmore Lang, commending a generation afterwards a system of emigration by which several families who were neighbours might sail together and settle as neighbours in the colony, recalled that in 1802 twelve Scottish Border families settled in this style at Portland Head on the Hawkesbury (*New South Wales Pamphlets*, Public Library of Victoria, vol. xxi, No. 4, p. 17).

83 in 1802, and 105 in 1803: more than 200 emigrants had applied for and received permission to leave England, precisely during the period of plenty when convicts transported were few; more than 60 per cent of the emigrants left during the period of peace.

Bearing in mind that emigrants and felons, coming for the most part from similar strata of society, were subject to the pressure of similar circumstances, we have to ask whether the probable explanation is that the emigrants had made their arrangements long before sailing—and the fact that a' substantial proportion drew back at the last might be an indication that they had waited for peace in order to get away, and preferred to stay now when plenty had supervened—or whether the comparative efflux might not have represented the dammed back intending emigrants of years past—in fact, those who sailed included many who had been in the colony and could not easily have returned to Sydney during the first war. But as there had been virtually no emigration of this (or any other) kind before 1801, and would be virtually none during the war period after 1803, we should scarcely be justified in even a tentative conclusion upon this interesting phase of the Anglo-Australian connection, were it not for the occurrence, as we find, in the peace interval of the only colonizing enterprise made by the Imperial Government between the pre-war period of the 1780's and the period of expansion nearly forty years later.

This was the attempted settlement of Port Phillip, on the southern coast of the Australian continent. The settlement was decided upon by Henry Addington's Ministry (March 1801 to May 1804) towards the end of 1802, during the peace. Lieutenant-Colonel David Collins, who sailed from Yarmouth in H.M.S. *Calcutta* on April 27, 1803, just before the resumption of war, to be Lieutenant-Governor at Port Phillip, took with him in the *Ocean* a number of free settlers. Lord Hobart had given twenty free persons, including seven men, permission to share with about 300 convicts the experience of founding a colony.[1] This feature of the expedition from England to Port Phillip seems, if taken in conjunction with the data given above, to be at least an indication that peace and a felt need of emigration were associated phenomena.

It is to be noted that even as Collins had trouble on the voyage with his free emigrants, neither Hunter nor King found, in the few free emigrants assisted to the colony, the qualities needed if the Governors were to establish there the mode of small farming that was becoming impracticable in England. King thought New South Wales farming would be advanced "if fifty respectable families, the heads of which ought to be good practical farmers, were sent here with the idea of staying all their lives." He gave a poor account of the immigrants already in 1802 in the colony, comparing them unfavourably with the "settlers from convicts." However, he gave each immigrant grantee two breeding ewes from the Government flock—a customary assistance to grantees which, he noted,[2] ate up the increase. Hunter, before him, had concluded that "very few of those sent out are likely to benefit the settlement." . . . "I wish they were in their own country again," he said[3] with feeling. It seems that often enough an immigrant farmer felt likewise; and some did return, just as after the first transports returned in Grose's time many ex-convicts had decided they preferred the poor rate in England to rations in Australia, and paid or worked their way home. But these deserters—expirees, disappointed emigrants, or soldiers of the original garrison who had resisted successfully the inducements offered to stay them in 1791–92—tended to find England a drearier land than the expected fields, which had seemed so green in the distance. And so many people in these categories reappear in the emigration returns. For

[1] *Vide* Frederick Watson's introduction to *Historical Records of Australia*, III, vol. i, and Sullivan to Collins, April 5, 1803; Collins to Sullivan, July 16, 1803, *ibid.*, pp. 18, 23–4.   [2] *Ibid.*, iv, p. 81.

[3] Hunter to J. King, April 30, 1796, i, p. 565; similarly, Hunter to Portland, August 20, 1796, i, p. 592. Who the many emigrants were of whom "very few" were desirable colonists, observably by 1796, is not known.

example, though one of the three ex-sergeants of the Royal Marine Service who had booked for the *Glatton* in 1802 missed the boat, Sergeants Knight and Stroud sailed; two "settlers to return" were on the *Calcutta* list in 1803, and two persons recommended by Hunter (now Vice-Admiral, living in retirement in England). Years later, Hunter would epitomize the feeling of such people as those: "When I returned to England (n.b. 1801), numbers applied to me for permission to go out again, for they said they could live there, but they could not live here."[1]

Nevertheless emigrants had shown little aptitude for the farming life of a raw colony. The Secretary of State was indeed doing his best to supply King with the best material offering, after King's repeated complaints of the calibre of early arrivals. "I have been particularly careful in the selection of the persons who have lately been permitted to proceed to New South Wales as settlers," Hobart wrote[2] in 1803, "and although I may have been in some instances deceived, I hope the trouble I have taken will not be altogether useless. . . . I cannot as yet give you much encouragement to expect settlers who possess property to any amount."

Yet, in spite of the minister's concluding phrase, within two months the first of a succession of persons of superior social and economic status would be putting down his name for New South Wales. The commander of H.M.S. *Calcutta*, Captain Woodriff, sailed with his ship, to leave it at Sydney in order to settle, with his family, on a special grant of 600 acres. An isolated forerunner of the propertied immigrants, another ship's captain who like Woodriff had had opportunity of gauging the possibilities of the colony had bought a farm, and staffed it with some of his ship's people, as early as 1796. This was Captain Hogan, of the *Marquis Cornwallis* convict

---

[1] The statement of Hunter is in *Minutes of Evidence*, 1812, Transportation Committee, p. 23. *Vide*, e.g., King to Sullivan, August 7, 1803, iv, p. 367, for "settlers to return."

[2] Hobart to King, February 27, 1803, iv, p. 35.

ship. In the year after his purchase (to renew an impression of some of the problems which Hunter and King had been attacking in the period between 1797 and 1803), at least 700 convicts had already completed their terms of transportation, and there were "not less than three hundred young persons already in the town of Sydney, very few of whom had been born in England." Expirees, emancipees, "currency lads" (as the native born were called) were giving the Governor an ever-increasing business of setting up farmlets. And this at considerable cost to Government, for though the Crown land was granted without cost to Government, it cost the Treasury about £138 to establish a settler, his wife and (say) four children and to maintain the household during the prescribed twelve months.[1]

In order to push on development, King found it desirable to seek "settlers who possess property." He had decided of the poor immigrants, "The bounty of Government is much imposed on by these applications," and urged that only recommended farmers be sent, instancing as an added burden which the emigrant ships were apt to bring, Bridget Heath. She had come in the *Glatton*, ostensibly to join her father; but her father was not in the settlement, and the man who had in fact sent for her left her destitute on her arrival. Such annoyances, and the poor performance of the early immigrants, led King to urge that more of the gentry be induced to settle and invest in Australia. Alexander Reilly and Dr. Luttrell had come in 1804, to shine in contrast with the lower orders. True, it had cost nearly £400 to settle Luttrell, his wife, and his seven children, and nearly £300 to establish the Reillys at the new settlement at Port Dalrymple in Van Diemen's Land, each on 600 acres (*cf.* 100 acres as a rule, to immigrants of the humbler ranks of society); but King thought the difference of capacity more than compensated Government for the greater outlay.[2]

[1] *Vide* for details of costs, v, pp. 126–7; for the mariner-settlers, *vide Historical Records of Australia*, 1, iv, p. xi–xiii, vol. ii, p. 24, and for the "Currency" lads and lasses, Collins, *op. cit.*, p. 366.

[2] *Ibid*, v, p. 127, iv, p. 367.

Curiously, on this ground Macarthur the arch-monopolist and King the anti-monopolist could meet at last. For, in England, Macarthur was at this time promoting just such an emigration as King, in New South Wales, now found preferable to the old. Encouraged in his wool schemes by the new Secretary of State, Lord Camden, by the committee for trade and foreign plantations, and by organizations of English woollens manufacturers, Macarthur returned to Sydney as a civilian, in June 1805, with an order of Whitehall for an additional grant of 5,000 acres and for the services of thirty convicts.[1]

Well, Macarthur had sold his commission in the army, and King had broken Macarthur's monopoly and could afford to receive him with the honours due to a producer and investor. "I offered Macarthur my hand, who very gratefully received it, and he is now farmer, shipowner, etc. . . . So much for our meeting after four years of suspense and vicissitude."[2] In fact King not only executed Camden's directions with regard to Macarthur, but also sold him 100 of the "finest woolled ewes from Government's stock," at £2 in grain apiece; and not only did he grant Macarthur's companion, Walter Davidson, the 2,000 acres ordered by Camden, but 1,000 more. Two Macarthurs, a governess, and Thomas and Edward Wood, wool sorters, had accompanied Macarthur and Davidson, and King wrote to Camden, "I cannot but consider it a valuable acquisition and advantage to the interest of this colony, when settlers of such description and uncontaminated mind as Mr. Davidson come to it. Unfortunately, those who have already arrived, with the exception of a very few, have generally been of that description, that many of them with their numerous families still continue to be a burthen to Government."[3]

So, reassembled, the Government flock that Macarthur as

---

[1] *Macarthur Records*, pp. 78 et seq.; *Historical Records of Australia*, I, iv, p. 163, Chapter 5 (a) infra for Macarthur's sheepbreeding.

[2] King to Banks (on "the hero of the fleece"), cit. *Macarthur Records*, p. 110. [3] King to Camden, July 20, 1805, v, pp. 108–9.

inspector of public works a dozen years before had dispersed, gave him of its increase now; the officer whom King had arrested in 1801, and who had organized his comrades to boycott Government House, was received as a civilian with honours at Government House: the two old antagonists—Macarthur now with backing for his pastoral projects, King with his ex-convict peasantry secure on the land—found themselves in accord.

In 1806 the colony gained another weighty addition when Gregory Blaxland and his family arrived in the *William Pitt*. Blaxland was given a pastoral grant of 4,000 acres, and his choice of the Government herd. He bought 80 head for £2,240, and King gave him, as he had given Macarthur and Davidson, all the convict labour that he sought. It would cost £1,300 to set Blaxland up at Government's charge, but still it would seem worth the money, to King. Six and a half years later, however, Macquarie found that the New South Wales Government had spent £4,500 on setting up John and Gregory Blaxland, and that the brothers were not worth the expenditure. Bligh, too, had considered the Blaxlands rather speculators than producers

Bligh, as Governor in 1806–7 and Macquarie after him from 1809, shared the view which Hunter and King had taken of immigrants as a class, although the late emphasis on gentleman settlers who were given special grants, had been expected to achieve a stimulus of colonial production. "The free settlers, hitherto, have been a thoughtless set of men," Bligh reported. ". . . Classes of plain sensible farming men, of moderate expectations, are the most valuable to come here." Similarly Macquarie, after three years as Governor, suggested a limiting of emigration; many emigrants arrived destitute, and the cost of establishing them was heavy. "I find it now becoming almost a constant practice for persons who wish to get rid of some troublesome connections, to obtain permission at the Secretary of State's office for their being allowed to come out here. By this means they relieve themselves and throw the weight of a most troublesome and useless set of persons on the Government of this country."[1]

But until Macquarie should attack his task of settling the outflow from servitude, and after him Brisbane and Darling supervise a balancing importation of capital and large settlers, King's regime would mark both the high-water mark of the 1787-89 Government policy, and the ebb of that policy from a land better suited to other tides. The high-water mark had been reached about 1803, when the farmers of New South Wales comprised 35 officials and officers, 84 immigrants and ex-soldiers, and 464 ex-convicts.[2] The emigrant, evidently, had been of small significance to date, for a dozen years earlier Phillip had settled almost as many ex-soldiers as now there were immigrants and ex-soldiers together. The transportation system had supplied most of the 1803 population of 7,000; officials, the garrison personnel, and the wives and families of functionaries and soldiers, including several hundred native-born children, made up most of the balance. Immigrants would for twenty years more be a negligible factor in the colonial population and economy. By 1820 the number of native born would be as great as the whole population of 1803, and there would be more adults among them than then remained in the colony of those who had come free since 1793. Still in those days the major elements of the population of New South Wales would be convicts and ex-convicts (more than 60 per cent) and native born (including, for purposes of comparison, all children; nearly 30 per cent).[3] And though Macquarie, like

[1] For the Blaxlands *vide*, e.g., King to Castlereagh, July 7, 1806, v (Gregory Blaxland arrived in New South Wales on April 14, 1806), Macquarie to Liverpool, October 17, 1812, vii, pp. 559, 560.

On the character of immigrants in general, *vide* Bligh to Windham, October 31, 1807, vi, p. 149, Macquarie to Liverpool, October 17, 1812, pp. 597-8.

[2] *Ibid.* iv, p. 396.

[3] For population figures at various stages from 1788, *vide* i, pp. 144, 203, 596; ii, pp. 615 *et seq.* ; iii, pp. 11, 313, etc.

For the population in 1820 *vide* Bigge's *Report on Agriculture and Trade in New South Wales*, p. 80.

King, put a wall about his ex-convict peasants, the economic power of the colony resided in the numerically small group which had secured its place in 1793–99, and thereafter been confirmed in it by the wealth which Macarthur's long experiments with wool gathered to it.

Appendix A

EARLY CURRENCY OF NEW SOUTH WALES[1]

The colony of New South Wales at its establishment was not equipped with a medium of exchange or any means of settling local debts. It had been considered that money would not be needed: necessary stores would be sent from England by the Transport Commissioners or the Victualling Board, the labourers being convicts would not be paid wages, and for other purposes the Commissary's Department of the Colonial Government might draw bills on the Commissioners of the Treasury in London "for Government services in New South Wales."

But when it turned out that supply-ships arrived but at wide and varied intervals, that recourse must be had for stores to the Dutch East Indies and China, besides British possessions in Africa and India, that money was needed for transactions with shipmasters calling at Port Jackson with cargoes on

[1] Some details of the development of currency makeshifts towards stability are given in this Appendix and in Chapters 5 (*b*) and 7 (*b*) and (*c*). It was found necessary to devote so much attention to the story of Australian money during the first forty years of settlement, in the absence of any reliable published account.

The evolution of a stable money system in the colony is readily traceable through the main stages: (1) a "Colonial currency" of promissory notes, etc.; (2) a regulated currency of banknotes and token coinage; (3) a Spanish dollar currency; to (4) sterling currency. But apparently the plenitude of data available has not been investigated hitherto.

The short account in *The Australian Banking and Credit System*, by A. L. Gordon Mackay (London, P. S. King, 1931), pp. 19–25, is generally erroneous; Professor R. C. Mills and E. Ronald Walker in their *Money* (Sydney, Angus and Robertson, 1935), pp. 223–4, make erroneous references to the "Colonial currency," early banking history in the colony, and the New South Wales history of the Spanish dollar's use. *The History and Practice of Australian Banking Currency and Exchange*, by H. E. Teare (Sydney, Alexander Hamilton Institute, 1926) gives on pp. 6–12 a series of substantially accurate references to New South Wales currency up to 1829, but fails to describe satisfactorily the process towards sterling.

speculation, that convicts working overtime for individuals, after their normal working day, had to be paid, and that the expiration (within two years of the landing) of the sentences of many transports of the first fleet threw upon the community a class of freedmen, the need for a currency became increasingly urgent. "The inconveniences attending the not having any money in the colony still subsist," Phillip wrote[1] late in 1791. Twelve months later, in November 1792 (just before Phillip left the colony), the first relief was made when the *Kitty* landed at Sydney Cove 3,870 ounces of silver in Spanish dollars, of £1,001 value.[2] (The Colonial branch of the Home Department had doubtless been taken aback somewhat to learn that the Commissary at Sydney had been forced to issue his own notes; and the dollars were forwarded as being good currency at the Cape of Good Hope and Batavia.) This coin, of 4s. 2d. sterling value, was the general counter of international trade, great quantities of silver dollars having been minted at Mexico City since the sixteenth century. A reflection of its use in the mixed currency of early Sydney is obtained in a letter written by the Reverend Richard Johnson, described by Major Grose as "one of the people called Methodists," to the Secretary of State in 1792. Johnson sought reimbursement in respect of £67 which he had spent on building a church—"sixty pounds of which I have paid in Spanish dollars and the remainder in provisions."[3]

Under the military administrations (1792–95) officers of the New South Wales Corps having accounts in England were able to draw bills, but these, like the Treasury bills drawn by the Commissary, were not a medium of internal currency. A makeshift currency was devised however on the basis of the notes issued by the Commissariat storekeeper in pledge of payment for farmers' produce bought for the establishment.

[1] Phillip to Nepean, November 18, 1791, *Historical Records of Australia*, I, i, p. 310.

[2] *Vide ibid.*, ii, note 142, p. 731, and *History of New South Wales from the Records*, vol. ii, pp. 226 *et seq.*; Sydney, New South Wales Government Printer, 1894. [3] Johnson to Dundas, September 3, 1793, i, p. 452.

Towards the close of Hunter's term these still, as he reported, "constituted our only current money."[1] Farmers holding such promissory notes, which were equivalent to sterling in the sense that they could be consolidated into Treasury bills drawn by the Commissary, could use their store receipts as a "reserve" against which to issue their private notes; and from such issues in good faith the custom was extended until this "base paper currency," Macquarie would find, was still (in 1809, and for many years after) "the only circulating medium, the lowest and most profligate persons issuing their notes of hand in payment of goods purchased, without having the means to redeem them when due."[2]

But the promises to pay of members of the New South Wales penal community were not good with visiting shipmasters; so that when, for example, the *Minerva* arrived at Port Jackson with convicts in January 1800, having articles for sale which her officers had bought at Rio de Janeiro, the colonists' muster for the market "drained the colony of every shilling that could be

---

[1] Hunter to Portland, July 4, 1799, enclosure, ii, p. 370.
The Commissary's notes had the form:

No. 2065   Sydney, *22nd October, 1799*

I promise to pay William Miller, or bearer, the sum of fifty-nine pounds five shillings on account of Government, being for two hundred and thirty-seven bushels of maize.

£59 5s. sterling.   (*Signed*) James Williamson,
    PAID   Acting Commissary.
Approved Jno. Hunter.

Cf. the form used at Hobart in the early days of Van Diemen's Land settlement (*Historical Records of Australia*, III, ii, p. 627):

No. 152   £5 0 0d.
Hobart Town.   *14th January, 1816*

Not to be Consolidated before the 24th June next.

I promise to pay the bearer the sum of Five Pounds Sterling.

Entd. H. C.   (*Signed*) P. G. Hogan, D.A.C.G.
Compared, Correct:—J. T. Campbell, Secy.

[2] Macquarie to Bathurst, July 27, 1822, I, x, p. 675.

scraped together."[1] In the year of the *Minerva's* arrival, the British Government delivered in the *Porpoise* and the *Royal Admiral* £1,200 in British copper coins; King issued them through the Commissariat store at 2d. colonial value for 1d., 1d. for ½d., etc. In a Government and General Order of October 19, 1800, he announced that when sufficient copper coin had been received, barter and the issue of promissory notes for currency was to cease; in the meantime, the export of the coins, in consignments above £5 value, was prohibited. The same order published colonial valuations set on the various coins which appeared from time to time at Sydney: an English farthing was to be a Colonial halfpenny, a halfpenny a penny, a penny twopence, one shilling 1s. 8d., a guinea £1 2s., the johanna £4, the gold mohur £1 17s. 6d., the ducat 9s. 6d., pagoda 8s., Spanish dollar 5s., rupee 2s. 6d., guilder 2s. (It is worthy of remark in this context that less than four years later, on July 10, 1804, an Imperial Act (44 George III, cap. 71) was passed to prevent counterfeiting Bank of England dollars at 5s. value (and Bank of Ireland 6s. tokens).) These "Bank dollars" were Spanish dollars, which were given an English stamp and issued in the period of acute shortage of metallic currency in England. Seven years transportation was the punishment for conviction of a charge of uttering counterfeits.

Generally, during the infancy of New South Wales in subordination to British transportation requirements, the colonist paid wages (to expirees and convicts working in their own time) in kind, and debts likewise or in promises. Actual grain was used as currency, and rum might be the form which truck wages took. "Colonial currency" (the private notes), barter, and a "property wage" were the extempore means by which the early farmers and dealers and employers hung a queer exchange economy about the skirts of the penal establishment. But in this lack of monetary order New South Wales was only a special instance of a general rule among all British possessions up to, and a little after, the beginning of

[1] Collins, *op. cit.*, p. 435.

the nineteenth century.[1] The Sydney community was in a monetary sense better ordered, in one respect, than some other British colonies. For at least, as a gaol, it was built on sterling.

But the sterling convenience for the settlement of overseas obligations did not meet the needs of local exchange, and when King, after the turn of the century, set up a Government retail store, as a measure against monopoly, the currency which he denominated as acceptable there was grain. The monopolists themselves had preferred to use rum as a means of exchange and a suitable means of wage payment (even to troops of the garrison), and even after King's first fruit of success against the monopoly the small settler often chose to convert his local grain currency into disproportionately small quantities of the "foreign" currency, rum. Teare says,[2] "From the first day of the landing, rum appears to have been the most acceptable form of currency." But there is a sort of poetic licence in this statement; for obvious reasons rum is not a reliable or handy measure of value.

When in King's time settlement was made in Van Diemen's Land, similar difficulties presented themselves. The Lieutenant-Governor there, "having no specie for salaries," issued Commissariat notes for £1 and upwards. In 1805, the *Lady Barlow* having arrived at the Derwent with articles for sale, Collins directed his Commissary to issue notes, up to £100, hypothecating salaries or repayable in two years in grain or stock. In 1808 Bligh directed the Van Diemen's Land Lieutenant-Governor to call in private notes circulating in the settlements and to order that, in the absence of specie, "military and colonial notes" (to be consolidated into Treasury bills) should be reckoned as sterling money; the use after February

[1] For a good account of monetary arrangements throughout the contemporary British Empire, vide *A History of Currency in the British Colonies*, by Robert Chalmers, *passim* (H.M. Stationery Office, 1893).

[2] *Op. cit.*, p. 6, *cf.* Phillip, October 11, 1792 (*Historical Records of New South Wales*, i, p. 665), replying to a notification that rum would be sent out for the troops' use: "The permitting of spirits among the civil and military may be necessary, but it will certainly be a great evil."

14, 1808, of private currency was to be punishable by £50 fine. But "notes of hand" for threepence and upward continued to circulate.[1]

More than three years after the arrival of the *Porpoise* and *Royal Admiral* coppers, King wrote to London appealing for a further £2,000 copper, together with £1,000 in sixpenny pieces, which he might put into circulation as shillings. The original "cartwheel" pennies of 1800 (each weighed one ounce) had not gone far towards assisting exchange among 7,000 people, nearly 60 per cent of whom supported themselves and drew or paid wages. But evidently the great pence were treasured, for Macquarie would report[2] that most of that copper was still in 1812 in the colony, having been stayed by the Commissary's reception of the pennies for "conversion" into sterling at the inflation.

The intervening period had evidently not been one of advance towards a stable currency system, if as was the case Macquarie's New South Wales was still almost without copper and silver change, still resorted to Colonial currency and truck wages, and circulated its diverse notes at a depreciation beside which the contemporary depreciation at home of Bank of England notes—up to 25 per cent in terms of gold and silver currencies—was a small matter. In fact, the shortage of currency in Britain, since the suspension of cash payments by the Bank of England in 1797 (until 1821), had given rise to an extensive token currency for retail trade and wage payments[3]—most of it not silver as were the Bank's own 1804 tokens—and during the wars the metallic stocks were in no condition to afford a surplus for currency in New South Wales.

[1] For Van Diemen's Land currency situation, *vide* Collins to Sullivan, August 8, 1804; Collins to King, December 8, 1804; King to Collins, September 9, 1804; Collins to Hobart, February 20, 1805; General Order, February 2, 1808; *Historical Records of Australia*, III, i, pp. 262, 293, 284, 308, 311, 561, 832.   [2] *Historical Records of Australia*, 1, vii, p. 606.
[3] *Vide Outline of the Economic History of England*, by H. O. Meredith, pp. 316-17, for an account of the contemporary English token currency (London, Pitman, 1908).

In general the colony rubbed along, during its first generation, with a currency compounded of grain, rum, store receipts, and Commissariat notes, private promissory notes, and premium pence—augmented as we shall see in 1814 by a token currency of mutilated dollars, in 1817 by New South Wales banknotes and metal tokens, and in 1824 by Spanish dollars as legal tender. When Treasury bills would not serve the needs of the establishment, the Commissary might draw such bills to an amount corresponding to what he required in Spanish dollars for the purchase of goods.[1] "The currency of the colony consists principally of Government paper and copper money," a select committee of the Commons would find in 1812, adding in wonderment, "At times indeed wheat and cattle have in the courts of justice been considered as legal tender in payment of debts."[2]

Chalmers considers[3] that four periods may be distinguished in the currency history of Australia: (1) "an age of barter and tokens," 1788–1822; (2) "the supremacy of the Spanish dollar as the actual standard and measure of value," 1822–29; (3) "the substitution of a sterling standard," 1829–51; (4) establishment of sterling after the gold discoveries of 1851, and the establishment of a branch of the Royal Mint in Australia.

[1] E.g., in 1804 the Commissary bought 7,500 Spanish dollars at 5s. each, to pay for stock, etc., for the Government farms (1, iv, p. 628).
For an example of the consolidation of store receipts into Treasury bills, vide King to the Secretaries of the Treasury, October 10, 1800, ii, p. 686, stating that the Commissary had consolidated such receipts during 1800 to a total of £2,215.   [2] 1812 Transportation Committee Report, p. 12.
[3] Op. cit., p. 242.

Appendix B

OBSERVED RESOURCES OF EARLY NEW SOUTH WALES

New South Wales made in its early years but a poor show of realizing Phillip's anticipation that it would prove "the most valuable acquisition that Great Britain ever made." Until, about 1804–1805, Macarthur's sheepbreeding experiments attracted some practical encouragement by industrialists and Government, the colony could not be regarded as a field for investment, except official investment in so far as it served as a dump for convicted members of the redundant population of England.

This is illustrated sufficiently by three views of the colony in 1798, after ten years' settlement. In Soho Square Sir Joseph Banks, who was usually wrong, wrote irascibly that no raw material of interest to British manufacturers had been discovered in New South Wales. In the miserable settlement by the harbour of Port Jackson Captain Hunter wrote that the colonial population walked naked, for it was two years since any clothing had been supplied. A select committee of the House of Commons determined that the colony was "already fully supplied with convicts."[1] No staple of production, no clothes, no accommodation even for criminals: this was the character of the colony at the end of its first decade.

However, already some signs had been remarked of natural resources and potentialities which, if they were developed, might offset to an extent the cost of the settlement to its promoters, the British Government. The only approximation to a staple of production which King found was the winning of

[1] *Vide* Banks to J. King, May 15, 1798, *Historical Records of Australia*, 1, ii, p. 231; Hunter to J. King, November 1, 1798, *ibid.*, p. 235; *Parliamentary Papers*, 1798, *cit. A Colonial Autocracy*, by M. Phillips, p. 5; London, King, 1909.

sealskins and whale oil; but he observed with hopeful interest the experiments of the sheepbreeders and could anticipate an exploitation, which might be profitable, of other means of wealth. It would be far into the 1820's before a vision of Australia as a gigantic spread of pasture was entertained by more than a few, but the suspense during forty years until then was not unrelieved by observation of economic possibilities.

Six months after the landing, Phillip, having had unfortunate experience of the depletion of his small livestock, disposed succinctly of what in the future would be the colony's major concern. "Sheep do not thrive in this country at present," he wrote.[1] But twelve years later King could remark upon the situation created by Macarthur's introduction of Spanish merino sheep (in the very year of gloom, 1798), "There is a promising appearance of a great quantity of wool being produced in a few years."[2] He noticed a steady improvement subsequently, and after Banks's favourable report in 1803 upon eight fleeces submitted by Macarthur, could be confident that the breeders were "getting of a finer wool every year."

Earlier, a secondary process auxiliary to the small wool-production was instituted, two convicts being set to weaving. The 1801 clip yielded material for 306 yards of coarse blanketing. Similarly the flax (which Phillip's original instructions had urged should be cultivated) in the colony was yielding thread for 1,400 yards of linen a year, woven by female convicts at their "factory" at Parramatta. Looms had been sent out in 1798.[3]

Phillip had planted some vines, which did well for four years but later failed through blight; the efforts during King's Government of two French vignerons were frustrated likewise

[1] Phillip to Nepean, July 5, 1788, *Historical Records of Australia*, 1, i, p. 45.
[2] King to Portland, September 28, 1800, ii, p. 612, *vide* also King to Hobart, May 9, 1803, iv, p. 81; March 1, 1804, iv, p. 481.
[3] Portland to Hunter, September 18, 1798, i, pp. 225 *et seq.*; King to Portland, March 10, 1801, August 21, 1801, iii, pp. 4, 125; King to Hobart, May 9, 1803, enclosure No. 12, iv, pp. 106 *et seq.*

through visitations not yet understood.[1] Indeed, the well-meant essays of Whitehall to make the colony fruitful were usually malapropos. Perhaps the most engaging instance was Lord Hobart's response, to King's report, early in 1801, that during the summer the rich Hawkesbury farmlands had been flooded on three separate occasions, so that, a shortage of grain threatening, the Governor had thought fit to send to Madras for rice for the public store. The Secretary of State recommended the cultivation of rice in the Hawkesbury meadows— for was it not a singularly happy dispensation of Nature by which "the plant rises in proportion as the water rises, without suffering material injury"?[2]

If flax, rice, and the vine were not ideal subjects of colonial enterprise, perhaps something might be done with minerals, which had been noticed *in situ* in various areas about the settlements. Portland had suggested to Hunter that coal be hewed and sent home; and when King assumed the administration he was hopeful of loading the *Porpoise* with some New South Wales black coal, within a year or so. Before the year was out, in fact, the *Lady Nelson* brought to Sydney 150 tons of "coal and wood" from the Coal River (modern Newcastle, New South Wales), on the coast north of Port Jackson; this was sold to a shipmaster bound for India, the while the settlement's only trained miner, given eleven convict assistants, bored 100 feet into non-bearing strata. Coals from the north, brought by the colonial vessels, were useful for barter with visiting shipmasters, in exchange for badly needed commodities, and King, having declared the discovered coal seams Crown property, established a coal-getting post at the Hunter or Coal River. Though further search had been made since in 1800 the known strata had been found inaccessible to ships, King had had men prospecting, and in the next year it was only lack of colliers for transport that limited his activities at

[1] King to Portland, March 1, 1802, iii, pp. 405, 406, 421 *et seq*.
[2] King to Nepean, March 10, 1801; Hobart to King, January 30, 1802, iii, pp. 76, 369.

"the rivers, where there are great quantities lying on the surface." In 1803 samples of iron ore found in the north were sent home, but French mineralogists in the colony gave their opinion that the iron content of the ore was not great enough to make production worth while.[1] Still, there was in any case a brick manufacture. Up to June 1789 the convict gang at the Sydney brickfields had turned out but 10,000 bricks a month, but then a new kiln was built in which 30,000 bricks might be burnt off at the same time.[2]

Early comers to New South Wales waters in search of sperm whales were adventurers from various North and South American whaling bases. In Phillip's time some of their ships, like the *Britannia* and *William and Anne*, were getting both whales and seals, and King saw a good prospect of development; it was irritating, however, that none in the settlement might buy supplies of the whaling masters, for the East India Company's charter protected the Company against whalers' sales in British possessions east of the Cape of Good Hope. Before settlement was extended from Sydney to the island of Van Diemen's Land (in 1803), the whaler was pioneering in Bass Strait, and, soon, the sealer was making his seasonal bases on the Port Phillip coast. In 1802, King, who would in due course circulate a questionnaire among colonial sheepbreeders as to the experiments they were making, put a questionnaire to three masters of English whalers operating in Australian waters.[3]

Such were some of the avenues explored in the early days of the colony. The abortive result of most early efforts to make the land commercially fruitful is no doubt especially curious against the background, slowly becoming defined, even in these times of public farming, peasant farming, and rum running, of the Australian pasture.

[1] For the early story of coal prospecting, etc., *vide Historical Records of Australia*, I, ii, pp. 609, 695 *et seq.*; iii, pp. 13, 14, 116, 257; iv, pp. 106 *et seq.*
[2] Collins, *op. cit.*, p. 57.
[3] Phillip to Nepean, November 18, 1791, i, p. 307; King to Portland, September 28, 1800, ii, pp. 612–13; iii, pp. 421 *et seq.*, 514 *et seq.*

Chapter 4

THE DISTURBED ECONOMY OF POST-WAR ENGLAND

(a) *English Agriculture to 1817*
(b) *Contemporary British Manufactures, and Labour Conditions*
(c) *Contemporary British Public Finance and Banking*
(d) *Radicalism and Rioting, 1816–17*
(e) *Second Period of "Impaired Liberty," 1817*
(f) *British Foreign Policy and the Vienna Settlement of Europe, 1814–15*
(g) *Third Period of "Impaired Liberty," 1819*
    Conclusion

WHEN the nineteenth century opened, the majority whether in the British Isles or in New South Wales were in sad condition. The colonial penal community could not even feed itself, and, as we saw, it was apt to short rations because supplies from outside were uncertain during the wars. At home, the pauper community was losing the habit of feeding itself, and in the conditions of war and readjustment it, too, was subject to experience of especial scarcity. The lot of the convict, abroad in New Holland, was not far sundered from that of his relations in the slums and shires of England. We saw that as the agricultural and industrial revolutions gathered force the British mass was being proletarianized, and that as the French Revolution gathered force the protesting spokesmen of the mass in England were being subjected to a repressive discipline which had much in common with the practice of the penal settlement. And if the amenities of life were sparse in Sydney, they were not conspicuous in London. In crucial undertakings for the safeguard of health, for instance, the nine millions of rural and urban English were indifferently served. London, which had not reached its first million of population, was still liable to scourges causing fearful mortality; it was still a settlement or camp as it were, within whose confines each year more died than were born. The very water supply was of the most primitive kind. As late as 1802 the New River Company, bringing from neighbouring Hertfordshire water by canal and aqueduct to supplement London's sewage-polluted supply, used wooden mains. "Water is conveyed three times a week," it was said exultantly,[1] "into almost every house by wooden pipes and is preserved in cisterns and tubs in such quantities that the inhabitants have a constant and even lavish supply." The early water mains were hollowed elm trunks, laid end to end; on each of the three days of lavish supply they would be subjected to water pressure for two or three hours, the while housewives left the tap turned on. In the poorer quarters where "company water" was not available, the inhabitants like their ancestors of Elizabeth's day drew their water from common pumps which tapped springs; and the pumps stood among innumerable cesspools.

(a) *English Agriculture to 1817*

The bulk of the population still lived outside the towns, however, though these were increasing in number, and numbers as factories using steampower were concentrated in the midlands and north, deserting the riverbanks by which the first factories were built for easy access to waterpower. Throughout the wars the rural population bore an ever-increasing weight as Parliament and the parishes pressed further burdens upon them by enclosures and pauper-worker systems, and as industrialists laid upon onetime cottage manufacturers the burden of the machine. For their relief there were stirrings of enquiry. Thus (*vide* Chapter 1) in the first year, 1795, of the Speenhamland system of semi-pauperized agricultural labour,

[1] Feltham's *Picture of London* (1802), *cit.* Buer, *op. cit.*, p. 100; *cf.* also Howard's slightly earlier description (*op. cit.*, pp. 131 *et seq.*) of hospitals which gave patients meat, porridge, and bread—no fruit or vegetables—and three pints of beer in the summer and a quart in the winter. The patients at Guy's got great quantities of beer from alehouses.

Pitt, the Prime Minister, secured the appointment of a select committee of the House of Commons to enquire into the high price of corn. The irony of this circumstance inheres in the broader accompanying fact that, while the corn committee sat, the rude sociology of the landlords was being applied to adapt the social-economic system to a permanent economy of profitable scarcity, which should be dependent precisely on the maintenance of prices at a high level; of this adaptation the House of Commons would be the chief instrument.

The Speenhamland system, which originated in 1795 after a harvest failure, was not particularly objectionable "as a temporary scheme to tide over the effects of a bad harvest," Barnes writes,[1] "but when the price of grain continued at a fabulous rate during the greater part of the next twenty years, the landlord interest found it profitable to support the labouring classes in this fashion and to absorb all the surplus themselves." (It was as if a wage standard, abandoned perforce during an economic slump, was permanently shelved as a matter of regular, not emergency, policy.) The alternative was to protect the labourer by some such means as the requirement of employers to pay a minimum wage, and this contrary system, safeguarding the labourer's interest, was actually advocated in the House of Commons by Samuel Whitbread, a Whig member, during Speenhamland year.[2] His motion was not supported by the majority.

Public control by less salutary devices grew during the Revolutionary and Napoleonic wars, indeed, into a system under which the labourers of England habitually lived. Not only by the Speenhamland recourse of the local authorities, but by Orders in Council and periodic legislation controlling the export and import of grain, the State and its delegate

---

[1] *Op. cit.*, p. 75.
[2] *Vide Parliamentary History, 1795–97*, xxxii, cols. 700 *et seq.* And *cf.* col. 687, on the day of Whitbread's introduction of his measure, December 9, 1795, the House of Commons accepted, *nem. con.*, its Corn Committee's recommendation that Members should undertake to reduce by one-third their families' breadstuffs consumption!

authorities pursued a policy which was generally favourable to the landowner and only in desperate need succoured the landworker. Yet in November 1795 Edmund Burke had warned Pitt of the final inefficacy of stopgap methods. "Of all things," Burke said,[1] "an indiscreet tampering with the trade of provisions is the most dangerous, and it is always worst in the time when men are most disposed to it—that is, in time of scarcity."

And in fact civil commotions became periodic, and frequent, throughout the country, as the Government and local authorities continued their extempore policy. Thus again in the last months of the century rioting was widespread, as in the early and middle 1790's, indicative of the popular resentment of the continued high price of corn, and in particular of corn dealers' practices. In various places the militia were called out. Another Commons committee produced more than a dozen reports on the corn position in 1800–1, while the price of breadstuffs rose steadily. The average price of corn for February 1800 was more than 100s. a quarter, for July, 134s. 8d., for March 1801, 154s. 2d.[2] Again there was rioting. Nevertheless respectable opinion was beginning to entertain some sympathy with the hungry. "The privations and sufferings of the lower orders," wrote a chronicler,[3] ". . . were so great, that every candid mind was less offended at the commotions of the populace, than struck with their forbearance and patience." Relief came, however, in this year of 1801, in the shape of a good harvest bringing a fall of prices, and the beginning of peace negotiations with France; but no relief by amendment of public policy, for during nine years of war and hardship "the Government had displayed the same hopeful inefficiency in dealing with the problems of the internal and external corn trade that it had shown in conducting the war."[4]

Peace was maintained from March 1802 until May 1803; then Pitt's Government had to face a more formidable France.

[1] *Cit.* Barnes, p. 79.   [2] *Vide* Barnes, *op. cit.*, p. 85.
[3] *Annual Register*, 1801, p. 1.   [4] Barnes, *op. cit.*, pp. 85, 86.

For Napoleon had seized the government in November 1799. Made First Consul for life by plebiscite of 1802, he was crowned Emperor in 1804. Pitt died in 1806. A "National" or Coalition Government of Whigs and Tories had to deal thereafter with the situation created by the French Emperor's Berlin Decree of November, by which Britain was declared to be in a state of blockade.[1]

The military disasters of Ulm and Austerlitz (a little mollified for the British Government and its allies by the naval victory of Trafalgar) and, nearer at hand, the turbulence of the starving, were Pitt's requiem. Nor had his Government been able to pursue consistently and, from the landlords' point of view, successfully, the chief design of its domestic policy—the protection of the English farmer against foreign competition by the virtual prohibition of the import of corn when prices should be low in England. Nature, by blighting the crops, had made Pitt's provision unnecessary, and his grain legislation, e.g. the Corn Law of 1791, passed expeditiously after the agricultural interest had returned him to power in 1790, was practically inoperative during the war period of poor harvests and high prices. Later, however, in the circumstance of a good harvest of 1801, the narrow constituency of landed persons began to feel the pinch of abundance. From 154s. 2d. in March 1801—the equivalent of nearly half a year's money wages of one of the new rural proletariat—the price of wheat fell to less than 50s. a quarter average late in 1804, when Nature was at successive harvests kind to the poor and discriminatory against the rich. So in 1804 (November 15th) a new Pitt Government brought into operation, as one of Pitt's last major acts, a new Corn Law, to sustain the agriculturalist by giving him bounties on his exported surplus and levying heavy duties on imported grain. "In reality," Barnes says[2] of this measure, "the Act of 1804 was merely a link between that of 1791, which marked the first decided use of

---

[1] Barnes, *op. cit.*, pp. 87 *et seq.*, for an account of the war-commercial policies of Britain and France.   [2] *Op. cit.*, p. 89.

political power by the landed interest to secure class legislation, and that of 1815, which marked the most extreme use of this power." Again, however, a providential crop failure in 1804 demanded and obtained the usual recourses of suspension of the restrictive Act's provisions and, on the part of the populace, rioting. By the spring of 1805 the price had climbed back to 100s.

England had had fifteen months of peace in 1802–3, the poor of England three years of less straitened poverty in 1802–4. But the following years saw the mass reduced to its now almost customary misery. In 1809–10, as we found, this position was mitigated in an unexpected way. The Napoleonic Government of France had to remark in that year a dangerous restlessness in the peasantry as prices for grain fell after a bountiful harvest, and the Government permitted a relaxation of the provisions of the Berlin Decree, to allow of the export under licence of French grain to the English enemy. (The harvest was again a failure in England.)

So French corn went to England, to the gain of French agriculturists—and English boots and greatcoats went to France (1807), to the gain of English manufacturers—while the armaments of England and France slaughtered French and British thousands on sea and land.

The whole history of the management of the grain trade during the wars to date was thus a history of expedients. But select committees had sat, and on May 11, 1813, the latest of them, having presented its report, received the House of Commons order to have its conclusions printed. This committee had deliberated under the chairmanship of the Irish landlord Sir Henry Parnell. It now recommended a return to the policy which it said had obtained prior to 1765, i.e. a policy of the restriction of imports and the encouragement of exports.

But Parnell's gay picture of steady high-price levels under enhanced protection was seen by the agriculturists in its brightest colours only when, months after its publication, the bumper harvest of 1813 had started English prices on a downward track. Now, a year after the Parnell committee's report, the House of Commons debated the Corn Laws in conditions very different from those which had ruled in mid-1813, when landlords and farmers, sleepy with the repletion of high prices, felt no stimulus to interest in the select committee's nostrums. "Instead of high prices, war, four successive deficient harvests, suffering in the labouring classes, and prosperity among the landlords and farmers, there were now low prices, peace, the most abundant harvest in years, a plentiful supply of grain, and distress among the farmers."[1] From 117s. 10d. in June 1813, wheat fell to 69s. 7d. average a quarter for May 1814, the month of a Commons debate on the Corn Laws; the month, too, of Napoleon's removal by the allies to Elba, after his defeat by Blücher at Laon, and his abdication.

Just as a flood of petitions from the north of England and the west of Scotland had come to Westminster against the protective duties imposed by the 1804 Corn Law, so now, petitions from Scottish manufacturing districts prayed that no increase should be made of the import duties on corn and breadstuffs. But in the House the landlords' spokesmen lauded the spirit of the Corn Laws of 1670 and 1689 and deplored the spirit which they said had animated more recent legislation, especially the Corn Laws of 1773 and 1791. "We should revert to the policy of the revolutionary laws," said one in the House of Commons; "we should give our farmers that confidence which they inspired, and thus again throw off all dependence on foreign countries."[2] But this reasoning failed to move the extra-parliamentary persons who would have to bear the weight of the fresh impost now in contemplation. One hundred and seventy petitions reached the House of Commons in early 1814, protesting against any increase of protective duties; there were one hundred and thirty others "respecting the Corn Laws." The Reverend Thomas Robert Malthus, who had taken holy orders a few months before publishing his alarming *Essay on Population*, re-entered the economic lists by publish-

[1] Barnes, *op. cit.*, p. 122. [2] *Cit. ibid.*, p. 125.

ing a pamphlet favouring a moderate duty, to conserve the agricultural interest which should have to save crowded England at last. But George Canning, still in the Tory back benches, advised the Government of Lord Liverpool against proceeding with a new and more onerous Corn Bill, in the face of such strenuous opposition as was being manifested outside Parliament. Ricardo and Hume, spokesmen of the manufacturers and the masses (whose interest was in this matter similar), made pamphlet-war on a grand scale against Malthus, Jacob, and Sheffield, the Government propagandists.

But Whigs and Radicals in Parliament, malcontents in the Government party room, and popular demonstrations, made little impression on a ministry which proceeded to show itself to be in the Pitt tradition. Through February and early March 1815 Parliament developed, in haste recalling the passage of the repressive legislation of 1795–99, the spirit of nine resolutions introduced into the Commons by "Prosperity" Robinson. (Robinson was a Tory member who as Lord Goderich would be Prime Minister and would, as Secretary of State for the Colonies, favour Edward Gibbon Wakefield's plan for the further colonization of Australia.) On March 6th a London mob assembled outside Robinson's house to express hostility to his nine resolutions for higher protective duties on food. Troops fired from his windows, killing three persons. On March 10th Sir Francis Burdett, himself a supporter of the Corn Bill, presented to the Commons London's petition against the Bill. It bore 42,473 signatures. Burdett spoke bitterly of the Government leader in the House of Commons, Lord Castlereagh, who as Pitt's Irish secretary had negotiated the Union of 1800 and who was the arch-opponent of parliamentary reform as Burdett was its arch-advocate. "Whatever falls from him," Burdett said,[1] "is received as if he were clothed in the mantle of the prophet; there he sits as an oracle and all the people bow obedience to him."

But "all the people" did not, for mobs were defying his

[1] *Cit.* Barnes, *op. cit.*, p. 137.

Government and sacking the town houses of the great landed gentry during the first three weeks of March, and there was gunfire in London streets.

However on March 23, 1815, the Bill received the Royal Assent. The Corn Law of 1815 (55 George III, cap. 26) enacted that foreign wheat might be let out of bond when wheat stood at 80s. a quarter on the English market; rye, peas, and beans might be released when the English price was 53s.; barley, beer, and bigg, 40s.; oats, 27s. The average of prices during one quarter of the year would be the determinant whether foodstuffs in any of these categories should be admitted to the English market during the next quarter. The colonial preference principle which was traditional in English commercial legislation was embodied in the new Corn Law, British North American wheat being allowed entrance when the English price should stand at 67s.; rye, etc., 44s.; barley, etc., 33s.; oats, 22s.

The historian of the Corn Laws assesses thus this last great victory of the agricultural interest, achieved in the period of peace before the wars' last brief flare of the Hundred Days: "There was no change of principle in 1765 or 1773[1] as the Corn Bill advocates had charged. The principle of the Act of 1689, which was to drain off the surplus grain when prices were low by paying a bounty on all which was exported, was destroyed by the Act of 1814;[2] and the principle of the Act of 1670, which was based on three scales of import duties varying with the price of grain, was destroyed by the Act of 1815."[3] (The Bill which became this "Act of 1814" was introduced

[1] Thus the Act of 1773, enacted after a period of prohibition of imports, empowered imports, when the English price of wheat should stand at 48s. a quarter, at the nominal duty of 6d. a quarter.

[2] 54 Geo. III, cap. 69, given the Assent on June 27, 1814, nine months before the 1815 Act, fathered the Corn Law, since (*cf. Annual Register*, 1814) after the accomplishment of the first Act there was to be seen " in the proposers a design of keeping up a price of corn adequate to the support of that extraordinary increase of rents which (had) taken place of late years."

[3] Barnes, *op. cit.*, p. 141.

into the House of Commons on May 16th of that year; the Commons passed it on May 23rd and the Lords on June 13th. This sudden measure permitted the export of grain and flour at all times without duty or bounty. It expressed the desire of Irish landlords and farmers to supply the West Indies and other colonies with grain,[1] free from liability to such prohibition as Pitt's emergency legislation after bad harvests, e.g. Act 36 George III, cap. 3, 1795. At other times, i.e. when the home harvest was good, the bounty would be worthless since the existing Corn Laws kept home prices so high that there could be no gain in overseas markets above the assured gain in the home market. In short, the 1814 Act, in the circumstance of the 1804 Act's assurance of a high minimum price in a good year, gave the agriculturist freedom of export when, even in a bad year, exports not subject to export duties might raise high home prices still farther and, in addition, permit of a profit on exports to non-agricultural British colonies.)

Thus these Acts of 1814 and 1815 represented an effort by the entrepreneurs of England's greatest industry, in the period of that industry's decline from first place, to secure by legislation a continuance in the post-war era of the prosperity which had been maintained generally through the war time.

(b) Contemporary British Manufactures, and Labour Conditions

The Corn Laws represented, too, a positive discouragement of the newer great interest, that of the capitalist-manufacturer. "The British manufacturer could not enter unprotected into a contest with his continental rival," a Whig Commoner would urge[2] in attacking the 1815 Corn Law, "while the chief means of his subsistence were kept up at an artificial rate, far above their cost in any other country of Europe." During the period of a few years after the end of the war and the enactment of the Corn Law, from time to time "the tables of both Houses" would be "covered, almost nightly, with piles of petitions,

[1] *Vide* Barnes, *op. cit.*, pp. 126, 141 *et seq.*
[2] *Vide Annual Register*, 1826, p. 49.

partly from agriculturists, praying that the (Corn) law might be allowed to stay as it was, but, in greater number, from artisans and manufacturers, praying for its instant repeal."[1]

So the Corn Law served to promote in industrialists and their workmen a feeling of common interest in a vital matter. The capitalist because the Corn Law kept up the costs of industrial production, the workman because the law taxed so heavily his basic food, joined in opposition to the system of the landowners and their great tenants. And these two classes in manufacturing industry, mutually hostile on other grounds, would make on this common ground a joint effort to secure reform of the parliamentary system. For by such reform, it seemed to them, it might be made possible to repeal the Corn Law. But we need to consult the development of the new large-manufacturing interest, in order to understand the three-party conflict which was going on now outside Parliament more than within it. This was the conflict between agriculturist and industrialist and the labour employed by both.

Already in 1816 social conditions incidental to the process of industrialization were engaging the attention of Parliament through select committees. Sir Robert Peel the elder could give evidence[2] then concerning a factory, in which he was financially interested, which "at one time" employed a thousand children. He said that the Factory Act (42 George III, cap. 87) which he had promoted in 1802 was inapplicable in the conditions which had developed since. Another Act was needed because, "owing to the present use of steampower in factories, the Forty-second of the King is likely to become a dead letter. Large buildings are now erected, not only as formerly on the banks of streams, but in the midst of populous towns, and instead of parish apprentices being sought after, the children of the surrounding poor are preferred, whose masters being

[1] *Vide Annual Register*, 1826, p. 44. *Cf. Annual Register*, 1816, p. 93, etc., on "distresses arising from the stagnation of manufacturers," especially, as the natural consequence of disarmament, in the iron districts, and in the coal districts as the iron foundries' demand fell off.

[2] *Cit. Select Documents* (Bland, Brown and Tawney), pp. 503, 504.

free from the operation of the former Act of Parliament are subjected to no limitation of time in the prosecution of their businesses, though children are frequently admitted there to work thirteen or fourteen hours per day, at the tender age of seven years, and even in some cases still younger." Again, before this Committee on Children in Manufactories, Robert Owen, a cotton manufacturer who had been in business for nearly twenty years at New Lanark in Scotland, gave evidence that in a Stockport mill a girl of four years had been employed, a boy at three years, "some at five, many at six, and a greater number at seven."[1] He said a sixteen-hour working day ruled in woollen and flax mills. Samuel Coulson would give evidence to a later committee that in cotton mills small girls worked from 3 a.m. until 10 p.m. "in the busy time," for 3s. 7½d. wages a week. "In the early time we had to take them up asleep and shake them, when we got them on the floor to dress them, before we could get them off to their work"[2]—where the overlooker's strap would stimulate their lagging faculties.

Robert Owen exerted himself, in the late war years and subsequently, to convince his fellow cotton magnates that the exploitation of child labour in this manner would not pay. Between 1813 and 1818 he published his *Essays on the Formation of Character*, in one of which, a pamphlet addressed to manufacturers,[3] he apostrophized the new industrialists: "Will you then continue to spend large sums of money to procure the best devised mechanism of wood, brass or iron; to retain it in perfect repair . . . and to save it from falling into premature decay? . . . And . . . will you not afford some of your attention to consider whether a portion of your time and capital would not be more advantageously applied to improve your living machines? From experience which cannot deceive me, I venture to assure you, that your time and money so applied . . . would return you, not five, ten, or fifteen per

[1] Cit. *Select Documents* (Bland, Brown and Tawney), p. 502.
[2] Committee on Factory Children's Labour, 1831–1832, *Minutes of Evidence*, cit. *Select Documents*, pp. 510, 511.   [3] *Life*, i, pp. 260, 261.

cent on your capital so expended, but often fifty, and in many cases one hundred per cent. . . . Give but due reflection to the subject, and you will find that man, even as an instrument for the creation of wealth, may be still greatly improved."

"Due reflection" was not likely to be given to side issues like the abuse of labouring children, in the scramble to extend the great profitable industries, chiefly cotton milling, which could now employ them. Owen himself in 1817 epitomized graphically the industrial revolution as far as it had gone, when he wrote,[1] "There is machinery at work in one establishment in this country (i.e. Scotland), aided by a population not exceeding 2,500 souls, which produces as much as the existing population of Scotland could manufacture after the mode in common practice fifty years ago." And if a revolution had thus made possible the multiplication a thousandfold of Scottish industrial production, that revolution had convulsed the neighbouring English counties too, where "certain mechanical inventions and the judicious exploitation of the geographical advantages of the west coast raised (the cotton industry) to the front rank in the course of two generations."[2]

Now this industrial capitalism which went stamping over the north-west of England and the west of Scotland during the wars, on the heels of the agricultural capitalism which promoted enclosures and the Corn Laws, was simply an application of a principle of capitalist production which was of old application in other fields than that of manufacturing. "Capitalism was not the result of machinery," we are reminded,[3] "it was rather, perhaps, one of its causes. The life of Europe was not revolutionized because a genius watched a kettle boiling over, but because a social organism had been evolved which encouraged invention instead of punishing it as treachery or witchcraft. That organism, which can be briefly described as capitalistic, had its beginnings in Italy in the thirteenth century and in England at least as early as the fifteenth century

[1] *Op. cit.*, ii, p. 54.   [2] J. R. M. Butler, *op. cit.*, p. 28.
[3] Buer, *op. cit.*, p. 57.

and probably earlier. Broadly speaking it may be defined as the system under which the handicraftsman does not own the raw material or the finished article, nor does he decide the quantity or quality of the goods to be made. These decisions were made by the *owner* of the goods, known to economists as the capitalist or entrepreneur. The early capitalist was usually a trader, and capitalistic organization tended to arise in industries which became dependent on distant trade, either for raw material or for markets for their finished products."

How far had such capitalistic industrialization of Britain gone, when the wars came to an end and the agricultural capitalists of Britain stood in sanctuary behind the gate of the Corn Law, locked and barred?

It was in the field of textiles, more than any other manufacturing field, that industrialism made largest strides in the wartime. It has been indicated (Chapter 1) that the last decade or two of the eighteenth century had seen a great change in the character of the British textile employment which for generations had offered the peasant a subsidiary income for his share in manufactures, especially of woollens. But the cottage spinning-wheel had been eliminated, like the cottage farm; as power mills, like large-farming, assailed the peasant basis. "By the year 1815," says Halévy,[1] "the entire series of phenomena characteristic of the industrial revolution had as yet appeared only in certain manufactures of a particular type—manufactures few in number but important owing to the quantity of labour employed. These phenomena consisted in the entire transformation of the mechanism of manufacture, a sudden alteration of the relations previously existing between masters and men, and popular risings caused directly by the break-up of the old economic order."

In heavy industry, on the other hand, the day of concentration of capital in large enterprises had not so much as dawned. There, as in most industries, the relation of a common skill,

[1] *A History of the English People in 1815*, by Élie Halévy, p. 239; London, Fisher Unwin, 1924.

the master-journeyman relation, still characterized the personnel of manufacture. In towns like Birmingham, working iron, factories with a capital of a few thousands sterling were exceptional, workshops each representing an investment of a few score sterling were the rule. "Neither in the mines nor even in the foundries had technical improvements sensibl affected either the size of the industry or the aggregation of labour. . . . Despite the disturbances which broke out in the mines and foundries in 1815 and 1816, no Englishman, at the date of the restoration of peace, would have been inclined to regard the mining and ironworking districts as hotbeds of industrial discontent."[1] It was not at what would become Britain's established centres of social protest—the iron and coal districts of South Wales, Durham, the Midlands, and Clydeside in Scotland—that the transformation of the labouring population, and of British economy, by machines and by industrial capitalism, was made first. It is true that troops were called out against rioters in South Wales in 1816, and that police turned back "hunger-marching" colliers from London;[2] but the source of this protest was the disability of peace, not of capitalism. Baron Dupin's impression of the ironbound Midlands, a decade hence, would be of a territory far more portentous than any outward sign suggested about 1816—"I have walked over this country in a dark night; the horizon about me was bounded by a circle of fire."[3] But not yet. During the wars and the first years of peace it was in Lancashire and only the western section of what would be Scotland's industrial belt, that the industrial revolution was proceeding at pace; there, that population was being concentrated, and capital, in cotton mills.

Today the spinner—it would be the weaver's turn tomorrow—driven from his cottage by enclosure and machines, was being subjected the first to the sad discipline of factory

[1] *A History of the English People in 1815*, by Elie Halévy, p. 239.
[2] *Vide Annual Register*, 1816, pp. 93, 94.
[3] *Cit.*, Clapham, *op. cit.*, i, p. 43.

production, his wife and children likewise, as factory workers. Of 10,000 hands in 41 Scottish mills in 1816, 4,581 were children, or young persons of fewer than 18 years, and 6,854 were girls and women as compared with 3,146 males. In the same year more than 60 mills were working in Manchester; before the machine age all Lancashire had counted only 41 by its streams. Two of the 60 employed more than a thousand workers; 24,000 men, women, and children worked in Manchester mills in the first year of peace. Here, in the cotton industry, was, too, the major concentration of capital—perhaps £20,000,000 in Lancashire—and here was the chief instance of greatly enlarged output. It was calculated in 1817 that about 100 million pounds of cotton thread was spun yearly.[1] Here, again, a depression of wages and working conditions was already evident. In 1792 the hand weaver had, as we saw (Chapter 1), earned above the average of the working population; by 1811 his wage was down to 11s. a week, perhaps to as little as 7s.[2]

After the wars the capitalist was undeniably master of the spinning and the spinners of Britain, and the power loom was giving him the mastery of weaving and weavers too.

In that little manufacturer's world now passing, the capitalist had been merchant and trader recently, as he had been since, early in the eighteenth century, an expansion of the English woollens industry had advanced the hand spinner and hand weaver. Sometimes the capitalist would own the material all through, letting the raw material out to the spinner, and then the spun thread to the weaver, paying each by the piece. Or he might buy yarn from the spinner and sell it to the weaver, then buy the resultant cloth. The water frame, the mule, and the power loom killed these cottage industries but elevated the capitalist from his function of merchant to that of producer.

[1] *Vide* Halévy, *ibid.*, pp. 243 *et seq.*, for these and other details of the contemporary cotton position.

[2] *Ibid.*, and *cf. Annual Register*, 1826, p. 56. Lord Liverpool said in the House of Lords that agricultural labourers who had received 17s. to 18s. a week were, at the end of 1816, receiving 7s. to 8s. a week.

In the process a proletariat was born: a class divorced from independent craft and from the land.[1] But as yet the portion of the new proletariat which was absorbed into industrialism was a small one: "cotton was the single industry into which industrial revolution had cut really deep by the 1820's," Clapham says.[2] But as early as 1813 some of its object-lessons were being realized by industrialists like Owen, with his sixteen years' experience of the conduct of mills. At New Lanark, he wrote,[3] "the practice of employing children in the mills, of six, seven, or eight years of age, was discontinued, and their parents advised to allow them to acquire health and education until they were twelve years old. (It may be remarked, that even this age is too early to keep them at constant employment in manufactories, from six in the morning till seven in the evening.) Far better would it be for the children, their parents, and for society, that the first should not commence employment until they attain the age of twelve, when their education might be finished, and their bodies would be more competent to undergo the fatigues and exertions required of them."

The British population after the wars thus included a proletarian mass whose adult units might earn a shilling a day or a little more, in field or factory, in the almost chronic "bad times" when bread was a shilling a loaf. The children of these unfortunates might add three or four loaves weekly to the family income by working 14 to 18 hours a day. But the bulk of industry, unmechanized still, employed artisans much more fortunate in their circumstances than the lowest order of workers, the labourers and "manufacturers" in field and mill. These were the people of England, whom a Utopian capitalist would have educated until each should attain the age of twelve years. To supplement our picture of their condition, we require a general understanding of the financial position of the British State after the wars which it had subsidized so lavishly.

[1] *Vide* Cole, *op. cit.*, pp. 28, 29, for a good statement of this theme.
[2] *Op. cit.*, i, p. 41.   [3] *Op cit.*, i, p. 281.

(c) Contemporary British Public Finance and Banking

British finance, though doubtless better tended than some sections of the population, was in a condition by no means healthy, after the strain of war. For the post-war situation repeated the experience of peace as it had followed other wars: that peace had her expenses, less readily met than war's. As in 1715, after more than a year of peace, the Speech from the Throne had "lamented . . . the injuries suffered by trade, and observed with surprise, that the public debt had been increased since the peace,"[1] so now in 1815-16 the financial rigours of peace were being felt in a similar vexation of increased debt and decreased trade. The beginning of war had found the annual expenditure of Government at £18-19,000,000, and the public debt at £240,000,000; now in 1815 public expenditure was £100,000,000 and the funded debt and floating debt totalled £876,000,000.[2] The Bank of England, which had been established in 1694, had been given a monopoly of joint-stock banking a dozen years later; i.e. it was by law the sole exception to partnership banks in England, though there were in Scotland banks with capital subscribed by many shareholders or "partners." As the Government's bank it had attended to war finance, and, facing in the aftermath a more complex world, it still had its joint-stock monopoly. By an Order in Council of February 26, 1797,[3] it had been empowered to cease making cash payments, and thereafter until 1821 did not give specie in return for its notes on demand. The war exigencies had, in the condition of this protection, induced a great expansion of the Bank's credit base; it discounted £2,946,500 of bills in 1795, £20,070,600 in 1810.[4] Subsidizing the allies had required a considerable drain of gold from England, as had the recurrent necessity of paying for

[1] *History of the Principal States of Europe from the Peace of Utrecht*, by Lord John Russell, i, pp. 315, 316; London, John Murray, 1826.
[2] *Outline of the Economic History of England*, by H. O. Meredith, p. 334; London, Pitman, 1908.
[3] *Vide Parliamentary History, 1795-97*, vol. xxxii, col. 1517.
[4] Meredith, *op. cit.*, p. 320.

large importation of grain after each of many poor harvests of war time. Thus it was in 1800, after the bad harvest of 1799, that the depreciation of the Bank's paper currency, now inconvertible, began. (It was not that England had "gone off the gold standard" in 1797, for the basis was not yet monometallic. In 1774 silver by tale was restricted as legal tender, but silver by weight was legal tender to any amount, until 1816.) An especially serious depreciation of the Bank's notes occurred in 1808–9, a period of particular stress because of the more effective French blockade of English trade then; the period saw, also, the beginning of English capital investment or speculation in Portuguese South America, entailing a further drain of specie.

Taxation now yielded £75,000,000 a year—but interest on the public debt claimed £32,000,000.[1] And merchants in the colonies, as well as at home, had lately traded under the embarrassment of a 25 per cent depreciation of Bank notes in gold terms.[2] Ricardo was already urging that the Bank should issue its notes against a reserve of gold in proportion to which the circulating note-issue should be kept stabilized, and in 1810 a select committee of the Commons had begun deliberations upon the "high price of gold bullion." But when the drains of war and emergency importation, and the depreciation of the chief paper currency, drew gold and silver coins out of circulation in the later war years, retail trade and the payment of labour in England had become vexing problems. Employers struck their own token coins to meet the deficiency. (But such private currency, having local circulation, did not achieve the curious universality of the contemporary system in use in New South Wales.)[3]

Again, the private banking institutions of England were not at all points found sufficiently tempered to stand the strain of peace. "To judge of the unsoundness of the present system,"

[1] *Vide* Dietz, *op. cit.*, p. 470; Meredith, *op. cit.*, p. 334.
[2] *Vide Historical Records of Australia*, series 1, vol. x, pp. 733 *et seq.*
[3] *Vide* Chapters 3 (Appendix A), and 5 (*b*) *infra*.

contemporaries would point out after the lesson of many disasters in the early post-war years, "it is only necessary to look at the fact, how easily many of the country banks have at all times been overturned."[1] A hundred of them had fallen to ruin upon the first shock of war in 1793; again, as the war machine moved by fits and starts from 1814 to rest in peace in 1816, nearly one-third of the 700 country partnership-banks failed.[2] This latest epidemic which closed bank doors followed the last stage of one of England's campaigns incidental to the great war, when Britain had spent £33,000,000 in prosecuting a war on the Iberian peninsula during two and a half years.[3] Indeed, susceptibility to sudden failure seemed endemic among the small banks, since a count showed[4] that during the war-years 1810–13 inclusive, 65 country banks had "commissions of bankrupt" issued against them; nor did this number represent the total of failures.

These facts may be accepted as indicative of some of the stresses to which the financial structure of England had been subjected during the long wars, and to which it was subjected markedly after the outbreak of peace.

The first important measure of reconstruction was undertaken in 1816 by an Act (56 George III, cap. 68) which provided for the minting of sovereigns and half-sovereigns (not to be currency for years yet), and which declared silver coins to be tokens, legal tender only up to 40s. (This Act is memorable in financial history as having for the first time made gold the sole monetary standard in Britain. In economic and social history it is significant in that, unanticipated by its promoters, its influence upon English commerce was a marked deflation until, in 1849–51, the Californian and Australian gold discoveries gave trade throughout the Western world a new buoyancy.)

[1] *Cit. Annual Register*, 1826, pp. 15, 16.
[2] *Ibid.*, and Mathieson, *op. cit.*, p. 143.
[3] *Cf.* Canning, speech in *Parliamentary Debates, New Series*, vol. viii, 1823, cols. 1516–17.   [4] *Annual Register*, 1826, pp. 15, 16.

(d) Radicalism and Rioting, 1816–17

We may usefully gather up, here, some of these diverse social threads, when we shall notice that by 1816, the first year of undisturbed international peace, Parliament had undertaken a readjustment of the public finances; that English agriculture had urged its claim so powerfully as to secure Corn Laws that would protect it from even a bumper harvest; that industrial capitalism had now a firm hold on the cotton manufacture though little on other industry, and small help or check by a legislature in which it was meagrely represented; that the masses of England, increased by perhaps a quarter-million discharged soldiers and sailors, were as depressed—economically, socially, politically—as was consonant with their utility for what work there was to do in the mines and fields and factories. Then, at the end of 1816, the consequences of a general crop failure began to be visited on England's people.

The wartime semaphore posts along the London-Portsmouth road might now wag their wooden arms to repeat an old tale of public violence and official violent reaction, of the usual pamphlets, petitions, and debates; but this was new, that a strange *mariage de convenance* of capitalist and pauper was being celebrated by these parties' joint assault upon the walls of parliamentary privilege still unshaken. Robert Owen was by speech and publication seeking to "pervade society with a knowledge of its true interests, and direct the public mind to the most important object to which it can be directed—to a national proceeding for rationally forming the character of that immense mass of the population which is now allowed to be so formed as to fill the world with crimes."[1] But, beyond his plan for the declaration of a minimum age of twelve years for industrial workers, Owen's chief suggestion for the nurture of the poor was the establishment of *ergastula*, pauper colonies on 1,200-acre blocks; herein the parish, the county, or it might be the national authority could, having spent £96,000 on each colony, set 1,200 men, women, and children to work at useful

[1] *Op. cit.*, i, p. 271.

agricultural and industrial employments.[1] But political agitation was rising and the poor—though Owen had not yet thrown himself into their fight as the promoter and supporter of trades unions—were being bidden to launch their strength against the constitution of the landlord Parliament. William Cobbett, an ex-Tory journalist, began campaigning in the autumn of 1816 in his *Weekly Political Register*, reduced in price to twopence so as to appeal to a wide public. In the next year Jeremy Bentham published his *Catechism for Parliamentary Reform*.

Meanwhile the agricultural poor burned ricks, the industrial poor wrecked machines, and in London men rioted, and, in the metropolitan manner now threatening to become standard, made lethal motions at Royalty as it drove through the streets. Cases of arson were reported in the agriculutral counties of Norfolk, Suffolk, Huntingdonshire, and Cambridgeshire, and an "organized insurrection" on the Isle of Ely was followed by several executions. Alarmingly widespread were "the discontents among the inferior ranks of people, occasioned by the want of regular employment, and by reduced wages."[2] We noted that serious riots occurred at this time in the coal districts; and there were instances of machine wrecking in the north-west. The years 1816 and 1817 were alive with menaces, and ameliorative proposals, which in any case were not numerous or well-supported, were ineffective. Thus a Royal person, the Duke of Kent, presided over a committee which sought to popularize with labourers and legislators Owen's

[1] *Op. cit.*, ii, pp. 248, etc.
[2] *Cf. Annual Register*, 1816, pp. 93, etc. The "Luddite" riots of 1811 in Nottinghamshire, which spread to Derbyshire, Leicestershire, Lancashire, and Yorkshire, derived from the introduction in 1809 of an improved stocking-frame. A bad harvest in 1811 aggravated the situation of workers whose market was narrowed by the machine, and a week's rioting in Nottingham, in November, led to the calling out of 2,000 troops to suppress the frame-breakers. At Manchester and in the West Riding mills were burned down. Frame-breaking, which had been punishable by transportation, was made a capital offence, in February 1812; 22 offenders were executed (*vide* Mathieson, *op. cit.*, pp. 136 *et seq.*).

scheme for modern workhouses. The committee dispersed having achieved nothing. For neither its proceedings, nor the Bullion Act, nor the publications of the Radicals, altered the basic situation that wheat, which had sold at 53s. a quarter early in 1816, was up to 110s. at the end of the year, or the fact that increased unemployment attendant on the thin harvest had depressed the wages of those who were still in work, or the fact that cotton manufacturers with many openings for children had few for men. It made little difference, again, that "with the peace, and with the distress which ensued, the advantage of colonies for the disposal of surplus labour began again to be recognized,"[1] for Government's encouragement of emigration at this pass achieved only the shipping of 200 Scottish mechanics and 700 or 800 ex-soldiers to the Cape. An increase of poor rates to yield almost double the £5,000,000 average from 1813—so that in 1818, when the population was 11,876,200, £9,320,440 was raised and £7,870,769 spent (equal to 13s. 3d. a head)[2]—solved no problem save of the desperate moment. The Association for the Relief of the Labouring and Manufacturing Poor, the select committee of the House of Commons on the Poor Law, and the independent pamphleteers were alike helpless to lead "the immense mass of the population" over the high fence of the Corn Law into a land of plenty or even sufficiency. "Forbidden to combine into unions and deprived of the old protection of the Elizabethan Statute of Labourers, which had been repealed during the war, the workers' first impulse in certain districts was to destroy the machinery which was taking the bread out of their mouths."[3]

So the riots in Lancashire, in the agricultural south and east, in the mining districts of South Wales and Durham, and in London (especially in Spitalfields, where the silk weavers were feeling the additional pinch of foreign competition), all as it were converged to a point when the life of the Prince Regent

[1] *Vide* Egerton, *op. cit.*, pp. 231, 234.   [2] Nicholls, *op. cit.*, ii, p. 470.
[3] *Vide* Dietz, *op. cit.*, p. 470.

was endangered by an attempt at assassination as he drove through London.

Government now set itself to govern after Pitt's book.

(e) Second Period of "Impaired Liberty," 1817

For the situation was all too vividly remindful of that dangerous period of the 1790's when agitation had inveighed against corn laws and landlords' parliaments. On the part of the lower orders faith in any political solution of their long-suffering had remained generally at zero after the suppression of the corresponding societies in 1799. But now some of the Whig minority in the Commons were raising their voices again to the pitch of 'ninety-three, and it might be profitable for Government to consult the measures which had been so effective then in silencing levellers and innovators.

Pitt was dead, but Lord Eldon, his senior by eight years, survived as Lord Chancellor. It was he who as Pitt's Attorney-General in 1793 had administered prosecutions of radicals for treason. Chief Justice of the Common Pleas in 1799, he had maintained his reputation as a willing servant of the State. He was now a hale man of sixty-seven years, with a dozen years' experience as Lord Chancellor behind him, and more than twenty years of life before him. He was able to recall some of the stratagems of that other period of national emergency. In February 1817, then, the Government leader, Lord Castlereagh, introduced into the House of Commons another *habeas corpus* Suspension Bill.[1] Strongly opposed by the Whigs, it nevertheless passed both Houses in a week, to become law as Act 57 George III, cap. 3. Three other Coercion Acts passed at this period (*viz.* 57 George III, cap. 6, 7, 19) restored the effect of the legislation which in the late 1790's restricted the right of public meeting, political association, etc.

[1] For Castlereagh's speech, *vide Parliamentary Debates*, vol. xxxv, cols. 590 *et seq.*

THE DISTURBED ECONOMY OF POST-WAR ENGLAND 175

(*f*) *British Foreign Policy and the Vienna Settlement of Europe, 1814–15*

With domestic problems so exacting, a Parliament which found no prescription for social troubles except coercion had a disinclination from complications abroad. Lord Liverpool's Government (1812–27) in fact committed itself during the first two-thirds of its course only to so much variation of either imperial or foreign policy as circumstance compelled. Portents of change were numerous enough, and ominous enough, at home. So having assisted at the international settlement of 1814–15 the Tories strove to be oblivious alike of the old tyrannies which they had striven successfully to restore and the new liberalism which almost at once began to tunnel under the despotic thrones of England's triumphant allies. After the final victory of the allies at Waterloo on June 18, 1815, accordingly, Parliament refused to allow the Prince Regent to subscribe to the arrangement, called the Holy Alliance, by which the sovereigns of Prussia, Russia, and Austria sought to assure the perpetuity of the settlement reached at the Congress of Vienna in 1814–15. This English shyness was in effect a withdrawal from Great Britain's commitment under the secret Treaty of Chaumont of March 1, 1814, by which the four Powers, about to dethrone Napoleon (April) and exile him to Elba (May), entered into an undertaking to stand together about the prizes of their military victory. The Treaty of Paris was signed on May 30, 1814, by the late belligerents generally. In the result, France was replaced in the European system as a Bourbon kingdom; and in deliberations at Vienna, interrupted only by Napoleon's last throw in the Hundred Days (March to June 1815), the victorious Powers realigned Europe under International Act completed on June 9, 1815. This was the settlement which Napoleon challenged unsuccessfully at Waterloo a few days later.

The Vienna settlement, which gave Prussia the left bank of the Rhine, was above all, in this respect, the work of the British Foreign Secretary, Lord Castlereagh. His object in this disposition of authority on the Rhinebank was to set Prussia, as the strongest of the German States in proximity, to police France and to buttress the new Kingdom of the Netherlands. Austria and Prussia made large territorial gains by the Congress decisions; most of Poland went to Russia, and a Bourbon King was restored to Naples as the ruler of the two Sicilies.

In this brief period before British policy beat a strategic retreat from constant responsibility for the new European concert, Castlereagh's "main object," we are told,[1] "was to obliterate the traces of the French influence over Europe, and to build up dykes against the perils of another French inundation. Hence he adopted too implicitly the views of Metternich (the Austrian Chancellor) . . .; in seeking to multiply the securities for peace, he overlooked the incidental evils which these securities engendered. The Congress of the three despotic Powers, which had been instituted for the purpose of keeping France within bounds, began to be used for the purpose of suppressing popular movements in other States, on the plea that revolutionary excesses might tend to war, and that Jacobinism might light up a conflagration in Europe. Hence the Holy Alliance (the principle of which Lord Castlereagh favoured) became a military league, not so much for the preservation of European peace, as for the suppression of European freedom, and the confirmation of European despotism. In this armed conspiracy of despots against the liberties of Europe, Lord Castlereagh was deemed to be an accomplice. . . . Justice to the weaker States was overlooked. . . . The military position of (Austria and Prussia) was the canon which determined the readjustment of boundaries, under his auspices, in 1815."

This is a fair account. And we may note that the Castlereagh-Metternich system of peace-by-preponderance-of-power stood

[1] *Essays on the Administration of Great Britain from 1783 to 1830*, by Sir George Lewis, pp. 426, 427; London, Longmans, 1864 (reprinted from the *Edinburgh Review*).

in contrast with Britain's earlier[1] policy of seeking to maintain a balance of power in Europe. But only when Europe had been placed in a strait-jacket so effective that there could be little free play in it for more than a generation, did the British Government affirm a new policy of isolation; nor did it return to a balance of power policy until, about the middle of the century, the old preponderance was untenable. This deft polity, a supernal sort of opportunism, was pursued in spite of such insistent Whig advocacy as that of Lord John Russell, the future Colonial Secretary and Prime Minister, who maintained that an early return to a balanced Whig world was preferable to the Holy Alliance "system of general and mutual guaranty of all the Governments now subsisting on the continent,"[2] a guarantee which rested on British complaisance. When in October 1818 Lord Liverpool recalled Castlereagh from the allies' congress of Aix-la-Chapelle, he was indicating to the Foreign Secretary (who in the Whig view "belonged to the illiterate school of politicians")[3] that though the fount of Jacobinism in Paris was now stopped, waters from it were still coursing along the channels of South Europe; here, they might assist the British interest, there, retard it: the foremost necessity for Britain was to refrain from begging the question of their potency. Thus before revolutionary outbreaks began in Europe with the 1820's, British foreign policy retired to that tower of "splendid isolation" from which, with incomparable success during the whole of the next hundred years, her ministers would manipulate the currents of the world in England's favour.

Britain's comparative advantage among the nations had been quite another affair in 1787–92, when she had recoiled nervously from even mild colonial experiment. But after

[1] *Cf.* Holland Rose, *op. cit.*, p. 8: "The formation (1788) of the important triple alliance between England, Prussia, and Holland, aimed at maintaining the balance of power in Europe against the attempts of France in the Netherlands and the encroachments of Russia and Austria on Poland and Turkey."
[2] *Cit.* Halévy, *The English People, 1815 to 1830*, p. 152.
[3] Lewis, *op. cit.*, p. 425.

Waterloo she was in a position to choose her routes in an imperial world from which her chief rival had been excluded and whence she might with cautious "lone hand" exclude others.

This would not, however, be a simple process. At home, for many years after the demobilization of the sailors and soldiers, social and political contentions would be maintained with bitterness and rigorous repression would be the order of many days. Nor would colonizing return an answer speedily to every domestic question (*vide* Chapters 5 (*b*), 7 *infra*). For instance, before an important modification of the policy for Australia was made early in the 1820's, another demonstration on the part of English working people would evoke yet another series of measures restrictive of their ancient rights.

(g) *Third Period of "Impaired Liberty," 1819*

The three contending interests whose struggle is the social story of the industrial revolution in Great Britain were coming into still more damaging collision, as the second decade of the nineteenth century drew to a close. The agricultural interest of great landowners and their capitalist tenant farmers represented the premier English industry and the landlords controlled the means of legislation and executive power. The landowners were the Lords and most of the Commons, the enfranchised minority, most of the educated class, the sinews of the English Church, universities, and fighting services. Vote after vote in Parliament had shown their essential solidarity in guardianship of their particular interest by particular direction of British policy. Secondly, the industrial-capitalist interest of cotton millers and manufacturers of clothing stuffs was increasing rapidly in the power of wealth, numbers, and in contribution to the national economy. The third broad section which was not at all a "third estate"—for it had neither estate nor political franchise—was beating impotently at the other two: rioting against the executive and its coercive forces, demonstrating against the Corn Law that buttressed the rulers, dissenting from the Establishment, whether of Church or Constitution, contending, too, with manufacturers and mineowners. For the most part neutral in this sharpening struggle, a quite numerous section remained of craftsmen in unmechanized industry.

The year of "Peterloo," 1819, was a year of the special intensity of these civil commotions which were sequels and accompaniments of the agricultural and industrial revolutions, and reactions from the class-nature of public policy. Economic difficulties were again pressing vexatiously in 1819, after another poor harvest. The customary riots culminated in the affair of Peterloo. At Peter's Fields, Manchester, on August 16th, a meeting of several score thousands of people heard speakers demand universal suffrage, vote by ballot, annual parliaments, and Corn Law repeal. A yeomanry charge interrupted the proceedings; eleven persons were killed and hundreds injured. "Peterloo" was the ironic designation given an affray by which the Duke of Wellington's fellow-Tories put down the pretensions of the people as he had put down the pretensions of Napoleon I at Waterloo four years before. This business, reported in *The Times*, raised a noise of indignation and protest throughout Britain. But more threatening, if less spectacular than ephemeral demonstrations like this Manchester mass meeting, was contemporary action by sections of the new industrial proletariat upon the idea of a "General Union" or "Trades Union" (i.e. an association of employees in several industries at several centres). In Staffordshire and London, as well as Manchester, an attempt was pursued in 1818-19 by the Philanthropic Society, or "Philanthropic Hercules," to establish a working-class organization of this kind—an anticipation of the "One Big Union" motive of twentieth century industrial unionism. It seems probable that the organization was dissolved during the period of general repression after Peterloo, though its later history is nowhere recorded.

In the sequel to Peterloo, at any rate, Lord John Russell, a young leader of the Whig remnant—"Radical Jack," as he was known to the miners of his Durham constituency—introduced a Reform Bill into the House of Commons, where it was deemed especially unseasonable. For the Liverpool Ministry had an extraordinary session of Parliament convoked for November 23rd. Sitting through Christmas until December 29th, Parliament carried a repressive programme which outdid Lord Castlereagh's own achievements of 1817, and vied with those of Pitt and Eldon in 1795-99. It authorized an immediate increase of the military forces by 10,000 men, and passed the notorious body of legislation which lives in history as, simply, "the Six Acts." These were:

1. 60 Geo. III, cap. 1—which prohibited meeting for drilling, under penalties of seven years' transportation for instructors, two years' imprisonment for other participants.
2. 60 Geo. III, cap. 2—a temporary measure for "the disturbed counties," empowering magistrates to enter private houses at any hour in search of arms.
3. 60 Geo. III, cap. 6—which was the first English Act to regulate exhaustively (by forty restrictive clauses) the right of public meetings: meetings of more than fifty persons must be confined to parishioners and landowners of the county, a bond of £100 must be deposited, and unlawful assembly was punishable by seven years' transportation;
4. 60 Geo. III, cap. 8—penalties for "blasphemous and seditious libels."[1]

---

[1] *Cf.* Cobbett (*Weekly Register*, March 27, 1824, vol. xlix): "Six Acts say that I shall be banished for life if I put upon paper anything having a tendency to bring (the House of Commons) into contempt." In the *Register* for May 15, 1824, Cobbett reproduced the petition of Joseph Swann, who had been in gaol since August 1819, having been apprehended for selling seditious pamphlets. Swann was convicted—by a bench of magistrates—on three charges, and was sentenced to imprisonment for 4 years 9 months. In 1824 the Home Secretary, Peel, refused to release him before the expiration of his term. (*Cf.* Peel's attitude in the "Tolpuddle Martyrs" case ten years later: "Further, when Peel became Prime Minister after the dismissal of the Whig Government at the end of 1834, he took no steps to remit any portion of the sentence" passed on the six Dorchester labourers (*Injustice Within the Law*, by H. V. Evatt, p. 14; Sydney, Law Book Co., 1937).

5. 60 Geo. III, cap. 9—which subjected political pamphlets, like newspapers, to a tax payment per copy sold.
6. 60 Geo. III, cap. 4—a procedure Act to enforce the other five.

Five days before the extraordinary session of Parliament which completed these arrangements, and three months after Peterloo, William Tooke, the friend of Ricardo, had set down his recommendation that the Association for the Relief of the Labouring and Manufacturing Poor should be wound up.[1] Only £8,000 had been collected, by the committee under the presidency of H.R.H. the Duke of Kent, towards the institution of a rationalized and economical system of dealing with the problem of poverty. Six months later, on May 8, 1820, the banker Alexander Baring presented to the House of Commons Tooke's petition for the restoration of stable conditions by the institution of a reformed fiscal system. "The maxim of buying in the cheapest market and selling in the dearest . . . is strictly applicable as the best rule for the trade of the whole nation."[2] And a petition from London merchants, on trade difficulties and the occasion of them, had been received by the Commons during the Six Acts debate.

The conjunction of these events directs attention to the manner in which the economists of the rising industrialist and commercial classes tried one expedient or principle after another, in representation to the Parliament of the landed. The while, the mass was crushed between the upper millstone of the Parliament and the nether stone of industrial capital, and a State power still serving particular ends used its old means of violence upon the poor and of rigorous repression upon would-be reformers. "If trade does not improve, there will be a war of the rich against the poor," Sydney Smith summed up in 1819.[3]

[1] *Vide* Owen, *op. cit.*, for the History of the Association.
[2] *Cit.* Halévy (*1815–30*), p. 120.
[3] *Cit. Dietz, op. cit.*, p. 471, *cf.*, for a retrospect of the prolonged situation of social acerbity, *Edinburgh Review*, vol. 59, 1835, pp. 227 *et seq.*: "Pitt, Whitbread, Sturges Bourne, Scarlett, and many others, have toiled for years seeking remedies, and finding none. Malthus has written, Chalmers has

At this epoch—as a few years before—almost the only plane of British life on which an effort was being maintained towards readjustment and reform was that of finance. We noted that in 1816 silver coins were declared tokens, to be legal tender up to 40s. only, that the Bank of England had not yet resumed cash payments and that gold and silver had been driven out of circulation accordingly. The 1816 Act (56 George III, cap. 68) was the first step taken in redress; it authorized the mintage of a gold coinage, and a silver coinage which should be token. A larger step was taken, now in 1819, by "Peel's Act" (56 George III, cap. 49), which required the Bank of England to resume payment of its notes in gold as from May 1, 1823, on a basis of the Mint price of gold, viz. £3 17s. 10½d. per oz. The two Acts would place Britain, alone of nations, on a gold standard. And actually the Bank of England resumed gold payment of its £5 notes on May 10, 1821. (A little earlier Britain's late enemy of the wars of 1775–83 and 1812–14, the United States of America, had made a somewhat similar readjustment. By Act of Congress, March 14, 1816, a United States Bank had been established, with right of issue restricted however to the amount of its capital (35,000,000 dollars) and a requirement to meet its notes in gold on demand, under a penalty of 12 per cent per annum interest. America, too, had experienced a loss of gold, together with difficulties with its system of small banks. So the historian of American finance tells us[1] of the debate on the United States Bank Bill of 1815, "Calhoun gave his support, together with a violent attack upon State banks, which he accused of circulating 170,000,000 dollars of bank notes on not more than 15,000,000 dollars of specie in their vaults. 'The metallic currency has left our shores,' said he; 'we have treated it with

preached; debate has succeeded to debate and Parliament to Parliament; and yet in the midst of all this intelligence and activity, the number of paupers has not as yet been reduced, and the admitted evil has as yet increased almost in the same proportion as the increasing alarm and despondency."

[1] *Vide Financial History of the United States*, by D. R. Dewey, pp. 149, 150; New York, Longmans, 5th edition, 1915.

indignity; it leaves us and seeks a new asylum on foreign shores.' It was in this debate that Smith, of Maryland, defending the local banks, said bitterly that during the late war they 'had been the pillars of the nation; now they were the caterpillars.' ") Alike in Britain, in her ex-colonies of America and her new colonies in Australia, the task was being performed of equipping or re-equipping the country's economy with a serviceable financial and monetary system.

The 1820's opened with so much of readjustment, and only so much, in train in Britain. There was, at the same time, a steady worsening of the condition of the masses who were crowding into the new industrial towns, or remaining in their rural squalor. "Speaking broadly," Clapham says[1] of the homes of the English people, "the houses of Britain grew worse the farther one went northward and north-westward.... In no part of the country was even the three-room cottage universal, and in places half the cottages were of the one-bedroom, 'hay-loft' type. . . . On the outskirts of the wastes in Surrey and Hampshire, in the 'twenties, were still to be found the turf huts of squatters—so long as the farmers tolerated them." The "common and waste" area was vastly contracted by the last series of enclosures, and now perhaps eight million acres of England's thirty-seven million was unenclosed; the rest enclosed for corn and rents.

In foreign policy, too, situations were developing to a point of urgency which would necessitate some definite line of British policy. Early in 1820 a Spanish army, assembled at Cadiz for embarkation to South America to suppress the colonial revolts there, mutinied and declared the restoration of the Spanish Constitution of 1812, which had been submerged beneath the post-war wave of reaction. In July, troops of the two Sicilies mutinied at Naples, forcing Ferdinand, the Spanish Bourbon King, from his throne and securing from his son, the Duke of Calabria, acceptance of a Constitution. Mutiny broke out in Portugal in August, and in November

[1] *Op. cit.*, i, p. 27.

the Spanish Constitution was adopted in that country also. Abortive revolt was made in Piedmont and Rome. To the south-east, where Turkey ruled Greece, the Morea in arms under Ypsilanti struck for independence.

These stirrings—constitutional, Liberal, "Jacobin"—were an answer of southern Europe to the three absolutist Powers which had met at Carlsbad in 1819 to devise means of repressing liberal movements; "to-day, outside the boundaries of the German Empire, the entire south of Europe had become Jacobin."[1]

British policy trimmed sails to the revolutionary wind. In May 1821 Lord Liverpool's Government protested to the allies against their proposal of intervention against the Constitution in Spain; the alliance, Lord Castlereagh had now to write, had not been designed to be "an union for the government of the world, or for the superintendence of the internal affairs of other States."[2] At the same time Castlereagh was showing reluctance in abandonment of his old policy of co-operation with the allies. "He had on a former occasion, in the face of the House (of Commons), entered his protest against the imputation that they (*viz.* Austria, Russia, Prussia) were actuated by a spirit of aggrandizement, because his experience of their character convinced him that the charge was wholly unfounded."[3] Nevertheless on January 19th he had laid down publicly Britain's subscription to a doctrine of non-intervention. For the Whigs Sir James Mackintosh urged that Britain should intervene in Spain, but on the side of the *liberales*. "It appeared to him that the allied powers, by their circulars from Laybach, had been guilty of the same attack upon the independence of nations as the National Convention (of France) had been, by its decree of July 1792, of which the overt acts were the seizure of Belgium and Saxony. In the same manner... had the members of the Holy Alliance attacked the independence of every nation in Europe, and thus had left the question

[1] *Vide* Halévy (*1815–30*), p. 126.   [2] *Cit. ibid.*, p. 129.
[3] *Parliamentary Debates, New Series*, vol. v, 1821, cols. 539–41.

of peace and war to them only as a matter of policy and prudence."[1] It remained for George Canning, who would succeed Castlereagh as Foreign Secretary and leader of the Commons, and who now sat behind him in the Tory benches, to state the Government's pragmatic philosophy. On March 20, 1821, two months after Castlereagh's enunciation of the principle of non-intervention, Canning said[2] in the House of Commons: "The monarchial and the democratic principle were now opposed to each other, as the old opinions and the new had been at the time of the Reformation. And did not the gallant virgin, Queen Elizabeth, side, it was asked, with the reformed opinions of Europe? Doubtless it would be little short of heresy to presume to break the spell which encircled the name of that illustrious heroine . . . but when . . . she came to be held out as an example, then her conduct must be subjected to examination. . . . Rapin had fully characterized Elizabeth. . . . Did he accuse her that, overlooking the wants of her own country, she plunged into wars of which she could see no end? No: Rapin said that Elizabeth followed those wars so long 'as they served her own interest.' . . . At the very time when the Treaty of Blois was in agitation, she was busy in stirring up the Huguenots; and, but a few months after the massacre of Saint Bartholomew, she was godmother to the child of Charles IX.

"Statesmen would not plunge the country into war unless its interests coincided with its sympathies."

From the policy stated in the last-quoted sentence the matchless diplomacy of Great Britain would derive an unfailing inspiration at every crisis to come. And if at this present more was needed than such a bald statement of *realpolitik*, to impress upon the Whigs that their manufacturing, commercial, and investing supporters would not praise them for running counter to those supporters' interest, Canning could supply the necessary reminder. "Freedom must ever be the greatest

[1] *Parliamentary Debates, New Series*, vol. iv, 1821, col. 1379.
[2] *Ibid.*, cols. 1372–75.

of blessings," he said,[1] "but it ceases to be a distinction, in proportion as other nations become free." It was not prudent, he implied, that a manufacturing, commercial, investing nation should spend its resources in order to secure for its competitors the advantage of political and administrative systems like its own, rational and flexible as compared with the systems imposed on Europe by the despots at Vienna, Berlin, and St. Petersburg.

In August 1822 Viscount Castlereagh, Marquess of Londonderry, cut his throat with a pocket knife; Canning succeeded him at the Foreign Office and in the Commons leadership, and England's post-war reconstruction was seriously undertaken at last, at home and abroad, by these more sensitive hands.

Conclusion

In what other respects did Britain of the post-war years differ remarkably from Britain of the previous generation? King George's subjects—increase from thirteen or fourteen to about twenty millions—and their Government made no move yet to use in imperial expansion their new strength magnified by the elimination of France, Portugal, and Spain, from the effective list of maritime Powers and by the virtual addition of the Netherlands to British policy. The empire comprised Canada, which in 1791 Pitt's Government had divided for administrative purposes into Upper and Lower Canada; in European waters Heligoland and Malta in addition to Gibraltar (1704); the Cape of Good Hope (formerly Dutch, legally British since the peace settlement); Ceylon (1802); much of India, and of the West Indies; in Australia Van Diemen's Land (1803) in addition to New South Wales.

But Australia, "not known until 1803 to be a single unit and not yet given that name,"[2] had been little enlarged in the

[1] *Parliamentary Debates*, New Series, vol. viii, 1823, col. 1521.
[2] *England in the Nineteenth Century (1806–1810)*, by A. F. Fremantle, p. 380; London, Allen & Unwin, 1930. *Vide* Barton, op. cit., pp. 87 et seq., for the origin of the name "Australia," probably the most usual description

British scheme during the wars. Little use could have been made of it while the country was at war. For instance, during twenty-five years after 1790 an inconsiderable number of convicts was, as we saw, transported to New South Wales; that colony had by no means solved the problem which it had been brought into being to solve. But that was consonant with the suspense, during the long war time, of almost every major consideration which had occupied Home Secretaries since the 1780's. True, a start had been made towards adjusting problems of finance. But expediency still dictated *pro tem.* measures to enable the wretched majority to live; enclosures were still expropriating the peasantry, village by village through the realm, and no means was seriously in view for the new proletariat's economic and social accommodation; practically no effort had been made to repair the fearful social loss attendant on the rapid development of machine industry; Parliament was still unreformed and government by restriction had but been carried to a farther stage, along the various roads of home policy, by the latest Corn Law and the latest Coercion Laws. In 1820 the British State was still substantially as it had been in 1787 when Phillip sailed. Only it had altered the shape of the world it could range, and which its people and capital would range before the new peace of Europe was very old. "Ever since 1815," writes Halévy,[1] speaking as if from a standpoint of 1820, "England had been sending out her swarms over the entire globe. Nobles and members of the middle class had betaken themselves to Paris or Italy to enjoy cheaper living, lighter taxation, a better climate, and more abundant pleasures. Unemployed labourers left England to find work on the virgin soil of North America, South Africa, and Oceania; and the revolutions which were breaking out well

of the country by about 1820. But confusion of nomenclature persisted. The Swan River Settlement on the western coast was founded in 1829 and given a Constitution only in 1890 as the Colony of Western Australia. But the title of an Act (5 & 6 Wm. IV, cap. 14) of 1835 uses the descriptions, "His Majesty's Settlements in *Western Australia* on the Western Coast of *New Holland.*"

[1] *A History of the English People*, (*1815–30*), p. 124.

nigh throughout the entire world afforded to all who were goaded by the spirit of adventure and found a life of peace insipid the opportunity of coming forward as the sworn champions of liberty."

The attention of some of these now outward-looking people of Great Britain was already given to New South Wales; more than one of England's suspended domestic problems would find their chief solution there; there, where the curious preoccupation of John Macarthur and others with sheep breeding was promising useful results, and where a normal economy was struggling through the penal system. There, in 1817, notes of a Bank of New South Wales had gone into circulation, with this provoking inscription:[1]

While we discharge our small Engagements in the Silver and Copper Specie of the Colony, we will with equal promptitude pay the greater either in Dollars, Store Receipts, or Bills upon the Treasury. This is our Pledge to the Public, and we will redeem it. Our Truth shall be inviolate, and no Man shall say with Truth, the Bank has not deserved a Good Name.

[1] *Vide Historical Records of Australia*, 1, x, p. 431.

Chapter 5

TRANSITION TO A FREE ECONOMY IN NEW SOUTH WALES, TO 1821

(a) *Sheepbreeding for Fine Wool*
(b) *Economic Consequences of Resumed Transportation*
    Appendix
        Government Accounts

(a) *Sheepbreeding[1] for Fine Wool*

WHILE in England the imperial authority grappled with its most vexatious financial, economic, social, and political difficulties—fobbing off reformers, clubbing demonstrators, hanging machine-wreckers, abrogating rights, executing this year's hasty statutes which would be contradicted by next year's, calling out the militia, calling in the taxes—while in short Whitehall whirled in the unaccustomed winds of a changing environment, the half-forgotten colony of New South Wales was being prepared in a way to solve some English problems.

Such preparation, but after his own motives, was the self-set task of John Macarthur the rum-runner turned sheepbreeder. We saw that his tireless advocacy of a pastoral use of New South Wales created some impression in England long before the

[1] This phenomenon of Australian history has, it seems, been somewhat oddly reviewed. Shann's *Economic History of Australia* does more than justice to Macarthur's work, his account being based, apparently, on little material other than the Macarthur family archives yielded in the collection, *Early Records of the Macarthurs of Camden*. Roberts's *History of Australian Land Settlement* scarcely mentions Macarthur, but quite the best example of the kind is in Arthur W. Jose's *History of Australia* (Sydney, Angus & Robertson, 1899; 13th ed., 1927), where the author writes (p. 39): "of course (Bligh) at once fell foul of the New South Wales Corps, more especially of its ringleader, John Macarthur, a man whose influence on the young colony was so important that it deserves a separate paragraph." Shann's account of Macarthur's work at the Cowpastures is probably the best which is easily accessible.

peace which released in England augmented energies. Indeed, for more than twenty years before British policy for New South Wales made its first great compromise with demonstrated facts of the colonial economy, Macarthur's alternative or supplement to the policies of 1787–89 gained ground steadily at Whitehall.

Macarthur sprawls across almost half a century of Australia's beginnings. He was the prime mover of each of the two major developments which distinguish the economic history of Australia in the fifty years after Phillip's initial settlement. Macarthur more than any other exploited after 1792 the human raw material which the English had dumped in New South Wales and forgotten in the stress of European war; and he, much more than any other, showed that as a wool producer the colony could be of far greater value to the imperial power than it could be as a prison and a smallholders' preserve. He is seen again and again in his oddly differing roles in the economic pageant of the time. We find him in 1796–98, the unscrupulous exploiter of the Crown (whose sworn officer he was) in its emergency, pretending an offer of relief to Government, and the representative of the Crown commenting bitterly on what Macarthur had done in fact: "The labouring servants of the Crown had been before my arrival in this colony given away, were scattered all over the country, and were employed for the benefit of private individuals." (Macarthur in a letter to the Secretary of State had written that he had offered to take one hundred convicts on assignment and find them bread, and Hunter's following comment refers to this offer.) "I was not in possession of the number he asked for, which I am convinced was the reason he applied for them."[1] Nevertheless in 1798 it is this sly trickster who alone has begun to divine a practicable way round the *impasse* which, Sir Joseph Banks considered, New South Wales had reached. Banks wrote,[2]

[1] Hunter to Portland, July 25, 1798, *Historical Records of Australia*, I, ii, pp. 160 *et seq.*; *cf.* Macarthur to Portland, September 15, 1796, *ibid.*, pp. 89 *et seq.*   [2] Banks to J. King, May 15, 1798, *ibid.*, p. 231.

"We have now possessed the country of New South Wales more than ten years, and . . . no one article has hitherto been discovered, by the importation of which the mother country can receive any degree of return for the cost of founding and hitherto maintaining the colony. . . . It is impossible to conceive that such a body of land, as large as all Europe . . . situate in a most fruitful climate, should not produce some native raw material of importance to a manufacturing country as England is." Banks wished the Imperial Government to send Mungo Park, who was just returned from his exploration of the Congo, to discover in New South Wales the staple, to serve England, that *must* be there. Mungo Park was willing to undertake the task for ten shillings a day and rations. But already Macarthur, a pioneer much more expensive to both colony and Crown, had seen the way.

He had reached the colony in 1790 with a detachment of the New South Wales Corps relief for the Royal Marines. Thirty years later he gave his own account[1] of the development which he initiated in Australia, of breeding sheep for fine fleeces. In 1794, he said, he had bought from an officer sixty Bengal ewes and lambs which had been imported from Calcutta, and from the captain of a convict ship two Irish ewes and a lamb. (Both varieties were customarily raised for meat and not for wool, the Indian sheep being covered with hair and the Irish sheep with wool of a coarse kind.) "By crossing the two breeds," Macarthur related, "I had the satisfaction to see the lambs of the Indian ewes bear a mingled fleece of hair and wool—this circumstance originated the idea of producing fine wool in

[1] Macarthur to J. T. Bigge, in 1820, *cit. Macarthur Records*, p. 59.

Chapter vi of Shann's *Economic History of Australia* draws heavily on the useful documentary material, and less cogent commentary, in that work. Miss Macarthur Onslow's collection of documents in the *Macarthur Records* supplies, too, the epitome given here of Macarthur's contribution to Australian economy. But the attempt has been made in this and other chapters to avoid isolating Macarthur's achievement from the context of social-economic conditions, in the colony and in Britain, without which it is apt to be misunderstood or seen out of proportion.

New South Wales." (n.b. It is to be assumed that the Irish lamb was a ram.) Two years later the warships on station at Port Jackson were sent to the Cape of Good Hope. Macarthur requested their commanders to enquire whether there were wool-bearing sheep there; they brought back to Sydney about twenty merinos, of which Macarthur bought six (four ewes and two rams). "In a year or two after" (n.b. 1801), he bought 1,200 sheep from Major Joseph Foveaux (with land, for £2,000) on Foveaux's transfer as Lieutenant-Governor to Norfolk Island.[1]

Then later in 1801—conveniently under arrest, for Government thereby incurred the obligation of paying the passage money of this man worth £20,000—Macarthur made his way by India to England, where, like his fellow officers disciplined by Captain King, he would not be court-martialled. An incident of his journey is worth relating as indicative, like his masterly circumventing of Government in the matter of his own and Foveaux's flocks,[1] of the direct, practical character of the "arts and intrigues" which King noted[2] were at Macarthur's command.

[1] According to King (King to J. King, November 8, 1801, iii, p. 321) Macarthur, who had "come to the colony in 1790 more than £500 in debt," was worth by this "at least £20,000." Prior to his arrest for duelling with Lieutenant-Colonel Paterson, Macarthur had offered his sheep and Elizabeth Farm to Government (ii, pp. 538–9). He had then 600 sheep. King referred the offer to the Secretary of State, who in June 1801 wrote authorizing the purchase of the sheep and cattle (iii, pp. 99 et seq.). But in November Macarthur, whose motive in offering his property for sale was, he said, his wish to leave for England, bought Foveaux's land and flock (King to Portland, November 14, 1801, iii, p. 329), though Foveaux, like himself, had offered his possessions for sale to Government. The Secretary of State expressed annoyance with the "highly censurable" action of Foveaux (Hobart to King, February 24, 1803, iv, pp. 37–8).

But Macarthur by this time was in England—his passage as far as Calcutta cost the Treasury £100 (King to J. King, August 21, 1801, iii, p. 275)—where he was urging his breeding projects before woollens manufacturers and departmental heads, while deputies managed his augmented flocks in the colony.

[2] King to J. King, August 21, 1801, iii, p. 246. The Farquhar incident is told in *Macarthur Records*, p. 62.

In India he met Sir Robert Farquhar, who was under official disapprobation for having attacked (unsuccessfully) the Dutch settlement at Amboyna. Macarthur dissuaded him from the course he proposed, of writing a letter of apology to the Indian administration. "Tell them," Macarthur urged, ". . . that you are determined to renew the attack. Having thus written, do so—and mind you take the place!" Farquhar took the advice, the place, and consequential promotion. This fell out well for his shrewd counsellor, the arrested officer of the ill-reputed Rum Corps, for it gave him access to influential circles in England. Farquhar's father was physician to the Prince of Wales (afterwards George IV), and a relative was private secretary to Lord Camden, who early in 1804 would succeed Lord Hobart as Secretary of State.

Macarthur's own account ran that in 1801 he took specimens of the wool of his merinos and crossbreds to England, where a committee of woollens manufacturers pronounced his merino specimens to be as good as any from Spain, and his crossbred specimens good. In England he bought nine merino rams and a ewe from the Royal stud at Kew (landing in New South Wales subsequently five rams and the ewe). "It is from these sources alone that my present stock has been raised," he wrote in 1820. Quite soon after he had written these recollections Macarthur, we may note in passing, sold some of his merino flock thus laboriously culled to the first great pastoral enterprise in New South Wales of British capital—the Australian Agricultural Company, which with the sheep bought of Macarthur and two shiploads of 700 pure merinos from Saxony, France, and England, built up the Peel River Estate flock. By 1835, the eve of the economic transformation of Australia which Macarthur's work originated, this famous flock grazed 24,000 head[1]—three and a half times as many sheep as were in all New South Wales when Macarthur sailed in 1801.

[1] *Vide Pastures New*, by R. N. Billis and A. S. Kenyon, p. 173; Melbourne, Macmillan, 1930.

In 1803 Macarthur secured the interest of a manufacturers' committee that was watching the progress of a Woollens Bill through Parliament. "The wool is of very superior quality, equal to most which comes from Spain," the committee found. "If Government will afford him the necessary encouragement, Captain Macarthur undertakes to return to the colony without delay and promote the objects to the utmost." In addition to this recognition, the committee circularized manufacturers, pointing out that Spanish wool was scarce and dear, the French having monopolized most of the best of it; and they advocated the development of colonial grazing as a means to English manufacturers' independence of the French-controlled Spanish supply. (By this time Macarthur's flocks, 3,000 to 4,000 head, included no rams but merinos. He anticipated that in twenty years New South Wales would be producing "as much fine wool as is now imported from Spain and other countries at an annual expenditure of £1,800,000 sterling.")

He had now some support for his case as represented to Government. He sought a sufficient land grant and a sufficiency of convicts for shepherds. But Banks, the accepted authority in England on New South Wales, though his knowledge was almost *nil* in respect of the place, adjudged Macarthur's merino wool "not equal to the best of old Spain,"[1] New South Wales grasses defective, and climate and soil not shown to be suitable; in any case, freighting wool from the colony would be a costly business. However, in February 1804, Macarthur wrote to Nicholas Vansittart, one of the secretaries of the Treasury in Addington's Ministry, proposing that a company should buy the Macarthur flocks at the price current in the colony for sheep for slaughter (£5 a head) and install the present owner as manager. (He had sold his com-

[1] But *cf.* Banks's comment on one of eight fleeces which Macarthur sent him in 1800—"nearly as good as the King's Spanish wool at Oaklands . . . worth 5s. per lb. . . . Could the colony produce such kinds of wools, it would be a great acquisition to our manufacturing in England" (*cit. Sydney Gazette*, March 26, 1803).

mission in the army.)[1] In May he applied to the Committee for Trade and Foreign Plantations for a grant of 10,000 acres and the assignment of thirty convicts. "I know no other person in the colony," he told the committee in reply to a question, "who has paid any attention to the improvement of the wool."[2]

The committee recommended Macarthur's company scheme to Lord Camden for reference to the Governor of New South Wales "with instruction to give every encouragement to the growth of fine wool"; Macarthur should have his grant, but for pastoral purposes only, Government reserving a right to resume. Camden accepted this direction, offering however an initial grant of 5,000 acres (Sir J. Banks having objected to the larger grant). Macarthur selected the Cowpastures, rich land on the Nepean River, about 45 miles south-west of Sydney.

When in June 1805 Macarthur reached Sydney on his return, King exerted himself to execute the new policy of settlement laid down in Lord Camden's instructions with respect to Macarthur and those he had brought with him. There were now 20,000 sheep in the colony where there had been but 7,000 on the principal owner's departure for England four years before. Macarthur's flocks totalled 5,000 head (including sixty pure merinos) by the spring of 1805. Resuming his work at the Cowpastures, under unwonted official en-

[1] *Vide* Adjutant-General Calvert to Under-Secretary Sullivan, enclosure in Hobart to King, February 24, 1803, iv, pp. 40–1, *cf.* Note 15, *ibid.*, p. 656.

[2] Probably Macarthur answered the question as a breeder, concerned to point out that there were no other serious breeders in the colony. But it would not be proper to accept a reading that no one else in the colony was actively interested in the advancement of breeding for fine wool. *Cf.*, e.g., King's references *cit.* Chapter 3 (Appendix B) *supra.*

Nevertheless, *cf.* Macarthur to Walter Davidson, September 3, 1818 (*cit. Macarthur Records*, pp. 317–18) and the colonists' negative answers to King's questionnaire (*cit. ibid.*) for evidence of the lack of interest among landholders in the progress of sheepbreeding. Macarthur wrote to Davidson, "My feeble attempts to introduce merino sheep still creep on almost unheeded, and altogether unassisted. Few of the settlers can be induced to take the trouble required to improve their flocks, or to subtract a few guineas from their usual expenditure (tea and rum) to purchase Spanish rams. Although mine is the only flock from which they can be had pure, I do not sell half a score a year."

couragement, he permitted himself the anticipation that "a plain arithmetical progression will prove that the present stock (n.b. 20,000 sheep in the colony) may increase in twenty years to five millions," giving twice as much wool as Britain bought now from Spain, at a cost of nearly two millions sterling.[1] (Actually it would not be until 1843 that the colonial flocks exceeded five million head; in 1827 New South Wales wool exported would bring only £24,000 out of £76,000 total exports.[2] It may be pointed out here, also, that a wrong construction may easily be placed upon Macarthur's account of the "circumstance (which) originated the idea of producing fine wool in New South Wales." The offspring of his 1798 Indian ewes by an Irish ram were not the progenitors of a breed of fine-woolled animals whose fleeces would be the Australian staple. The chief factor was the acclimatization of the merino in Australia. Nor did the merino thrive in the coastal district where Macarthur experimented, a district that still today is rich dairying country. The merinos flourished on the great dry inland plains; but these were undiscovered when Macarthur took up his Cowpastures pastoral grant.)

Captain King, during whose term Macarthur had pushed successfully the pastoral claim, sailed from Port Jackson in H.M.S. *Buffalo* on February 10, 1807, having handed over the government to Captain Bligh on the previous August 13th. Four days after King's departure Bligh issued a regulation against the use of rum as currency; within a year he was removed from office by the New South Wales Corps. John Macarthur, as usual in the disciplining of the colonial authority after assault of authority upon the major economic interest, provided the occasion. Just as, years before, he had advised Farquhar how to re-establish himself with the Government of

---

[1] Camden's instructions, in a despatch of October 31, 1804, to King, are in *Historical Records of Australia*, 1, v, p. 163, and *Macarthur Records*, p. 102.

[2] For the figures of sheep in the colony, value of wool exports, *vide Macarthur Records*; Darling to Huskisson, April 10, 1828, xiv, p. 134; and *Official History of New South Wales*, p. 127.

India by direct action, now, a civilian, he gave similar counsel to Major Johnston, the officer commanding the New South Wales Corps. It is related[1] that on January 26, 1808 (the twentieth anniversary of Phillip's landing from Sydney Cove), Johnston appealed to the ex-captain: "God's curse! What am I to do, Macarthur? Here are these fellows advising me to arrest the Governor!"

Macarthur's answer was: "Advising you? Then, sir, the only thing left for you to do is to do it. To advise you on such matters is legally as criminal as to do them."

There were now more than 700 small farmers in the colony —and more than 25,000 sheep. Nearly 400 of the 700 had publicly repudiated an address which Macarthur, "for the free settlers," had presented to Bligh on Bligh's arrival; after the Rum Corps' rebellion under Johnston they objected, equally, to Macarthur's appointment to be Secretary to the Colony in the extempore military administration set up after Johnston had followed Macarthur's advice and arrested the Governor. "We believe John Macarthur has been the scourge of this colony by fomenting quarrels between His Majesty's officers, servants, and subjects," five hundred and forty-six farmers joined in declaring. "His monopoly and extortion have been highly injurious to the inhabitants of every description." The fight it seemed was not yet wholly lost of peasants and old policy against the interest represented by the man whom Bligh spoke of as "the public enemy, Macarthur."[2]

But the rebels were firmly in the saddle. John Palmer, whom King had substituted at the Commissariat for James Williamson of the old officers' ring, was sentenced to three months' gaol for delivering Bligh's proclamation, dated March 17, 1808, which declared New South Wales to be in a state of

[1] Editor's introduction to vol. vi, *Historical Records of Australia*, 1, pp. xxii–iii.

[2] *Vide* Bligh to Castlereagh, June 30, 1808, vi, pp. 568 *et seq.*, 572–3, 578–9, 583. The first full account of the truth of the Bligh-Macarthur situation is in H. V. Evatt's *Rum Rebellion* (Sydney, Angus & Robertson, 1938), published after the present work was completed.

rebellion. Johnston suspended Palmer from office[1] and reappointed the complaisant Williamson, who in spite of King's hopes of 1801 (*vide* Chapter 3 (*b*) *infra*) was again in the colony—"with a pedlar's pack." Johnston conducted the rebel administration from January 26, 1808, until July 31st, when Lieutenant-Colonel Foveaux, that first large sheepowner, who had sold his flock to Macarthur in 1801, as Johnston's senior officer succeeded him. Foveaux was in charge until September 9, 1809. Then Lieutenant-Colonel Paterson, who had governed in 1795 in the officers' interim administration but later had supported King against Macarthur and the officers, assumed control, until the end of the year. By that time the Imperial Government had appointed a successor to Bligh.

Having as King had prophesied turned the colony topsy-turvy, Macarthur left for England in the *Admiral Gambier* in June 1809. After the rebellion had been investigated, he was forbidden by the Imperial authorities to return to New South Wales, in punishment for his part in the revolt, and, in fact, he was absent from the colony until 1817. A few months after his departure, the government of the colony was assumed by a man who would seek, as King had done, to develop New South Wales after the original policy of smallholding; a system which, as was by this time assured, could not be compatible with the end towards which Macarthur had made: a pastoral base of the colonial economy. Nevertheless, Colonel Lachlan Macquarie, who took office on January 1, 1810, was driven by the requirements of his execution of the smallholding plan to hasten the adoption of Macarthur's contrary plan. It was the inadequacy of the known coastal strip as a terrain for Macquarie's battalions of emancipee-settlers, Roberts points out,[2] which "forced Macquarie to open the lands between the river and the mountains." That is, much

[1] *Vide* Johnston's Government and General Order of January 27, 1808 (the day after the New South Wales Corps' march on Government House, Sydney), vi, p. 271; Bligh to Castlereagh, June 10, 1809, vii, p. 130.
[2] *Op cit.*, pp. 28–29.

of the known area between the Hawkesbury and Nepean Rivers and the Pacific coast was unsuitable for farming, and if peasant-proprietors in numbers were to be settled, the western barrier of the Blue Mountains would have to be surmounted. In May 1813 Gregory Blaxland, that early gentleman-settler so derided of Governors, W. C. Wentworth, who would be a director of Macquarie's Bank of New South Wales, and was a son of the rum-running surgeon, D'Arcy Wentworth, and a surveyor named Lawson, crossed the mountains and so showed the colonists the way to the rich Bathurst Plains to the west; in July Macquarie set volunteer convicts to make a road in the explorers' wake.[1] After this the narrow bounds within which the King's writ had run were extended steadily, until questing sheepmen penetrated far beyond authority's "boundaries of location" and, from about the year of Macarthur's death (1834), thereby relegated to history Whitehall's old dream of a peasant Australia.

Before Macquarie, settlement had been confined to a tiny area. As early as 1798, indeed, attempts had been made to cross the Blue Mountains, and men had sought those "vast rivers, capable of being navigated far into the interior," the discovery of which Sir Joseph Banks awaited impatiently in Soho. Another attempt was made, in 1802, with the first fully-equipped land exploration party, led by Ensign Barrallier, King's *aide de camp*.[2] But the successful 1813 expedition was the first significant step taken towards a Greater New South Wales. The colony which Macquarie left in 1821 was twenty times the size of the territory he had come to rule. For not only were the Bathurst Plains beyond the mountains tapped during his time, but Charles Throsby and Hamilton Hume in March 1818 explored the Jervis Bay hinterland, to the south, and the

[1] Macquarie to Bathurst, October 7, 1814, June 24, 1815, viii.

[2] *Vide* for those very early journeys *Historical Records of Australia*, I, ii, note 92, p. 721; Banks to J. King, May 15, 1798; *ibid.*, p. 231; King to Hobart, November 11, 1802; iii, *cf.* map of settlement in 1817, opposite p. 28, Roberts, *op. cit.*

Goulburn Plains; to the north settlement spread beyond the outpost which King had established at the Hunter River for the getting of coal. "The triple penetration," as Roberts calls it,[1] raised the known territory to three million acres by 1828 (*cf.* a total, of Crown and granted land a quarter of a century earlier, of about 125,000 acres).[2] Macquarie's Surveyor-General John Oxley opened the Liverpool Plains in 1818, and traversed in boats 120 miles of the Macquarie River, to the swamps of the interior. In 1821 stockmen, "looking not for glory but for grass,"[3] found the long watercourse of the Murrumbidgee River, anticipating Hamilton Hume, who crossed it and the Murray on his way to the southern coast of the continent at Port Phillip, with William Hilton Hovell in 1824, and Captain Charles Sturt, who in a series of exploring journeys in 1828–30 disclosed something like Banks's dream—"a vast river system draining a territory of 414,253 square miles, which is about the size of France and Germany combined."[4] Allan Cunningham's journey of 1823 and his journey of 1827 opened the Darling Downs, in the north, to grazing.

When we correlate the implications of these extensions with the facts that Australian wool was first sold in London in 1817 and the first wool commercially exported was sent to England in 1821, and that by 1831 wool exports were fifteen times the export of 1821,[5] we understand the more readily how Macarthur's establishment of a pastoral industry, and Macquarie's efforts to find room for a peasantry, made towards the same goal of an extended New South Wales.

On Macquarie's part there was, too, some active encouragement of the attempt to establish flocks of fine-woolled sheep. A good example is to be found in the early economic history

---

[1] *Op. cit.*, p. 31.

[2] For the territory surveyed in King's time, *vide*, e.g., iv, pp. 498 *et seq.*, v, pp. 774–75.

[3] For a good brief account of exploration at this period, *vide The Cambridge History of the British Empire*, vol. vii, part i, chapters iv and v, by Ernest Scott. The quotation is from p. 123. [4] *Ibid.*, p. 132.

[5] *Vide* Chapter vii *Cambridge History* (chapter by S. H. Roberts), pp. 185–86.

of Van Diemen's Land of this correlative effort, made in this case consciously, of Macquarie and Macarthur in front of the changing background of British policy for Australia in the post-war years.

In the first year of Australian wool export, 1821, the thirty-three year old colony of New South Wales and its eighteen year old dependency of Van Diemen's Land sent nearly 200,000 lbs. of wool to England. After separation, the colony of Van Diemen's Land could export almost double this quantity—though the only market found for the early Tasmanian clips had been the Colonial Government, which bought wool at 3d. lb. for stuffing mattresses.[1] When J. T. Bigge was in Van Diemen's Land as Commissioner of Enquiry in 1821, a grazier answered his question as to what became of the local wool produced: "It has hitherto all been thrown away. The settlers have begun to attend to it very lately, and the ship *Regalia* I believe has taken a little (for sale in England)."[2] But on the eve of the radical alteration which the *Regalia's* cargo portended, John Macarthur in 1819 notified Macquarie, who passed on his notified offer to William Sorell, Lieutenant-Governor of Van Diemen's Land, of his preparedness to sell to Government 300 merino ram lambs, for retail to Van Diemen's Land graziers.[3] Before this plan was executed, the best sheep in the island, which had flocks of more than 100,000 (for meat) already in 1817,[4] were Leicesters and improved Teeswaters, the Teeswaters being the issue of some sent to Major Johnston by the Duke of Northumberland; Lieutenant-Colonel Paterson had bought some of Johnston's lambs and sent them to Port Dalrymple in Van Diemen's Land.[5]

Sheep for fine wool were now introduced into Van Diemen's Land when Macquarie bought Macarthur's proffered merinos

---

[1] *Historical Records of Australia*, III, iv, note 15, p. 929.
[2] *Ibid.*, iii, p. 353, evidence of G. Gatehouse before Bigge.
[3] *Cf.* Sorell to R. W. Loane, grazier, Nov. 22, 1819, III, ii, p. 744.
[4] *Historical Records of Australia*, III, iii, p. 584.
[5] *Ibid.*, iii, p. 251, evidence of J. Gordon before Bigge.

at five guineas apiece.[1] In September 1820 the 181 survivors—there had been heavy losses *en route* from Port Jackson—were sold by Government at seven guineas apiece (the extra two guineas to cover freight costs) to forty-three Hobart and Launceston graziers, Macarthur having been paid by the New South Wales Government in land at 7s. 6d. an acre.

This significant transaction was slowly brought to completion as the Imperial Government commenced the execution of a new colonial policy: the encouragement of the emigration of small capitalists to the Australian colonies.

(b) Economic Consequences of Resumed Transportation

Study of the portentous changes which were made in British colonial policy in the 1820's, and of the work of Macquarie (1809–21) who governed New South Wales during the post-war period of transition, requires a résumé of the New South Wales problem. For when we come to examine the events of the second half of Macquarie's government, we approach the reorganization of what had been a quite minor colonial undertaking into a most important one.

Now, in the twenty-two years' history of New South Wales before Macquarie became Governor fewer than 10,000 British convicts were transported there, a number less than the total for his last five years of office. Ill-selected for the rigours of pioneer colonization—ranging in age from twelve years to more than seventy, averaging two female to seven male felons—they were distinguished above all by an appalling death-rate, and at the beginning of 1810 there were fewer than 8,000

---

[1] *Cf.* the erroneous account of this important business, in Shann, *op. cit.*, p. 92: "While Governor Macquarie was shortsightedly spoiling his emancipists, Lieutenant-Governor Sorell grasped the magnitude of McArthur's idea. Early in 1820 he bought 300 of the Camden ram lambs at five guineas a head and induced the island settlers to use them by an offer of prizes for the finest wool."

Shann gives as the source of this story Sorell's letter of February 4, 1820, to Macarthur, in the *Macarthur Records*, pp. 343–44. The instance is a salutary example of vital error made by deduction from inadequate data, and suggests that the *Macarthur Records* should be used with gingerly hands.

adults in the colony, of whom more than a thousand were soldiers. But when Macquarie left after a dozen years, there were nearly 30,000 people in New South Wales: more than half of them were under or had served sentences; only 1,300 had come, during a whole generation, as free emigrants from Great Britain or elsewhere. The nine administrations before Macquarie had granted only 117,000 acres of lands; he granted 240,000 acres. Under him the cost of government was no greater than the cost would be under the "economy" administrations which succeeded him, and, comparing his expenditure on public works in 1815 (which year may serve to mark the resumption, with the peace, of large-scale transportation) with his maximum expenditure in 1819, we may find that the difference between £7,000 and £16,500 is a sum not incommensurate with the difference between a thousand convict arrivals in the year of Waterloo and three thousand in the year of Peterloo.[1]

The all-important inference from this series of contrasts is that the colonization of New South Wales, whether for prison or other purpose, was not very seriously undertaken until, during Macquarie's term of office, a sustained flow of convicts required a large expansion.

For this reason the problem which confronted the early Governors is not more closely comparable with Macquarie's problem than is the problem of administering in 1850 the little pastoral town of Melbourne with the problem of administering in 1853 a Melbourne which was become a terminus of gold-seekers from all over the world. To draw a less serious analogy:

[1] *Vide* for these facts J. T. Bigge's *Report on Agriculture and Trade in New South Wales* (1823), pp. 10, 33; and his *Report on the State of the Colony* (1822), p. 140 and *Appendix: Return of the number of persons transported as criminals to New South Wales, since the first establishment of the colony (1810)*, p. 59; Barton, *op. cit.*, p. 463; *Colony of New South Wales for the Year 1828* (official), p. 32; *Report from the select committee on transportation (1812)*, pp. 3, 22; *A Colonial Autocracy*, by M. Phillips, pp. 109, 132; *Official History of New South Wales*, pp. 29, 31; Macquarie to Bathurst, July 22, 1822, *Historical Records of Australia*, I, x, pp. 671 *et seq.* Several different statements of Macquarie's grants are given in the present section.

the minutes of evidence given before the parliamentary select committee of 1812 on transportation begin with the question put to Vice-Admiral Hunter, "You was Governor of Botany Bay?" By 1822, when Major-General Macquarie was on the imperial carpet, the form would be, "You were Governor of New South Wales?" That may be taken as an indication of a great change. The change consisted originally in the optimum use of New South Wales for receiving criminals when, and when only, after the Napoleonic Wars, the project of 1786–87 could be appreciably advanced. All the rest must be derivative from this: Hunter, King, and Bligh had ruled an insignificant half-forgotten settlement, where Macquarie was required at once to conduct a great gaol and make a colony for an ever-increasing number of freedmen.

Hence it is meaningless to assert, "Macquarie deliberately adopted the principle that New South Wales was for the convict and not for the free colonist, and the story of his Government is largely the story of the momentary success and final defeat of this policy."[1] For it was not Macquarie, but the Imperial Government, which adopted this principle, which Macquarie, like King before him on the smaller scale, had to execute; and Macquarie's term is the subject of no such "story," for during the twenty years after his recall 50,000 convicts were transported to New South Wales—and it was *that* policy which connoted its own defeat, for the great majority of those transported were under sentence of only seven years, would stay, being freed, in the colony, and would force by their presence a free colonization which would make further penal colonizing impracticable in New South Wales.

Shann's criticism[2] is equally invalid. Macquarie's "vacillation about public agriculture," he writes, "suggests that a laird's paternalism prevented his seeing the economic futility of convict labour in public employ." It suggested nothing of the kind to Commissioner Bigge, no friend to Macquarie and his policies, who found that the great increase of transportation

[1] M. Phillips, *op. cit.*, p. viii.   [2] *Op. cit.*, p. 78.

in Macquarie's time "has certainly exceeded during the last three years . . . the positive demands of the settlers for labour."[1] That is, whatever Macquarie "saw," or failed to see, conditions forced upon him the public employment of convicts for whom there was no call in the private labour market.

Important misconceptions like these have arisen from a confusion of issues. It is true that a factor which had been present early persisted throughout Macquarie's time: a view of the colony as simply a prison farm and a scene of a peasant economy was challenged by a few free persons who strove rather to lay there a large owner basis of a free economy. This challenge the early Governors, well instructed that their commission was "not to build up a free community, but to hold in check the criminality of an empire,"[2] tried to meet. Hunter, King, and Bligh had all failed essentially to meet the challenge with effect. Macquarie in his turn had to meet it. But in his time both basic considerations were immensely magnified: not only was the "pure merino" challenge more formidable as England grew interested in Macarthur and his wool, but the colony was being converted, at an accelerated pace, into a *milieu* presenting the problems of a great gaol and a great labour exchange of time-expired convicts to whom a land still scarcely touched in an economic sense offered scant employment. His correlative problem was not different from that of his successors, save in that he essayed it first and longest. From 1810 to 1821 he administered the colony consciously with a view of its emergence as a *freed* society from its penal swaddlings. He did not invent "emancipists" or "public works policies"; the system of transportation produced these phenomena in New South Wales, and he sought to adapt it to them, them to it. It follows that protagonists of the private interest like John Macarthur were at odds with

---

[1] *State of the Colony*, p. 53.
[2] The phrase is used of Sir George Arthur, Lieutenant-Governor of Van Diemen's Land, 1824–36, in *The History of Tasmania*, by John West, i, pp. 178–79; Hobart, 1852.

Macquarie as they had been with Hunter, King, and Bligh; but for this new reason additionally, that he from the eminence of his public responsibility of office saw the developing society as a wider thing than they saw it from their homesteads. To them the colony was, or ought to be, a minority of enterprising business men and a majority of rightless servants—but in their service, not the Crown's. To Macquarie the colony looked much as in fact it was—a few thousand convicts destined to the service of Government or settlers, more thousands of expirees who by the weight of their numbers and the enterprise of some of them, must in his time be the major consideration of Government. The roads he had built to the farmlands of Liverpool and the Hawkesbury, and to the newly-discovered Bathurst Plains, were open to freemen and freedmen and their flocks and stock, his 250 public buildings were more appropriate to the service of 30,000 than the 1810 waste had been to the needs of the 10,000 population of that day; and indeed he and Macarthur made, each after his fashion, towards the further stage of a free community. No doubt Macarthur did more than any other to generate the economic power which would free the colony; and there is not less doubt but that Macquarie performed the essential auxiliary service of financial and commercial readjustment by which Macarthur's current might be transmitted. But because of social and similar complications of their passing environment the two were often enough, and seriously enough, at odds to leave an impression of their fundamental conflict, whereas in fact they were unwitting partners in an enterprise of nation building in Australia. The effort of each of them was towards the expansion of New South Wales, and each worked for such expansion with a calculated aim of broadening the colony to accommodate English needs—Macarthur being concerned with economic needs chiefly, Macquarie with needs that were in a secondary sense economic but that primarily were social needs: the absorption of British outcasts in a British colonial society which should be developed sufficiently to take them in. If this relation of Macarthur's significance and Macquarie's significance in Australian economic history is not understood, the perfectly "natural" transition of Australia from a prison to a colony must continue to seem an act of God or a spontaneous expression of some unique ability in English-speaking people to create bread and butter to give substance to the forms of political democracy.

Macquarie found the colonial community a version, debased in many respects, of the New South Wales of Captain King. The assignment of convict labour had been placed by King on a regular basis in 1804, and Macquarie continued King's system. Under this, convicts received, in return for fifty-six hours' work a week, lodging, clothing, food, and a wage of £10 a year. From the wage £3 might be deducted if the employer found the labourer's clothing.[1] The wage took as a rule the form of an allowance of tea, sugar, and tobacco, and perhaps rum. (Here, perhaps, had its origin a general sybaritism among the colonists of which General Darling was later[2] to find evidence in the statistical abstract of commodities imported.)

The "property wage" was well enough in the outlying districts, where barter was the ordinary means as between landowners themselves in their purchases; but where, in the centres of closer settlement, the master had not his own store of luxuries for distribution as wages, but paid his assigned servant as he paid his grocer's bills, i.e. by promissory note, in such cases "the amount of the wages varied with the fluctuating value of the paper money in which all payments were made." Bigge, the Commissioner of Enquiry who made this note,[3] referred to "the custom of paying the largest proportion of wages in New South Wales in articles of consumption" at prices which he said were raised to levels 25 to 40 per cent

[1] Macquarie's Government and General Order of September 10, 1814, republished King's regulations, and his G.G.O., September 7, 1816, added the clause allowing a deduction for clothing found.

[2] *Vide* Darling to Huskisson, April 10, 1828, I, xiv, pp. 131 *et seq.*

[3] *State of the Colony*, p. 75.

above Sydney retail rates. In this way, it appears, the convict servant who did not lose on the swings of Sydney custom 25 to 40 per cent of his wages paid in his employer's depreciated notes, lost as much on the roundabouts of country custom—the employer's adjustment of prices to depreciate the value of his labourer's truck wages.

But clearly the convict-labourer was not the only sufferer from the vagaries of a defective business system of makeshifts. "Petty banking," as Macquarie styled the private currency system, excited his shocked apprehension from the beginning, and he recognized almost as early the desirableness of strengthening the economic base of this crazy society by promoting the use of the land. Writing to Lord Castlereagh[1] ten weeks after he had taken over the Colonial Government, Macquarie cited the success of the Government Loan Bank at the Cape of Good Hope, as a model for New South Wales. (The British had been in effective possession of the Cape colony, lately Dutch, since 1803, and would retain it after the wars. The Cape bank had been founded in 1782 by the Dutch East India Company. Macquarie said its contemporary practice was to advance money to landholders at 6 per cent interest on mortgage. It maintained a circulation in the colony of rix dollars.)

But the committee for trade and foreign plantations[2] was not prepared to sponsor a bank. Accepting the necessity, however, of redressing the currency shortage, it recommended

[1] *Historical Records of Australia*, I, vii, p. 264.

[2] When under Burke's Act of 1782 (22 Geo. III, cap. 82) the department of the Secretary of State for America was abolished, the Committee for Trade and Foreign Plantations, within the Home Office, was given the conduct of colonial affairs. It was quite another organ than the Board of Trade, with which Shann confuses it (*op. cit.*, p. 54). For the long sustained confusion of Colonial administrative authorities, vide *A Hundred Years of English Government*, by K. B. Smellie, especially pp. 102–3; London, Duckworth, 1937: "A question about the transportation of convicts," for instance, "would involve the Treasury, the Home Office, the Ordnance Dept., the Inspector of Prisons, and the agent of the colony! All financial despatches had to be referred to the Treasury; all tariff despatches to the Treasury or the Board of Trade; all convict despatches to the Home Office; and all the questions of land and emigration to the Commissioners concerned."

the despatch to New South Wales of £10,000 in Spanish dollars from India. The Prime Minister, Lord Liverpool, advised Macquarie that this recommendation would be acted upon;[1] these tidings arrived late in 1811, and nine months later Liverpool's second reference to the currency matter was read in Sydney. Liverpool then suggested that the Cape Colony had retained its sound currency in circulation by banning its export, and that New South Wales, when it should have specie, might do well to follow suit, especially if it was the case as reported that American shipmasters visiting Sydney were gathering such dollars as the colonists had, for their commerce with China.

On November 12, 1812, the promised supply of dollars reached Sydney in H.M.S. *Samarang* from India, whence they had been despatched by the East India Company upon the Imperial requisition. Determined to retain the currency nucleus for which, thus, he had waited nearly three years, the Governor was able to report by June 1813 that, to the end of maintaining local circulation of the dollars, he had ordered the construction of a machine to punch a small disc of silver from the centre of each coin. The residue (the "holey" dollar) would be put into currency at 5s. declared value, the smaller piece at 1s. 3d., each stamped with Colonial marks. This value would be proclaimed, under guarantee of the exchange of the tokens into Treasury bills, at the premium, within two years of issue. By late April 1814 the experiment was launched of a token currency for New South Wales. Most of the *Samarang* dollars were in circulation by then,[2] with the undertaking however (by Order of February 5, 1814) that quantities of the dollars would be consolidated into Treasury bills quarterly, instead of after two years. On July 8, 1815, the Governor proclaimed by another General Order that the consolidation would be made monthly by the

[1] July 26, 1811, vii, p. 365.
[2] For Liverpool's advice *vide* Liverpool to Macquarie, April 22, 1812, vii, p. 479; for Macquarie's account of his token scheme preparations and actions, Macquarie to Liverpool, Nov. 11, 1812, Macquarie to Bathurst, June 28, 1813, *ibid.*, April 28, 1814, viii, p. 145.

Commissary-General.[1] In this way New South Wales was supplied with the nucleus of a silver token currency backed by sterling (which in 1814 was itself, as represented by Bank of England notes, into which, only, Treasury bills could be exchanged in London, at an average discount of 25 per cent).[2]

There remained two associated problems of currency to be settled. With tokens of 5s. and 1s. 3d. in authorized circulation at those values, the colony still lacked small change; and would not the circulating bad money of the private note drawers drive the new good silver into the hands of the "sinister hoarders" whom Bligh had remarked, according to the law promulgated by Sir Thomas Gresham as long ago as Elizabeth's day? As for copper coin, Governors King and Bligh had placed a colonial value of twopence on each penny of £2,500 worth sent from England. Twelve years after King's proclamation of 1800 setting this premium value on British pence Macquarie reported[3] to Lord Liverpool that the 1800 expedient had been largely successful. Only some of the pennies had left the colony, the rest having been stayed by the advantage of their reception at the Commissariat, where the Deputy Commissary-General would count King George's pennies as tuppences in making up accounts to be met in his bills on the Treasury. More than two years before this, Macquarie had requested[4] that he be sent another £5,000 copper, for circulation at 100 per cent premium, and his vindication in November 1812 of King's measure was made in reply to a Whitehall enquiry arising out of his request of October 1810. (Similarly, silver for currency which the Governor had sought by letter of March 1810 did not reach him until November

---

[1] Macquarie to Bathurst, March 15, 1821, sub-enclosure No. 5; *Historical Records of Australia*, I, x, p. 427.

[2] *Cf.* Colonial Secretary Goulburn to the President and Directors of the Bank of New South Wales, May 16, 1822, *Historical Records of Australia*, I, x, pp. 733 *et seq.*

[3] Macquarie to Liverpool, November 11, 1812, *Historical Records of Australia*, I, vii, p. 606.

[4] M. to L., October 27, 1810, *Historical Records of Australia*, I, vii.

1812. These incidents suggest some of the difficulties under which the early Governors laboured in attempts to give commercial interchange within the colony a medium.) It does not appear that Macquarie was supplied with the small change he required for the colony, but fifteen years later another Governor received a cargo of coppers from a Treasury which, after a dozen years of peace, had command once more of a copper surplus. As for the nagging difficulty of the private currency, three months after his March 1810 letter to Castlereagh on the currency question Macquarie attempted to regulate by proclamation (June 30th) the private issues, requiring some assets to support the promises; it was an appropriate level from which to launch a reforming administration. But in spite of his strictures the men of straw continued to pour forth their promissory notes, and on November 23, 1816, Macquarie published another proclamation which admitted that earlier regulations had not been observed, and attempted more effective regulation. As he informed the Secretary of State,[1] still more considerable measures were called for; accordingly it would be well to encourage private persons of substance in their design for a Bank of New South Wales. Indeed, he made known, such persons had subscribed already—by March 29, 1817—£7,000 in £100 shares towards a nominal capital of £20,000 which should sustain a Sydney bank. Whitehall might have been surprised to read a set of rules and regulations[2]

---

[1] Macquarie to Bathurst, March 29, 1817, ix, pp. 216 et seq.

[2] *Ibid.*, pp. 224 et seq. The Charter, which limited the liability of shareholders, was repudiated by the Colonial Office (Bathurst to Macquarie, October 29, 1818, ix, p. 840), but nevertheless it was renewed on October 11, 1823, by Brisbane (Brisbane to Bathurst, May 14, 1825, xi, pp. 579 et seq)—it had been granted for seven years—although a Colonial Office instruction of July 31, 1823 had required its cancellation. On the strength of this instruction Darling in 1826 refused the Bank's request for permission to seek new capital (Darling to Bathurst, May 1, 1826, xii, pp. 268–9). However, the Bank continued to exist and Darling made Government loans to it in 1826 and 1828. In 1828, after the Imperial Act (7 Geo. IV, cap. 26, 1826) which terminated the Bank of England's monopoly of joint-stock banking, a New South Wales Act of Council (9 Geo. IV, No. 3) gave the Bank a new con-

amounting to a charter, which the Governor himself had laid before the promoting shareholders. They had been unanimous in their endorsement, and within a few days their bank would be open for business. The Bank of New South Wales would be empowered to issue its notes for 2s. 6d., 5s., 10s., £1, and £5, and so at length the nuisance of a multiple currency system would be abated.

It will be useful to remind ourselves at this point that the promotion of sound trade dealings among the free community through a bank of issue and official manipulation of an inflated coinage, could not be the sole major occupation of a New South Wales Governor. In Macquarie's time and for twenty years after it, the Governor's primary responsibility was still for the thousands of convicts under servitude on public works and on assignment to free settlers. So Macquarie had dealt almost together with the settlers' affairs and the convicts', when in late 1816 he had published his regulation of private currency and his regulation fixing the wage to be paid convicts on assignment. Again, the maintenance of a large programme of public works, entailing the employment of numerous convicts, was a policy of his which was designed as well to enable the development of the colony. "Making permanent roads and bridges is one of the first steps towards improving a new country,"[1] he held. Further, he had to keep a constant concern for a store of foodstuffs sufficient for the establishment. That still, after a quarter century's settlement, this was not to be taken for granted is suggested by Macquarie's report of 1814[2] that, in consequence of certain steps taken, "the dread of actual want is for the present removed." He had earlier reduced

stitution as a joint-stock undertaking. Macquarie's 1817 Charter, in protecting the shareholders "against all risk and liability beyond the amount of the shares . . . taken up by each," was about half a century ahead of the law of England in limiting the liability of banking companies.

[1] *Cit. An Economic History of Australia*, by Edward Shann, p. 66; Cambridge University Press, 1930.

[2] Macquarie to Bathurst, April 28, 1814, *Historical Records of Australia*, I, viii, p. 144.

from 10s. to 8s. a bushel (King's 1800 figure) the maximum price which the Commissary might give for settlers' wheat; but a poor harvest in 1813, requiring a large call on stores for current provision, had made necessary an increase to 15s. a bushel.[1] By April 1814 the Commissariat contained six months' stores, but Macquarie ordered wheat from Bengal, at 8s. a bushel, to make a larger provision against another emergency. (The Indian wheat was weevily, and inferior to New South Wales averages in quality, and the Governor restored to 10s. the Commissariat price for local wheat, even after recovery in 1814.) But under Macquarie the Colonial Government's bills on the British Treasury "for Government services in New South Wales," i.e. for the supply and maintenance of the penal establishment, were attaining alarming annual totals. Before him, the average annual total of the Commissary's bills was only £29,415 for 1806–9; but in Macquarie's first year, when the population somewhat exceeded 11,000, he caused to be drawn bills on the Treasury to the amount of £72,600. In his last full year of office, 1820, the figure was £181,376 (but the population, of New South Wales proper and Van Diemen's Land, was then nearly 39,000).[2] The increase of colonial expenditure, and rising murmurs, heard at home, against Macquarie's policy of encouraging emancipated convicts to regard themselves as entitled to consideration in the country

[1] Cf. *Colony of New South Wales for the year 1828*, p. 176, for an illustration of the remarkable fluctuation of wheat prices even in the free market after 40 years' settlement. In March 1828 wheat was 7s., in Sept. 14s. 9d., Dec., 7s. 9d. Cf. *Historical Records of Australia*, III, iii, p. 584. After bad floods at the Hawkesbury in 1817, wheat to the amount of 22,000 bushels was sent to Port Jackson from Van Diemen's Land. Similarly, cf. *Historical Records of Australia*, III, iv, p. 5, after Hawkesbury 1820 floods, 20,000 bushels from Van Diemen's Land to Sydney.

[2] Vide *Historical Records of Australia*, I, xii, p. 831. Frederick Drennan, who arrived at Sydney in January 1819 to relieve David Allan as D.C.G., abolished store receipts and issued his own notes in payment for produce. Macquarie disapproved of the system, as did Sorell, Lieut.-Governor of Van Diemen's Land, vide Macquarie to Commissioners of Treasury, March 24, 1819, *Historical Records of Australia*, I, x, pp. 102 et seq.; Macquarie to Sorell, May 15, 1819, *Historical Records of Australia*, III, ii, p. 396.

in which they had been released, had their sequel in the despatch by the Secretary of State, Lord Bathurst, of J. T. Bigge as a commissioner of enquiry. Bigge's terms of reference were strictly limited by the Minister's implication that the Imperial Government preferred to ignore the situation, inevitable in the circumstance that for more than thirty years thousands of men and women had been sent to the colony with the prospect of being freed there within a term of years, that a freed community was already in existence in New South Wales and must be provided for. Bathurst said flatly that "the settlements in New Holland must clearly be considered as receptacles for offenders," and that so long as transportation thither was maintained "their growth as colonies must be a secondary consideration."[1]

At any rate, before Bigge presented his reports, and before Macquarie was recalled because his view of the scope of "Government services in New South Wales" was deemed distorted or too wide, he had made an extraordinary revision of the circumstances in which the colony lived and worked and traded. Before him the preoccupation of the majority was the

[1] Bathurst to Bigge, January 6, 1819, *Historical Records of Australia*, I, x, p. 4. Shann, who quotes these instructions (*op. cit.*, p. 69) cites Macquarie's Treasury Bill totals for 1814 and 1817 (£227,000 "and almost £240,000"). He does not give indication of the great increase of population, chiefly by convicts, ex-convicts, and their children, during Macquarie's term 1809–21, and the concomitant increase of the weight of the establishment and its expenses, together with the absolute contingency on the Governor of securing a livelihood for the freed. Further, Treasury Bill totals for two selected years have little meaning in themselves. Sir Thomas Brisbane was sent out as Governor to institute economies, and yet the bills drawn for his last year of office amounted to £170,899 (*Historical Records of Australia*, I, xiii, p. 923, audited accounts of New South Wales), although the Colonial revenue, swollen since the institution in 1824 of land sales, was double, at £71,682 for 1825, the 1821 total (*Official History of New South Wales*, p. 36). After Brisbane's recall, Sir Ralph Darling was sent as Governor to make economies, but in 1827 and 1828, after his initial attempt at reducing the expense of the colony, his Treasury Bill totals were £175,050 and £175,898, when the population in his charge (Van Diemen's Land now having a separate Administration) was 35,623 and 36,598 (*Historical Records of Australia*, I, xiv, p. 130; *Colony of New South Wales for 1828*, p. 32; *Official History*, p. 48).

imminent arrival of another of John Macarthur's rum cargoes, of the minority, the progress of Macarthur's experiments in sheep breeding at the Cowpastures. Now under Macquarie rum indeed retained its potency and its special place in the common estimation—but the traffic in it would build a hospital[1]—and the crossing of strains for finer wools gave still brighter promise for the future—but the building of Macquarie's roads and bridges, churches and dwellings, gave a present prosperity and introduced a transformation of the gang-studded wilderness into a colony. Upon the system of convict transportation seen from a perspective of the 1820's Egerton has commented,[2] "From the colonial point of view it rendered possible those preparatory works without which free settlement would remain impossible." And if this sound judgment justified Wakefield (*vide* Chapter 6 *infra*) it might be pronounced especially upon Macquarie among the administrators of the system, for before him the colonial governors had made little use of their convict charges in "preparatory works." And, apart altogether from the question of provision of this kind in the colony for persons who might emigrate from England—that is, provision of roads and bridges and wharves —the very evolution of the system itself required such provision if the persons who in due course were freed of servitude were not to become as a pauper population a dead weight upon the State that had sentenced them to exile for set terms. By Macquarie's disbursements, therefore, whether on account of the insignificant Colonial Revenue (or police fund, *vide* appendix) or on account of the British Treasury, he marked his practical recognition of an inescapable duty of New South Wales administration at this stage. That was the responsibility of the Crown in New South Wales to the freed community it had brought into being there. It might have been hoped in 1787, when Phillip was sent to found the penal settlement, that New South Wales would become self-supporting; but that was an old chimera, unrealized under the direction of

[1] Sydney Hospital in 1811.   [2] *Op. cit.*, p. 227.

Macquarie's predecessors, and he had simply to deal with the situation as he found it. What he found was a starveling community of free and bond and freed, unequipped with the means of seeking self-support. And during the second half of his term the volume of transportation from Britain, which had not exceeded a few hundreds of convicts in any year since 1791 (when 2,407 were sent), rose to about 3,000 a year in 1818–20 from the resumption of the practice on a large scale on the advent of the first peace with Napoleon in 1814 (when 1,097 convicts were sent). In addition to this rapidly accumulated prison population, the accumulation of freedmen presented Macquarie with a nicer and a novel problem. Most of the survivors of nearly twenty years' transports worked out their sentences or could earn remission during his dozen years in New South Wales. Here were nearly 30,000 persons, before the Imperial Government recalled Macquarie; most were propertyless, and many worked for shelter, rations, and a doubtful dole for the minority of a few hundreds who grew (insufficient) foodstuffs and grazed a few score thousands of sheep in unfamiliar conditions.

Nor did Macquarie's special problem rest exclusively in this formidable enough list of calls upon his ingenuity and steadfastness. The post-war flood of emigrants did not neglect New South Wales.

Persons of small capital were allowed, even encouraged, to emigrate on favourable terms to New South Wales, before any instruction or means had been supplied by which the Colonial Government might prepare for their reception; and this at a time, indeed, when the Secretary of State was having an enquiry made into the colony viewed as a "receptacle for offenders." As early as 1812 Robert Peel, as under-secretary for the Colonies, had on Liverpool's instruction prepared a circular letter for intending emigrants who might seek land grants under the old New South Wales system. "No persons are allowed to go out as free settlers to that colony," ran the circular, "unless they can prove themselves to be possessed of sufficient property to establish themselves there without the assistance of Government. . . ." Macquarie's protestations from Sydney brought in 1814 the relief of a reduction of the period during which the Commissariat must maintain the immigrant (from eighteen months to six months), and in that year the system of giving emigrants free passages on convict ships was abandoned—on account, probably, of the convict pressure on available accommodation. But in 1816, after the last peace, all restrictions on emigration were removed, and three years later the Government began to encourage emigration by an extension in New South Wales of the policy of granting land. Now an intending emigrant convincing the Colonial Office—apparently no difficult matter—that he possessed £400 or £500 worth of capital available for colonial farming, was passed; and the Governor had to find land and settle him on it.

This liberalization of the emigration policy of Whitehall came at a time, 1816–20, when Macquarie had to accommodate in New South Wales proper more than 11,000 male convicts. The transports had to have most of the Governor's attention, and he dropped perforce his former practice of personal investigation of each free immigrant's claim for land. He drew up a scale of grants in proportion to capital claimed (the claim was often fictitious).[1]

[1] M. Phillips, *op. cit.*, pp. 111–46, gives an excellent account of the factor of immigration in Macquarie's system.

Macquarie made many complaints of the practice of making fictitious capital claims, and in Van Diemen's Land Colonel Arthur, the Lieut-Governor, was making similar complaints, as late as 1825 (*cf.* Arthur to Bathurst, August 11, 1825, *Historical Records of Australia*, III, iv, p. 319).

Macquarie's schedule of proportional grants (recommended by Bigge) is in *Historical Records of Australia*, I, x, pp. 570 *et seq*. A settler with £100 capital was entitled to a grant of 100 acres; so *pro rata* to £500; £2,000, 1,500 acres; £3,000, 2,000 acres. Bathurst approved of Macquarie's maximum of 2,000 acres (Bathurst to Sorell, December 20, 1821, III, iv, p. 45, Sorell having received on July 24, 1820, instructions to follow Macquarie's scale (Sorell to Henry Goulburn) March 1, 1823, III, iv, p. 69).

As instances of Macquarie's system for immigrants, *cf.* his grants of 800 and 500 acres respectively to George Read and William Bunster, who came

If in such arduous circumstances "total incapacity" was as Bigge the Commissioner said Macquarie's distinction among Governors, some undisclosed providence must have directed him in his work of supplying New South Wales with a sufficient emergency currency system to meet conditions of emergency, setting up a bank to be the centre of reference of a commercial community which had had none but the Government Commissariat, rationalizing the system of assigning convict labour, transforming Sydney from a camp into an ordered town—articulating, indeed, the monetary, productive, social body which had been flung, with scant consideration for its guidance during growth, into the unknown Australian continent. John Macarthur and others were meantime giving this body the means of livelihood. But if Macquarie had omitted to provide his institutions of a free economy, their pastoral development must have been carried out with great difficulty and its achievement of a wool staple of export delayed. The lawyer whom Liverpool sent to examine New South Wales grasped little of all this, and Macarthur was singularly narrow in his view of the factors which were present in the transition stage of the colony. "John Macarthur was clearly not ill-pleased," says Melbourne,[1] "to be informed by Bigge's assistant that they looked to his evidence 'as the key or touchstone of the truth of all they had heard,' and he did not fail to pass on to his son the advance decision which was communicated to him, that there was but one excuse to be offered for the Governor, namely, 'his total incapacity.'" What did the Commissioner of Enquiry find in the colony to lead him to his conclusions?

J. T. Bigge, who went to New South Wales in 1819 as the

out recommended by the Secretary of State. He gave Read four and Bunster two convict servants, and gave each settler six months' free victualling (*Historical Records of Australia*, III, ii; Macquarie to Sorell, November 17, 1819.)

[1] *Early Constitutional Development in Australia*, by A. C. V. Melbourne, p. 84; Oxford University Press, 1934. The doubly quoted phrases are from *Macarthur Records*, pp. 325, 324.

Liverpool Government's commissioner of enquiry, and stayed there about two years, presented three reports of a voluminous kind to the Secretary of State for the Colonies, Earl Bathurst. One report related to judicial establishments in New South Wales; the other two, *Report of the Commissioner of Inquiry into the State of the Colony of New South Wales* (ordered by the House of Commons to be printed, June 19, 1822) and *Report (etc.) on Agriculture and Trade in New South Wales* (ordered to be printed, March 13, 1823), contain much valuable information relating to the economic aspect of the colony about 1820.[1]

Bigge made his economic and administrative survey in conditions which tended to make it unlikely that his estimates would be of enduring value. Before his departure from England the British Government gave him a pair of spectacles to wear, through which he must see New South Wales as now and indefinitely into the future a penal colony, and after his arrival John Macarthur had him don another pair, through which the colonial countryside appeared as if patterned with grazing flocks. Bigge's *Reports* are a strange medley of his impressions of the colony, now as seen through Lord Liverpool's dark lenses, now through John Macarthur's roseate ones. However, he was a patient compiler of returns, and the hundreds of his folio pages are an unsurpassed *Picture of New South Wales*.

The Commissioner's view of Macquarie was a happy adjustment of a Colonial Office view that the Governor cost too much and a sheepbreeders' view that he was, intolerably, assisting competitors into the "exclusives'" field. The first essential was to frame his report in accordance with his instructions, which were sufficiently definite:[2] "The settlements in New Holland must clearly be considered as receptacles for offenders. . . . So long as they continue to be destined to these purposes . . . their growth as colonies must be a secondary consideration, and the leading duty of those to

[1] The three reports, originally published as Miscellaneous *Parliamentary Papers*, are available in the Public Library of Victoria, bound together in a volume which contains much other relevant contemporary material.
[2] Bathurst to Bigge, January 6, 1819; *Historical Records of Australia*, I, x, p. 4.

whom their administration is entrusted will be to keep up in them such a system as may render transportation an object of serious apprehension." That is, Bigge must examine the colony with a prospect of it as an effectively terrible prison—which it could be only now that the wars were over, and must be, now that solution of the British social and political problem, including crime, was being attempted. And Bigge's commisson gave him power to direct the Governor to the ends of this policy. So far, so good. Bigge could write[1] with confidence: "In the expressions of Governor Macquarie, there may be traced that determination which he has never relinquished under any circumstances, of adhering to a system recommended more by motives of humanity than of reason." It was all very well, even by the light of "reason," for the Governor to pursue the system initiated by Phillip, of planting expirees on a small grant of land, very well, indeed, for him to add a marriage portion of land, as the earlier Governors had done; when the expiree could afford marriage—for "it is the opinion of the Rev. Mr. Marsden (n.b. senior chaplain and sheep-breeder) that marriage, even in New South Wales, operates as a corrective of vicious propensities."[2] But was it conducive to rendering transportation "an object of serious apprehension," that the Governor should interpret generously the implied power given him under Act 30, George III, cap. 47, to remit prisoners' terms and join them, perhaps untimely, to the free community? Why, out of 324,251 acres of land granted by Macquarie and his predecessors, each of whom had followed Phillip's 1789-92 precedent of settling expirees, 83,502 acres were, on July 12, 1820, in the hands of ex-convicts.[3] Of this area 54,673 acres was held by expirees, but 8,585 acres was

---

[1] *Report on the State of the Colony of New South Wales*, p. 83.
[2] *Ibid.*, p. 104.
[3] *Report on Agriculture and Trade in New South Wales*, p. 33, figures correcting those in *Report on the State of the Colony of New South Wales*, p. 140. Bigge made yet a third statement of this position. John Oxley, Surveyor-General under Macquarie, Brisbane, and Darling, wrote in 1826 that Macquarie granted about 400,000 acres, *cf.* 177,000 granted by all his predecessors (*Historical Records of Australia*, I, xii, pp. 379 *et seq.*).

held by holders of absolute pardons, 19,459 by holders of conditional pardons, and 765 acres by convicts holding tickets of leave.[1] Surely in granting thirty absolute pardons in 1819–20, 251 conditional pardons, and 570 tickets of leave, the Governor had been mitigating unwarrantably the designed severity of British punitive policy?[2] During the whole of his term to 1820 he had granted 366 absolute pardons, 1,365 conditional pardons, and 2,319 tickets of leave. About one quarter of these remissions had been accorded in "exception to the regulations" published by Macquarie himself in General Orders of June 1811 and January 1813, by the latter of which prisoners under life sentence might apply for free pardons, presenting certificates of their good conduct, after having served fifteen years at least, and prisoners serving a term of years must have served three-quarters of their term before application; similarly, conditional pardons (or "emancipations") might be applied for after ten years by life sentence men, and by others after having served two-thirds of their term. Too many instances of clemency, without these conditions having been satisfied, had issued in the enlargement of the emancipee class—who with the expirees had admittedly to be provided with the means of livelihood from the land—to a considerable element in the colonial population. "By the last muster taken by the magistrates of New South Wales, and by the muster taken in Van Diemen's Land, there were 3,617 male and female convicts whose terms of sentence had expired, 182 whose sentences had been absolutely, and 1,170 whose sentences had been conditionally remitted, out of a population that amounted to 29,407 souls.[3] One-sixth of the population were ex-criminals,

---

[1] An absolute pardon signified the absolute remission of the rest of a prisoner's term; a conditional pardon remission if he stayed in the colony during his term; convicts under ticket of leave might employ themselves independently during good behaviour or the Governor's pleasure. Bligh had given tickets to "gentlemanly convicts" on arrival (*Report of 1812 Select Committee, Minutes of Evidence*, p. 29).

[2] *State of the Colony*, pp. 119, 120.

[3] *Ibid.*, p. 140. Cf. *Report on Agriculture and Trade*, p. 80, where figures for New South Wales only are given.

a swarm like locusts on land of their own! Here Bigge doffed his Liverpool spectacles and donned those proffered by Macarthur and "the private interest" of "exclusives." For in New South Wales proper the adult population was about 18,000. Half were convicts and another third had served their sentences or had them remitted or were conditionally at large on tickets of leave (three in these classes, to every four ex-pirees). The residue of adults who had never been convicted was thus only about one-sixth of the whole, and more than half of them had been born in the colony; it was for the golden product of the process of refinement, the seven per cent or so[1] who had come free from Britain, the "pure merinos," that Bigge now agitated himself. It was true, of course, Bigge reported,[2] that even Macquarie in his system of allocating land-grants had not neglected provision for this backbone class. His scale of grants according to capital held by permitted immigrants[3] (during a period of little emigration, and that by persons with the Secretary of State's permission and a recommendation to the Governor, the first at least being contingent on the possession of capital)—his scale of grants provided for 100 acres for each £100 capital up to £500, by a graduated scale up to the immigrant with £3,000 capital, who might be granted 2,000 acres. But the sheepbreeder *in loco* was deserving of especial consideration. Colonial flocks had been tripled between 1810 and 1821, when they stood at almost 300,000[4] head, and of these John Macarthur, that "key or touchstone of the truth of all we have heard," owned 6,800, including 300 pure merinos. One of Macarthur's bales had fetched

---

[1] Analysis of Bigge's figures in *Report on Agriculture and Trade in New South Wales*, p. 80.

[2] *Ibid.*, p. 146.

[3] In 1819, 22 emigrants received Lord Bathurst's permission to go to New South Wales to settle.

[4] *Cf. Report of the 1812 Transportation Committee*, p. 3; *Report on Agriculture and Trade in New South Wales*, p. 16; and Macquarie to Bathurst, July 22, 1822, I, x, p. 675. Macquarie wrote that New South Wales grazed 25,888 sheep in March 1810, 290,158 in October 1821.

10s. 4d. a lb.,[1] and the colony's wool export to England in 1821 was 175,433 lbs. Now by Act 59 George III, cap. 52, the present duty of only one penny a lb. on colonial wool would be raised to threepence after January 5, 1823, and to sixpence after the corresponding date in 1826.[2] Freight and other charges amounted to another 1s. 0½d. a lb. To encourage the sheep man bearing this heavy load, so that his enterprise might support many assigned servants and thus relieve Government of expense, would it not be advisable to reconsider these heavier imposts so that the colonial exporter might not be discouraged? Bigge had pointed out earlier[3] that of 11,767 male convicts who arrived in the colony between the beginning of 1814 and the end of 1820, 4,587, including 1,587 mechanics or skilled workers, had been "taken by Government." Now the cost of a convict's upkeep in Government service was £29 14s. a year; if wool duties were not raised to the heights determined upon by Parliament at home, then the sheepbreeders would be able to employ another 2,000 convicts,

[1] *Report on the State of the Colony of New South Wales*, p. 162. And *cf.* John Macarthur to his son John, February 20, 1820, *cit. Macarthur Records*, p. 323: "In the course of conversation with the Commissioner he has three or four times touched generally upon the affairs of the colony, and I could easily discover that the opinions I expressed . . . were in conformity with his own."

[2] The increased duty under 59 Geo. III, cap. 52 was not continued. The *Edinburgh Review* (vol. 58, No. cxx, October 1833, p. 50), speaking of the "obloquy and abuse heaped on Mr. Huskisson for the part he took in reducing the wool duties" (n.b., in December 1825), pointed out that although home-grown wool—"by far the largest portion of the raw material of the (English) woollen industry" still—was produced in increasing quantities, imports of wool continued to rise (except in 1826 after the general economic crisis of 1825). Prices, too, had gone up steadily, in spite of the reduction of duty on colonial wool.

Cf. also *Minutes of Evidence*, 1833, Select Committee on Manufactures, Commerce, and Shipping, and House of Lords Committee on the Wool Trade, 1828. The Lords Committee's report found no reason for any increase of duty. From the late 1820's English wool imports were about 30,000,000 lbs. annually, e.g. 29,669,908 lbs. in 1831, when the policy of granting land was discontinued in New South Wales.

[3] *Report on the State of the Colony of New South Wales*, p. 21

thus saving the Government £49,400.[1] (But it would be only later in the 1820's that authority could entertain the likelihood, already stated to Bigge by Macarthur, that "by storing the country with fine-woolled sheep a most valuable export would be obtained, the returns of which would . . . in time enable (the colonists) altogether to provide for their own expenditure."[2] In 1828 the Governor, General Darling, would, following the now approved policy of extensive grants which Macquarie had initiated, grant nearly 3,000,000 acres, the colony's flocks would aggregate more than half a million head; and even then "the increased export . . . of the great staple commodity of the colony, viz. wool, (to) more than double the export of any former year"[3] would be only 834,343 lbs. Although Bigge was very properly persuaded to advance the claims of the developing wool interest, he was over-optimistic in forecasting that an adjustment of English wool duties would save the Imperial Government nearly £50,000 expenditure on the upkeep of 2,000 convicts assigned to sheepmen's service. For the value of wool exported in any one year was not to be nearly so large a sum, for several years yet.)

Bigge made,[4] towards the end of his survey of New South Wales, a statement which may be taken as a sufficient indication of his double-vision of the colony—that is, his attempt to satisfy his instructions and at the same time to advance the free settler against the emancipated settler, or the intruding factor against the inevitable factor, where Macquarie had sought to satisfy *his* instructions by keeping the gaol inmates busy about the gaol, while making provision for the rapidly growing expiree and emancipee groups. Bigge wrote, "Convinced of the rectitude of his own intentions, and not probably calculating upon the possible evils of resistence in quarters where co-operation was absolutely necessary for the success of

[1] *Report on the State of the Colony of New South Wales*, p. 162.
[2] *Cit. Macarthur Records*, p. 328, John Macarthur to his son John, February 29, 1828.   [3] *The Colony of New South Wales in 1828*, p. 175.
[4] *Report on the State of the Colony of New South Wales*, p. 147.

his measures; fortified also with the approbation of the Parliamentary Committee of 1812, Governor Macquarie has not only continued his support to the emancipated convicts, but has manifested on public occasions towards them a larger share of attention than he has manifested towards those of the free class."

This was the indictment. It may well be that a reading of the social history of the period shows that Macquarie did err in discriminating overmuch against "the free class," and that he did cast the light of official favour on emancipated persons whom he ought to have left to serve their sentences. But the "resistance" of the seven per cent "pure merino" element must, however urbane the social policy of a Governor of this period of resumed transportation and of the expiry of the sentences of many, have obstructed and deterred the only economic policy which such a Governor could have pursued if he was to cope with the local situation and the imperial policy's consequences. The short term aspect of that policy, which was Macquarie's policy, was the employment of surplus convicts on public works, the long term aspect was the settlement of expirees and emancipees, as a major duty of government. Macquarie may have over-emphasized both aspects.

No doubt, had Macquarie been a man of instruction and exceptional foresight in matters of primary production—and, further, had the practical sheep visionaries like Macarthur been men of less reactionary political and social proceedings—Macquarie's pattern of colonial reconstruction might have included more strands of wool, which was soon to be the economically significant factor in Australia. But Macquarie was an administrator—and Macarthur was a reactionary. His son thought it no shame to admit[1] that in politics John Macarthur was of the school of Pitt, and that among the figures of history whom he admired Coriolanus stood high. Again, in practice Macarthur contemplated no other solution of the developing problem of colonial economic and social organization than

[1] James Macarthur's appreciation of his father, *cit. Macarthur Records*, p. 471.

that, "if this colony is continued a receptacle for convicts," the transportees should be committed to the tender mercies of settlers. No doubt some settlers would abuse their power. Still, such an arrangement, involving the granting of large estates, of (say) 10,000 acres, to men who would become an aristocracy, ought to be made. Inevitable class hatred, which Macquarie was accused of having aroused by his policy, would not be important if aroused by Macarthur's policy—"the democratic multitude would look upon their large possessions with envy and upon the proprietors with hatred. As this democratic feeling has already taken deep root in the colony, in consequence of the absurd and mischievous policy pursued by Governor Macquarie, and as there is already a strong combination amongst that class of persons, it cannot be too soon opposed with vigour."[1] But establish a sheep aristocracy—and Britain would have a monopoly of the raw material of woollen clothing, and some of her major problems would be solved by the colony's taking "any number of convicts or paupers Great Britain and Ireland may send forth."

Here were the elements of sound prophecy. But although the chief constituents of Australian economic society after Macarthur's death in dementia in 1834 did assume shapes very like those which he had declared fitting, this aftermath can have little relevance in any judgment upon Macquarie the Governor. His instructions were to accommodate in New South Wales transports and those who, having been transported, earned their freedom by servitude or by behaviour which merited emancipation from servitude. After the war this task was one of unexampled difficulty, for more than 18,500 convicts were sent out in the years 1814–21. This was roughly four times the annual average of the pre-Macquarie period. Bearing in mind that in 1817 the number of convicts sent passed two thousand, and that by 1820 the number for the year was three thousand five hundred, we can find the essential

[1] "Suggestions" of Macarthur to Bigge, February 7, 1821, cit. ibid., pp. 349 et seq.

flaw in the judgment passed upon Macquarie by an historian as well disposed to his memory as Professor Roberts. Roberts writes,[1] "The arbitrary treatment of (free) settlers in his last few years . . . was merely retarding progress. . . . Clearly, Macquarie's best work was in the years before 1817, and that work was manifest." It is manifest, too, that in those years his task was remarkably easier of performance; nor was the establishment of the Bank of New South Wales merely a retardant of progress. Roberts continues, "His attitude to free immigration, after 1817, was irrational, and he departed from the wisdom of his former policy." But there was little free immigration before 1817, to be wise about, and at that Macquarie had suggested in 1812 a strict limitation of such immigration as there was—of ne'er-do-well persons of gentility (*vide* Chapter 3 (c) *supra*). But the basic factor to be considered in all these enquiries must be the volume of transportation, and most misunderstanding of early Australian history no doubt derives from a failure to take this factor into account. In the particular case there is no evidence that Macquarie suddenly became irrational, about 1817, and took out his eccentricity on immigrants; simply, he was too busy to bother about them.

Another factor of great importance from this period of transition was the economic stature to which ex-convicts had grown in the colony—in part because of the pursuit of the original policy of establishing them as farmers, in part because of the advantage which they took of the pastoral development. When Macquarie was recalled, and Brisbane sent out as Governor, the largest economic interest in the colony was vested in persons of the ex-convict class, in spite of the monopoly advantages which the officer-settlers had enjoyed, especially in 1793–1800 and 1808–9. In October 1821 the emancipees themselves made the following comparison[2] of the economic position of the free and freed classes:—

[1] *Op. cit.*, p. 25.
[2] Petition of the emancipated convicts, enclosure Macquarie to Bathurst, October 22, 1821. *Historical Records of Australia*, I, x, pp. 549 *et seq.*

	Freed Persons	Free Persons
Number of adults in colony	7,556	1,558
Number of their children in colony	5,859	878
Land in cultivation	29,028 acres	10,787 acres
Land (owned) in pasture	212,335 acres	198,369 acres
Sheep owned	174,179	87,392
Estimated capital	£150,000	£100,000
Estimated property of all descriptions, valued at	£1,123,600	£597,464

From 1820, when the ex-convicts, having Macquarie's support, had (some of them) made for themselves great holdings in New South Wales, pressure was increased against them as owners, by two means notably. In the first place colonial judicial decisions[1] ruled that emancipees could not hold property, or enjoy other basic rights of citizenship, until their pardons were listed in a general pardon under the Great Seal. In the second place, the administrative policy of Whitehall was swung quite away from the conception of the colony as a settlement for convicts and ex-convicts, to the conception of it as a field for investment by unconvicted persons. The orchard was too rich now to be left to the boy who once stole a windfall from its ground.

The fundamental change of Government policy is shown interestingly in contemporary instructions to the Governor. When Macquarie was recalled and Sir Thomas Brisbane given his instructions, in 1821, Bigge's reports (ordered to be printed, 1822 and 1823) were not available, and the Colonial Office's directions to him on February 5th followed the traditional pattern in requiring him to make grants to emancipees (30 acres, *plus* 20 acres for wife, 10 for each child, with subsistence, etc.), and to free immigrants (about 100 acres). But from this year the system was extended rapidly by which persons of substance were provided, before leaving England,

[1] E.g. *Eager* v. *Field*, April 4, 1820, *Eagar* v. *De Mestre*, September 15, 1820; I, x.

with orders on the Governor for land grants. In 1822 the new Governor, carrying out the Whitehall policy of diverting convicts from public to private service, required settlers to maintain one convict for a year, *per* 100 acres granted.[1]

Three years later, when Bigge's reports had been sent to Brisbane, and he was fully informed of the Government's expectation that he should follow them, he considered Bigge's recommendation that "no grants, beyond ten acres, be in future given unless to those possessed of property." Brisbane's comment was: "Attended to as far as considered expedient to due encouragement to that class of inhabitants, combined with the means they possess of doing justice to a grant of land."[2]

The next Governor, General Ralph Darling, received his instructions two months after Brisbane had sent the despatch containing this comment. The provision was not in his instructions that ex-convicts should be settled on the land in New South Wales. Grants might be made to "private persons," in addition land was to be sold, and no grant less than 320 (or more than 2,560) acres was to be made.[3]

This date, July 1825, thus marks the official termination of the policy which in fact Macquarie had been the last to execute —the accommodation in New South Wales of the small man as an owner—and the institution of a new policy—the accommodation of the large owner. The process was commenced, with intensity, when Bigge wrote his reports in 1820–21, when he and the ex-convicts alike were outspoken concerning the accumulated interests of that class; it achieved a system in 1825–26, when capital outflow from Great Britain was a

---

[1] For Brisbane's instructions *vide Historical Records of Australia*, I, x, pp. 596 *et seq.*

Vide x, pp. 373 *et seq.*, for a list of persons of substance given orders on the Governor's consideration in 1821.

For the maintenance of convicts as a condition of grant, *vide* Brisbane to Bathurst, April 10, 1822, x, p. 630.

[2] Brisbane to Bathurst, May 14, 1825, xi, p. 579.

[3] For Darling's instructions *vide* xii, pp. 107 *et seq.*

phenomenon of English economy only less remarkable than the concentration of capital in great industrial and farming enterprises at home.

One hundred and one grants were made or confirmed by Darling in 1828, aggregating more than 150,000 acres. Ten of them averaged 67 acres, another eight, 354 acres. The remaining eighty-three averaged nearly 2,000 acres per grant. The smallholder was vanishing from the colonial scene, and nearly 4,400 square miles had been alienated in New South Wales, as compared with considerably less than 300 square miles when Macquarie came, and considerably less than a thousand square miles when he left. In Brisbane's and Darling's years to 1828, 3,500 square miles would be granted or sold, as compared with less than 300 square miles in 1788–1809.[1]

Trimming of the official sails of England to the wind and the currents of British capital, and the suitability of New South Wales as a port of call for capital—rather than any personal dissimilarity between Governors—is the explanation of the proceedings of the Imperial Government with regard to Brisbane and Darling as we shall see (Chapter 7 *infra*), as well as to Macquarie. This nice navigation was conducted in the period from 1822, the period of an expansion of England now to be considered.

[1] *Vide* xii, pp. 379 *et seq.*, xiv, p. 671.

Appendix

GOVERNMENT ACCOUNTS

"The revenues collected within the Colony of New South Wales from its establishment until the commencement of the administration of Governor Macquarie in 1810, were raised in support of the 'Gaol' and 'Orphan Funds' respectively," General Darling's civil service found in 1828.[1] Thus in 1805 (King, Governor) gaols and orphans shared local revenue in the proportion of 2 : 1. (The collected revenue totalled £2,783 0s. 6d. for the year.) This revenue, the sources of which were determined absolutely by the Governor, was levied at rates which he determined. So Captain Hunter during his term (1795–1800) decided that spirits imported should bear a Customs duty of one shilling per gallon, wine, sixpence, and beer, threepence, in addition to a wharfage duty of sixpence on each cask or package landed. (This was not the germ of the Australian tariff system of Protection, for no Governor showed a desire to establish a local distilling industry—"the consumption of Ardent Spirits" was never deemed "a great Blessing" by authority in New South Wales, though brewing was, as the lesser of two evils.)

Hunter applied the revenue from spirits to the gaol fund, though the orphans benefited from permit-fees for the landing and removal of spirits after King's campaign against rum-runners was opened in 1800. (King established an Orphan Home for the colonial foundlings.) Licences to sell liquor, and a duty of one and a half per cent on all goods sold at auction, were other means by which King raised money to support the Orphan Fund, in addition the fund received the proceeds of an *ad val.* duty of five per cent on all goods imported from centres east of the Cape of Good Hope (1802), from fines and

[1] *Colony of New South Wales for the Year 1828, Revenue and Expenditure*, p. 3.

fees on land grants, and from quit rents (up to January 1, 1805), and from harbour dues.

Soon after Macquarie's arrival he renamed the Gaol Fund. It was now the Police Fund. Three-quarters of the proceeds of all duties, etc., were to be paid into the Police Fund, and one-quarter into the Orphan School Fund (except that all charges on spirits were to be paid into the Police Fund). This was directed by ordinance of March 31, 1810. On June 21, 1817, an ordinance reduced the orphans' proportion to one-eighth.

After the war, the Imperial Government required British parliamentary sanction for the New South Wales Government's revenue resorts, and an Act of 1819 (59 George III, cap. 119) which made this provision legalized the Governors' actions in the field during the twenty-odd years preceding. Other Acts of 1822 and 1823 (3 George IV, cap. 96, and 4 George IV, cap. 96—the second of which also gave the colony a legislative council and civil judges) increased the taxing powers of the Colonial Government.

In 1823 the picturesque "funds" lost their identity, becoming the "Colonial Revenue" after the 1822 Act's requirement that the accounts of such revenue should be rendered to the Imperial Treasury.

And it is an oddity of Australian history that this practice had scarcely been instituted when the Treasury officials in London had to marvel at the spectacle to which they were treated, of the accounts of the British Government at Sydney made up, not in the familiar sterling terms, but in terms of dollars and cents—or rather, dollars and decimal fractions, including even those "damned little dots" of recurrent decimals, the like of which would puzzle a Chancellor of the Exchequer of two or three generations later.

Chapter 6

THE POST-WAR EXPANSION OF ENGLAND, AND FURTHER COLONIZATION IN AUSTRALIA

(a) *British Foreign Policy and European Constitutionalism, from 1823*
(b) *British Trade and the Navigation Laws*
(c) *The Penal Code and Transportation*
(d) *"Combinations of Workmen"*
(e) *Economic Crisis, 1825*
(f) *Emigration, and Van Diemen's Land, North Australia, Westernport, and the Swan River Settlement*
(g) *Slavery in British Colonies*
(h) *British Foreign Policy and British Trade, 1826*

(a) *British Foreign Policy and European Constitutionalism, from 1823*

IN his five years' direction of the British Foreign Office and the House of Commons, George Canning attempted the task of "calling a new world into existence to redress the balance of the old." That is, he saw that British statecraft was required, if it was to serve the ruling and the rising interests of the State at this time, to undertake a drastic reorientation of its fundamental policies. It had to balance the European preponderance of power system by encouraging national growth in the Americas. It had to breach, if still it might not burst, the walls which contained the enterprise of England within too narrow limits. It had to recognize that another and even more portentous revolution had followed the agricultural revolution, and, conscious of the new factor of industrialism, serve it by whittling away the corn laws and navigation and fiscal laws which had been placed in position about a narrower and simpler economy. It had to direct its subsidies, at this new epoch, no longer towards the support of European combinations for military purposes, but towards the freed Spanish-Portuguese colonial world and the scarce-developed colonies which remained under the English Crown. It had to undertake the rationalization of penal laws which no longer reflected the actual requirements of the State, and it had to realize that policies must be formulated to accommodate the augmented "reserve army of labour" which an antiquated system of poor rates could no longer support. The task of British statesmanship in the 1820's was, in short, the revision of almost every important canon of foreign, imperial, and commercial policy.

This gigantic programme was largely fulfilled by George Canning as effective leader of Lord Liverpool's Government after Castlereagh's death, William Huskisson, President of the Board of Trade, and Sir Robert Peel, Home Secretary. The evidence of their words and deeds, in the records, shows that they were generally conscious of the nature of the problems set them and the implications of their solutions. In association, the three went far towards laying the required new nineteenth century basis for British policies, and we may find that later Whig or Liberal Governments did not depart from the principal lines along which the new Tories directed England during the 'twenties.

Canning, flexible where Castlereagh was stiff, saw the advantage which Britain might gain of all European parties by joining none. He saw that European "Jacobinism" could not triumph while England held her hand, yet that the Great Powers must be preoccupied with their liberal revolutions while England would be free to profit from a field of development and trade thus left exclusively to her. He understood that the new capitalists and industrialists would be with the old privileged class a bulwark against Jacobinism in Britain—though he resolutely opposed their enfranchisement. After Canning succeeded Castlereagh he sometimes paid lip-service to Whig rather than to Tory ideas. For example, in 1823 he spoke in the House of Commons in favour of a balance of power;[1] but

[1] For his speech *vide Parliamentary Debates, New Series,* 1823, vol. viii, cols. 897 *et. seq.* Upon the lead given subsequent Liberal Ministries by

no more than Castlereagh did he dream of basing British foreign policy on this Whig conception; it suited English interest better that the Holy Alliance preponderance should quiet the world for English trade. Yet he designated the balance of power system "the only safeguard of nations," and, ignoring the contemporary struggle of Constitutionalists all over Europe against the Holy Alliance despotisms, he found a balance to be "the protection of the weak against the strong, the principle by which small States flourished in the vicinity of great ones." This, while divided Poland lamented her lost national identity, and in Italy and Spain the weak struggled, unaided by Britain that had indeed helped to forge their chains, against the great States of the Alliance!

But such grim irony was as much the habit of this very "un-English" Londoner as the apperception which dictated, for instance, the terms of his refusal to lend England to an enterprise by which Bourbon France (admitted to the Alliance in 1818 at Aix-la-Chapelle) proposed to put down the Spanish Constitution by intervention. "Be yours," said Canning to the French Ambassador, "the glory of a victory followed by diaster and ruin, be ours the inglorious traffic of industry and ever-increasing prosperity."[1] The effect was that France, England's most formidable rival in the world's markets when she should be free to compete, would spend her resources to weaken Liberal Spain, and would thus herself be weakened; at the same time Britain would in theory support the assailed

the Canning-Huskisson-Peel policy, *cf.* Halévy (*1830–41*) on Palmerston's foreign policy *circa* 1834 (pp. 67 *et seq.*), Poulett Thomson's reduction of duties, 1832–34 (p. 90), and Brougham's law reforms, 1832–33 (pp. 95–96). Grey's Whig Foreign Secretary, President of the Board of Trade, Lord Chancellor, pursued international, fiscal, and legal reconstruction after the Tory triumvirate's pattern, just as Melbourne, the Whig Home Secretary in Grey's Cabinet, moved briskly against popular demonstration (*cf. ibid.*, p. 13), using a severity comparable with the Eldon-Peel method. In the 'thirties, indeed, it was Tory Nonconformists, like Richard Oastler, Michael Thomas Sadler, and Ashley, who sought by organization outside Parliament, and agitation within it, to mitigate the lot of the working classes under Liberalism (*cf. ibid.*, pp. 100 *et seq.*).

[1] *Cit.* Halévy (*1815–30*), p. 173.

Spanish Constitution while in fact she detached rich colonies from a weakened Spain. Canning could exclaim piously, "God forbid that, if honour, or good faith, or national interest required it, we should decline the path of duty because it is encompassed with difficulties."[1] But in the Spanish case British "national interest" lay in Spain's loss of her American colonies, a loss that would be hastened by Spanish civil strife and foreign intervention in Spain; and "honour" and "good faith" were perhaps not parliamentary expressions after all. Moreover, Canning pointed out to the Whig advocates of British intervention on the side of the Spanish Constitution, the last Peninsular War had cost Britain £33,000,000 in two and a half years. In formulating British foreign policy in the Spanish affair of 1823, Canning went on to use language of a directness which has come to be associated with the name of Bismarck who was but a later pupil of Machiavelli than Canning: "But let us not deceive ourselves. The general acquisition of free institutions is not necessarily a security for general peace. I am obliged to confess that its immediate tendency is the other way."[2] Prodigal at the same time of moral support of the Spanish Constitution—a Tory following the best Liberal tradition—Canning actually collected £500,000 from the Spanish Cortes or Parliament, compensation by this friendly, constitutionally ordered society for British losses by piracy in the Caribbean Sea,[3] and he persuaded the Cortes to recognize the independence of the revolted Spanish colonies in America. He would not amend the Foreign Enlistment Act of 1819 to permit English volunteers to fight for the Spanish Constitution; but he declared traffic in arms to be lawful, thus giving British manufacturers a wide market with the Bourbons, the Spanish *liberales*, and the revolutionary Governments in South America. He lured towards England, in this wise, a late ray of the commercial sunshine which had shone during the long summer of the great war now over.

[1] *Parliamentary Debates, New Series,* 1823, vol. viii, cols. 1516, 1517.
[2] *Ibid.,* cols. 1520, 1521.   [3] *Vide* Halévy (*1815–30*), pp. 176, 177.

The House of Commons might well thank him for his direction of policy. "The mention made in the Speech (from the Throne)," said a chronicler a little later,[1] "of the conclusion of a treaty with the Republic of Columbia called forth . . . many expressions of admiration at the masterly . . . policy by which Mr. Canning had solved the difficult problem of connecting ourselves with the new Governments of South America as independent States." (Nor was it out of his character that when objections were raised to sections of the Brazil-Portugal treaty by which Portugal, upon British mediation, acknowledged Brazilian independence, Canning should have passed on the blame for the offending clauses and stated that he had no intention of seeking Parliament's ratification of the treaty in this form.)

A dexterous use of the conflicting importunities of the Great Powers on the one hand, the Spanish, Portuguese, and Italian Constitutionalists on the other, with a consequent increase of British commercial opportunities, were phenomena of Canning's statecraft which did not exist in isolation but were part of a State policy now being remarkably revised. Canning had (*vide* Chapter 3) urged the withdrawal of the Corn Bill of 1815, unavailingly against the Tory majority, nor could he now during his term of power do more in regard to its oppressive incidence than to mitigate this in the manner of his predecessors, by suspending the Act at critical periods. Indeed, a quarter of a century would pass before British statesmanship, responsive to the industrial interest which by then would have relegated the agricultural interest to second place, could scrap the immemorial protective system of the Corn Laws. But the Tory reformers who with him were readjusting British policy to the changing needs of the post-war industrial era, were able to make a salutary change of policy which would have an extraordinarily revivifying effect on the British trade connection with the rest of the world.

[1] *Vide Annual Register*, 1826, p. 6.

(b) British Trade and the Navigation Laws

Now that the world carriage of goods was the lesser, the world supply of goods the greater hope of English business, it became clear to the far-sighted that a modification was necessary of the Navigation Laws which restricted trade with Britain and her colonies. A reform of this restrictive system was undertaken by Huskisson, the President of the Board of Trade, by Act of 1825 (6 George IV, cap. 114). Of the policy which this measure introduced, the standard authority (Egerton) writes:[1] "For the theory of monopoly a new theory had been substituted—that of reciprocity—to be ever connected with the name of Huskisson. The shadow of the mercantile system, it is true, long survived to amuse politicians. . . ." In fact, the Navigation Laws, like the Corn Laws, were not finally repealed until 1849; but the carrying economy of eighteenth-century England, seriously disturbed when Britain recognized in 1783 her American loss, was adapted now, by Huskisson's Act, to a growing national economy which would depend to a greater degree on production in England, for export to further or more numerous markets. After his reform, carriage of goods between England and British colonies was retained as the prerogative of British shipping, but his Act modified the Navigation Laws which had conferred this prerogative, by opening the commerce of all British colonies to States which, having colonies, gave reciprocal treatment to British shipping.

Again, Huskisson's tariff reforms are indicative of the new Tory attitude. The old Whig tariff, ranging from 18 to 40

[1] Egerton, *op. cit.*, p. 222. Note applications of this statute (and the 1827 Customs Act, 7 & 8 Geo. IV, V. 56) to foreign trade with New South Wales. Orders in Council of April 28, 1828, and April 7, 1830, dealing with trade concessions to Spain and Austria respectively, empowered ships registered in those countries to traffic in imports into British colonies and to carry British colonial exports to any country. The Governor of New South Wales was instructed accordingly in letters from the Secretary of State, August 19, 1828, and April 10, 1830 (*Historical Records of Australia*, I, xiv, pp. 342 *et seq.*; xv, p. 410).

FURTHER COLONIZATION IN AUSTRALIA

per cent and contained in 1,100 statutes, was reduced by him to eleven statutes in 1824-25, levying a scale of duties of from 10 to 30 per cent. This was at once to rationalize the tariff system and to modify it by lessening the discouragement of foreign exporters contemplating the British market.

Huskisson had become President of the Board of Trade in 1823 and would be Colonial Secretary four years later. It is important for our special study that we recognize him, therefore, as one who would regard colonies less as conveniences than as assistants in British enterprise.

(c) *The Penal Code and Transportation*

As the son of the author of the first Factory Act, and a member of a family with large interests in mechanized industry, Sir Robert Peel might have been expected to be alive to the significance of some of the changes which the new industrialism demanded of British policies. And indeed he lost no time, from 1822, when his association as Home Secretary with Canning began, in broadening the base and scope of his department's policy in a manner consistent with the foreign and imperial strategy of Canning and Huskisson. Peel found subsequently[1] that England's grand total of 14,437 convictions during 1825 included 12,530 convictions for theft, or about 85 per cent, and that during the seven years to 1826 British justice had had to rebuke—the order is of the Home Secretary's own—247 persons for forgery, 111 for murder, 50 for arson, 43 for perjury, and no fewer than 43,000 for larceny. And the 200 offences which were still by statute capital crimes included

---

[1] *Vide Annual Register*, 1826 (*History of Europe*, p. 114), for Peel's speech on the subject, in the House of Commons; *ibid.* (*Chronicle*, p. 324) for a statement of capital executions in the City of London and County of Middlesex, in the 11 years 1816-26. The total of 245 included 7 females executed. Of the 245, 14 were executed for forgery and 46 for uttering forged notes = nearly 25 per cent for these two offences; 138 (56 per cent approx.) were executed for various forms of theft (including 70 for burglary or house-breaking and 40 for highway robbery). Thus more than 80 per cent of capital sentences executed, 1816-26, were in respect of offences against property. *Cf.* Chapter 2 (*a*) *supra*.

scores of varieties of theft, which nevertheless the courts would not punish with death. The first step of reform was therefore to equate legal theory with judicial practice. In the event, Peel undertook a rationalization of the penal code correlative with Huskisson's undertaking in respect of the tariff laws. He compressed 92 old statutes concerning theft into a single measure of 32 pages, a single clause of which accounted for a dozen old statutes. Four of his Acts abolished the death penalty for a total of 100 offences.

Here, with a policy which had the appearance of mitigating the savagery of the law, a policy which at the same time recognized as fundamental the prevalence of offences against property, was a very different tone from that which the Tory Government had used as recently as 1821. Then, the Whig Sir James Mackintosh's three Bills for taking away capital punishment of forgery (except of Bank of England notes), stealing from dwelling-houses and stealing from navigable rivers, had been rejected by the Commons after short debate. The Solicitor-General had deprecated "this new-fangled scheme of philanthropy," comparing it unfavourably with the retributive "policy sanctioned by time and by great names." Though this British Minister agreed that the existing code was severer than codes in force on the Continent, he argued that it was more effective. (His predecessor under Pitt in 1785 had been more apprehensive of actualities; *vide* Chapter 1). Another point of view was taken by Dr. Lushington in the House, who, drawing attention to the fact that forgery of a marriage register was still in 1821 a capital offence, could find no reason for this anomaly of the existing law "except our extraordinary anxiety for the multiplication of capital punishments."[1]

But within a year or two of these exchanges the progressive group in the Tory party had stolen the Whig thunder. In Castlereagh's day it was Whigs like Ricardo and Mackintosh who had urged in the House economic and social reforms; now the ruling Tory trio were adopting Whig and Liberal causes

[1] For an epitome of the whole debate *vide Annual Register*, 1821, pp. 52 *et seq.*

which their party majority had repudiated so recently. In 1823–24 Peel made sweeping reforms of the English penal and prison systems in a series of Acts (3 George IV, cap. 64; 4 George IV, cap. 64; 5 George IV, cc. 19, 84). And the long inefficacy of British Ministers under George III (who had died with the advent of the 'twenties) was redressed now, additionally, by a reordering of that policy which had made the reception of criminals the Australian colonies' *raison d'être* and the chief reason for their maintenance. Peel modified the transportation system, too, during the era of his penal reforms. This system, Halévy points out,[1] "was impossible to continue in its existing form now that free colonists were emigrating to New South Wales." Accordingly an 1823 Act promoted by Peel (4 George IV, cap. 96), recognizing the rising significance of a free community in Australia, reformed the New South Wales administration by the appointment of civil in the room of military judges, and the appointment of a Legislative Council of five, six, or seven members by the Governor to advise him. The Act separated the administration of Van Diemen's Land from the Sydney Government and empowered separate penal settlements for those who offended in the colonies (section 38). The assignment of convicts to private service in New South Wales, which had been made at the Governor's discretion from the beginning, was now to be regulated (section 41). (In 1826 the Governor, Sir Ralph Darling, set up accordingly a board of control of assignments.)[2]

[1] (*1815–30*), p. 190. An oddity of Peel's association as Home Secretary with the Duke of Wellington's Ministry in 1830 would be his deviation in a solitary instance from the revised emigration policy, of the encouragement of people of substance to emigrate *vice* poor persons, which he and his colleagues had instituted on the large scale a few years earlier. Thus *vide Historical Records of Australia*, I, xv, p. 572, for a letter to R. W. Hay, Under-Secretary of State for the Colonies, from Phillips, Under-Secretary of State for Home Affairs, requiring, at Sir Robert Peel's instruction, a free passage to New South Wales for one John Wild, in the *Royal Admiral*. There had been scarcely any emigration of this kind for a quarter of a century past.

[2] For Peel's general overhaul of the transportation system, *vide* Acts 4 Geo. IV, cc. 47, 82, 96, and 5 Geo. IV, cc. 19, 84. For Darling's Land and

242   BRITISH IMPERIALISM AND AUSTRALIA

The Canning-Huskisson-Peel policy of the early 'twenties then evidently sought by several significant transformations to provide for an England that was finding itself under new necessities of expanded markets for its wider production, and colonies. So in the year of Huskisson's Reciprocity Act, 1825, New South Wales appeared for the first time in the emigration returns. In that year, 485 emigrants sailed for Australia, out of 14,891 emigrants in all.[1] As the general volume of emigration from Britain increased, so did the inflow into New South Wales, whither Britain sent, between 1825 and 1829, 4,460 emigrants. In 1820 there had been in New South Wales only 1,307 persons who had gone there free.[2]

(d) "Combinations of Workmen"

Emigration was increasing because—among other reasons—for the new British proletariat prospects of employment at home were narrowing, in spite of the increase of factories. The Poor Law statistics show that the taxpayers of an English and

---

Assignments Board, vide *Historical Records of Australia*, I, xii, pp. 252-53. The principal statutes relating to transportation, passed during the hundred years to 1816, were 4 Geo. I, c. 2 ("for the more effectual transportation of felons and unlawful exporters of wool"), 6 Geo. I, c. 23; 8 Geo. III, c. 15 ("for the more speedy and effectual transportation of offenders"), 19 Geo. III, c. 74; 24 Geo. III, c. 61; 27 Geo. III, c. 2 (denominating New South Wales as a transportation terminus); 28 Geo. III, c. 24; 30 Geo. III, c. 47 (giving the Governor of New South Wales power to remit sentences); 43 Geo. III, c. 15; 55 Geo. III, c. 146 (in force until May 1, 1816); 56 Geo. III, c. 27 (in force until May 1, 1821).

Francis Forbes (later knighted) was the first Chief Justice of the Supreme Court of New South Wales; he sailed for Sydney in August 1823, a year after his appointment and a month after the passage of "the New South Wales Act" (4 Geo. IV, c. 96), and vide *Historical Records of Australia*, I, xv.

[1] *Vide* Nicholls, *op. cit.*, ii, p. 467. The Secretary of State recommended three emigrants to the Governor of New South Wales in 1821, and gave orders for grants of land to 125 persons who were to emigrate; the number of persons thus furnished in 1822 was 212; in 1823, 6 were recommended; in 1823, 13 and 43 (*vide Historical Records of Australia*, I, x, pp. 373 *et seq.*, 603 *et seq.*; xi, pp. 1, 190, 191.

[2] *Vide Report of the State of Agriculture and Trade in New South Wales*, by J. T. Bigge (1823), p. 80.

Welsh population of about 12,000,000 in 1818 and about 12,500,000 in 1824 paid £9,320,440 and £6,836,505 in poor rates in those years. The amount actually spent on poor relief, per head of the English and Welsh population, was 13s. 3d. in 1818 and 9s. 2d. in 1824. Thus what might have appeared a natural, if disagreeable consequence of peace was acquiring the character of a permanent burden. For the middle 1820's were, as Mathieson writes,[1] "years of deficient and ill-paid employment; and the failure of the masses to improve or even to maintain their condition by industrial effort caused, or was soon to cause, a revival amongst them of the demand for parliamentary reform which had been dormant since 1819."

However, wheat had fallen steadily in price from January 1819, when it stood at an average of 80s. a quarter, to 63s. 2d. a year later, to 46s. 2d. in December 1821, down to 42s. 6d. in July 1822.

Another burden was lifted with the repeal in 1824 (by Act 5 George IV, cap. 95) of the Combination Laws. These Acts of 1799 and 1800 (39 George III, cap. 81, and 39 and 40 George III, cap. 106) had prohibited combinations of workmen or trade unions, making membership of such bodies punishable by three months' imprisonment, etc.

Unfortunately, however, the price-fall and the repeal of restrictive legislation did not coincide. For in December 1822 —" a critical date in the economic history of England"[2]—a rise in the corn price had begun, to reach in May 1825 a maximum of 69s. 2d. a quarter as compared with 34s. at the end of November 1822. The natural corollary was that after the repeal of the Combination Laws working men used their associations to demand wage increases commensurate with the increased cost of living. In 1825 strikes occurred in many industrial towns; the Port of London, for instance, was made idle for a time by a strike of shipwrights. A hasty enactment of new (though lighter) methods of controlling working class use of the now legal weapon of trade unionism was made during

[1] *Op. cit.*, p. 225. [2] Halévy (*1815–30*), p. 193.

the year. An Act (6 George IV, cap. 129) made "molestation," "destruction," etc., offences punishable by three months' imprisonment. It was at this time that Cobbett made a statement[1] which foreshadowed the doctrine of a class war, which Karl Marx would soon be preaching to Europe.[2] "The working classes," Cobbett saw, "combine to effect a rise of wages. The masters combine against them. The different trades combine and call their combination a *general union*. . . . Here is one class of society united to oppose another class."

However, the 1824 repeal Act was of great importance in making it lawful for working men to combine to protect their interests, and it is interesting to find that, if its passage was not due to the initiative of the great Tory trio, at any rate its sponsor, Francis Place, through the assistance of Sir Francis Burdett and Joseph Hume in the Commons, secured through an exploitation of the Tories' liberalism that it should become part of the law of the land. That is, he embedded the matter of combinations in a Bill which, in conformity with the Huskisson policy, removed restrictions upon the export of machinery and the emigration of skilled artisans (as well as upon the combination of workmen).[3]

But "the immediate result of the Act," as Halévy points out,[4]

---

[1] *The Weekly Political Register*, August 27, 1825, vol. lv, pp. 519, 520.

[2] *Cf. Selected Letters of Marx and Engels*, p. 57: Marx said in 1852, "No credit is due to me for discovering the existence of classes in modern society, nor yet the struggle between them. Long before me bourgeois historians had described the historical development of this class struggle and bourgeois economists the economic anatomy of the classes" (London: Martin Lawrence, 1934). [3] For this account, *vide Dietz, op. cit.*, pp. 474–75.

[4] (*1815–30*), p. 206. *Cf.* the interesting analysis in *The General Theory of Employment, Interest and Money*, by J. M. Keynes, pp. 5, 6 (London: Macmillan, 1936). Just as, in Halévy's historical account, industrial workers remained unconvinced of economic law which operating in a free market would bring wages to a "proper level," so in his analysis of "fundamental postulates of the classical theory of employment," Keynes disputes the validity of contemporary economic assumptions made by Ricardo, the economico-jurist from whose exposition the working men dissented, according to the lessons of their experience.

Keynes finds two bases, practically undiscussed, of the theory with which

"deceived the expectations of the Liberals. They had believed that the moment the workers ceased to feel themselves at war with the law of the land, they would realize that their combinations were powerless against the operation of the laws of nature, and would therefore cease to form them. Unfortunately, economic conditions remained the same as before, and the workmen were obliged to demand a rise of wages to correspond with the continued rise in the cost of living. It was in vain that Joseph Hume addressed a public appeal to the working class... (pointing out) . . . 'it will require time, under the operation of a free market for labour, to bring both (i.e. hours of work and rates of wages) to their proper level.' "—In vain, for the period had closed already during which (1822 to mid-1825) a steadily sustained increase of foodstuffs prices had given the dominant interest a surplus with which it could be generous. This period had seen the great changes of British economic and social policies which we have just discussed. Therefore the date of the commencement of the price-rise is indeed an im-

Hume, for instance, failed to confute the wage earners' *a posteriori* argument. These bases were: "*I. The wage is equal to the marginal product of labour . . . II. The utility of the wage when a given body of labour is employed is equal to the marginal disutility of that amount of employment.*" Keynes explains the second postulate as conveying that "the real wage of an employed person is that which is just sufficient (in the estimation of the employed persons themselves) to induce the volume of labour actually employed to be forthcoming" —subject to wage-earners' combination as a factor of disturbance (the gravamen of Hume's appeal).

Keynes proceeds to state factors which diminish the status of the two classical postulates as a comprehensive account of the basis of employment and wages.

Detailed consideration here of his position is not appropriate, but the student of the nineteenth century will find Keynes's analysis extraordinarily stimulating, especially in the context of the economic history of the period.

Contemporary thought, too, struggled with the classical postulates, e.g. Owen's anticipation about 1813 (*op. cit.*, i, p. 285) of Marx's doctrine of a reserve army of labour "when the general demand for labour throughout the country is not equal to the full occupation of the whole." *Cf.* also Clapham's citation (*op. cit.*, i, p. 557) from the newspaper *Northern Star*, of June 23, 1838—a second anticipation of a doctrine which attempts to qualify vitally the classical theory of employment and wages.

portant one in English economic history, inasmuch as it marks an opportunity for domestic reconstruction by enlightened ministerial policy, yet—because of the reaction of labour to the price-rise—portends a terminus of the period during which the fundamental problems of English society could be attacked without direct recourse to a very large, public-controlled policy of emigration.

Naturally the brief period of sustained high prices had bred the usual distresses. The poor labourer, paying in May 1825 for a loaf double what he had paid in November 1822, must leave England for New South Wales or elsewhere, as felon or free emigrant, to find more and cheaper bread; and he would find in New South Wales a community which Huskisson's 1825 Act had empowered to trade more freely with its natural markets and suppliers. But a mighty problem remained with a great section of British people, for the State to solve. Between 1823 and 1827 Lancashire, the English county to which most Irish immigrants drifted in search of work, paid the passages home to Ireland of 20,000 Irish paupers whom its industries could not accommodate.[1] (There was still room for children in the factories, however. In February 1826 a Macclesfield (Cheshire) newspaper printed an advertisement[2] which called for 4,000 to 5,000 young persons between the ages of 7 and 21 years. The advertisement was addressed sufficiently "to the Overseers of the Poor and others.") In May 1826 Parliament suspended the operation of the Corn Law of 1815, giving the Government power to admit foreign foodstuffs during the parliamentary recess. Even in this emergency there were landed members to oppose such action, though the Prime Minister, Lord Liverpool, had painted movingly to the House of Lords the situation into which labourers were plunged.[3] And next year, when Canning was Prime Minister, his Bill

---

[1] *Vide* Clapham, *op. cit.*, i, p. 59, for this citation from the *Report of the Select Committee on Irish and Scottish Vagrants*, p. 4.

[2] *Cit. Annual Register*, 1826, p. 62.

[3] For Liverpool's speech, *vide Annual Register*, 1826, p. 56.

drastically to amend the Corn Law by reducing from 80s. to 60s. a quarter the statutory level at which foreign corn might be admitted, was rejected by the Lords though it passed the Commons. The agricultural interest was evidently fighting to the last ditch, even as the machine aggravated the ruin of the class which its enclosures had now disinherited almost entirely. In 1826 John Williams said in the House of Commons[1] that of 20,000 silk weavers employed in Macclesfield in 1825, 8,731 had lost their work in six months, so that 1,600 additional families were placed on poor relief—in Macclesfield that now was so avid for child labour. The 10,688 broad-silk looms of the town were now (May 1826) reduced to a remnant of 4,111.

Foreign competition, as well as the machine and the child labour policy, contributed to such displacements, and while Huskisson administered a lower tariff-scale, representatives like Williams of industrial constituencies sought to have it raised, if only to protect these poor victims of industry.

(e) *Economic Crisis, 1825*

Contributory also to the especial misery of the working classes in 1826 were sequels of the disastrous financial slump which, from late in 1825, disturbed the equilibrium of a British economy expanded in one direction too far and too quickly. Speculation in South America was the chief cause of this sharp crisis, which followed the three years' boom. "The manufacturers had dumped in South America their entire surplus production, the capitalists had lent money to the new Governments[2] and had floated companies to exploit the mineral wealth of Mexico and Peru. It was calculated that in this way no less than £150,000,000 had crossed the Atlantic."[3] This process

[1] *Vide* for his speech *Annual Register*, 1826, p. 59. Napoleon's continental system had encouraged French manufactures, but England's control of the seas had limited French supplies of raw material, the French had been unable to prevent English smuggling into Europe, and French manufacturers had not been able to satisfy alone the European demand.

[2] E.g. in loans by the bankers Baring, Barclay, Rothschild, etc.

[3] Halévy (*1815–30*), pp. 225, 226.

had been continuous ever since, about 1810–11, France's continental system had proved especially effective in restricting British enterprise. Canning's astute foreign policy had, as we saw, facilitated British exploitation of the old Spanish and Portuguese colonies in America, and the reorganization of English finance since the Acts of 1816 and 1819 and the Bank of England's resumption of gold payments in 1821 had made a base from which English capital export could be undertaken in some security. It had been largely availed of. "The passion for establishing joint stock companies," we learn from a contemporary source,[1] "which had raged like an epidemical disease in 1825, had overflowed the table of the House of Commons, during that session, with petitions for private bills" (i.e. for the registration of companies). Six hundred companies had been floated during the boom period late 1822 to mid-1825, with £500,000,000 aggregate capital,[2] to undertake public utilities services in Britain, South America, and elsewhere. New South Wales, now coming in for some other regard than as a prison, had shared in the endowments of this capital expansion. The Australian Agricultural Company had been given a charter on November 1, 1824; it was to receive great areas of land at a nominal quit rent, in return for its investment of £1,000,000 capital in the colony, and its accommodation of the Establishment by employing convicts.[3] Lord Bathurst, Liverpool's Colonial Secretary, gave the Australian Agricultural Company a monopoly in coal-getting in New South Wales, with its charter, and the Colonial Government turned over to the company its coal mines and machinery at Newcastle, New South Wales.

[1] *Annual Register*, 1826, p. 103.

[2] Halévy, *op. cit.*, p. 231; with his statement of the boom position *cf.*, however, the account in *A Complete View of the Joint-Stock Companies formed during 1824 and 1825*, by H. English, cit. *The Pound Sterling, A History of English Money*, by A. E. Feavearyear, p. 218 (Oxford, Clarendon Press, 1931): "In 1824 and 1825 over 600 new companies, with a total capital of £372,000,000, were floated, in addition to numerous foreign loans, particularly to South American States."

[3] *Vide Historical Records of Australia*, I, xi, pp. 563 *et seq.*

The crisis in England which succeeded these great movements is particularly interesting to us as an indication that where once a poor harvest at home had been the chief cause of the labouring classes' affliction, and the stimulus for their violent demonstration and unavailing agitation for political reform, now the experience of capital released for overseas investment could bring similar woes upon them.

The 1820's had opened, we saw, with England, alone among nations, basing its currency on a gold standard. Equally it was the only country in which the central bank (the Bank of England) had a monopoly of joint stock banking, or banking enterprise upon the capital of numerous shareholders. (On the other hand, in Scotland, for example, conditions differed. Thus in 1826 there were thirty Scottish banks, of which seven were chartered, seven joint stock, and sixteen partnership undertakings. There, too, the chief banks had gone in for branch-banking, especially since 1774, and in 1826 the Bank of Scotland had sixteen branches and the British Linen Company twenty-seven.)[1] After the 1825 crisis, the Bank of England lost its joint stock monopoly by an Act (6 George IV, cap. 91) by which joint stock banks of issue were permitted subject to the provision that they established no branches in London or within sixty-five miles of it. (There were about sixty banks other than the Bank of England in London; unlike the country banks they did not issue notes but used those of the Bank of England.) Another Act of 1826 (7 George IV, cap. 6) forbade the issue of further £5 notes by the country banks after April 5, 1829, and ordered that no more be stamped for circulation after the date of the Act. In the Commons the great trio, Canning, Huskisson, and Peel, together with the London banker Baring, had opposed the suggestion that the current depression be alleviated by the allowing of three years' further currency to the small notes of the small banks—for, as they pointed out,[2] seventy-six such banks, or perhaps ten per cent of those in operation at the crisis, had had "commissions of

[1] *Vide Annual Register*, 1826, p. 33.   [2] *Annual Register*, 1826, pp. 15, 16.

bankrupt" issued against them before 1825 was out, and to realize "the unsoundness of the present system" it was only necessary to consider that 233 small banks had failed between 1810 and 1825. A London bank, too, had failed at the end of 1825; like most of the others, it failed because of its irrecoverable loans to South American Governments.

The Bank of England began immediately in 1826 to execute its new statutory right to establish branches outside London, but banking reforms had not now, any more than in 1816 or 1819 after crisis, the immediate effect of righting the economic and social structure. The trade figures seemed to reflect a healthy condition which was no longer present. Thus, during 1825 Britain imported more than £36,000,000 of goods and exported £58,000,000, including £10,000,000 of re-exports of foreign and colonial merchandise.[1] But after crisis the huge drain to South America was diminished, and English buying with it. Of the public finances, the necessity of dealing with civil commotions was requiring increased charges on account of the coercive machinery of State, and in 1826 the country supported 30,000 sailors and 9,000 marines, and 87,240 soldiers (an increase of military since 1822 of 17,152). Irish unrest kept twenty-three of the eighty-three line regiments in Ireland, whither the paupers were being shipped back in thousands from England, and there were nine regiments in England, Wales, and Scotland.[2]

But still public discontent grew, and expressed itself in organization as well as demonstration—in spite of banking

[1] Official figures in *Annual Register*, 1827, p. 278. But the figures may be made up of the "official values" of goods imported and exported, i.e. rates fixed in 1794 and not altered until 1854, when, with the publication of the *Statistical Abstract of the United Kingdom*, declared values, i.e. at current prices, were given. Official values were generally far higher than declared values. In 1825 British wool imports rose to 41,000,000 lbs., in 1826 fell to 18,000,000 lbs., *cf.* a usual annual importation during the 1820's of about 30,000,000 lbs. (New South Wales wool export was commenced in 1821.) *Vide Minutes of Evidence*, 1833, Select Committee of the Commons on Manufactures, Commerce, and Shipping.

[2] *Vide Annual Register*, 1827, p. 231.

reform, increase of the Services estimates; in spite alike of repeal and part-re-enactment of the Combination Laws; in spite of Corn Law suspension and an increase of the poor rate.

Other opinions, other remedies. In 1823 John Stuart Mill formed a group of young Utilitarians, pledged to advocate *laissez-faire* as the panacea of social and economic ills; next year Jeremy Bentham founded the *Westminster Review* to promulgate similar doctrines; in 1825 the Radicals brought into being the University of London to give higher education to the new industrial middle class, and Mechanics' Institutes to civilize the new industrial working class. But "the name of Bentham," William Hazlitt wrote in his *Spirit of the Age* published in 1824, "is little known in England." And though Hazlitt said it was known better in Europe, where liberalism was fighting absolutism, and "best of all in the plains of Chile and the mines of Mexico," reaction was none the less strong against it in England. And although 40,000 of Bentham's political works might have been sold in Argentina, Guatemala, and Columbia,[1] and although he had "offered constitutions for the new world and legislated for future times," the English had no such constitution as he advocated for the Guatemalans, and the need of their masses was immediate, not to be satisfied by future legislation. So a sort of socialism was germinated in the working-class movements, in the alternative, even as the first co-operative society, after Robert Owen's advocacy, was founded at Brighton in 1828. "Thomas Hodgskin and William Thompson," Halévy records, "starting from the principle of the Utilitarian philosophy, and even accepting certain postulates of Ricardo's political economy, had failed to discover in this system of economics either a scientific explanation or a moral justification for the capitalist's profit, and had begun to elaborate the doctrine, not slow to find adherents among the working class, which maintains that the worker has a right to the entire capital produced by his labour. . . . Indifferent to the political question, they looked to Robert Owen to solve

[1] *Vide* Halévy (*1815–30*), p. 189.

the social problem by the foundation of . . . co-operative societies."[1] Again as in 1818–19, in 1826 economic distress began to close the ranks of the suffering working classes, and a second attempt was made at a General Union of industrial workers. The *Herald of the Rights of Industry*, of Manchester, would recall in its issue of April 5, 1834,[2] "In 1826 a Trades Union was formed in Manchester, which extended slightly to some of the surrounding districts and embraced several trades in each; but it expired before it was so much as known to a large majority of the operatives in the neighbourhood."

The Government, nominally under Lord Liverpool until Canning became Prime Minister in April 1827, after Liverpool's death, sought in emigration a solution of the country's difficulties.

(f) Emigration; and Van Diemen's Land, North Australia, Westernport, and the Swan River Settlement

"Emigration as a cure for redundancy became fashionable in the 'twenties," Clapham puts it.[3] "Restrictions on the emigration of skilled artisans were swept away in 1825, though no one complained of redundant skill. The first parliamentary enquiry into emigration, 'this comparatively unexamined subject,' . . . was made in 1826–27. The tide of emigration from the United Kingdom was flowing strongly from 1829 to 1833. But even including the high figures of 1829–30, the average annual outflow from the year of Waterloo to 1830 was only about 25,000 . . . (the 1826–27 committee) signed a peroration about Emigration as a National System and left the matter. . . . No system was ever adopted. Individual need

---

[1] *(1815–30)*, p. 279. According to the *Edinburgh Review* (vol. 59, 1834, No. cxx, pp. 341–42) many co-operative societies had fallen into a decline by the early 'thirties. *Cf.* K. B. Smellie's comment (*A Hundred Years of English Government*, p. 16; London, Duckworth, 1937) on the early English socialists of the 1820's.

[2] *Cit. The History of Trade Unionism*, by Sidney and Beatrice Webb, p. 115; London, Longmans, 1920 edition.

[3] *Op. cit.*, i, pp. 53 *et seq.*

and individual enterprise continued their work of filling the new worlds, at a price."

But this is somewhat less than fair as a judgment; again, it contains errors concerning fact. In the first place, an expert in this phase, having examined contemporary evidence, gives quite another account and interpretation of Government policy towards emigration. Egerton says:[1] ". . . If there could be at the time (i.e. the 1820's, when British enterprise was preoccupied with the new independent States of South and Central America) little desire for the colonies on grounds of trade, what other reasons were there to promote colonial development?" Egerton finds abundant evidence to show that the reason perceived was "the advantage of colonies for the disposal of surplus labour." Huskisson's Reciprocity Act of 1825 and the 1823 Act (4 George IV, cap. 96)—especially article 38 providing for the segregation of colonial offenders— are among the indications which he cites of the Government's active policy of encouragement of colonial (i.e. chiefly Australian and Canadian) establishments. He concludes that "by all these means (the British Government) endeavoured to encourage and develop that tendency to emigrate which followed the close of the great war." Further, it is clear from the parliamentary debates that Government did something more than heed fashion and note perorations. "During the last four years," it was recorded[2] in 1826, "Government on more occasions than one had lent its aid to emigration to Canada. The general misery which prevailed during the present year increased tenfold the claims of emigration upon its notice as a means of relief."

Thus in 1823 Parliament voted £50,000 to remove 268 free settlers to the North American colonies, and in 1825 promoted and financed the emigration thither of 2,024 Irish paupers, at a cost of £20 per head. Clapham's statement that "no system was ever adopted" is utterly erroneous if it means what the

[1] *Op. cit.*, pp. 223–31.
[2] *Annual Register*, 1826 (*Chronicle*), p. 43.

words mean. For the appointment of an Agent-General for Emigration, and Emigration Commissioners, and a Board of Colonial Land and Emigration Commissioners, during the next decade, was quite systematic. If he means that no system was adopted by Government in the 1820's he must have dismissed consideration of a sufficient explanation in 1826 of the official attitude:[1] "It had never been in the contemplation of Government to supply all the expenses necessary for carrying such experiments further: their object was to show by a few trials, to those who might be interested in forwarding such a system, and in removing a redundant population, the ease with which it might be carried into effect, without any very great expenditure of funds, and the beneficial consequences resulting from it."

In any case, a system, to meet the situation of officers of the army and navy demobilized after the war, was devised as early as 1818, and a corresponding arrangement for any of the hundreds of thousands of disbanded rank and file.[2] It is, however, true that when R. Wilmot Horton (the chief emigration theorist before Wakefield, and a member of the Commons

[1] *Annual Register*, 1826 (*Chronicle*), p. 44, vide also *Emigration from the British Isles*, by W. A. Carrothers, Chapter iv (London, P. S. King, 1929), for an account of emigration experiments in the post-war period. Carrothers mentions, *inter alia*, the emigration to the Cape of Good Hope in 1818 of 2,000 to 3,000 distressed knitters from Nottingham (which had been the centre of "Luddite" riots); grants in 1818 to individuals who contracted to place emigrants in employment at the Cape or in Canada; emigration of 1,200 Glasgow weavers, 1820, and of 1,883 Scottish weavers next year to Upper Canada; various grants to assist emigration, 1823–5–7. The chapter contains much other interesting evidence of a definite, sustained effort by the Imperial Government to find a system fit to cope with the problems of British and Irish pauperism and contingent social problems.

[2] *Cf.* instructions to the Governor of New South Wales, to give land grants on special terms to recommended ex-officers (Bathurst to Macquarie, July 24, 1818, *Historical Records of Australia*, I, ix, pp. 823–24). New South Wales Government Orders of June 8, 1826, May 16, 1827, and August 24, 1827 (*ibid.*, xii, pp. 585–86; xiii, pp. 485–86, 596) applied this instruction, and many officers emigrated; *cf.* Murray to Darling, November 16, 1829, in which the Secretary of State noted that the number who had gone out "fully answered the proposed object" (*ibid.*, xv), *cf.* also Chapter 7 (*a*) *infra*.

who had been Under-Secretary for the Colonies until 1825) moved on March 14, 1826, for the appointment of a select committee to enquire into emigration he was snubbed. But perhaps this is not important in view of the fact that within a few weeks a similar Government motion was carried into effect.

In 1826 more than 20,000 emigrants left England, by 1832 the number to leave during the twelvemonth would be more than 100,000. (A few minutes' scrutiny of the emigration account given in Sir George Nicholls's *History of the English Poor Law*, from which these figures are taken, will dispose of any misconception that authority merely enquired, then "left the matter" of emigration. Nicholls was the chairman of the Poor Law Commission which, from 1834, reorganized the system of poor relief, after a principle made practicable by a concurrent encouragement of emigration.)

In fact a climax of several years' intense theorizing, accompanied by some practice, was reached in the publication in 1829 of Edward Gibbon Wakefield's *A Letter from Sydney*. Goderich, when Secretary of State for the Colonies at a period (the opening of the 1830's) of transformation of British colonial policy to meet requirements of capital and population expansion, "adopted from Wakefield," as we are told,[1] "the idea that if the colony's lands were sold, the proceeds of the sales might fitly be applied to introducing that labour without which the land itself would be of little value." But during fifteen years before the *Letter* was published, 313,913 emigrants[2] sailed from the British Isles—a number equivalent to about one and a half per cent of the population after Waterloo, and approximating to the number of sailors and soldiers thrown on the British and Irish labour markets after the war. And naturally this great

[1] *Labour and Industry in Australia*, by T. A. Coghlan, i, p. 218.
[2] Nicholls, *op. cit.*, and Carrothers, *op. cit.*, *Appendix I*, give emigration figures for this period. Their pre-1840 figures are from Customs returns; and "from other sources" Carrothers gets a figure of 2,518 emigrants "to Australia and New Zealand" (i.e. to New South Wales and Van Diemen's Land), in 1821–24.

efflux did not take place without the formulation of principle and the creation of administrative organs. Indeed Malthus had been by no means alone in apprehensive examination of what seemed a concrete instance of the principle of "redundant population" which he had enunciated in 1798. He wrote[1] in 1820 of "the powerful stimulus given to population during the war," and, heavy with foreboding increased by the social disturbances of 1816-19, he found that "for the four or five years since the war, on account of the change in distribution of national produce, and the want of consumption and demand occasioned by it, a decided check was given to production, and the population under its former impulse has increased, not only faster than the demand for labour, but faster than the actual produce. Though labour is cheap, there is neither power nor the will to employ it all." Proposals were legion for a practicable means of alleviation.[2]

Especially in Ireland the problem bore crushingly upon the landlord economy. Wilmot Horton gave un-Malthusian evidence before an 1825 committee on the state of Ireland. Unemployment and distress there, he conceded, were due less to inadequate productivity than to limitations of the landlord system. Malthus advised that famine would solve the problem of Irish "redundancy," but that Britain would have to find relief in an emigration of her human surplus, the while cottage holdings were being consolidated into large estates. But these elements were, even in the 1820's, rather history than prophecy, and Horton was no doubt nearer the kernel of the matter when he maintained[3] that population might be redundant in relation to means of employment yet not to means of subsistence. He found that to be the situation in the United Kingdom, and his solution lay in controlled emigration. Emigrants should be

[1] *Principles of Political Economy*, pp. 493-95; London, 1836.
[2] *Cf.* e.g. *Reports* of select committees on the Irish poor (1823), payment of wages from poor rates (1824), emigration (1826-27), and state of Ireland (1825).
[3] Carrothers, *op. cit.*, pp. 38 *et seq.*

established in the colonies, having been supplied with initial capital not in money but in kind.[1]

However, as we saw, the British Government had had peasant plantation of the sort in mind, for a generation or more, and had practised or tried to practise in New South Wales, with ex-convicts and recommended free emigrants, the mode of colonizing which Horton now urged.[2]

At this time the Commons committee on emigration was finding it to be fact (*a*) that in England, Ireland, and Scotland communities existed in which there was "a very considerable proportion of able-bodied and active labourers beyond the number to which any existing demand for labour could afford employment"; and (*b*) that in North America, the Cape of Good Hope, New South Wales, and Van Diemen's Land much land lay unappropriated which could support this surplus element in Britain. The committee's reports of 1826 and 1827 advocated, accordingly, the assisted, voluntary emigration of paupers.

But how was authority to make such emigration practicable?

On April 17, 1828, Horton presented his solution when he sought leave to bring in "a bill to enable parishes in England, under given regulations, and for a limited period, to mortgage their poor rates, for the purpose of assisting voluntary emigration."[3] Horton's line of argument is indicative of the new realism pervading minds which French political philosophy and English political economy had sharpened. There was no more direct relation, he told the Commons, between wealth and numbers, than between health and blood supply. But while involuntary unemployment[4] existed in Britain it was sound

[1] *Cf. ibid.*, and Horton's *Enquiry into the Causes and Remedies of Pauperism* (1830).

[2] *Cf.* Horton's speech in *Parliamentary Debates, New Series,* vol. xxvi, col. 480.

[3] *Vide* for the debate on Horton's Bill *Parliamentary Debates, New Series,* 1828, cols. 973 *et seq.*

[4] The use of this term has a special interest. Note that Keynes's 1936 analysis (footnote 4, p. 244 *supra*) finds the factor of "involuntary unemployment" to be a notable omission from the theory of employment which in Wilmot Horton's time was novel.

doctrine that the excluded labour power should be transferred, when it could not only pay the cost of transfer but could create new wealth. Somewhat in advance of the official position, Horton advocated his principle of hypothecation, "not," he said, "under the patronage but I may say rather in the teeth of His Majesty's Government." Chairman of the select committee on emigration, and earlier the author of the experimental emigration already mentioned, of Irish paupers to Canada, Horton found the crux of the contemporary problem in the necessity of a bloodletting by emigration from Ireland; only thus could the congestion of workless Irish in England be dispersed.

Apparently the general principle of hypothecating poor relief collections to finance the emigration of paupers came from the London parish of Marylebone. This local authority had sought Crown opinion whether the parish was competent to advance to twenty female paupers desirous of emigrating to New South Wales, an amount equivalent to two years' maintenance from the poor rates. Horton now sought a two years' experiment in emigration on such terms as Marylebone had considered. His proposed emigration of 100,000 paupers would cost £60,000 in a year, in respect of them, whereas an expenditure of £300,000 from the rates would be required for a year's maintenance for that number at home.

Criticism of Horton's proposal was concentrated on the authority given parishes, under the Bill, to secure loans on their poor rates; on the unlikelihood of the success of pauper-immigrants in colonial conditions which demanded able persons; on the danger of reproducing in the colonies the British situation of redundancy (Huskisson); and on the unlikelihood of a speedy increase of colonial wealth by the arrived emigrants, unless a large expenditure had been made first on, e.g., roads and bridges in the colonies (Peel). The Bill was rejected by the Commons, nor did fresh consideration in 1830 and 1831 of its proposals lead to its enactment.

William Cobbett, thundering in his *Weekly Register* against the "colonizing, or transporting, or getting rid of" method, gave a particularly pungent criticism[1] in 1824 of the whole argument that the promotion of colonization was the only means of relieving the condition of the "redundant" masses, especially of Ireland. Satirizing the favoured argument (drawn to what fine threads in strange patterns after Adam Smith, Malthus, and Ricardo) he wrote, "In England, it was the poor rates that caused the redundant population. Take away the poor rates, said Malthus and Scarlett, and that will prevent improvident marriages and check population.[2] But in Ireland there are no poor rates, and there they marry earlier than they do in England. . . ." Similarly, the Irish multiplied because they were poorly educated, but in Scotland, "where everyone is a saint, a moralist, a philosopher," there was over population. Long internal tranquillity accounted for English over population; doubtless it was precisely the long and bloody revolution which accounted for the over population of France; and so on.

However, there would not be a social revolution in England because Cobbett and his like made discomforting references to the entire practicability, given such a revolution, of a settlement without emigration of the redundancy problem. There was not enough in Britain to go round, in the old proportions —so the poor must be "thinned" as an orchardist thins his peach branches to ensure a few fat fruit. Let the theorists come forward with a technique that practical men could use.

Such a one was forthcoming in the person of Wakefield, gaoled in Newgate for abduction. It was in the last year (1829)

[1] *Weekly Register*, June 19, 1824; *cf*. Sir Francis Burdett's speech in the House of Commons, May 7, 1824: "Colonization on a large scale is the only remedy for this redundant population."

[2] *Cf*. the argument in an anonymous pamphlet of 1819 (attributed to Sir William Elias Taunton, "of Oxford," according to a review in the *Gentleman's Magazine*, June 1819, vol. lxxxix, pp. 537 *et seq*.). In this publication the contemporary redundancy was put down "partly to the facility afforded by the poor rates, and the provisions so profusely supplied by them, to early improvident masses amongst the lower classes; and partly to other subordinate causes; amongst the principal of which is the saving of human life by the discovery of the art of inoculation."

of the long Tory dominance of English politics that his book was published which gave England most of the essentials of an emigration policy which would serve Liberal and Tory Minister alike until the middle of the century. *A Letter from Sydney* is eloquent of a high order of economic and social understanding and of appreciation of contemporary problems. Wakefield saw the possibilities of colonial development to British benefit, at this era of the release of powerful forces which demanded room for their operation. He visualized from extraordinary insight the dangerous division of English society (made rapidly and recently) into a tiny minority in control of capital and, over against them, a huge proletarianized mass. Aware that a solution of this ominous situation was impracticable, as the social tides ran, within Britain itself, he taught the Imperial Government how it might be found abroad. Wakefield reawakened consciousness of the advantage of colonies, to an intensity which Huskisson and Wilmot Horton had not aroused it. He taught that this advantage was evidently to be gained by a full use of colonial land, and that use required the export of capital and people. More than forty years' practice of using New South Wales for transportation had, he pointed out, prepared the colonial ground for the more profitable exploitation which he now advocated. "We owe everything," he said,[1] "over and above mere subsistence, to the wickedness of the people of England. Who built Sydney? Convicts. Who built the excellent roads from Sydney to Parramatta, Windsor, and Liverpool? Convicts. By whom is the land made to produce? By convicts. Why do not all our labourers exact high wages, and by taking a large share of the produce of labour prevent their employers from becoming rich? Because most of them are convicts. What has enabled the landowner readily to dispose of his surplus produce? The demand of the keepers of convicts....

"But will transports continue to exert the same happy influence on our condition? I think not. If for every acre of

[1] *A Letter from Sydney* (1829), pp. 37, 38, Everyman edition.

land that may be appropriated here there should be a conviction for felony in England, our prosperity would rest on a solid basis; but, however we may desire it, we cannot expect that the increase of crime will keep pace with the spread of colonization. . . . Every day . . . sees an increase in the quantity of land, whilst the quantity of labour remains the same."

This wholly admirable statement of the position—the clearer, perhaps, for the author's remoteness from the scene his book purports to describe—may not be bettered by the verdict of history given a century later. Certainly Egerton's conclusions assess the factors in much the same way. He writes,[1] "Undoubtedly, from the point of view of the Mother Country, transportation was an economical measure, while from the colonial point of view it rendered possible those 'preparatory works' (e.g. roads and bridges and wharfage) without which free settlement would remain impossible. . . . It would seem that the (transportation) system encouraged free emigration by providing the settler with markets, and above all by 'assigning' him cheap and efficient labour. It is reckoned that, in the first thirty-four years of Australia, more than ten million pounds were expended in it by the British Government. Can anyone suppose that the spending of this money was not of advantage to the free colonists?"

Transportation having then in this manner prepared the colonial field for a British society now under a pressing necessity of expansion, how should British enterprise plant seed that should return an abundant harvest? Wakefield offered a system.[2] The requirements of a systematic colonization according to him were these:

(1) The declaration by authority of a fixed price per acre of land; this should be a "sufficient price" in the sense of an amount

---

[1] *Op. cit.*, p. 227.

[2] Wakefield, *op. cit.*, pp. 100 *et seq.*; *cf.* K. B. Smellie, *op. cit.*, p. 91, on the "tremendous complications of the legal and political tradition" through which "rationalizers" like Wakefield, Owen, etc., had to force their ideas.

which should be high enough to prevent a person without capital from soon acquiring land from wage-savings.
(2) All land grants should be taxable on their rent.
(3) The proceeds of land sales and taxation should be devoted to an emigration fund for providing labourers with free passages to the colony.
(4) The trustees of the fund should be empowered to borrow on the security of the constant fund.
(5) The immigrant labour supply should "be as nearly as possible proportioned to the demand at each settlement, so that capitalists should never suffer from an urgent want of labourers, and that labourers should never want well paid employment."
(6) Young emigrants should be preferred and a proper balance of the sexes maintained.
(7) Colonists paying an emigrant's passage should be reimbursed from the emigration fund.

With two minor specifications these articles made up the nine commandments of colonization according to Wakefield. We may infer from the content of his writings that he could not have devised his system had it not been for the observed condition of British society on the one hand and the several British colonial societies on the other, at a time of over-supply on the part of the first and under-supply on the part of the second. He would not have been listened to with the immediacy of attention which was in fact given his ideas, had authority in Britain not been uneasily aware of the difficulties which he proposed to resolve—redundant population imposing an increasing economic and social burden, and capital lacking sufficient attractive ground for investment on the one hand; on the other hand inadequate population and capital, and in consequence insufficient development of land and resources. The application or adaptation of Wakefield's ideas in Canada, New Zealand, and several of the Australian colonies represents the first major impulse of British colonization in the nineteenth century. The foundation in 1829 of a settlement at Swan River, Western Australia, by a syndicate reduced in practice to Thomas

Peel, a cousin of Sir Robert Peel, and some individuals, was permitted by British Government grants of land there. There was no settlement about that coast at this time, and the impracticable scheme was a costly failure. With the foundation of a colony of South Australia in the middle 'thirties, however, and a radical alteration of land regulation in New South Wales and Van Diemen's Land in 1831, colonization somewhat after Wakefield's pattern received trial over wide areas. However, the suitability of Eastern Australian land above all for sheep breeding would qualify seriously the usefulness of Wakefield's scheme, which had contemplated colonial agriculture rather than grazing, as applied to these colonial territories.

The chief matter for present consideration, however, is the broad reform of colonial policy which the Liverpool Government achieved by Canning's and Huskisson's measures of the 1820's. And this reformed policy provided, as it were, a taking-off ground for Wakefield's theory of colonization. The reciprocity principle which by 1825 Huskisson had substituted for the old mercantilist principle of monopoly, in his Act 6 George IV, cap. 114, had been established against strenuous opposition. "Notwithstanding the difficulty . . . to Mr. Huskisson's admission into the Cabinet," Canning's intimate, Stapleton, wrote[1] of changes in the Liverpool Ministry in 1823, "Mr. Canning did not rest long without securing it." Canning had himself gained pre-eminence in the Ministry only upon Castlereagh's death in August 1822. Next year Frederick ("Prosperity") Robinson, who would be Viscount Goderich, then Earl Ripon, was promoted from the Presidency of the Board of Trade to the vacant Exchequer, and Canning called Huskisson to Robinson's vacated department. "There was considerable divergency of opinion between Mr. Canning and some of his colleagues," Stapleton records, "as to the principles on which the foreign policy of the country was to be conducted; but Mr. Canning, supported, as he was, by the Premier and

[1] *George Canning and His Times*, by A. G. Stapleton, p. 576; London, Parker, 1859.

Mr. Peel, and afterwards by the King, succeeded in carrying his own views." Huskisson had been expeditious in practising in the field of his department the flexible policy which Canning advocated. Already in 1823 he had by two Acts (3 George IV, cc. 44, 45) thrown open commerce between British colonies and all American States in British ships or ships of the American country supplying the colonies. In 1825 followed his Reciprocity Act, and various measures designed to assist that more extensive use of colonial land which Wakefield would soon be advocating. Such measures were an Act giving a charter to the Van Diemen's Land Company (6 George IV, cap. 39) and another giving a charter to the Canada Company (6 George IV, cap. 75). In the same year the Home Secretary, Sir Robert Peel, secured a further Act (6 George IV, cap. 96) regulating the segregation of second offenders from the New South Wales community and regulating the powers of magistrates.

Again—and second only to the Reciprocity Act in the manufacture of the new colonial system—the Order in Council which the triumvirate secured from George IV on March 23, 1825, sought to gather the scattered colonies into an imperial system by requiring the Colonial Governments to abandon for sterling the old international monetary basis which all of them had used or were using at various levels of inflation. This was the Spanish or Mexican dollar, which had then 290 years' history as the accepted counter of international trade. The Order in Council of March 23rd declared,[1] "with a view of securing the circulation of . . . (British) money in those colonies . . . in all those colonies where the Spanish dollar is now, either by law, fact, or practice, considered as a legal tender for the discharge of debt . . . a tender and payment of British silver money to the amount of 4s. 4d. should be considered as equivalent . . . to one Spanish dollar." We shall see (Chapter 7) that in the sequel of this measure New

[1] The Order in Council is reprinted in *Historical Records of Australia*, I, xi, 637, 638, and in *A History of Currency in the British Colonies*, by Robert Chalmers, p. 425; London, H.M. Stationery Office, 1893.

South Wales was given for the first time a financial basis comprehensive enough and secure enough to serve the enlarged needs of a free, instead of a prison, economy. Also, on the day of the publication of this Order in Council which grouped the colonies with Britain on sterling, Huskisson addressed[1] the House of Commons on the methods, objects, and implications of his imperial policy, in a speech which conveys clearly the wide new view which the New Tories were taking of the post-war world.

A conscious effort to promote emigration went with such statements and enactments of an expanding colonial policy. Three weeks after Huskisson's speech on imperial policy the House of Commons voted £30,000 to finance the emigration to Canada of Southern Irish poor—pursuing, again in this later instance, the policy of encouragement which, whether of colonial trade or colonial peopling, had been embarked upon in 1823. On this occasion Robinson, the Chancellor of the Exchequer, stated[2] in his turn the Canning policy which saw a situation which must be resolved without delay. Speaking in reply to a suggestion that the House ought to appoint a committee to enquire into emigration, before it made specific votes, he said that such a committee would be appointed— but that must not serve as an excuse for the shelving of the immediate vote of funds. The House voted the money. (A member, Spring Rice, gave during the debate this interesting view of the contemporary position, "Emigration is an experiment which has been tried and has failed; and now it is asked to try the same experiment again. . . . Formerly, the peasantry of Ireland looked on this system of emigration as only a genteel mode of transportation; but now they were anxious to emigrate to any place where they could find an honest mode of subsistence.")

With a lively sense of the basic issues of British home,

[1] *Vide Annual Register*, 1825 (*History of Europe*), pp. 99 *et seq.*, for his speech.
[2] *Parliamentary Debates, Second Series*, vol. xii, 1825, cols. 1358 *et seq.*

foreign, and imperial policy, Canning and his coadjutors established a system by which the British colonies including New South Wales, and the former Spanish and Portuguese colonies in America were advanced in population, finance, and trade; and they established this system of expansion, not out of altruism but out of their realization of the urgent needs of British population, finance, and trade. "I delighted in raising these people into States," Canning wrote[1] in October 1825, referring to the ex-colonies in South America . . . "This time twelvemonth it was a question whether there should be any new States at all." And he stated his view that an occasional rap over the knuckles was salutary in reminding the Mexicans, the Columbians, and the Guatemalans of the reason for and the contingency of their existence as citizens of independent States.

So with the Australian colonies; although as prisons these were still valuable, the Government understood that they might serve a larger need, and if it did not "delight" in raising New South Wales from prison to colony, at least Huskisson and Goderich assisted in that process in a recognition of its value to the British interest. When Robinson became Viscount Goderich and, as Colonial Secretary in Lord Grey's Whig Ministry, adopted quickly Wakefield's conception, he was simply taking advantage of a proffered form for that content which he and his fellow assistants of Canning had perceived years before *A Letter from Sydney*; "and so," as Canning said,[2] "behold! the New World established, and, if we do not throw it away, ours!"

The Australian sphere of that New World was not however established with anything like the rapidity with which Canning's policy was able to convert the American sphere into something resembling a British economic establishment. Several experiments of colonization in Australia were made even as the early freighters of the Australian wool trade from

[1] Canning to Lord Granville, October 11, 1825; *cit.* Stapleton, *op. cit.*, p. 445.   [2] *Ibid.*

Sydney and Hobart astonished the ports of call on the long homeward route. Some of the experiments were abortive—the second attempt, on the shores of Westernport, at Port Phillip settlement, and two attempts to make a settlement in North Australia, and, for the most part, two attempts at settlement in Western Australia.

Nevertheless the inflow of capital into Australia from the early 1820's (*vide* Chapter 7 *infra*) proceeded uninterruptedly, and this phase of the economic history of Australia represents a very good example, comparable in essential respects with the South American examples, of the investment accompanying the flag which trade followed throughout the nineteenth century. Great companies were chartered, in the expansive years after recovery from the post-war slump, to invest hundreds of thousands of pounds in Australian pastures, farms, and mines. India and the East Indies had long been the scene of operations of the greatest of all chartered companies, the East India Company. Then in 1825 a New Zealand Company and in 1826 a Canada Company were chartered, in addition to the Australian Agricultural Company and the Van Diemen's Land Company. It might turn out that the three Australasian colonies, and Canada, were not, in their undeveloped condition, perfect ground for the kind of enterprise represented by the chartered company; the convicts whom the Australian Agricultural and Van Diemen's Land Companies were to employ on the huge areas granted them were not serviceable substitutes for the docile native labour which the East India Company could conscript, and it was found that empty lands not obviously studded with natural riches were fields rather for individual adventurers than for shareholders in Bayswater or Edinburgh. But fields had to be found, which could be made to yield dividends on the enormous capital available for investment in the hands of British entrepreneurs. And Canada, New South Wales, and Van Diemen's Land almost exhausted the waste lands then claimed by the British; the Dutch had pioneered at the Cape of Good Hope, and the observed prospect of investment there was now very straitly limited; Canning's shrewd game with the decayed mercantile empires of Spain and Portugal in South America opened a vast prospect there, but in South America, too, as the investors of hundreds of millions in company shares and bank loans learned to their cost in 1825, all that glittered was not gold.

Such hard lessons were it seemed becoming the "normal" lot of post-war investors every hundred years—with the melancholy examples of John Law and the *Banque Royale*, *Mississippi Scheme* and *Compagnie des Indes*, and the South Sea Bubble a century before the South American bubble burst, and with Hatry, Kreuger, Stavisky and Insull to come a century after Canning's time. But indeed peacetime from 1815 had been a period of anxious questing on the part of British holders of capital, for territories which might be used for production and trade. The East India Company itself, deprived under the peace settlement of its wartime gains made at Dutch expense, was restless on its narrowed terrain, and, perforce handing back in 1816 the rich prize of Java, was glad enough to have Thomas Stamford Raffles, Governor of Java from 1811, buy Singapore in its behalf, from a native potentate, in 1819. Still, the English were naturally not *persona grata* with the restored masters of the Indies, and when one W. Barns proposed in 1823 the establishment of a British trade base on the northern coast of the Australian continent, handy to the East Indies and Malaya, John Company lent an ear. There was now no British possession of value in the Indies, Barns pointed out;[1] "the Dutch are consequently fully engrossing the whole of that trade, and having shut all their ports to the British flag"—evidently in ignorance of Huskisson's wish for reciprocity—were seeking to maintain a monopoly of the island riches.

---

[1] Barns to Wilmot Horton, September 25, 1823, *Historical Records of Australia*, III, v, p. 737.

North Australia

In the same year P. P. King returned a survey of the North Australian coast, and the Company's East India Trade committee supported Barns's representations to the Colonial Office.[1] The committee argued that a North Australian settlement might be at once a useful base for trade with the Malays and a naval station in a strategically good position. The Secretary of State saw the point, with the sequel that in July 1824 Captain J. J. G. Bremer, in H.M.S. *Tamar*, arrived at Port Jackson *en route* to the north. The Governor, Brisbane, was prompt in the execution of his instructions[2] to forward the expedition, and within a month the ships *Countess of Harcourt* and *Lady Nelson* sailed with H.M.S. *Tamar* for the Gulf of Carpentaria. Troops, convicts, four civil officials, and three free labourers, to a total landing party of seventy-six, sailed in the colonial vessels. The area claimed by Britain in Australia was augmented by a shifting of the imagined frontier line six degrees westward, and a settlement was made on Melville Island in the Gulf. Brought under the New South Wales Government in 1825, at the close of Brisbane's administration, North Australia did not profit for that, and in April 1826 Bathurst sent out a second expedition, under Captain James Stirling in H.M.S. *Success*, to make a settlement at another point. He arrived at Port Jackson in November, and Darling, the Governor, following his instructions,[3] sent three other ships north with the man-o'-war, to make a settlement at Raffles Bay in June 1827. The newer settlement did not prosper more than the older. Relief was sent from Sydney in March 1828, and in May the Secretary of State ordered the removal to Raffles Bay of the whole establishment at Melville Island,

---

[1] Most of the matter in this summary account is to be found in the editor's introduction to *Historical Records of Australia*, III, v, pp. i–xvii.

[2] Bathurst to Brisbane, February 17, 1824, *Historical Records of Australia*, I, xi, pp. 227 *et seq.*

[3] Bathurst to Darling, May 30, 1826; *ibid.*, xii, p. 339.

This was carried out in January 1829, but in May the evacuation of Raffles Bay in its turn was carried out after Whitehall's instruction of November 1828.[1] Neither Melville Island nor Raffles Bay had been a magnet to the Malays, and still one hundred and ten years later men would be discussing the imperial strategy's urgent need of a naval base in North Australia.

Hokianga

But the *Lady Nelson* brig that sailed with Bremer, and that Captain Stirling who commanded H.M.S. *Tamar*, played parts in colonization of, ultimately, a more remunerative kind. Before passing to the colonization of Van Diemen's Land and Western Australia, those comparatively successful establishments, we may note that developing New South Wales was itself strong enough, about this time, to provide capital and personnel that would seek to turn another English loss, of the expansive era, into a colonial gain. The New Zealand Company, formed in London in the year of boom and crisis 1825, had sunk £20,000 in futile effort, from the end of 1826, to exploit the hinterland of Hokianga Harbour, at the northern extremity of the unsettled North Island of New Zealand. After a few weeks the company pioneers abandoned the territory which they had bought of the natives, and sailed across the Tasman Sea to Port Jackson, where they arrived in February 1828. They sold their stores and equipment in Sydney.[2]

In April, Darling included in his half-yearly report the note, "A kind of trading establishment has lately been formed by two merchants of Sydney at the port of Shukianga (n.b. Hokianga) on the north-west coast of New Zealand for the purpose of securing New Zealand flax and pine logs, which

---

[1] *Vide Historical Records of Australia*, III, vi, pp. xix *et seq.*; I, xiv, pp. 214–215, 411.

[2] *Historical Records of Australia*, I, xiv, note 42, p. 912, and Darling to Bathurst, April 10, 1828; *ibid.*, p. 133.

promises some success." The Sydney venture had a 40-ton schooner for trade, and another, of 150 tons, building; some of the New Zealand Company's stranded workmen had joined the new company.

The little Hokianga enterprise is of interest here as indicating the degree of stability to which the reorganization of New South Wales during the 1820's must have attained, that merchants of Sydney should be setting up already as merchant adventurers beyond their own shores. Men who in lean seasons sent ships to Valparaiso for wheat, and to the Cape, Mauritius, and Calcutta for meat, who were reluctantly forgetting the feel of Spanish dollars, Dutch guilders, and sicca rupees, and who were brothers to the exploring adventurers of the far-off rivers and coasts of an unsurveyed continent, might, it is true, have been expected to think in terms of the broadest horizons. But their investment of what Mr. Wemmick called portable property in remote speculation could scarcely have been possible without an enhanced security at home in the old colony.

WESTERNPORT

Similarly animated, the Colonial-born Hamilton Hume had set out in October 1824 from his holding at Lake George, New South Wales, on a journey through untrodden country to the southern coast of the continent. There, at the entrance to Port Phillip Bay, Lieutenant-Colonel David Collins had attempted half-heartedly, in 1803-4, to make a Crown settlement; he had left, "by no means satisfied with the prospect." Along the coast a little to the east, Westernport had been discovered by George Bass in 1798; James Grant and Francis Barrallier had surveyed the area, landing from the *Lady Nelson*, three years later, and in 1804-5 John Oxley and Charles Robbins had reported against any attempt to make a Government settlement there. Hume, with Captain William Hilton Hovell, reached the southern coast, having crossed the great Murrumbidgee and Murray Rivers and the breadth of what would be called Victoria, and believed himself, after Hovell's calculation, to have emerged on the shores of Westernport. (What the explorers believed to be Westernport until, in 1826, Hume visited the actual Westernport,[1] was in fact Corio Bay, an indentation of the shores of Port Phillip Bay.) Hume reported[2] the country traversed as being "as fine a country as we had ever seen in any part of the colony." This journey was, truly, a harbinger of adventures on a larger scale than Thomas Raine's at Hokianga. "The discovery of the highly promising territory south of the Murrumbidgee," says Professor Scott,[3] "was in itself the most important occurrence of its kind since the crossing of the Blue Mountains eleven years before." The authorities of Sydney, however, made no more of Hume's account of fertile soil inland than an inducement to plant convicts by the seaside; but another Colonial, John Batman, New South Wales born and settled in Van Diemen's Land, saw larger possibilities. An associate in the settlement which Batman made subsequently at Port Phillip related[4] ". . . Batman telling me that when he was in Sydney, he had heard from a schoolfellow, Hamilton Hume, who with Captain Hovell had explored the neighbourhood of Port Phillip, that the country there was of the finest description, and that this information had dwelt in his mind."

Meanwhile, Darling's Government, instructed[5] by the Secretary of State, sent its expedition to Westernport. The Government party arrived on November 24, 1826, six days after the departure in *l'Astrolabe* of Dumont d'Urville, the

[1] *Vide The Cambridge History of the British Empire*, vol. vii, part i, p. 124.

[2] *Sydney Gazette*, February 10, 1825, *cf.* Sydney *Australian*, January 27, 1825: "They report the country from latitude 36 degrees (n.b., that is, from the Murray River south) to Westernport to be remarkably rich, and much superior to the county of Argyleshire or Bathurst" (n.b., in New South Wales).

[3] *Vide Cambridge History of the British Empire*, chapter v, for Professor Scott's account.

[4] . . . to James Bonwick, *vide* his *Port Phillip Settlement*, pp. 124 *et seq.*; London, Sampson Low, Marsden, Searle and Rivington, 1883.

[5] Bathurst to Darling, March 1, 1826, xii, pp. 193 *et seq.*

latest French voyager to haunt the dreams of Whitehall with figments of competitive colonization in Australia. The party of soldiers and convicts found two acres in cultivation on Phillip Island in Westernport, representing the labour of sealers who had come there from Van Diemen's Land a few months earlier. The country behind Westernport on the mainland was so obviously unsuitable for settlement that the site was abandoned by Darling's men in January 1828, the Governor having earlier advised Whitehall that it would be useless to continue.[1]

To date, then, the Crown's moves had been remarkably ineffective, in the second period of peace. Actually the less elaborate efforts made in 1802-3, in the pause between wars, had been much more successful—as their memorial, the now separate colony of Van Diemen's Land, could show. While the ill-conceived convict settlement at Westernport was dragging out its existence—in literal fact "solitary, poor, nasty, brutish, and short"—the principal need of the Tasmanian settlements on the southern side of Bass Strait was more convicts. Surely a felt need of labour, in a colony not much more than twenty years old, augured well.

Van Diemen's Land

The original settlement of Van Diemen's Land (Tasmania) had been made with the object, *inter alia*, of forestalling the French. For as in the later and longer peacetime, so in 1802-3 it had been apprehended that, the strain of war removed, England's last serious competitor as a maritime, colonizing power for the mastery of the world would bid again for unappropriated areas. In May 1802 King had suggested[2] a settlement at Port Phillip. He argued, from the favourable reports of the place by Captain Matthew Flinders and Lieutenant

[1] Darling to Bathurst, April 6, 1827, xiii, pp. 239, 240.
[2] King to Portland, May 21, 1802, I, ii, p. 490; enclosure No. 2, p. 491, gives details of the Port Phillip establishment proposed.

Murray, that it seemed advantage might be derived (1) by the cultivation of the good soil there; (2) by a distribution for safety of the numerous convicts who must be expected after a termination of the war (peace had been made in March, but King could not know that until much later); and (3) by anticipating French colonizers. It may not be without significance, as an additional factor, that the possibilities of the Australian whale fishery were in King's consideration at this time. For all these reasons (and no others were given) the settlement of Port Phillip was decided upon by the British Government and King was so notified by despatch of February 24, 1803.[1]

The Port Phillip district which King had named after the first Governor of New South Wales, under whom he had served and in whose office he now found himself, would be of especial value in supplying an alternative place of reception for convicts, while King was proceeding with his task of reorganizing New South Wales after the military oligarchy.

Lieutenant-Colonel David Collins, appointed in England to be Lieutenant-Governor of Port Phillip, sailed in H.M.S. *Calcutta* from Yarmouth on April 27, 1803 (just before the resumption of war with France) and arrived at the heads of Port Phillip Bay on October 9th. (Collins, an officer of the Royal Marines, had as Judge-Advocate, comported himself outside the Sydney officers' trading ring.) King had anticipated imperial approval of his proposals for further settlement, for the French exploring ships *Le Géographe* and *Le Naturaliste* cleared Port Jackson on November 17, 1802, and the Governor, fearful of designs on the unsettled island of Van Diemen's Land in his Government, decided to make a settlement on the Derwent River, in the southern part of the island.[2] His reasons were precisely similar to those advanced for the Port Phillip settlement being organized in England. An expedition was fitted out in haste at Port Jackson, after the arrival of H.M.S. *Glatton* on March 11, 1803, had provided the means. Lieutenant

[1] Hobart to King, February 24, 1803, I, iv, pp. 8 *et seq.*   [2] I, iv, p. 249.

John Bowen and Jacob Mountgarrett were borrowed from her to be commandant and surgeon respectively at the Derwent.[1] Three months after the *Glatton's* arrival they set off in the *Lady Nelson* for Van Diemen's Land. Settlement was made at length at Risdon Cove, near modern Hobart, by troops, convicts, and free settlers,[2] landed in September from the *Lady Nelson* and the *Albion* whaler. But Collins, having found "not . . . fit for a settlement"[3] the rocks and sands of Sorrento near the entrance to Port Phillip Bay, landed at Risdon Cove on February 16, 1804, from the *Ocean* convict ship, in which he had brought his convicts and free settlers from England for Port Phillip settlement. Four days later he condemned Bowen's site, and selected the site of modern Hobart in the alternative. Assuming command as Lieutenant-Governor, Collins mustered a party at least five times the numerical strength of the personnel King had sent. His people comprised 26 troops, 6 civil officials, 13 free settlers, 178 male convicts, and three other men (including a botanist), 15 women, and 21 children.[4]

The first settlement of Port Phillip was attempted, then, and the first settlement of Van Diemen's Land made, with free emigrants in addition to convicts. Other free persons (many of them ex-convicts) were evacuated from Norfolk Island during the years following. (The Norfolk Island establishment was considered too expensive and too difficult of access.)[5]

---

[1] For Bowen's instructions *vide* I, iv, pp. 152 *et seq.*
[2] For the free settlers *vide* III, i, p. 804.
[3] King to Bowen, November 26, 1803, III, i, p. 206. The *Journal* of the Reverend Robert Knopwood, chaplain in Collins's party, contains a useful account of the abortive colonizing attempt at Port Phillip and the happier Tasmanian venture.
[4] Collins to King, February 29, 1804, enclosure No. 2, III, i, p. 227; according to Collins to King, November 5, 1803 (III, i, pp. 26 *et seq.*), Collins had 299 male convicts with him at Port Phillip and 47 marines.
[5] *Vide* for the Norfolk Island operation Hobart to King, June 24, 1804, I, iv, p. 304; King to Foveaux (Lieut.-Gov. at N.I.), July 20, 1804, I, v. pp. 24 *et seq.*; Foveaux's General Order of May 8, 1804; Collins to Castlereagh, August 20, 1808, September 1, 1808, May 10, 1809; Collins to Foveaux, October 10, 1808; III, i, pp. 399, 400, 403, 421, 407; Liverpool to Macquarie, July 26, 1811, I, vii, p. 363; Macquarie to Davie, January 30, 1813, III, ii, p. 17.

The Norfolk Island farmers were to be re-settled on favourable terms. The first of them to be transferred arrived at Hobart in the *Lady Nelson* on November 28, 1807 (three years after receipt of the instruction from Whitehall), others next year in H.M.S. *Porpoise* and the *Lady Nelson*, *Estremina*, and *City of Edinburgh*, to a total of 202 settlers. These, with their families, and 23 Norfolk Island convicts, made a grand total of 554 persons removed from Norfolk Island. But the changes had been rung in New South Wales administration, through King, Bligh, Johnston, Paterson, and Foveaux, and Macquarie was Governor, while still (until 1811) the Imperial Government was issuing orders for the evacuation. Actually the operation was completed only after nine years, when in early 1813 the last of the Norfolk Island farmers were removed to Port Dalrymple, the northern Van Diemen's Land settlement. (Norfolk Island was re-established as a penitentiary on June 6, 1825, by Major R. Turton, after instructions of July 1824.)

The early story of the Tasmanian settlements' struggle for subsistence is very like a repetition of the story of early Sydney, saving the important particular that the little encampments on the Derwent and the Tamar could be succoured from an Australian headquarters. Collins's officers were asking for land grants, and complaining of their lack of convict servants, within six months of the arrival of the *Calcutta* and the *Ocean* at the Derwent River.[1]

But whaling experiments from Phillip's time now gave Van Diemen's Land hope of a means towards self-support, and the Hobart harbourmaster, William Collins, began whaling operations off southern Van Diemen's Land in the first year of the new settlement. In the July-September season, he pointed

[1] *Cf.* Collins to King, August 1, 1804, III, i, p. 255, and note General Order of August 11, 1804, *ibid.*, p. 522, forbidding officers in Van Diemen's Land to engage in trading. This was in expectation of the arrival of the *Lady Barlow*, whose cargo for Van Diemen's Land was ultimately sold at 50 per cent profit from the Hobart Government store, according to the practice instituted in New South Wales after Lord Hobart's instruction of January 1802.

out,[1] black whales were numerous in those waters, schools of fifty or sixty having been sighted from Hobart itself; a good trade might be had if a small whaling fleet were fitted out. The Lieutenant-Governor gave William Collins permission in early 1805 to establish whaling stations, and a year later made regulations for the conduct of the people employed at the station, at Relph's Bay, which William Collins had made his base. By 1810 John Oxley could report[2] that oil up to 600 tons was got in a successful season. And when the season for chasing sperm whales was over, that for black whales began, and sealing was an auxiliary enterprise.

Farming had been engaged in without delay. In the first seven years of Tasmanian settlement King, Paterson, and Macquarie granted more than 5,000 acres to about 40 settlers.[3] Nearly 300 farmers had more than 2,000 acres in cultivation in 1813. By 1817 the area under crop exceeded 4,500 acres and Van Diemen's Land was able to send 22,000 bushels of wheat to New South Wales after the Hawkesbury floods had diminished the old colony's yield. In 1819 a population of 4,000, more than 8,000 cultivated acres, and flocks of nearly 200,000 sheep, measured the progress of Van Diemen's Land.[4]

Government encouragement of breeding for fine wool was forthcoming early in Van Diemen's Land, as in New South Wales, where King was from early 1805 following Camden's directions. When Lieutenant Lord of the Royal Marines, deputy-commandant in Van Diemen's Land, took ewes with him from Sydney to Hobart, King "made him a present of a ram as near the Spanish breed as Government is in possession of," and sent two more for the Government flock at Hobart. "The amelioration of the wool throughout these colonies (being) an object much recommended by his Majesty's Government," King wrote, it would be desirable that the Hobart flock

---
[1] III, i, pp. 276 *et seq.*
[2] Oxley's *Report on the Settlement of Van Diemen's Land* (late 1810), *ibid.*, p. 580. For other details of whaling *vide* Collins to Hobart, February 26, 1805, *ibid.*, p. 316, General Order of March 10, 1806, *ibid.*, p. 539.
[3] For details *vide ibid.*, p. 568.   [4] III, iii, pp. 583, 585, 821.

should be furnished with rams nearer the true Spanish breed, "when they can be obtained from the individuals who now possess them."[1] Fifteen years later Macquarie bought 300 merinos from John Macarthur (*vide* Chapter 5 (*a*) *supra*) and sent them for sale to Van Diemen's Land graziers for the improvement of flocks.

About the period of this last transaction emigrants purporting to have some capital were being encouraged to settle in the island, Government following the Macquarie-Bigge system of land grants in proportion to capital held. King had foreshadowed this system as we saw (Chapter 3 (*c*) *supra*) by giving to immigrants of gentle birth larger grants than were customary. Thus in 1804, only a few months after the beginning of settlement at the Derwent, he had made a special grant to Alexander Reilly.[2] Further, as the free settlers accompanying Bowen's original landing party received special privileges, and as the hundreds transferred from Norfolk Island were given each approximately double the acreage they had held, Van Diemen's Land may be said to have placed emphasis, from its early years, on a free farming community. From 1821 more particularly, when 71 emigrants arrived with letters of recommendation from the Secretary of State (and four ships brought nearly 700 convicts), the free population was augmented. Free people were actually in the majority in 1823, to increase in greater ratio than the bond population thereafter, except in 1830–31 and 1834–35, years of exceptionally busy transportation activity.[3] In England the under-secretaries had to receive many aspirants for Tasmanian land grants, and in 1825 a circular for intending emigrants was made available at the

[1] King to Collins, September 26, 1805, III, i, p. 326. Collins's reply (November 2, 1805, *ibid.*, p. 335) ran: "I purpose, and indeed always intended, to pay particular attention to the growth and improvement of wool. . . . If Palmer (n.b., John Palmer, Deputy Commissary-General at Sydney) has, as he promised, sent me any ewes on my own account by the *Sydney*, I shall assign a Spaniard to their use, and carefully mark the amelioration of the wool."

[2] *Historical Records of Australia*, I, v, pp. 126–27.

[3] III, iv, pp. 1, 2, and *cf. Governor Arthur's Convict System*, by W. D. Forsyth, p. 103; London, Longmans, 1935.

Colonial Office.[1] The typical letter[2] approving an emigrant would read: "I am directed by Lord Bathurst to acquaint you (n.b. the Lieutenant-Governor) that his Lordship has granted permission to Mr. —— to proceed as a settler to Van Diemen's Land, and I am to desire that you will make him a grant of land proportioned to his means of cultivation and to allow him any reasonable indulgence in the selection of it." When the arrived emigrant's selection had been approved by the Government surveyors, his application would be forwarded to Sydney, together with a recommendation by the Lieutenant-Governor. A grant would be made then by the Governor of New South Wales in the prescribed form.[3]

In this post-war period the flow from the British Isles was increasing, to both Australian colonies. Not only more con-

---

[1] *Cf.* Bathurst to Arthur, September 28, 1825, III, v, p. 382; for copy of circular, *vide* I, xii, pp. 454 *et seq.*

[2] Horton to Arthur, January 6, 1824, III, v, p. 104; *et vide* I, xi, pp. 83 *et seq.* for Bathurst's instructions in respect of additional grants of land in Van Diemen's Land.

[3] Specimen form of grant of 1,500 acres (*vide History of Tasmania*, by John West, i, p. 141; Hobart, 1852):—

> "Whereas full power and authority for granting lands in the territory of New South Wales are vested in his Majesty's captain-general and governor-in-chief . . . (etc.) . . . under the royal sign manual, bearing date respectively the 25th day of April 1787, and the 20th day of August 1789:
> "In pursuance of the power and authority vested in me as aforesaid, I do by these presents give and grant unto   his heirs and assigns, to have and to hold for ever 1500 acres of land lying and situate in the   district . . . bounded . . . (etc.) . . . to be had and held by him the said   his heirs and assigns, free from all taxes, quit rents and other acknowledgments, for the space of five years from the date hereof; provided always, and it is hereby expressed to be understood that the said   the grantee in these presents named, shall in no ways directly or indirectly sell, alienate, or transfer any part or parcel of the land hereby granted within the said term of five years; and also provided always that the said   shall clear and cultivate . . . within the said term of five years, the quantity of 75 acres of the said land hereby granted, otherwise the whole of the said land hereby granted shall revert to the Crown . . .(the grantee shall pay) an annual quit rent of 30s. after the term of five years. . . ."

victs and more small capitalists were coming, but larger capital, whether in the form of enterprises like the Van Diemen's Land and Australian Agricultural Companies, or in individual enterprises like that of Timothy Nowlan, the Tasmanian later counterpart of Macarthur's protégé, Walter Davidson. Nowlan, an Irish woolgrower, brought with him in the *Mangles*, in 1822, fifty merino sheep, with two shepherds and two woolsorters. Bathurst recommended him for special consideration. Nowlan, like the directors of the Van Diemen's Land Company, was interested in the island primarily as a scene for fine-wool production.[1]

The Van Diemen's Land Company, given letters patent on November 1, 1825, and a charter on November 11th, under Act 6 George IV, cap. 39, was floated with a capital of £1,000,000. It was to have remission of quit rents on lands granted to it, according to the number of convicts for whom it found employment. Special Commissioners were appointed for the selection of land for the company. In March 1826 a panel of Commissioners for the Survey of Lands in Van Diemen's Land was appointed to survey the colony at large. (The first Commissioners were Edward Dumaresq (Chief Commissioner), Peter Murdoch, and Roderic O'Connor.) Edward Curr, agent in Van Diemen's Land for the company, wished the company's selections to be limited to pasture and arable land, but Arthur, the Lieutenant-Governor, preferred to make a larger grant, inclusive of barren land in respect of which no quit rent would be charged. In 1826 the company established itself at Circular Head.[2]

At about this time, too, land grants to expirees were discontinued.[3] In sum, Van Diemen's Land was erected, like the

[1] Bathurst to Sorell, April 20, 1822, III, v, pp. 51–52

[2] Bathurst to Arthur, June 2, 1825, Arthur to Bathurst, November 15, 1826, III, v, pp. 271 *et seq.*, 398 *et seq.*

[3] *Cf.* Arthur to Hay, March 23, 1827, enclosure, Minutes of the Executive Council of Van Diemen's Land, evidence of Major James T. Morisset; III, v, pp. 665 *et seq.*: "The practice of giving grants of land to prisoners, merely because they had become free by servitude, has been discontinued," *et vide* (*a*) *supra*.

older colony, into a terrain for unconvicted persons of some means, able to employ ex-prisoners of the Crown. So, of more than 63,000 acres granted in 1826 to 119 persons, five-eighths was granted in parcels of at least 500 acres, to 24 persons.[1] There were now more than 6,000 convicts in Van Diemen's Land, of whom about five per cent became free by servitude each year.[2]

The colony was, nevertheless, short of labour, while its farmers were exporting wheat to New South Wales, the Cape of Good Hope, and the Dutch East Indies, and wool to England.[3] And although in 1826 the Van Diemen's Land economy suffered some ill effects, after two successive harvest failures and the changeover from a dollar to a sterling currency system,[4] Arthur could refuse an application by the great Van Diemen's Land Company for even twenty-five convicts.[5] Replying to the application, made under clause 5 of the company's charter (relating to remission of quit rent), Arthur wrote, "His Excellency deems that in forming such an arrangement with the company, His Majesty's Government laboured under a misapprehension as to the state of the colony; for, instead of a pecuniary allowance being made to individuals for relieving the Crown by employing convicts, it is not to be denied that, at this time, settlers would cheerfully give a bonus for a very considerable number of men of good character." During Sorell's term of seven years, before Arthur, as Lieutenant-Governor, more than 5,000 convicts were sent to Van Diemen's Land (early 1817 to early 1824); in the six years 1824–29 the number sent was nearly 6,000, and in the five years 1830–34, more than 10,000.[6] In the first year (1824) of

[1] 1826 return, III, v, p. 709.   [2] *Ibid.*, p. 295.
[3] *Vide* III, v, pp. 700 *et seq.*
[4] By Van Diemen's Land Act of September 22, 1826, corresponding to the New South Wales Dollar Act Repeal Act of the month before (7 Geo. IV, No. 3 (Van Diemen's Land), ditto (New South Wales)).
[5] Acting Colonial Secretary Hamilton to Edward Curr, October 6, 1826, III, v, p. 397; *cf.* Bathurst to Darling, April 2, 1827, I, xiii, pp. 220–21, for the similar position in New South Wales.
[6] For these and the following figures, *vide* Forsyth, *op. cit.*, pp. 99, 102. The Governments of Van Diemen's Land and New South Wales were

Arthur's term, the number of free and bond persons in the colony was almost equal, at 6,000; in his last year (1836), there were 26,000 free persons as compared with 18,000 convicts in a population (including soldiers) of 43,886. The percentage of convicts in the total population was:

1822	58 %	1828	40·4 %	1833	43·4 %
1824	46·8 %	1829	40·2 %	1834	41 %
1825	46·9 %	1830	41·6 %	1835	42·1 %
1826	43·7 %	1831	44·7 %	1836	40·1 %
1827	42·9 %	1832	43·7 %	1838	39·6 %

Now, too, at the change of emigration policy after the advent to office in England of Grey's Liberals, Van Diemen's Land was to receive some of the stream of farm labourers from England, and the consequential situation was to contribute towards the restriction of transportation, which, however was, not diverted from Van Diemen's Land until after 1852.

Earlier, impulses felt in England and in New South Wales had brought to a sort of fruition yet another enterprise of British colonization in Australia. The Swan River Settlement, made in 1829 on the western coast of the continent, came into being as the nucleus of a more profitable colonial undertaking than could be achieved in North Australia.

THE SWAN RIVER SETTLEMENT

Anticipation of the French[1] in what was believed to be their design of colonization in Australia was at length a decisive

separated in 1826. From September 25, 1826 the Commissariat Department of Van Diemen's Land was separated from that of New South Wales, the Acting Commissary-General in Van Diemen's Land thenceforward corresponding with the Treasury through the Van Diemen's Land Lieut.-Governor, instead of through the Governor of New South Wales (who was still titular Governor of Van Diemen's Land), *vide* Darling to Secretary Harrison, July 22, 1826, I, xii, pp. 424–25.

[1] *Cf. History of Western Australia*, by J. S. Battye, p. 57; Oxford, 1924: "There is little doubt that the settlements at King George's Sound and Swan River were in the first place due to the activity being displayed by the French in Australian waters."

motive in a settlement of Western Australia which at first the Imperial Government did not wish to undertake or encourage. In 1827 Captain James Stirling, having presented to Darling a glowing account of his observations made along the western coast, applied for the command of a settlement to be made by the Swan River. Although in November of that year the imperial authorities denied that it was their intention to form a settlement there, Huskisson advised Darling in the following January that the project was to be made. Then Huskisson's successor as Secretary of State, Sir George Murray, gave his attention to a memorial from Thomas Peel, Sir Francis Vincent, E. W. H. Schenley, and Colonel T. P. McQueen seeking the Crown's patronage of a private colonization upon which they wished to enter at the Swan River.

This grandiose Peel scheme included a proposal to take out 10,000 emigrants at a cost of £30 a head, the promoters to be paid "for their trouble" in Western Australian land, calculated as worth 1s. 6d. an acre, to an equivalent value; cotton, tobacco, and (the obsession of Whitehall when the Botany Bay settlement was proposed more than forty years earlier) flax would be grown; and the syndicate would contribute more than a mite towards the realization of a self-contained empire—as Macarthur had promised seven years before of his New South Wales great estates plan[1]—by supplying from Western Australia "that produce for which, at the moment, the Government are indebted to Powers which would be their policy to suppress, were they in a condition so to do."

The Colonial Office gave attentive hearing to proposals so harmonious with the spirit of this age of expansion. (Earlier, sites at King George's Sound and Shark Bay had been inspected as possible settlements of reconvicted persons from New South Wales, and Major Lockyer had landed with a few convicts on the shores of King George's Sound in late 1826.[2]

[1] *Cf. Macarthur Records*, pp. 350–51.
[2] *Vide* Battye, *op. cit.*, pp. 59 *et seq.* Lockyer's instructions are reproduced in *Historical Records of Australia*, I, xii, p. 701.

This convict settlement was abandoned after Stirling assumed the command at Swan River in 1829.) At the end of 1828 the Imperial Government approved of a modified Peel plan, undertaking to grant land in proportion to capital invested, and offering the syndicate a million acres. Peel's three associates withdrew, but in January 1829 Peel accepted the Government's terms, which allowed him 250,000 acres if he should land 400 emigrants at the Swan River before November 1. Stirling had been appointed Lieutenant-Governor on December 30, 1828,[1] and on June 18, 1829, landed in Western Australia. In September the first allotments of land were made on the sites of Perth and Fremantle, and by the end of the year more than half a million acres had been granted, including 25,000 acres to Peel, who had arrived with immigrants in mid-December.

Peel's private venture failed and the colony made small progress in its early years. Immigration raised the population only from 652 in 1829 to 1,800 in 1834; and in 1840 it was still only 2,311.[2] More than a million acres was granted in 1829–30; but Western Australia at this stage offered so little inducement to persons of capital, as compared with New South Wales or Van Diemen's Land and especially, from 1834 and 1836, Port Phillip and South Australia, that Western Australian land granted in the ten years 1831–40 did not reach half a million acres more. Half a century would pass before the sorry little Swan River Settlement, at length metamorphosed by the discovery of gold in its territory inland, would as the Colony of Western Australia cut a figure in the British world.

(g) *Slavery in British Colonies*

If the Liverpool Government by the agency of Peel and Huskisson and Goderich was working out a colonial design in which Australia and British North America should be

---

[1] Battye, *op. cit.*, pp. 77 *et seq.* for digest of relevant documents in the Record Office, London, and pp. 454 *et seq.* for Stirling's instructions.

[2] *Statistical Register of Western Australia* (1900).

represented otherwise than by convict symbols, an abuse of colonization which was even less attractive than transportation was recognized as such during these years. This was slavery as practised by West Indian planters. They used slave labour upon their sugar plantations, under worse conditions than those usually accorded their assigned convict servants by the graziers and farmers of New South Wales.

On May 15, 1823, the House of Commons resolved that the various colonial legislatures of the West Indian islands should take action to ameliorate the condition of the slaves. No such action following, Orders in Council were promulgated in 1824. Still, the colonial councils did little. In six West Indian colonies whose Governments took no action whatever, there were 80,000 slaves;[1] these worst offending colonies were Antigua, Bermudas, Montserrat, Nevis, St. Kitt's, and Tortola, including the Virgin Islands. Small amelioration had been attempted even in the foremost colony, Jamaica, with 340,000 people, most in bondage, and a like reluctance was maintained by Barbados, with 70,000 to 80,000 slaves, Grenada, Demerara, and St. Vincent's. Only St. Domingo had emancipated its slaves.

This situation, like that of the transportation system as concerned New South Wales, would have to await resolution until the next decade. What concerns us at this point, however, is the evident introduction in the 1820's of an imperial policy which would require, before long, the abolition of chattel-slavery in one part of the British Empire, as it would require the abolition of assignment-slavery in another, to assist the modernizing in all its members of the world's leading producer and trader.

(h) *British Foreign Policy and British Trade, 1826*

Perhaps enough has been described of Canning's imperial and foreign policies to make readily understandable a view of those policies as harnessed to draw George IV's State carriage,

[1] *Vide Annual Register*, 1826 (*History of Europe*), p. 158.

which in Canning's unromantic vision was simply the vehicle of British economy. British interest drove the horses of imperial and foreign policy—now one, now the other—harnessed with the needs of British trade. Alone, neither the British Empire nor the international system had vitality for England's service; in harness with trade policy, either could advance untiringly along the highroads of the world. Canning's unerring direction from the box seat of the Commons and the Foreign Office secured that this should be so. In one of his letters to Granville he described a typical stage of one such typical journey. Completing at once the firm establishment of the new Republic of Columbia and a British trade connection with it, at the end of 1825 he brought Señor Hurtado, Envoy Extraordinary and Minister Plenipotentiary of Columbia, to wait upon King George IV. Canning wrote of this audience,[1] "I then told the King (in the presence of Hurtado) that I had received from Hurtado the most positive assurance of the disposition and desire of his Government to cultivate the relations of peace with all the world, but expecially with the new States of America, and especially, among *them*, with the State more immediately under His Majesty's protection, Brazil. To which Hurtado bowed, and muttered his assent, and His Majesty added, 'I rejoice to hear it,' and, turning to Hurtado, 'Peace, peace by all means and above all things. We have had thirty years of convulsions—let us all now conspire to keep the peace.' And so the audience ended." Then Canning added his conclusion already quoted, "And so, behold! the New World established, and, if we do not throw it away, ours!"

An even better instance than description of his Columbian policy could provide, of this undeviating motive of Canning's —British prosperity, British aggrandizement, as the author of every policy—is furnished by the events of 1826, of international significance, in Portugal and Spain.

That French army of intervention in Spain, with which Canning had refused to co-operate in 1823, was still in occupa-

[1] Canning to Granville, November 21, 1825; *cit.* Stapleton, *op. cit.*, p. 447.

tion. The Constitution had been suppressed and Spain's colonies lost, according to Canning's anticipation. (Indeed, he had but now disposed of another of them as planned, while Señor Hurtado replied in execrable French to George's trenchant English.) Already Britain was reaping profit from the new markets thus opened to her production (though indeed her financial magnates had made but a clumsy maiden essay of exploiting this new field for their investment: they had squandered more than £11,000,000 in highly speculative loans, mostly to South American Governments, during a few months' frenzy in the previous year).[1] But now a political crisis on the Iberian Peninsula followed the death of John IV, King of Portugal. The heir was his son Pedro. But Pedro was Emperor of Brazil, Canning's Brazil, and under the new Brazilian Constitution (which Canning had helped prepare) the sovereign of Brazil might not at the same time be sovereign of Portugal whose colony Brazil had been until lately. Pedro elected to retain his new empire, and nominated his infant daughter for the throne of Portugal. At the same time he offered the draft of a Portuguese Constitution.

Here was an opportunity for the Bourbon-Hapsburg partnership which held the power in Spain. The despotic alliance seized as best it could this opportunity of bringing Portugal on to the reactionary side in Europe. Part of the Portuguese army revolted against the proposed Constitution and crossed to Spain, where, in defiance of treaty obligations, the reactionary Government succoured them and encouraged them to return to Portugal, equipped to upset the Constitution. Now, under the 1815 Treaty of Vienna Britain was bound to go to the assistance of Portugal in the event of attack on that Government. Here then was Canning's opportunity. Spain was not a formidable adversary, and in any case was most unlikely to fight. A mere show of British force should suffice; and Canning might make a brave speech, which he did with

[1] *Vide* for a detailed statement of speculative British payments in 1825, *Annual Register*, 1825 (*Public Documents*), pp. 48 *et seq*.

eloquence in the House of Commons, to avow England's respect alike for treaty obligations and for the application of the sacred principles of freedom even to foreigners. He might, equally, frustrate the advancement of French influence on the Peninsula and prevent such restoration of Spain among the nations as Ferdinand's overrunning of Portugal would bring. All these desirable objects Canning might attain at a minimum of expense and risk. This was a situation in which positive action on the Peninsula would pay Britain best, as the 1823 situation had been one in which the guiding star of British interest pointed to negative action as best.

So, eight months before his death, England's veriest Machiavelli was able to drive the State carriage-horses of foreign policy and trade at a gallop once more. Liberals, he said gently to their representatives in the Commons, ought not to inveigh against the continued presence of French troops in Spain; was not their presence the best safeguard of the beaten Constitutionalists, who otherwise might be sacrificed to the fury of their reactionary countrymen? Nor need anyone fear that the Foreign Secretary was committing England to a fearful war. Spain was not now the redoubtable antagonist of a century ago. "Is it indeed the nation whose puissance was expected to shake England from her sphere? No, Sir, it was quite another Spain—it was the Spain within the limits of whose empire the sun never set—it was Spain with the Indies that excited the jealousies and alarmed the imaginations of our ancestors."[1] Therefore it was safe to send to Lisbon British troops numbering 5,000 in all. Successive detachments were landed on Portuguese soil from Christmas Day 1826 to New Year's Day 1827. There was no fighting. Spain ceded the point. The troops returned home. At small expenditure Britain had strengthened her hold on Portugal and Brazil, prevented Spanish revival, checked any increase of the power or influence of her chief maritime rival, France. "Statesmen

[1] *Vide* for this speech *Annual Register*, 1826 (*History of Europe*), pp. 202 et seq.

will not plunge the country into war unless its interests coincide with its sympathies," Canning had said. . . .

Canning carried his masterly policy of expedients literally to the end. In final illustration that the primary concern of his foreign policy was Britain's commercial advantage, the development of the Græco-Turkish struggle may be mentioned. Greece's struggle with absolutism, which like the struggles of the Italian and Iberian peoples had been intense since 1820, was by 1826 a matter of urgent import in British international policy. Britain was an ally of the Sultan of Turkey, and was opposed, moreover, to the extension of Russian influence by the Tsar's support of the Greek Constitutionalists against the Turkish tyranny—for it did not commend itself to Whitehall that another Great Power should sprawl over the Balkans to show teeth in the Mediterranean, whose littoral was a main field of British trade. Yet, to balance these considerations which weighed against British assistance to the Greeks, Turkey too was still a major European Power bestriding the Levant and the eastern end of the Mediterranean because of the Sultan's advantage of alliance with the Egyptian sovereign. Assessing the factors by his invariable standard of interest, Canning decided[1] that the reduction of Turkish interest should be the first advantage of England, and his policy now in 1826 was that "every engine short of war (which no English minister in his senses would dream of incurring at this time out of reverence to Aristides or St. Paul) is to be applied to beat down Turkish obstinacy"—and to establish a Greek Government which would subsist (as in the event it did subsist) in British protection. Accordingly Canning engaged Britain in a treaty with absolutist Russia and France to enforce Turkish abstention from further denial of Greek independence. A combined fleet of the three Powers, this Unholy Alliance for Freedom, patrolled the Mediterranean off the scene of hostilities. The English admiral, Codrington, commanded. It is no doubt a fine irony of history that Canning's careful precautions against

[1] *Vide* Halévy (*1815–30*), pp. 185 *et seq.*

a too active homage to Aristides and St. Paul should at last, three months after his death in August 1827, have been brought to naught by the eagerness of his admiral. The manipulator dead, the puppet lost his balance, fell on the armaments of the Sultan and the Khedive, and bloodily scattered them.

Canning had encouraged Constitutionalism and rebellion where and when it suited his country's material interest, and ignored fine causes when ignorance seemed a prudent assumption; refused to intervene with absolute Powers when he foresaw that intervention would not pay, and intervened, with despots for company, when intervention seemed likely to pay: he had sought successfully in Greece, Italy, Portugal, Spain, and South America always the commercial advantage of England. In the issue "an ever increasing prosperity" was as he had posited England's portion from his policies; France's portion, great outlay and small return; Spain's and Portugal's the assisted loss of the colonies they were less able than Canning's England to exploit; Prussia's, Russia's, and Austria's the expensive lot of maintaining without English assistance the despot's order in a Europe which Britain had helped to divide among them.

Canning had had just five years of power after Lord Castlereagh's suicide in August 1822. During the last four months of his life he was (after Lord Liverpool's death) Prime Minister of England. Sir Robert Peel, his assistant in so many successful designs, had joined Canning as Home Secretary in 1822. At last he deserted his leader, over the question of Catholic emancipation which Canning favoured. This was in April 1827, when the old Tories were saying of the new Prime Minister that Whig "sentiments coincided with his own convictions."[1] (Canning had knighted the Whig James Scarlett and made him Attorney-General in a reconstructed Ministry.) But Canning still recognized Peel's and his unity of attitude in all things essential. "It is a pride, as well as a comfort to

[1] *Vide Annual Register*, 1827 (*History of Europe*), p. 103.

FURTHER COLONIZATION IN AUSTRALIA

me," he wrote[1] to Peel after Peel's resignation, "to know that . . . you would willingly have continued to sit by my side in the House of Commons; and to share with me the defence of all those other great questions, and of all those principles of external and internal policy—in respect to *all* of which (with the single exception of that *one* question) we agree." Peel agreed in this epitome also—"I have hitherto acted in concert with you on all points, save the one which now compels our separation."[2] (It might have amused Canning's ghost to learn two years later that the Duke of Wellington, the High Tory with whom Peel sided in 1827, should have felt impelled by circumstances to grant Catholic emancipation against his views.) And Peel would live to complete some of the policies of the triumvirate.

Huskisson, who joined Canning's 1827 Ministry after four years' previous service at the Board of Trade, was like Peel a member of the short Ministry of Lord Goderich (1827–28) which, after Canning's death, was so torn by internal Tory dissensions that it resigned without having met Parliament. Huskisson resigned in 1829 from the Duke of Wellington's Ministry of 1828–30. In 1830 one of the new railway trains killed him who had done so much to lay its track. But like his leader of 1822–27 Huskisson was able to refute his opponents, during his last years, with proof of his policy's worth. His legislation of 1825, opening to foreign shipping some British colonial carriage, had brought to the Commons shipowners' petitions against measures which they said had caused loss to British shipping. Huskisson replied[3] that during 1824, 19,164 British ships, aggregating 2,360,000 tons, had entered the ports of England, and 5,280 foreign ships, 66,940 tons; in 1825 the number of British ships entering was 21,986, 2,786,844 tons, of foreign ships 5,661, 68,192 tons. The greater increase of

[1] Canning to Peel, April 15, 1827, *cit.* Stapleton, *op. cit.*, pp. 590, 591. Canning had been commissioned on April 10th to form a Ministry.
[2] Peel to Canning, April 17, 1827, *ibid.*, p. 594.
[3] *Annual Register*, 1826 (*History of Europe*), p. 65.

British shipping activity during the year, as compared with foreign, was he said the odder, if the argument of the shipowners was sound, for the fact that 1825 had given an unusual scope for world carriage, "in consequence of the unprecedented extent of speculation in almost every branch of commerce." So he went a little farther, to secure from Parliament modification of the Navigation Laws, in 1826, in respect of Columbia and the United Provinces of Rio de la Plata (Argentine), with which new South American Governments Britain had made commercial treaties.

These men had made "Constitutions for the New World and legislated for future times" in a sense at least as real as Bentham's. We shall find in contemporary New South Wales, surely, some indices of the changes which they envisaged and helped to bring to pass.[1]

[1] For a contemporary estimate of Canning and Huskisson which attributed to them most repressive acts of Pitt's and subsequent Governments to 1822 (allowing them thereafter some small reform) *vide* the Liberal *Westminster Review*, October 1831, vol. xv, pp. 281 *et seq.*

Chapter 7

IMPORTATION OF CAPITAL INTO AUSTRALIA
FROM *circa* 1822

(*a*) *Land and Emigration Policies, 1822–31*
(*b*) *The Dollar System, 1822–25, and Economic Crisis, 1826*
(*c*) *Reorganization on Sterling, from 1826*

NEW SOUTH WALES had been transformed, during the first half-dozen post-war years, from a derelict prison and the happy hunting ground of a caste, into a colony which was the scene of a considerable, unique society. Because of this in general, and in particular because of its deepening pastoral colour and England's intensifying need of new ground, the colony was by 1822 a factor to be given due weight in considerations of imperial policy. Macarthur and Macquarie between them had ensured so much by their labour—the one to make something of what the land offered, the other to make something of what the convict-ships offered. It would be strange if, in the circumstances which we have noted of English economic and social pressure outward, the imperial march neglected the roads that Macquarie had made to the sheepruns that Macarthur had made. In fact, Australia was looked to by the imperial authority as a territory in which British labour and capital might find elbow room. For the alternatives were seen to be limited. In North America a strip of the Canadian west coast was effectively British, and a large triangle marked by lines from Hudson's Bay, the Great Lakes, and the St. Lawrence. When Macquarie left and Brisbane came to Sydney, Canning's policy had not yet made South and Central America British preserves. In Africa the Cape Colony offered a prospect strictly bounded. India could give little scope to the independent capitalist or the redundant labourer. Accordingly, the Australian continent, especially the part-developed south-eastern fringe, was an obvious resort for British interest in the time of reconstruction.[1]

The Australian Agricultural Company, chartered by Act of 1824 "for the cultivation and improvement of waste lands in New South Wales,"[2] may serve us as an indication of the circumstances in the light of which the colony would be adjusted to British needs, in the 1820's, during the terms of Brisbane and Darling as Governors. The company represented a formidable muster of British capital for overseas investment; its plans subscribed to that other expression of contemporary mood, i.e. the removal of redundant population; and it had genesis, not only in such circumstances but in a recommendation of Bigge's reports and in the notion which Macarthur had propounded, twenty years before, for an English capital undertaking which should utilize his expert services in a development of New South Wales for depasturing flocks bred for fine wool. The Australian Agricultural Company project contained, thus, most elements of a revised system for the use of New South Wales. In its execution it was even more nearly representative of most impulses of British imperialism having effect upon Australia. Macarthurs were numerous upon its list of shareholders, and British Government encouragement of it was conditioned by the requirement that it employ convicts in numbers, in return for great grants of land. Again, its activities sought to feed from New South Wales other British industries than woollens, and the imperial insistence upon the Colonial Government's transfer to the company of the public coal mines[3] at Newcastle (New South Wales) is, like the accompanying

[1] For the distribution of colonial possessions among European Powers after the wars, *vide* map in *Modern European History*, by C. D. Hazen, p. 488; New York, Holt, 1917.

[2] A useful account of the Australian Agricultural Co.'s history is in Roberts, *op. cit.*, pp. 52 *et seq.*, and his *Appendix I*.

[3] For the Australian Agricultural Co.'s lease of the Newcastle coal mines *vide Historical Records of Australia*, I, xii, pp. 237–38; xiv, pp. 32, 272 *et seq.*, 538 *et seq.*; xv, pp. 714–15, etc.

insistence on the Governor's abandonment of public farming, evidence of official endorsement of the new capitalism's ideology of *laissez-faire*. John Macarthur was the company's early adviser in New South Wales.

The policy for New South Wales development which the Australian Agricultural Company idea represented, and for which British Governments from Canning's stood, required (1) the emigration of men of substance; (2) the grant to such of large areas of land, to be used for pastoral and agricultural purposes; and (3) the absorption, in their undertakings, of convicts who otherwise would be a charge on the Treasury *via* the New South Wales Commissariat. The emphasis for the present, during the 1820's, was on the practices, believed to be mutually serviceable, of capital export from England, convict export from England, largeholding in the colony. The profitable association of these elements was to be assisted by the employment of expirees and emancipees, no longer as independent small settlers, but as workers for wages for capitalist landholders; and this policy, which had been approaching the forefront in the latter part of Macquarie's term, marked the final discarding of the imperial idea of 1787-89.

That no feature of the old system for the colony should interfere with the free operation of the new, Government control in every department of economic activity was to be made consistent with the principle now in Brisbane's time approved. A suitable currency system must be fitted to colonial business; the inelastic produce market of the Commissariat store was to be swept away and competitive demand given room to determine price variations; Government farming was to be discontinued; public works should be done by contract instead of by departmental enterprise as hitherto; in the disposal of land, competitive bidding at auction should be given scope, before areas were granted.

These departures, all made at Whitehall's instance, constitute the effort made by the Imperial Government in the 1820's to use New South Wales.

The early direction of the required transformation was entrusted to General Sir Thomas Brisbane, who arrived in the colony to be Governor, on December 1, 1821. Macquarie left for England in February 1822. Before we examine the working out under Brisbane of the new imperial policies, it will be appropriate to notice in Lord Bathurst's reply to Colonel Macquarie's account of his administration evidence of the Imperial Government's perfect comprehension of the persistent basic difficulty with which Macquarie had had to deal. Bathurst's tone suggested that Brisbane would be less taxed than Macquarie had been, to try to meet impossible demands by those in charge[1] of transportation from England. Bathurst wrote,[2] "If, as a place of punishment (New South Wales) has not answered all the purposes for which it was intended, this is certainly not owing to any deficiency of zeal or solicitude on your part, but is mainly to be attributed to the many difficulties in which the rapid and unprecedented succession of convicts, transported of late years to New South Wales, appears to have embarrassed your Government, and which progressively required a change of system, which you could not have contemplated in the earlier periods of it, the necessity for which, however, continued to increase by such slow and

[1] Transportation was the affair of a branch of the Home Office. The British Government Department of the Secretary of State for America was abolished in 1782 by Burke's Act (22 Geo. III, c. 82), and from 1784–1801 the responsibility for colonial affairs lay with one or more Under-Secretaries of State for the colonies and with the committee for trade and foreign plantations. The Transport Commissioners and the Victualling Board, auxiliaries of the Home and War Departments respectively, had some of the responsibility for the convicts and garrison of New South Wales. Then the War and Colonial Departments were amalgamated under one of the "Principal Secretaries of State," not to be separated until 1854. After Castlereagh and Liverpool, Earl Bathurst became Secretary of State in June 1812, Viscount Goderich on May 30 1827, William Huskisson on September 23, 1827, Sir George Murray on May 23, 1828, and Goderich in November 1830. Cf. *A Hundred Years of English Government*, by K. B. Smellie, pp. 102–3; London, Duckworth, 1937, for the complex administrative agencies dealing with matters of colonies and transportation.

[2] Macquarie's *apologia* is reproduced in *Historical Records of Australia*, I, x, pp. 671 *et seq.*, and Bathurst's reply, of September 10, 1822, in the same vol.

imperceptible degrees as not necessarily to force itself upon your attention."

If this "change of system" that was required was a reduction of costs by the employment of a greater proportion of convicts outside Government, such a change could in fact be achieved only by a diminution of the convict influx and an increase of immigration into the colony of potential settlers with capital: these two factors had to be adjusted to each other. The adjustment was tried for Brisbane: the number of transports sent during his first two years, 1822–23 (1,683), was only 47 per cent of the number sent in Macquarie's last full year, 1820 (3,563 transports); and more than 1,400 immigrants, hundreds of whom were recommended for land grants in proportion to their capital, entered the colony in 1822–23, as compared with a number for 1820 too insignificant to be given in any return.[1] At that, neither Brisbane nor his successor Darling (1826–31) was able to reduce the annual Commissariat bill, and at the end of 1829 the Secretaries of the Treasury recorded mournfully, against a convict bill for 1828 of £100,000, the note, "We believe an idea was formerly entertained that the convicts might be employed or let to hire to such an extent as to become the means of raising a fund equal to the amount of the expenditure necessary for their maintenance."[2]

(a) *Land and Emigration Policies, 1822–31*

As to how much land had been granted in New South Wales in the thirty-four years 1788–1821, that is from the original settlement to the close of Macquarie's administration, no reliable indication exists.[3] John Oxley, who held high office

[1] Transportation figures from Barton, *op. cit.*, emigration figures from Carrothers, *op. cit. vide* this chapter (a) for further account of settlers with capital.

[2] J. Drinkwater and W. L. Herries to Commissioners of the Treasury, December 30, 1829, xv, p. 831. The amount of Treasury Bills drawn in New South Wales in 1828 for Government services in respect of convicts, was stated by them at £98,469.

[3] The records are apparently a hopeless jumble. Precise figures of Phillip's grants are not available (*vide* Chapter 2 (b) *supra*), Grose and Paterson seem

as a Government surveyor in three administrations from Macquarie's, calculated in 1826 that up to Brisbane's time nearly 600,000 acres had been granted (1788–1821); and his figure may be accepted as giving, with however a probability

to have granted about 15,500 acres between them (*vide Historical Records of Australia*, I, i and ii), the figure of 28,279 acres for Hunter's grants is evidently excessive (*vide* footnote 1, p. 119 *supra*), but King wrote that in August 1806, 166,565 acres was "held" (I, v, pp. 774–75)—although even if his grants, 1800–06, were known it is unlikely that they would add up, upon those of his predecessors, to anything like this figure (*cf.* his recorded grants August 1805–August 1806, the first year of large pastoral grants to "gentlemen settlers," of 22,498 acres, I, v. p. 776; prior to that period his grants for the most part were small parcels to expirees and emancipees). Bligh made only one grant, and the three New South Wales Corps Administrators after him granted 74,496 acres (according to Macquarie: Macquarie to Castlereagh, April 30, 1810, I, vii), or 67,475 acres (according to Frederick Watson: Introduction to I, vii, p. xix). Bligh wrote in October 1807, before the military Administrations, that 142 square miles (equal to 90,880 acres) had been granted in all up till then (I, vi, p. 144).

Thus, accepting *pro tem.* King's 1806 figure as accurate, and adding Macquarie's figure for 1808–9, grants up to the end of 1809 would total 241,061 acres. Substituting Bligh's figure for King's, the total would be 165,376 acres. (Using Watson's figure, the total in each case would be 7,021 less.) But the Surveyor-General in 1826, John Oxley, calculated (I, xii, pp. 379 *et seq.*), that the total of grants 1788–1809 inclusive was 177,500 acres. For this period, therefore, we are given a range of choice for total grants, of from 158,355 acres to 241,061 acres.

The confusion persists into Macquarie's time (*vide* Bigge's various estimates of grants up to and including Macquarie's term, e.g. 324,251 acres—(Bigge gives three different figures in his *Reports* and *Appendix*)—but Oxley calculated that Macquarie granted 400,000 acres.

Darling in due course gave contradictory figures—e.g. according to *The Colony of New South Wales in 1828*, p. 175, grants to the end of 1828 totalled 2,906,346 acres; according to his *return* elsewhere (I, xiv, p. 671) the figure is 2,894,929.

There appears to be room for a careful piece of research into this not uninteresting contingent aspect of Australian economic history. Roberts's account (*op. cit.*, pp. 33 *et seq.*) does not attack the factual basis, and upon the period under review here he writes: "In the early twenties, however, several factors turned the attention of persons shedding their own land to New South Wales. Chief among these were Bigge's report, Wentworth's book, the opening of the new land beyond the mountains, and comparisons with American conditions." According to this author, "in the early twenties, a change (of land policy) was brought about by two factors—the waste of the old system and the new element of free emigration." But this was not the sequence.

of large error in the amount stated, a general notion that something a good deal less than a thousand square miles of New South Wales land had been granted in the entire course of the first stage of Australian economic history.

But during Brisbane's four years' administration which introduced the second stage of Australian history within the British imperial economy, almost as much land was granted; and in Darling's first three years (1826-28) grants were made totalling more than three times the acreage granted in the whole of the first period. That is, in the seven years 1822-28, about four times as much land was granted—in addition to several hundred square miles sold—as had been granted, from the earliest days, by Phillip, Grose, Paterson, Hunter, King, Johnston, Foveaux, and Macquarie under various modifications of the old system for New South Wales.[1]

Suddenly, then, New South Wales was expanded as Britain expanded. A population (in New South Wales without Van Diemen's Land) of about 30,000 (29,783 in 1821, 33,675 in 1825, Brisbane's last year) found that its Colonial Revenue stood at nearly £72,000 for the fourth year of the new order, as compared with a little more than £36,000 for the last year of the old. This revenue was got chiefly from land fees and import duties; the doubled income evidently, therefore, mirrored an extension of land alienation, or an increased buying from overseas, or both. The last was in fact the position.[2]

Quit rents were increased (from the 1789 figure of 1s. per 100 acres, to 3s. per 20 acres, from late 1823), and recommended immigrants bringing goods sent up the Customs

[1] The comparisons are based on Oxley's and Darling's figures *cit. supra*.
[2] *Cf.* New South Wales Land and Assignments Board to Darling, March 30, 1826 (I, xii, p. 424). Land revenue was of "increasing extent in all its branches, by the sale of Crown lands and yearly receipt of quit rents"; and Darling to Huskisson, April 10, 1828 (xiv, p. 131): It seemed, from the great excess of imports over exports (1827, imports of £362,324, *cf.* exports of £76,314) "that capital is in the course of being transferred to the colony." Probably the trade figures, prior to 1827 are unreliable. However, apparently a similar position of great excess of imports, e.g., about £200,000 in 1825, prevailed during Brisbane's term (*cf. Statistical Register, New South Wales, Summary, 1866*).

revenues. But fees on grants were a subsidiary source of income (although the increased quit rent, not payable until after six years in the case of grants made before November 1823, was payable from acceptance of grant in the case of new grantees), and then on August 12, 1824, an important novelty of land policy was introduced, when Brisbane authorized the sale of up to 100,000 acres, at 5s. per acre, such land to be more than forty miles from Sydney.

Sale was not (until Goderich's regulations of 1831) to supersede the system of granting land, but to exist side by side with it. Evidently, however, it was hoped that the costly business of collecting quit rents might be lessened, and revenue from land collected in greater amounts and more quickly, for in March 1825 Brisbane announced that the annual quit rent of 3s. per 20 acres was redeemable at twenty years' purchase. (This meant that the holder by grant of (say) 100 acres could enter into full ownership of his property, free of quit rent, by payment of £15; cf. £25 payable by the buyer of 100 acres under the regulation of August 1824.) In the same Order of March 31, 1825, Brisbane fixed at 4,000 acres the maximum quantity of land which an individual might buy (and members of any one family, 5,000 acres). Sales would be of unlocated areas in the County of Cumberland (about Sydney), or west of the Nepean River. The price now fixed was 7s. 6d. to 10s. per acre; 10s. deposit was required, and the balance was payable in six-monthly instalments during three years. A few weeks later Brisbane published a further set of conditions, after instructions to make an official division of the colony into counties, hundreds, and parishes. Valuation of land for sale was to be made parish by parish, and land bought was to be paid for in four quarterly instalments, a rebate of ten per cent being allowed for cash payment. Interest of one per cent per quarter was charged on current balance due.[1]

[1] *Vide* for the facts of these two paragraphs *The Colony of New South Wales in 1828, Sydney Gazette* for General Orders of November 5, 1823, March 31, 1825, May 18, 1825.

IMPORTATION OF CAPITAL

With these proceedings, Brisbane did not hold his hand from grants, and up to November 1825, when he was superseded by General Ralph Darling, grants made just half of more than a million acres that he alienated—534,000 acres granted, 200,000 acres reserved to the Crown, 334,000 acres sold.[1] The New South Wales he left was grown to eight counties, of 35,000 square miles (*cf.* 309,400 square miles of the modern State of New South Wales), divided into eighty "townships" or parishes. Eight per cent of the land of the parishes had been alienated or reserved. But payers of deposits were not always payers of due instalments, individual immigrants and the Australian Agricultural Company were giving the colony an access of capital to encourage excessive speculation, Brisbane had instituted a currency system (*vide* (*b*) *infra*) which was making extraordinary dislocations of colonial business; and though the Imperial Government had used the colony tenderly throughout the initial stage of experiment in landsale-*cum*-capital importation, sending in 1822–25 only a few dozen more convicts (3,599) than it had sent Macquarie in the single year 1820, the burden on the Treasury was scarcely lighter (*vide* footnote,[1] p. 214, *supra*) than in Macquarie's most expensive days. (The accumulated convict personnel from the Macquarie years of large transportation could not be got off the Commissary's hands in a year or two, even though Brisbane had made it a condition of his land grants that each grantee should assume responsibility for one convict per 100 acres granted.) The Imperial Government, facing some of these untidy facts, sent a new broom to sweep them away.

Darling sought to co-ordinate with the recently altered land policy the policy, which the Imperial Government was impatiently expectant of pursuing once more, of large transportation. On May 5, 1826 (while the first rumblings were audible of the colony's first general economic crisis), he set up a board

[1] Figures of this and the next two sentences are from Oxley's, I, xii, pp. 379 *et seq.*

to administer affairs of land and the assigned service of convicts[1] (in terms of Act 5 George IV, c. 84).

Tightening up further, by ordinance, the regulations for the use of the land and payment in respect of it, Darling announced in August the termination from March 1, 1827, of the system of issuing tickets of occupation (the permission, used by the early Governors, for landowners to graze stock on Crown land); instead, grazing licences would be issued, on payment of £1 rent per 100 acres of Crown land, under a liability to quit at six months' notice. A week later, it was ordered that quit rent should now be charged at five per cent on the assessed value of land granted and would be redeemable at twenty years' purchase—the equivalent of straight-out buying as under Brisbane's land-sale regulations of 1825. But in November the sale of land was declared suspended until after survey by officials expected to be sent from England.[2]

Sale by auction—where sale by tender of blocks selected by the tenderer had been practised since 1824—was introduced nearly two years later, when in August 1828 Darling announced a resumption of landsales. Lands still unsurveyed might, however, be secured at £1 quit rent per annum per 100 acres, with an acquittance at 20 years' purchase, i.e. at 4s. per acre. Grants—which were being made in greater number and acreage than before, under Darling—were subject now to payment of a quit rent of 2s. per acre per annum, save that recommended officers might receive grants free of quit rent. An order of October 1828 again revised the conditions of permissive occupancy, reducing from six months to one month the period of

[1] For the Land Board *vide Historical Records of Australia*, I, xii, p. 266; xiv, *note* 156, p. 929. The persons appointed to the original board were the Lieutenant-Governor (Stewart), the Colonial Auditor (W. Lithgow), and J. T. Campbell, who had been Macquarie's secretary.

[2] Government Notices and Orders of August 29, 1826, September 5, 1826, November 10, 1826. "Lands purchased, to be held in free and common socage" were the subject of a payment of "a yearly quit rent to the Crown of one pepper corn" (*The Colony of New South Wales in 1828*, p. 13).

legal notice to quit, but reducing from £1 to 2s. 6d. per 100 acres (of unlocated land only, adjoining the permissive occupier's property) the annual rent payable. Buyers under Brisbane's initial scheme of landsale had now to be provided for, too, and in the same month such persons, if they had not paid their 5s. per acre, might hold their land at a quit rent of 2s. per acre—i.e. 5 per cent interest on 3s. 4d. per acre, *plus* the payment of any difference between 3s. 4d. and the 5s. per acre originally contracted for.[1]

The position as viewed from a point of vantage in late 1828 was then that a policy of landsale, as supplementary to a policy of grants which it might supersede, had been in spasmodic operation over four years, subjected to frequent amendment as it became clear that the 1824 system of sale by tender of unsurveyed land might be analogous to placing the cart before the horse. In fact, landsale was discontinued as we noted during 1827 and most of 1828, except for special cases (covering sales to £2,275 in 1827, and £5,005—all sales—in 1828). Land had been disposed of much too generously for the Crown's profit: the wheatlands and the pastures had been parched by drought in the 1826-27 and 1827-28 seasons, the "Old Bank" of New South Wales had been in serious trouble much of the time, and by the end of the year Darling had not only to succour the Bank from Government funds, but had to carry more than £33,000 of arrears of quit rents, land purchase price instalments, etc., while he saw wheat imports for the year mounting to nearly £55,000.[2]

Had the Imperial Government, so far, experience or promise of its revised land policy as an aid to providing for transported convicts? Having "held out inducements to respectable capitalists and men of family,"[3] had Government experienced

[1] Sale by auction was instituted by Government Notice in *Sydney Gazette*, August 21, 1828. Other regulations mentioned—Government Orders, etc., September 23, October 16, October 23, 1828.

[2] Vide *The Colony of New South Wales in 1828*, pp. 47-48.

[3] *A History of New South Wales* (etc.), by T. H. Braim, i, p. 53; London, 1846. This is an artless work.

a transfer of some of its expenses, as well as of its lands, to such persons?

A despatch[1] of early 1827, from the Secretary of State to the Governor, suggests some uneasiness in Whitehall, after two years or so of landsale and the accompanying phenomena. Earl Bathurst wrote, "The indulgence which by the former instructions is given of allowing every grantee to have credit for one-fifth part of the sums which he may have saved to the Government by the employment and maintenance of convicts, I admit to be a privilege which there cannot be any necessity, under the present altered state of the colony, of allowing to the settler. The system of grants laid down by Sir Thomas Brisbane, by which every grantee was bound to receive and maintain one convict for every one hundred acres of land, first led His Majesty's Government to adopt the regulation now in force, by which a bonus is offered for the employment of convicts; but it now appears that a total change has taken place in the circumstances of the colony, and that, instead of a great number of convicts being thrown on the hands of Government, the supply falls infinitely short of the demand for their services. . . . Such a competition exists among the settlers to obtain them . . . that it is no longer necessary to hold out any premium to ensure their being taken off the hands of the Colonial Government." (A similar situation had arisen as we saw—Chapter 6 (*f*) *supra*—in Van Diemen's Land, in consequence of the immigration stimulated by the imperial policy of promise of grants in proportion to capital held by persons prepared to emigrate.) In this circumstance, Darling was instructed to suspend the allowance of the settlers' fifth.

For Whitehall had opened the colonial lands, for lease or sale (quit rents on grants were no longer nominal as we found), had diminished the transportation stream to assist the reorganization of the colony, and had successfully encouraged the emigration to New South Wales of persons of property. The

[1] Bathurst to Darling, April 2, 1827, I, xiii, pp. 220–21.

time had come for the colony to reply in kind, by making a decreased demand for funds on the Imperial Treasury. In fact, the old Adam Smith–Sheffield doctrine that colonies did not pay seemed to be receiving late confirmation in the balance sheet of the Colony of New South Wales. "I must impress upon you," Bathurst wrote further on this theme, "the difficulty I feel in reconciling the scarcity of assignable convicts, of which I have received accounts from all quarters, with the enormous and increasing expense with which this country is still being charged on account of the prisoners who are transported to that part of the world. I have always been given to understand that when a convict is assigned to a settler the Government from that moment are relieved from all further charge on his account, so long as he may remain in the service of that master. But if the bills which are drawn from the colony, connected with the convict establishment, continue of the same, if not of larger amount, as when fewer persons were employed and supported by private individuals, there must be some latent defect in the system, or at least there is an apparent inconsistency which requires explanation."

The Imperial Government, Darling might have reflected impatiently, evidently expected its Antipodean Rome to be built in a day. He could, however, say little in reply except ask for more—settlers and their money from England. Having explained[1] something of the colonial situation to Bathurst's successor, Huskisson, he forwarded to the Colonial Office a month later a circular letter[2] for distribution among intending emigrants who might come over to New South Wales. (For it was not as Rome but as Macedonia that he saw his territory.) Such helpers should apply on their arrival to the Governor for

---

[1] Darling to Huskisson, August 2, 1828, *Historical Records of Australia*, I, xiv, pp. 284 *et seq.*; vide Darling to Hay, September 1, 1928, *Historical Records of Australia*, I, xiv, p. 376.

[2] *Vide* Darling to Hay, September 1, 1828, *Historical Records of Australia*, I, xiv, p. 376.

a grant of land; and "when the Governor shall be satisfied of the character and respectability of the applicant, and that the amount of capital which he can command, and intends immediately to apply to agricultural purposes, has been duly ascertained, he will receive the necessary authority to select a grant of land proportionate in extent to the means he possesses." The proportion would be a grant of one square mile (640 acres) for every £500 available for investment, with a maximum of 2,560 acres and a minimum of 320 acres. In case of the immigrant's wish to buy land, the block selected by him would be advertised for two months and then auctioned. The maximum quantity which any individual might buy was 9,600 acres, in 1,920 acre lots. In the meantime, bills on the Treasury on New South Wales account would remain steady at about £175,000 a year.[1] But Darling did not include this pill in his circular, although in a descriptive publication which he had prepared a little later the fact was made clear, together with evidence of the positive extension of the colony under the new regime—with 3,000,000 acres granted, 70,000 acres in cultivation, more than a quarter of a million cattle and half a million sheep grazing upon its pastures.[2]

Prior to brief note of the kinds of men who were sharing in the task of extending the colony to and beyond the stature suggested by those figures, we may note, too, the reflection in the trade figures for Darling's years 1826–31 of the evident quickening of the colony in the new focussed rays of the imperial sun. The table below[3] conveys the position, in terms of trade, from Darling's first year in New South Wales to the year, 1831, of the introduction of a further important change in colonial land policy, which we shall need to consider in due course:

[1] Totals of Treasury Bills drawn in New South Wales were £175,050 in 1827 and £175,898 in 1828 (*vide* Darling to Huskisson, April 10, 1828, xiv, p. 130; *The Colony of New South Wales in 1828*, p. 32).

[2] *Ibid.*, p. 175 (the grants included 1,280 acres each to William Hovell and Hamilton Hume, the explorers).

[3] *Official History of New South Wales*, p. 47.

Year	Population (N.S.W. proper)	Imports	Exports
1826	34,649	£360,000	£106,600
1827	35,623	362,324	76,314
1828	36,598 (census)	570,000	90,050
1829	41,450	601,004	161,716
1830	46,302	420,480	141,461
1831	51,155	490,152	324,168

The low export figures for 1827-28 reflect a particularly bad two years' drought; the main item of the comparatively high export figure of 1831 is wool, exports of which increased vastly from the end of the 1820's. With regard to the import figures, it is to be remembered that sharp crises, like those of 1826 and 1828, in the infant colonial economy, showed belatedly in the returns as having been responsible for a contraction of buying, for, of course, there was as yet no telegraphic communication between Sydney and London, still divided by several months' sail. Increasing immigration, especially of persons of capital (totals, 903 and 715 for 1826 and 1827 respectively, as compared with 1,056—and these including many larger capitalists—in 1828), could obviate the effect of the 1826 local contraction, as far as the import figures are concerned.

What, then, was the personnel of this expansion?

The cases of Flanaghan, "who was a tailor" in Ireland, and Michael Hyams, "a perfect Jew," both of whom sought land unavailingly in the face of a careful policy which cherished "respectable capitalists and men of family," bring out the conscious direction of New South Wales towards a largeholders' haven. In 1827 Flanaghan presented to Darling "one of the usual letters from the Colonial Office, recommending him to the Governor. "I informed him," Darling reported,[1] "that it was not the practice to give land to people of his class,

[1] Darling to under-secretary Twiss, March 17, 1829, xiv, pp. 677-78, *vide* for the rest of the correspondence of Flanaghan and Hyams Darling to Twiss, January 28, 1829, *ibid.*, p. 618; Twiss to Darling, xv, pp. 77, 308.

and recommended him to attend to his more immediate business." Apparently the Irish tailor rested content in his shop until, nearly two years later, Michael Hyams, a shoemaker, presented credentials from the Chancellor of the Duchy of Lancaster, and Flanaghan heard that this applicant had been given land. Upon this, "considering his pretensions as good as the shoemaker's," he renewed his application for a grant. But in fact Darling had not been more encouraging in his reception of Hyams than of Flanaghan. "In order to establish his claim to a grant," Darling wrote, "Hyams has associated himself with a hosier; and thus, by uniting their respective investments of shoes and stockings, he hopes to obtain a grant." Darling's attitude in these cases was not simply that of the Lieutenant-General to the tradesman; it was affected by his doubt whether the tailor's stated capital of £2,353 6s. 2d.—including book debts, beds and bedding—was in the sense of the land regulations "available for agricultural purposes." A similar consideration applied to the other applicant, with his £2,000 said to be at hand; and Darling, enquiring what was the Colonial Office's mind, interpreted his own role correctly when he declared himself against grants to such people "until they have done making shoes and selling stockings"—until, in other words, their applications for land might more likely be dictated by a wish to produce, than by an intention of speculation. The Colonial Office endorsed this attitude, with the brief intimation that it was not the policy for New South Wales of His Majesty's Government that tradespeople should be given land.

Flanaghan was not the only applicant to seek land on the strength of inapplicable capital. "The statement of Mr. Flanaghan's capital, available for agricultural purposes," Darling had told the under-secretary, "will give you some idea of the pretensions of individuals who come out claiming land in proportion to their property. More than one instance has been known . . . of individuals having borrowed a sum of money for a day or two, which they lodged in one of the banks, and drew again as soon as they had 'verified their capital' at the Land Board." But, given unquestionable evidence of the financial weight of the applicant, an application for land would be another story. The type of investor that the Imperial and Colonial Governments wished to encourage is suggested by the history, so different from the history of Flanaghan or Hyams, of Richard Jones as an applicant. Jones was already a landholder; in addition, a merchant of Sydney, a member of the Legislative Council, and president of the Bank of New South Wales.

He had been a pioneer in applying capital to the getting of Australian wool and Pacific whales. Part owner of five whalers which had cost £25,000, and importer since 1824 of Saxon merinos and other pure-bred sheep, to a value of £20,000, he held, nevertheless (in 1829), "only 6,000 acres of land," of which he had bought two-thirds during Brisbane's administration. "I should presume there can be no objection," Darling wrote home, ". . . in extending his grant of 2,000 acres to the amount which other considerable capitalists have been authorized to receive." The Secretary of State agreed, confirming Darling's grant to Jones of 10,000 acres additional land.[1] For "to him that hath shall more be given" was a principle to be observed strictly by Government if, as was hoped, the policy of extending settlement was to result in the inexpensive accommodation of the growing class of convict transports, from whom, to that end, was taken away even that which they had had: the prospect of a new life as colonial peasant-owners.

Jones was but one of many rich men to be entertained as desirable colonists by the new policy of Government in the 'twenties. Another outstanding beneficiary was J. B. Montefiore, who brought £10,000 to the colony (leaving £8,000 in

[1] For the proceedings with regard to Richard Jones, *vide* Jones to Sir George Murray, May 18, 1829; Darling to Murray, May 19, 1829, June 28, 1829; Murray to Darling, Dec. 22, 1829: *Historical Records of Australia*, I, xiv, pp. 267, 299, 758–59.

England), helped to promote the coming pastoral boom of the late 'thirties, and went into bankruptcy at last in the crisis which succeeded the boom. Montefiore got 5,000 acres. The Marquis of Sligo and James Browne, M.P., scenting spoil, applied successfully to Huskisson for grants, of 10,000 acres apiece. Robert Campbell, who nearly thirty years before had sold cattle to King, aiding an attack on the fat men of that earlier colonial day, got 1,060 acres, to bring his total grant up to 7,560 acres; he had already more than 7,000 sheep and had invested £20,000 in the colony. Macarthur's companion of 1804–5, Walter Davidson, an absentee since 1809 though he had kept up his 2,000 acre grant of 1805 as a pastoral property and had spent £10,000 on it, applied for 20,000 acres; Darling gave him an additional 5,000 acres, on the eve of the cessation of the system of grants.[1]

So proceeded the onset of those whom a later Governor would call lords of principalities; drawing strength and sustenance from England and authority, they would bulk even larger, in a greatly enlarged colonial economy, than the officers who a generation earlier had made New South Wales their particular corner. Macquarie's emancipees could not predominate economically, in such impressive company. The bent of policy towards the capitalist is shown by Darling's use of his provision of October 1828 by which landowners might extend their grazing operations by using Crown land, at a charge of 2s. 6d. per 100 acres per annum. Under this provision, a list of thirty-three persons was published early in the next year; the persons named might have permissive occupancy of nearly 100,000 acres.[2] The "revolutionary scribbler,"

[1] For the instances of Montefiore, Lord Sligo, Browne, Campbell, and Davidson, *vide* xiv, pp. 195–6, 245; xv, pp. 411, 803–4; xvi, p. 33, etc.

[2] The application in 1828 of A. McD. Baxter, Attorney-General in Darling's Government and later puisne judge of the Supreme Court of Van Diemen's Land, serves to indicate the usual form (xiv, p. 781):—

"September 8, 1828

"I beg you will be pleased to submit to His Excellency my request that I may be permitted to rent, until the same can be put up for sale,

E. S. Hall[1]—who edited the Sydney *Monitor*, chiefly from gaol—pointed out that of the favoured thirty-three ten were civil officers or magistrates; the Macarthurs had between them 60,000 acres of the colony, yet James Macarthur, J.P., was in the permissive list for another 1,920 acres, where also Mrs. Bunker ("a married lady") was down for 15,000 acres.

In fact these short term leases of Crown land were aimed uncompromisingly at the small man, as if to remind him that

> (5,000) acres of land, under the regulations contained in the Government Order, No. 35, dated 5th September, 1826. I am now in possession of land to the following extent, viz.:—
>
> "By grant .. .. (2,560)
> "By purchase of the Crown .. .. .. —
> "By reserve .. .. —
> "By private purchase, gift, or inheritance .. —
>
> of which   acres are cleared.
>
> "I also possess live stock as under, viz.:—
>
> "Horses .. .. (2 head)
> "Horned cattle .. (140 head)
> "Sheep .. .. (500 head)
>
> and available money capital to the amount of (five hundred pounds).
>
> "I possess buildings on the lands of the following description and value, viz.:—(a hut and stockyard of the usual value).
>
> "I have completed   miles of fencing and have employed and maintained during the last year (ten) convicts and (part of it two) free servants, and have otherwise fully complied with the conditions annexed to the above lands."

Cf. Government Notice, April 22, 1829 (xv, p. 62), *re* the regulation of October 16, 1828, of permissive occupancy; Act of Council 10 Geo. IV, No. 6, 1830, Resumption of Crown Lands Act, repeated the 1828 Order's announcement of a month's notice required, instead of six months, as under the 1826 Order.

[1] Darling to Murray, July 6, 1829; *cf.* Hall to Murray, May 2, 1829, xv, pp. 53, 63; on the 33 permissive occupiers of 1829, *cf.* Hall to Murray, enclosure Darling to Murray, January 2, 1829 (xiv, p. 580), alleging discrimination in land grants, against the native born, some of whom by this time were middle-aged. Hall spoke of "the mortification our adult youths must feel, when they find their countrywomen forming connections with the emigrant and freed colonists as wives and concubines, while themselves, from obtaining no land or land in inadequate quantities, are unable to marry."

New South Wales was no longer, under Government, set aside for him. Darling put it that the system of permissive occupancy was "calculated to operate as a check upon the cattle stealers and prevent the farms of established settlers being grazed upon by the herds of itinerant individuals, who, having no land of their own, traverse the country."[1] Moreover, within a few months past two Acts of the Council which men like Jones and Macarthur filled, had tightened the largeholder's grip on the small man. These measures (9 George IV, Nos. 11 and 12, passed July 24th and August 2, 1828, respectively) required the establishment of pounds and the sharing between neighbours of the cost of dividing fences. Well enough in themselves, the acts could make a present burden on the remaining peasantry. High fees and fines in respect of straying stock, and the opportunity given largeholders to place small neighbours in debt to them by insisting on fencing—say immediately after a harvest failure—might be heavy loads on labouring backs.

It is not surprising to find that the colonial large owners approved of Darling's execution of the imperial policy. In July 1829 one hundred and fifteen "landed proprietors and merchants of New South Wales" presented him with an address[2] of commendation. "Sir" John Jamieson (son of Phillip's surgeon), Robert Campbell, Richard Jones, John and Hannibal Macarthur were among the signatories, who indeed included forty-five magistrates. Radicals in the House of Commons made bitter comment on this unanimity among 115 persons, in a colony of more than 30,000.[3]

The administration had always in mind the extension of pastoral holdings on a large scale, so that when Darling made grants to two daughters of clergymen, of two square miles each as marriage portions, the Secretary of State approvingly

---

[1] Darling to Murray, July 6, 1829; xv, p. 53.   [2] xv, p. 71.
[3] *Cf.* Darling to Murray, December 22, 1830 (xv, pp. 853 *et seq.*), in reply to Joseph Hume's criticism as reported in *The Times* and the *Mirror of Parliament* (House of Commons debates, edited by J. B. Barrow).

instructed him to embrace "the daughters of all respectable persons" within a like privilege.[1] (The marriage portion of Government to the convict bride of yesteryear was twenty acres.) Each intending settler who had satisfied the Colonial Office of his financial position might have of Darling's Land Board—as this generous system approached its apex and its termination—"the usual grant of 2,560 acres of land, at his option."[2] Now small grantees did not figure in the returns; even the minimum grant under the regulations (320 acres) was seldom made. For in these closing years of the 1820's Whitehall was not encouraging the emigration to New South Wales of poor persons—though 30,000 were leaving the British Isles each year, for various parts of the empire—who might have sought small grants; and as for the convicts they were drafted into private service as fast as the largeholders could take them, some to realize their share in a reorganized colony when they subscribed to such depositions as this:[3]

James Davis maketh oath and saith, I came by the ship *Eliza* and am assigned to Mr. David Hayes; I swear I have had no rations since Friday except part of a loaf; a two-pound loaf was shared amongst five of us.

His
James × Davis
Mark

When in the winter of 1828 wheat stood at 15s. a bushel in Sydney, after drought, and chartered foodships had not yet returned from South America and South Africa, Darling stressed in a Government notice the need for conserving stocks

---

[1] Murray to Darling, August 28, 1829; xv, p. 149. This system was abandoned in 1833, after the Secretary of State had refused to endorse grants of 1,280 acres each to the two daughters of the Reverend J. Cross, on their marriages (xvi, pp. 792–93). Darling had discontinued the general marriage portion grant on the publication of the 1831 landsale regulations. Goderich now ordered that clergymen's daughters, too, should forgo their customary benefit.   [2] E.g., Twiss to Darling, November 4, 1829; xv, p. 241.
[3] xv, p. 315.

of breadstuffs; as a practical step in this direction he recommended to landholders that they reduce their assigned servants' rations.[1]

Short rations for unlucky assigned convicts, impounding of stock, and enforced indebtedness, for ex-convict peasants, gaol for "radicals" like Hall—this was the reverse of the medal of a capitalist economy in New South Wales. Darling found at the opening of 1830 that "the radical press and its supporters" were "now miserably reduced"; Hall had been in gaol for the last six months, during which retirement four more actions for libel had been decided against him![2] The Governor could rejoice to notice "the humiliating condition of my few Radical opponents, who are in fact driven from society."

And at the opening of the 'thirties it was clear that New South Wales was being converted into a great settlement, by impulses of British capital acting in the pastoral environment which Macarthur and Jones and their kind had made. The instruction[3] given Brisbane in July 1825 to appoint commissioners to survey and value all waste lands, could be taken a stage farther, by May 1830, when the Secretary of State empowered the Governor to revoke the commissions and transfer the functions of the Commissioners to the Surveyor-General of New South Wales. Major Thomas Livingstone Mitchell, Surveyor-General after John Oxley, had now in his department deputy Surveyors-General, four surveyors (including Robert Hoddle, who half a dozen years later would plan Melbourne), eighteen assistant surveyors, and seven draughtsmen. Trade, too, had been developed, so that in 1830 producers could recall[4] a vividly contrasting stagnation: 'Ten years back, a ship of 300 tons transported the whole of

---

[1] Government Notice of June 12, 1828; cf. Darling to Hay, January 13, 1830; xv, p. 333.

[2] Cf. Darling to Hay, January 13, 1830; xv, p. 333.

[3] xii, pp. 133 et seq. For the later arrangements vide Murray to Darling, May 6, 1830, May 8, 1830; xv, p. 468.

[4] Petition of landed proprietors to Sir George Murray, January 23, 1830; xv, pp. 341 et seq.

IMPORTATION OF CAPITAL

our exportable produce for that year to England"; but from June 18, 1828, to June 18, 1829, 24 ships, aggregating 6,752 tons, sailed for England with New South Wales exports of £154,614 value; and exports to other places were of £30,100 value for the twelvemonth. (Imports over the same period were £508,430 from England and £170,229 from elsewhere.)

Laissez-faire as applied to Australia was now to be denied in no avenues which Government could clear. Very soon after Goderich took office with the Liberals in 1830 he required Darling to institute the performance of public works by contract instead of by Government gangs directed by civil servants.[1] Earlier in the year Goderich's Tory predecessor, Sir George Murray, had instructed Darling[2] to persist in his policy of getting rid of those public farms which remained, even though it should be impossible, as the Governor had represented, to get a fair price for the Government stock.[3] By the end of 1828 Darling had dismissed the Government farm superintendents at Bathurst, Port Macquarie, and Rooty Hill, transferring several thousand acres of the last-named public holding to the Church and School Corporation. The process was fast approaching completion, of which Macquarie had spoken in anticipation, more than ten years before.[4]

[1] Hay to Darling, December 14, 1830; xv, pp. 828 *et seq.*
[2] Murray to Darling, April 21, 1830; xv, pp, 432–33.
[3] Darling had tried twice, in July, August 1828, to sell the Government herds, but had been unable to get offers for them (after drought). He was discontinuing the Government farm at Bathurst and had reduced each of the other establishments. At the same time, he had found it his duty to point out that Whitehall must not anticipate a money saving by this course that it had instructed him to pursue; it would be dearer to buy bread for the convicts in the open market than to feed them from Government grain delivered to the Commissariat (*vide* Darling to Huskisson, September 23, 1828; xiv, pp. 401–2).
[4] *Cf.* Macquarie to Sorell, January 10, 1818; III, ii, pp. 294, 298: "It does not appear to be the wish or intention of his Majesty's Ministers to continue either a stud of Government horses, or flocks or herds, in this territory or its dependencies much longer. I have reason to believe they will be discontinued altogether soon."

Cf., however, Macquarie to Davey, April 12, 1816; III, ii, p. 142, rejecting

Nevertheless, Government expenditure on account of the colony was, as we found Bathurst complaining, still very high —even after four years of a modified *laissez-faire* under Darling. The garrison cost £64,000 in 1829, the convict establishment £122,000, stores from England another £20,000—totals recalling Macquarie's administration of New South Wales as a semi-public undertaking. Certainly the policy of large land transfer had brought in fees, duties, etc., enough to raise the colonial revenue for the year to £107,262; but this sum represented little more than a third of the public expenditure for the year of £313,262.[1] The originating circumstance of much of this expenditure was the second resumption of large-scale transportation, after a period of quiet during Brisbane's Government and Darling's first period. Then in 1829 Government had to accommodate 3,329 male convicts who arrived; the total convict arrivals for 1829, 3,664, aggregated more than twice the figure, 1,823, of Darling's first year, 1826, and exceeded the maximum of 1820, when Macquarie was Governor. The new arrivals could not all be removed from the Commissariat responsibility by assignment to settlers, nor could those of them who were assignable be placed without delay. "Of the convicts who arrive," Darling pointed out,[2] "many from their extreme youth, old age, blindness, and other bodily infirmities, would be totally useless to settlers; and therefore they are necessarily otherwise provided for," i.e. at public expense. Seven years' men of good conduct would receive ticket of leave (enabling them to seek private employment) after four years, fourteen years' men after six years, and life-sentence men after eight years. Even so, the proportion— even of the able-bodied, some of whom had to be retained for

---

Davey's advice as Lieut.-Governor that the Van Diemen's Land public herd should be sold: "It is a fixed principle with me to study the interests of the poor as well as of the rich." [1] xv, p. 439.

[2] Darling to Murray, December 22, 1830; I, xv, pp. 853 *et seq.*, especially p. 861. Darling's figures for convict arrivals for each year 1826–28 differ somewhat from Barton's (Coghlan's compilation, *op. cit.*), but Barton's figure for 1829 agrees.

public works, etc.—that had to be retained on the ration list involved a heavy charge upon the Treasury through the Commissariat. Moreover, Government establishments had to be kept up at the old Macquarie centre, Emu Plains, at Wellington Valley at the western extremity of the colony (for "educated convicts" during probation), Moreton Bay, Port Macquarie, and Norfolk Island. With the exception of Emu Plains, an exceptionally good farming area which it was prudent to keep up during these years of drought, and Wellington Valley, each of these was a penal settlement for New South Wales offenders.[1]

For such reasons, the colony was not yet to cease laying a burden on the Imperial Treasury, though at home Tories and Liberals alike embrace *laissez-faire*.

At any rate, when Darling had completed his set task of reshaping the colony to receive well-to-do emigrants, by opening up waste lands, putting in motion a machine for the assignment to private service of a majority of transports and for the early release of men under sentence, and by stabilizing the currency (*vide* (c) *infra*), Whitehall recalled him.[2] A Liberal Government was now in power in Great Britain, Viscount Goderich had the keys of the Colonial Office (since November 22, 1830), and a reorganized colony was required to render wider services to its imperial sponsor. Darling, like his predecessors, had served as best he could the current purposes of Whitehall after its interpretation of the most profitable use for New South Wales; in the process he had inevitably made enemies: so at length, like Macquarie and King

[1] The Imperial Act 6 Geo. IV, c. 69, of 1825, after Order in Council of November 11, 1825, gave the authority for retransportation of colonial offenders, which by Act of Council 7 Geo. IV, No. 5 (August 16, 1826) was used to denominate Port Macquarie, Moreton Bay, and Norfolk Island as colonial penal settlements.

[2] Darling was recalled by despatch, Goderich to Darling, March 15, 1831. This despatch is not available (*vide Historical Records of Australia*, I, xvi, p. iii). He acknowledged his recall on July 26, 1831 (xvi, pp. 314 *et seq.*), and left New South Wales on October 22nd. Colonel Patrick Lindesay, O.C. garrison, was Acting Governor until the arrival on December 2, 1831, of Major-General Richard Bourke to be Governor.

who had been relatively successful in performance of their set tasks, and like Bligh and Hunter who had failed, he was packed off home. The stern realists of the Colonial Office had an uncompromising way with their pro-consuls. And Goderich's first major despatch[1] to Darling furnishes one more instance of the awareness of ministers that the colony existed to serve contemporary British social and economic purposes. Goderich in a brief comprehensive review found (1) that the existing land regulations had not prevented large areas from passing to persons who could not improve or cultivate them; (2) that the existing land system was "founded upon an erroneous view of the true interest both of the colony and of the Mother Country." The quit rents system was unsatisfactory, experience having shown that the rents were hard and costly to collect, and in any case, assuming a productive New South Wales, an unimportant item of revenue. Upon the second point, Goderich believed the design of the 'twenties to have been the encouragement of persons of capital to emigrate to New South Wales; but "the mere removal of capitalists" did not give England the relief of bloodletting which it required emigration to give. So now another phlebotomy was called for: "emigration of the unemployed British labourers."[2] It was unsatisfactory that the capitalist immigrants should have "spread themselves over so great an extent of territory";[3] they would

[1] Goderich to Darling, January 9, 1831; xvi, pp. 19 *et seq.*

[2] As illustrating the fact that immediate British, not continuing Colonial needs were of primary consideration, note, e.g., that nine years before, Sorell had written to Henry Goulburn, under-secretary (*Historical Records of Australia*, III, iv, p. 37), to announce in pleased surprise that 170 convicts arrived in the *Malabar* "comprised an unusual number of useful men of the agricultural class, which has enabled me to distribute generally assistance in farming labour, a point so essential when the emigrant settlers are proceeding to the occupation of their lands."

[3] *Cf.* S. H. Roberts (cap. vii, p. 193 *Camb. Hist. cit.*): "By the end of the 'twenties there were three classes of graziers in New South Wales, two of them outside the law. The only legal ones were those who had annual licences within the boundaries of the nineteen counties; those who illicitly occupied lands within the surveyed area and those who had crossed the boundaries for the unknown outside were alike unrecognized."

have done better to farm, and in a small area; that was to say, the policy of the 'twenties had settled hundreds of owners who had been desirous of scope in the colonies, and that was very well; but at the moment the urgent English problem was how to clear the agricultural parishes of the South of England of their hundreds of thousands of pauperized farmers and farm labourers, and "the formation of a class of labourers for hire" was the imminent duty of the Governor of New South Wales. Goderich, in fact, could not see the progress abroad for the paupers at home. He set about recasting the imperial policy for New South Wales in English terms: New South Wales must be what it was not, and could not be—a country of farms—simply because the rulers of England were driven to wish it so. For how, if the colony were not what they persuaded themselves it was or might be, could "the redundant mass" be shipped afar from the subversive reminder of the enclosed fields of their fathers? New South Wales was still to receive convicts, and more than ever before—the peak was reached in 1833, with 4,136 convict arrivals in New South Wales; 1834 was the year of maximum transportation to Van Diemen's Land, with 4,515 convicts; nevertheless emigration must surpass the 1829 total of 2,016, to reach 4,093 in 1833, and pass 15,000 per annum before the end of the decade.[1]

This consummation, the employment in New South Wales of British capital to sustain droves of paupers and convicts as farm labourers, could be reached, Goderich believed, by a "simple and easy measure." Government in England would assist by paying part of the passage money of each emigrant labourer; Government in New South Wales must do its part by terminating the system of granting land, disposing of land only by sale—this to be at auction, at an upset price of 5s. an acre, 10 per cent of the purchase price to be paid down and the balance payable before the buyer should take possession. "When land was formerly disposed of by sale," the minister

[1] Barton, *op. cit.*, pp. 463–65; Forsyth, *op. cit.*, p. 99; Carrothers, *op. cit.*, p. 305 for these figures.

held, "the plan seems to have failed in consequence of the long credit that was given." (But only a year before, landowners had petitioned Goderich's predecessor, pointing out that in spite of the indulgence by which their wool was allowed into England duty-free, their pastoral undertakings were, because of low prices and three dry seasons, barely payable. Also, two years before that, Darling had had to give Brisbane's buyers (of land at 5s. an acre) time to pay £40,000 which they owed on their land, in a period of low export prices for timber and wool; he gave similar concessions to grantees who were behind with their rent-payments.[1] It would be odd, then, if short term instead of long term credit should more nearly meet the case of producers operating in such circumstances.)

Three weeks before Darling acknowledged the despatch which recalled him, and three months before he committed the administration to Colonel Lindesay until General Bourke should reach the colony, Darling was able to announce that the new system was introduced. He promulgated on August 1st a Government Order providing for a system of the sale by auction of 640-acre blocks after three months' advertisement. A month earlier he had published the general declaration that lands would henceforth be disposed of at auction only, and that the colony would be surveyed in counties, hundreds, and parishes (the delayed undertaking of 1825), each parish to be of an area of twenty-five square miles. This Government notice[2] reiterated the Brisbane regulation that applicants might select blocks and apply for their selections; at the sale, land offered might be acquired by a deposit of 10 per cent (as under the 1824 arrangement), the balance to be paid within a month, before the buyer secured possession or title. The great Crown reserves appropriated to the Church and School Corporation would be opened for sale, and the corporation dissolved.

[1] I, xiv, pp. 207–8; xv, pp. 341 *et seq.*; *The Colony of New South Wales in 1828*, p. 48.
[2] *Sydney Gazette*, July 1, 1831; *Historical Records of Australia*, I, xvi, pp. 850–51; Darling to Goderich, September 28, 1831, xvi, pp. 380 *et seq.*

Now the problem was how to adjust the emigration system to the amended land system. Goderich's instruction of 1831 by which the sale system was made exclusively the means of acquiring land required the Colonial Government to assist the emigration of distressed farm labourers either with the proceeds of a tax on employers receiving convicts on assignment—there were more than 13,000 convicts on assignment this year[1]—or by advances on the part of free settlers towards the passage money of emigrant labourers, and by applying to emigration the proceeds of land sales. In cases under the second category, the settler might recover his advance either by reserving a quarter of the immigrant labourer's wages until the debt was satisfied, or by conditions of a seven-year indenture of the labourer's services to him. (Most of these ideas were derived from Wakefield's *A Letter from Sydney*, which had been published less than two years earlier.) Again, grantees who assisted emigration in this way might be recouped by a rebate on their due quit rent. (This was a policy used in 1827 in respect of the Van Diemen's Land Company, which was allowed a reduction of its rent of £16 for each male, and £20 for each female immigrant introduced.)[2]

Darling instituted without delay a system for the remission of quit rents. A Government notice of August 26, 1831, announced that a rebate would be allowed of £35 for each family brought out, £15 for each woman, £12 for each man, and £4 for each child, not exceeding two in any family.[3] The Colonial Secretary circularized all members of the Legislative Council, for information upon employers wishing to subsidize emigration, with details of the numbers and classes wanted, and of wages which the settlers might be prepared to pay. At the London end, the minister announced on July 9, 1831, the

[1] Executive Council minute, enclosure No. 2, Darling to Goderich, September 10, 1831; xvi, p. 349.

[2] Hay to directors, Van Diemen's Land Company, May 23, 1827; III, vi, p. 94, *et vide* Chapter 6 (*f*) *supra* for the Lieutenant-Governor's refusal of a request, under this provision of the Company's charter, for a few convicts.

[3] *Cf.* xvi, pp. 346 *et seq.*

appointment of an Emigration Commission.[1] In September the Commissioners reported that many applicants had come forward for passages to New South Wales and Van Diemen's Land, but few with their passage money. The Commissioners believed that a 10s. tax, on employers of convicts and on holders of a ticket of leave, in respect of each of the 14,000 to 15,000 convicts on assignment or ticket in New South Wales, and each of the 7,000 to 8,000 in Van Diemen's Land, should yield about £20,000. On the security of this fund (they were Wakefieldian in their terminology) Government might furnish a thousand families with advances of £20 each towards passage money; mechanics might be the material of experiment in the first instance. (It was only seven years since the law of England had been amended so as to remove an absolute prohibition of the emigration of skilled workmen.) But the Commissioners' plan, although endorsed by the Imperial Treasury, seemed fantastic to the Council in New South Wales, which appreciated the difficulty of collecting such a direct tax from employers, many of whom had scores of convicts on assignment. However, Bourke, the new Governor, advised[2] the minister that the Colonial Treasury had £6,400 available (in February 1832),

[1] xvi, pp. 296–97, 410–11. The first Commissioners were Lord Richmond, Viscount Howick, and R. W. Hay (Under-Secretaries of State for the Colonies), F. Baring, and H. Ellis.

[2] xvi, pp. 532–33. Upon the cost of an emigrant's passage, cf. *Sessional Papers of the House of Lords*, 1847, vol. xxx, p. 499; 7th general report, Colonial Land and Emigration Commissioners—steerage passages had been £35 to £40 each to New South Wales or Van Diemen's Land; in 1831 Government arrangements secured a reduction to £20, sometimes £15. The report includes the further interesting statement, "Of the emigration to Australia, one peculiarity has been that it entirely originated in Government. Usually, the part of the Government, for obvious reasons, has been to follow in the course of private enterprise, and supply any amount of direction or control which circumstances may require. But no one had ever thought it worth while to provide accommodation to Australia for emigrants of the humblest class. . . . It was only after the Government had resolved in 1831 to try the experiment of disposing of its lands in Australia by sale, and applying the proceeds to emigration, that shipowners were induced by communications from the Government to make the experiment of providing steerage passages of the cheapest description."

representing £8 per family towards the cost of removing 800 families from the South of England. In April 1832 the Council appropriated £10,000, to be used by the Emigration Commissioners as an emigration fund. Of this sum £6,400 should be used to finance the emigration of young women of from eighteen to thirty years of age—the Commissioners had recommended six months earlier that the Colonial Legislature should immediately apply proceeds of landsales, to the amount of £10,000, to this purpose—and the balance to finance the emigration of skilled workmen and labourers.[1] The last class of grantee remaining—the discharged soldier—was not regarded more favourably as an immigrant by Bourke than he had been by Macquarie. Three hundred ex-soldiers had been worrying the Governor during 1832; "they are not of a description of persons whom it is desirable to see here," Bourke said.[2] It would be preferable if Government would promote the emigration of four or five hundred women every year. John Dunmore Lang, the formidable forerunner of Presbyterianism in Australia, had his own notion of a proper emigration for the relief of Britain and the gain of the colony. Before the imperial authorities began to practise their new scheme of emigration, he was on his way to Sydney with eighty Scottish mechanics in the *Stirling Castle*, of 350 tons. Upon his arrival, in October 1831, he was promised by the Colonial Government £1,500 towards the cost of his venture. Two years after his experimental Odyssey, Dr. Lang gave in the temporary hall of the Australian College in Sydney (on May 9, 1833) his theories upon the constitution through emigration of "a numerous industrious and virtuous agricultural population." (The lecture, reprinted as a pamphlet, merits the attention of the curious, if only for its graphic illustration from Nature: "Go to the bee, ye would-be political economists!")[3]

[1] Commissioners of Emigration, October 10, 1831, xvi, p. 408; Bourke to Goderich, April 11, 1832, xvi, pp. 608 *et seq.*
[2] Bourke to Goderich, September 24, 1832; xvi, p. 759.
[3] For Dr. Lang's venture *vide* Lang to Howick, May 3, 1831, xvi, pp. 258–259; Lindesay to Goderich, November 18, 1831, *ibid.*, p. 449; *New South Wales*

Thus the Wakefieldian associations of land and labour, landsale and emigration, farming and restricted settlement, the wastes of New South Wales and the enclosed fields of England, were already by 1831–33 translated practically into a British policy for Australia which was as different from the Pitt-Sydney-Dundas policies of 1787–89 as were contemporary British social and economic situations from those of the days before three revolutions had changed English life. The steady onset since the war of British society's demands upon its Australian territories had already, through Bathurst and Huskisson, Macquarie and Brisbane, transformed New South Wales into a system susceptible of extensive use to meet the widened needs of the rich crowded society at home. We have a sense of a stability in the colonial society, in contrast with the semi-chaos of most of the years 1788–1818, when we read the terms of the Governor's pronouncement of April 1832:[1] "The (convict) tax is not actually necessary if it be intended to allow the revenue derived from the Crown lands to be appropriated as heretofore to colonial purposes. A sum of ten thousand pounds is voted for the encouragement of free emigration in this year, and will be forthcoming if required. The expenditure of the colony is now assuming a regular form; the separation of the military and convict establishments from the colonial is nearly complete, and the expense of the latter could at once be defrayed without the aid of the military chest, if the concourse of criminals was averted from the colony and its establishments placed on the reduced footing which would then be sufficient." Within half a dozen years the Imperial Government would arrive, reluctantly, at appreciation of this necessity of terminating the use of New South Wales as a penal settlement —for within two years from Bourke's review the controllers of British capital would have entered upon an exploitation of the Australian pastures which would write *finis* to artless

Pamphlets collection in the Public Library of Victoria, vol. xxi, No. 4. There is a reference on page 3 of the pamphlet to the "transportation system" said by Dr. Lang to be used by bees.

[1] Bourke to Goderich, April 30, 1832; xvi, pp. 624 *et seq.*

official objections to the habit sheepmen had acquired of "spreading themselves" beyond the bounds drawn by Government for the accommodation of its short-view policies.

(b) *The Dollar System, 1822–25, and Economic Crisis, 1826*

The contrast between the impressively large trade dealings of New South Wales of the 1820's, and the meagre dealings of the isolated, sluggish little settlement of earlier times, is so marked as to suggest to the student of land or commercial transactions at these epochs that some radical adjustment of the means of exchange must have been necessary. The crude, extempore machinery of the colony's first thirty years was inadequate measured against the requirements of Macquarie's post-war years, and as we saw he had established a token coinage on the eve of peace, and a bank a couple of years after the peace settlement. How much more urgent must be the need, now at the period of immigration and extension of settlement, for an effective financial articulation of the colony. There had been supplied from home since 1812 no other means of conducting internal trade than the 40,000 dollars which Liverpool had sent and Macquarie had manipulated into a token coinage. But still the private note currency of the earlies eked out the tokens and the notes of the Bank of New South Wales. So the Sydney Chamber of Commerce, born of the first major difficulty of the emerging free community in 1826, would recall[1] that at Brisbane's advent the colony's resources could be counted in £150,000 in Treasury drafts, £15,000 in notes on the Commissary-General, £20,000 in Commissariat store receipts, £15,000 in notes of the Bank of New South Wales, and £10,000 in notes of "respectable private individuals." The bank's specie on July 19, 1820, had consisted of £4,170 in 16,680 holey dollars, £1,750 in 7,000 (unmutilated) Spanish dollars, £368 15s. in 5,900 dumps, and £12 9s. 5d. in coppers.[2] There was no British gold or silver in the vaults. This was the

---

[1] *Historical Records of Australia*, I, xii, pp. 518 *et seq.*
[2] Francis Williams (cashier New South Wales Bank) to J. T. Campbell (Macquarie's private secretary), July 19, 1820; I, x, p. 434.

character of the makeshift system which Brisbane found. To correct it he originated "what was known at the time as the 'dollar system.' "[1]

The steps by which Sir Thomas Brisbane tried to establish the Spanish dollar (the unmutilated coin) as the unit of currency and legal tender in New South Wales may be given summarily, at the outset, as follows:

1822 1. He had the Commissary import dollars from India, probably up to 400,000 dollars.[2]

2. He discontinued Commissariat payments in store receipts (i.e. sterling promises) and, instead, made payment for wheat, etc., in Spanish dollars at 5s. each.[3]

3. He authorized the payment of quit rent and Customs duties in Spanish dollars, receivable at 5s. each.[4]

[1] Chalmers, *op. cit.*, p. 246. The enumeration of steps to crisis, which follows, is after Chalmers, with additional matter and with departures from his account where this appears incorrect or misleading.

[2] This is inferential from contemporary references, but there appears to be no record of the actual orders and transactions, *cf.* President of Sydney Chamber of Commerce to A. Macleay, Colonial Secretary, August 15, 1826, I, xii, pp. 509 *et seq.*; Bank of New South Wales to Brisbane, May 10, 1822, I, x, p. 737: "The first purchase of dollars was completely a private (n.b., that is secret) transaction. It was in no way made known to the public or the Bank that dollars were to be the mode of payment in the future. . . . No public notice was ever given by the Commissary that it was intended to exchange bills on the Treasury for specie." *Cf.* also Chalmers, *op. cit.*, pp. 246 *et seq.*

[3] *Vide* Brisbane to Bathurst, September 2, 1822, I, x, pp. 729 *et seq.*, in which the Governor announces the institution of a system of paying in dollars instead of store receipts, "with a view to a diminution of the expenses of the colony." In enclosure No. 1, Bank of New South Wales, to Brisbane, May 10, 1822, reference is made to "the present mode of payment in dollars recently had recourse to on the part of Government." Brisbane's expedient was sanctioned by the Secretary of State—Bathurst to Brisbane, March 31, 1823, I, xi, p. 73.

[4] By General Order of May 9, 1822, *cit.* Chalmers, *op. cit.* This Order is not copied in *Historical Records of Australia*, but evidently some such arrangement was used, *cf.* 1832 Act of Council 2 Wm. IV, No. 6, requiring payment in sterling of certain fines, which had been payable in Spanish dollars.

IMPORTATION OF CAPITAL

4. About mid-1822 the Commissariat valued dollars paid into it at 4s. 2d. each.[1]

5. The Commissariat put up Treasury bills for sale by public tender. (They were sold at a premium, and a public memorial of August 1822 protested against the new Commissariat practice of paying in dollars at 5s. valuation and placing a premium on Treasury bills by receiving dollars only at the 4s. 2d. valuation.)[2]

6. The Governor called in holey dollars, offering to receive them at the Macquarie valuation of 5s. each during six months only, July-September 1822.[3]

7. He called in dumps, offering to receive them at the Macquarie valuation of 1s. 3d. each during six months from November 15, 1822; from the close of that period, their declared value would be 11½d. (holey dollars, 3s. 9d., being "three-fifths of the Spanish dollar").[4]

1823 8. The Governor ordered that Government accounts should be kept in dollars and official salaries paid in dollars.[5]

---

[1] *Vide* Bank of New South Wales to Brisbane, May 10, 1822, in which the Bank complains of its loss through "the Commissary's declining to give bills on the Treasury in exchange for those dollars, at the sterling value of which he has . . . paid them away in the purchase of stores and provisions, . . . the Government being the greatest, if not the sole purchaser of the surplus agricultural produce of the colony." *Cf.* Bank to Colonial Secretary, May 30, 1822, *ibid.*, "The Bank will lose 10d. on all dollars received at 5s. and paid by the Bank at the reduced value"; *cf.* also Colonial Secretary Goulburn to the Bank of New South Wales, May 16, 1822, I, x, p. 736; Memorial from the Colonists to Brisbane, I, x, p. 739.

[2] *Vide* references in last footnote, and public memorial of August 21, 1822, *cit.* Chalmers, *op. cit.*, p. 247.

[3] Proclamation, July 25, 1822 (not in *Historical Records of Australia*).

[4] Proclamations, November 15, December 31, 1822 (not in *Historical Records of Australia*).

[5] General Order, February 5, 1823 (not in *Historical Records of Australia*). Chalmers, who quotes this Order (and the others mentioned as not in *Historical Records of Australia*), says that official salaries were to be paid in dollars valued at 4s. each (which of course meant a considerable inflation of salaries), and that the soldiers of the garrison were paid in dollars at 4s. 8d., while the Commissariat paid out dollars at 5s., receiving them at 4s. 2d.

Something like the suggested confusion is reported by the Lieutenant-

9. By these means and from other causes Brisbane was able to reduce drawings of Treasury bills to £95,828 in 1823, compared with £181,376 in 1820.[1]

1824 10. The Legislative Council declared the Spanish dollar legal tender in New South Wales, and the same month (September 1824) a committee recommended the official valuation of the dollar at 4s. 4d.[2]

So New South Wales came to count its resources in dollars, under a system introduced rapidly by the Governor, with the sanction of the Imperial Government, during a little over two years from May 1822 to September 1824. When Brisbane came, the colony's trade appears to have been flourishing on the

Governor of Van Diemen's Land (Arthur to Horton, September 28, 1824, *Historical Records of Australia*, III, iv, p. 226): "The duties are demanded in dollars at their sterling value (n.b. about 4s. 4d.). The courts exact the dollars at 4s. The Government disbursements are paid in dollars at 5s. The troops are paid in dollars at 4s. 8d., and the colonial salaries in dollars at 4s. Such is the present state of the currency!"

There is no doubt about the two scales of valuation of the dollar by the Commissariat; and troops on colonial duty were generally paid in dollars at 4s. 8d. Again, Brisbane's statement to Bathurst, September 2, 1822, that the Commissariat was paying in dollars at 5s., when because of "large importations" of dollars, the colonial value of the coin stood at 4s. 2d., was answered approvingly by the Minister, March 31, 1823, Bathurst, however, stipulating that wheat should be sold to the Commissariat by tender instead of at a fixed price.

But the confusion was probably not greater than this. *Re* the valuation of salaries, etc., in dollars, Brisbane wrote to Bathurst on February 9, 1825 (I, xi, p. 518), that he had made it a system to make and receive payments in dollars, "and in those cases where it may be necessary to express sterling money, to specify that the dollar shall be taken nominally at 5s." (He added that the contemporary silver value of the dollar was apparently 4s. $3\frac{4}{5}$d.) "The better way to fall in with a (dollar) system which is becoming general" was, he said, to "stipulate that the payment of all taxes, as well as the salaries of public servants and other engagements, shall be made . . . at five shillings."

[1] Brisbane to Bathurst, June 3, 1825; I, xi, p. 624; note, xii, p. 831.

[2] The Dollar Act, 5 Geo. IV, No. 1 (the first Act of the first Legislative Council of New South Wales), was passed on September 28, 1824. It applied to Van Diemen's Land, which had as yet no Council. Note that a public complaint was made to Brisbane that his dollar system might make it hard for farmers to pay their assigned convict servants the £10 a year "which by the ordinance of Government they were compelled to do" (I, x, p. 740).

energy pumped into it by the Treasury bills by which the Imperial Government paid for Macquarie's public works, and by the old means of inflation, the Commissariat fixed maximum price of 10s. a bushel for wheat. Brisbane's problem, immediately, was to reduce the cost of the colonial establishment to the Treasury, and his overvaluation of the dollar in Commissariat payments was evidently a deliberate attempt to bring about such reduction in costs. But his problem was, further, to sustain the extended economic machinery of the extending colony—the scene, from about the time of the passage of the Dollar Act of 1824, of great transactions in landsale. The British Government gave him assistance by approving his abolition of the store receipt system and substitution of dollar payments, and by diminishing the flow of convict transports to be a charge and responsibility to Government. But his drastic imposition of two values on the dollar, according to whether the Commissariat, the chief colonial market, was paying (5s.) or receiving (4s. 2d.) the coin, threw the new economic machinery out of gear, and impeded the Governor in his execution of the expansive policy dictated to him by the Imperial authorities.

Brisbane, thus, imported great quantities of dollars from India early in 1822, soon after taking office as Governor: this with the evident intent of breaking down the structure of guaranteed price on which had rested the commercial relations of Government and producers. In the first half of the year he released these dollars in quantity from the Commissariat, in payment for farmers' wheat and meat—but refused dollars at the Commissariat except at 4s. 2d. valuation—and authorized tax payments to the Colonial Treasury in dollars at 5s. Later in the year he made an open market for Treasury bills, which naturally sold at a premium now that the colony's dollars were effectively deflated in the market, and called in Macquarie's token coinage by paying for tokens at the Macquarie premium. Early in 1823 he ordered that Government accounts should be kept, and Government salaries paid, in dollars.

Of these interesting expedients, those practised first about April and May 1822 demand attention first. At that time, within six months of Brisbane's arrival at Sydney, we find the colony's only bank protesting against the introduction of a dollar instead of a sterling standard at the Commissariat. While there were comparatively few Spanish dollars in the colony the Commissary had accepted them at 5s., equally with the Macquarie tokens, making the Imperial Treasury bear the cost of colonial inflation. But, now that dollars were circulating in quantity, maintenance of the premium value must be at a "ruinous loss" to the Treasury; but Brisbane had no intention of laying an extra burden on the Treasury. His view, in the alternative, that dollars were worth 4s. 2d. for Government to buy, but 5s. for it to sell (to those who had no other market) was, of course, repellent to a commercial community thus required in effect to bear the cost of a change of Government currency policy. For the settler receiving at the store a nominal 10s. for a bushel of his wheat found his two dollars worth only 8s. 4d. outside—or within, if he sought to buy Treasury bills of the Commissary or (after an open market was made) of colonial holders. The resultant premium on Treasury bills hit the importer hard. "Our property is at one blow depreciated at least 20 per cent," the colonists complained,[1] ". . . and it will be impossible for the fluctuating value of that article (n.b. the dollar) according to the demand for it to regulate with any degree of precision the sterling prices of articles." Treasury bills being scarce on the market, and at a premium, as Brisbane pushed his retrenchment programme and deflated the dollar in relation to sterling, the importer would seek specie in which to make his due overseas payments. But there was almost no specie available except in Spanish dollars; and the purchase of these in the colony could be made only at a severe loss. The importer had at credit with the bank (say) 400 dollars, acquired at 5s. But the transfer of that credit could not meet his obligation of £100 at Rio de Janeiro or Calcutta, for,

[1] I, x, p. 739.

when the cashier had paid him his 400 dollars he would still be much short of the number required to buy a £100 Treasury draft. If he sent his dollars as specie, he would find, after having paid freight and brokerage, that he had cleared only £79 3s. 4d. of his debt.[1] In fact, the bank represented to the Government, the old security of sterling standard, made accessible by Macquarie's and his predecessors' inflation of the dollar, was no longer the condition of New South Wales trade. The Colonial Secretary's reply to these representations was a nice essay in evasion. He pointed out that Bank of England notes had been at a discount of 25 per cent in 1814. The New South Wales farmer of that time might have received from the Commissary a £100 Treasury bill for his wheat. But if he wished to make an overseas payment with this, he could convert, in London, only into Bank of England notes, receiving the equivalent of £75 in terms of undepreciated currencies. The bank replied that an indubitable loss in 1814 seemed to provide no adequate reason for enjoyment of a loss in 1822. "We grant," wrote the directors sadly, "that we were among the colonists to whom the 'adventure' alluded to in your letter 'occurred,' and why for that reason should we 'not be the first to exclaim' against an arrangement by which a nearly similar adventure will occur to us? It rather appeals to us that it is for that reason that we should." The bank directors preferred to the introduction of the dollar system that if the Government would not itself carry the burden of its changed policy, at least it should make a direct reduction of the Commissariat price for wheat from 10s., rather than use a subterfuge which deranged the whole exchange economy.

But Brisbane sought Whitehall's endorsement of his method, and, securing it, abolished in 1823 the fixed price system and substituted a free market by requiring farmers to tender their produce. It was September 1824 before the Governor committed himself to the further step of legalizing the dollar by Act. This confirmed his order of February 5, 1823, that

[1] I, x, pp. 730 *et seq.*

Government accounts should be kept in dollars. (In accordance with this practice, Brisbane quoted[1] the 1824 revenue at 167,900.31 3-12 dollars.) But it marked Brisbane's bow to the colonial protest, for as we saw his practice now was to receive payments to Government in dollars at the 5s. valuation. No valuation was named in the Act; such valuation was made in orders, sufficiently. Then for nearly two years until 1826 this double peculiarity characterized the British colony of New South Wales: that its legal tender was the Spanish dollar of Mexico, at a premium on the sterling money of the realm. After the Dollar Act was repealed (*vide* (*c*) *infra*) Government cashiers were instructed to value dollars at 4s. 4d. for reception. By then, Bathurst had sent[2] a large consignment of British silver coins for a new Governor to let into circulation for the redemption of the colony's dollars at their silver value.

Before this came to pass, however, the colonial mercantile community, its confidence restored in 1824 at the expense of the Treasury, was encouraged by notable acts of the policy for an extended New South Wales to plunge vigorously into land and stock dealings, the natural accompaniment of extending settlement. Brisbane's regulations of August 1824 for the sale of land on easy terms were published just before Brisbane vouchsafed the scared business community the ungainly but sufficient reassurance of the Dollar Act. There were buyers forthcoming, before the end of the next year, for 334,000 acres, much of this area having been bought in parcels for a rise; and sheep and cattle were imported and exchanged as local entrepreneurs like Richard Jones and John Macarthur secured and offered the means of using land profitably. Colonial revenue

[1] I, xi, p. 622. Bligh had told the 1812 transportation committee that the dollar was legal tender in New South Wales in his time; theoretically Brisbane's Dollar Act was a *de jure* acceptance of a *de facto* position.

[2] Bathurst wrote to Brisbane on June 5, 1825, notifying him of an Order in Council of March 23rd, fixing at 4s. 4d. the value of the Spanish dollar in all British colonies (this was an error of 2d. in the Treasury calculation of the value of the silver content of the coin), and notifying that £40,000 in British silver was being sent, with "a proportionate supply of copper" (xi, p. 731).

as compared with 1820 doubled, as we noted, in 1825 under the condition of stimulus given to trade. Then, late in 1825, the Australian Agricultural Company began to exploit the princely concessions made under its charter of November 1, 1824. The company bought stock for its great acreage of granted land to the north of Sydney district, and its entering the buying field was an important promoting factor of the "mania for the possession of flocks and herds" which seized the community.[1]

The favourable condition of a policy which gave due weight to a recognition that New South Wales was no longer merely a prison "gave rise," as the first Australian Chamber of Commerce found,[2] "to a spirit of undue speculation, and especially a mania, as it has been called, for building. In the excitement caused by the general success, the production of any profitable articles of export was almost neglected." For a time, the Bank of New South Wales was unable to cope with the rush of speculators seeking accommodation, and the Waterloo Company, a mushroom house to be a model for the landbanks of the 1840's and 1890's, came into being to share in the trade. The Waterloo Company had notes for 16,000 dollars in circulation when it disappeared, as suddenly as it had appeared, in 1826.[3]

The Bank of Australia, which would have a somewhat longer career than the Waterloo Company, was formed in the first half of 1826. But by this time the gay bubble of the colony's first adventure in commercial intemperance was about to

[1] The charter of the Australian Agricultural Co. (*vide* Bathurst to Darling, April 29, 1826, enclosure No. 2, *Historical Records of Australia*, I, xii, pp. 237–238) provided, e.g. that all payments of quit rent by the company (at 30s. per £100 worth of land) could be abrogated after twenty years if by then the Treasury had been "exonerated from a charge equal to £100,000," i.e. by the company's employing convicts.

The reference to a "mania for the possession," etc., is from *Official History of New South Wales*, p. 38.

[2] Chamber of Commerce, Sydney, to Macleay, Colonial Secretary, August 15, 1826; xii, p. 508.

[3] *Vide New South Wales Year Book, 1904–5*, p. 474.

burst; the Bank of New South Wales was in trouble; and the Sydney Chamber of Commerce had to offer the reflection:

"However striking and anomalous it might appear in the hitherto prosperous colony of New South Wales, with large tracts of the finest soil, and a climate and natural resources inferior to no country in the globe, to see its active and intelligent pepulation plunged into difficulties of a pecuniary nature, they are satisfied that such will inevitably be the result unless some immediate aid is given to the commercial community."

The "Old Bank" of New South Wales was the storm centre. In May 1826 it found its situation dire. This time, the chief cause was not, as in May four years earlier, to be ascribed to Government action disruptive of the tentative free economy of the settlement—though Government policy was the immediate cause of crisis. The bank itself had been encouraged to adopt an ultra-generous credit policy by Brisbane's capitulation in 1824 to the pressure of the business people against the dollar system in its first form. Between May 1825 and May 1826 the bank had increased its discounts and note issue to an amount equivalent to ten times its specie capital. On May 9, 1825, its loans on bills amounted to 196,397·3 dollars; on the corresponding date of 1826, to 440,344·9 dollars. With about 125,000 dollars of notes in circulation, it had now 565,000 dollars of its paper out, as compared with a paid up capital of 50,000 dollars and a reserve of dollars varying from 37,780·88 dollars in August 15, 1825, to a maximum of 165,959·36 dollars on January 30, 1826. From the maximum the bank's dollar holdings fell to 4,739·11 dollars on May 10, 1826. More than half the total of bills due to the bank had been issued to three persons, who were liable between them for 249,046 dollars.[1] The position in May was thus that a bank with paid up capital of £12,500 and metallic reserves of about £1,000 was owed £110,000 by persons to whom it had given accom-

[1] *Report* of the Commission of Enquiry into the affairs of the Bank of New South Wales, May 10, 1826, *Historical Records of Australia*, I, xii, pp. 300 *et seq.*

modation (including £60,000 to three persons) and had notes for £30,000 in circulation.

This interesting state of affairs was sharpened by the situation which had resulted in the silver supplies of the bank being tapped, so that in a little more than three months from the end of January 1826 it lost more than 97 per cent of its dollars. Darling had replaced Brisbane in the previous November, and it was known that the Colonial Treasury held a considerable quantity of British silver, some of which had already been put into circulation. An Order in Council of March 1825, declaring the value of the Spanish dollars in all British colonies to be 4s. 4d. (*cf.* 5s. in New South Wales) must soon be made operative in this colony; and the bank's customers were tumbling over each other to get dollars and use them before general realization of the impending depreciation of the currency brought down prices. Treasury bills were again at a premium, as in 1822, in a flight from the dollar. Again, a rival producers' and merchants' group of "pure merinos" was forming the Bank of Australia, and capital subscribed for it was required to take some other form than Bank of New South Wales notes, which the Bank of Australia promoters would not accept in subscription. So on May 10th the old bank had on hand only £2,000 in British silver and gold, £2,000 in rupees, and £1,000 in Spanish dollars, besides £400 in store receipts which could be "consolidated" into sterling in Treasury bills. And how was the bank to recover the £110,000 in bills and mortgages due to it in May–August 1826? "It is supposed by those who profess a knowledge of finance," Darling explained to Whitehall,[1] "that the British money here, £30,000, is not

[1] Darling to Bathurst, May 20, 1826, *ibid.*, p. 298.
Shann finds (*op. cit.*, p. 101) a "boom of 1826," and "a financial crisis which followed. . . ." but is apparently under the impression that the major crisis (after a boom in 1825) happened about 1828–29. "The boom (of 1826)," he writes (p. 102), "may best be described as it appeared to the critical eyes of John Dunmore Lang, the fiery Scots parson whose zeal for Australia, though marred by a bitter sectarianism, burned with a flame that consumed many a sham. . . ." Shann then quotes Dr. Lang's description as it is reproduced in

sufficient to supply the necessary circulating medium and to purchase the means of procuring bills for remittance." It was at any rate clear to the directors of the old bank that their remaining £5,000 specie could not satisfy many further demands for remittable currency, while supporting a £30,000 note issue. In April the bank had appealed to Darling for permission, under the renewed charter granted it by Brisbane on October 11, 1823, to seek £21,000 in fresh capital, to be subscribed by deposit of £30 on each of 700 £50 shares. But Darling, preferring another solution as a means of steering the colony back to sterling according to his instructions, disinterred a Colonial Office instruction of July 31, 1823, which declared against a renewal of the Macquarie charter. Armed with this, he protested his inability to oblige.[1] On July 12, 1826, the Spanish dollar was officially devalued, to 4s. 4d. "A sum little short of £200,000 in promissory notes in the hands of banks and merchants," the Chamber of Commerce reported early in August, "is almost immediately beginning to fall due, and the largest estimate we are enabled to make of the amount of British sterling specie at the present in the whole country would very little exceed £10,000." And some £20,000 left in the colony in dollars at 4s. 4d. would not lift much of this "impending weight of engagements."

Darling's deflation would however be carried out more successfully than Brisbane's, and the banks would survive the crisis.

(c) Reorganization on Sterling, from 1826

Evidently the four or five years 1822–26 had been as eventful in terms of finance as in terms of land. Brisbane had in

Rise, Progress, and Present Position of Trade and Commerce in New South Wales, by Edward Pulsford (1893).

The crux of Dr. Lang's given analysis is perhaps "It pleased Divine Providence to visit the colony in the midst of these speculations with an afflictive drought of nearly three years' continuance, the effect of which, combined with the natural result of the sheep and cattle mania, was to open the eyes of the colonists to their own folly and madness, to blast the golden hopes of thousands and to bring many families to poverty and ruin."

[1] Darling to Bathurst, May 1, 1826; xii, pp. 268–69.

1822–23 tried to establish a dollar currency equated to sterling; in the effort he had, as we saw, perturbed the New South Wales bank and merchants. In 1824 he had seemed to give the dollar a stable value in sterling, and bank and merchants had felt able to share extravagantly in the profits possibly to be derived from the influx of capital encouraged by the contemporary changes in land and emigration policies. This boom was at its height in 1825, by the end of which year the bank backing of speculation had been drawn to an extent much beyond the ability of the colonial currency to reach. Then in early 1826 Darling commenced the process of deflation anew, with the object of banishing the dollar currency and making the internal currency system stand in direct relation to sterling, sweeping away the traditional market support which the Imperial Treasury had long given. The Bank of New South Wales, in its difficulty made acute by the promotion of the Bank of Australia, gave him the opportunity of taking the first large step in the direction desired by Whitehall.

As the Governor had anticipated when he refused the bank's request of April 1826 for permission to gather fresh capital, a second application sought assistance in the form of a direct loan—of £20,000 British silver from the Colonial Treasury. This offered Darling a useful means of getting his silver into circulation, for in the ordinary course he could not issue his silver except to the extent of routine Government expenditure. He made the loan.[1] Clearly, however, further specie supplies would soon be required from England, for much of the silver lent to the Bank of New South Wales would be withdrawn for the purpose of buying Treasury bills to meet the overseas engagements of importers sharing in the tremendous increase of colonial trade.

In the meantime the loan to the Bank of New South Wales in May sufficed to meet the demands of the bank's customers. On July 1st the Bank of Australia was opened for business,

[1] It was repaid within a few months, cf. Darling to Bathurst, February 26, 1827; vol. xiii.

having rescinded its refusal to accept Bank of New South Wales notes as good currency. On July 12th the Legislative Council repealed Brisbane's Dollar Act,[1] declaring 4s. 4d. sterling money full discharge per dollar contracted for in previous engagements, and prohibiting the issue of small notes by the colonial banks. The Bank of New South Wales discounted bills on a more moderate scale, as a condition of Darling's loan to the bank; and now the tide was on the turn to sterling. Still, the reduction of Government expenditure since Darling's arrival (wheat for instance cost the Commissariat an average for 1826 of only 6s. 9d. a bushel, bought by contract),[2] the restriction of bank credit, and the drain throughout the first half of the year of specie to pay for heavy importations of wheat from China, left the colony's finances straitened. So in February 1827 Darling asked[3] for approval of his action in having authorized the Commissariat Department to issue Government notes for £5 and £10, to augment the internal currency. The measure, he said justly, "had the effect of supplying the market with money to the extent required by Government, and prevented the necessity of withdrawing from immediate circulation the coin which had been issued. Had not notes been substituted, the coin would necessarily have been collected, to the great inconvenience of the public at large, by persons having occasion to purchase bills."

The Commissariat notes, issued to the amount of about £6,000, could all be withdrawn in the following year, after the arrival of further British silver; and the plates were destroyed. The expedient retains interest as the first direct issue

---

[1] The Spanish Dollar Act Repeal Act, 7 Geo. IV, No. 3 (*cf.* repeal of the New South Wales Dollar Act in Van Diemen's Land by Act of Van Diemen's Land Council 7 Geo. IV, No. 3). The New South Wales measure was "an Act to repeal an Act, intituled, 'An Act to make promissory notes and bills of exchange payable in Spanish dollars (etc.)' and to promote the circulation of sterling money of Great Britain in New South Wales."

[2] xii, pp. 205 *et seq.*

[3] Darling to Bathurst, February 28, 1827; xiii, pp. 130 *et seq.* The Darling notes, to the value of £6,160, were all redeemed, and the plates destroyed, by

IMPORTATION OF CAPITAL

by Government in Australia of paper money, as Macquarie's 1814 silver token was the first Australian metal coin.

Darling had successfully carried out his instructions under the Order in Council of March 23, 1825,[1] by which the Spanish

January 1828. The dates of issue were October 11, 1826 (£5 notes) and September 20, 1826 (£10 notes). *Vide* xiv, p. 323.

The notes had the form:

```
T   No. ........        NEW SOUTH WALES              No. ........
E
N       By Command of His Excellency Lieutenant-General Ralph Darling,
                           Governor-in-Chief, etc.
P
O            On Demand I promise to pay ................ or Bearer
U                          Ten Pounds Sterling.
N
D          This Note will be received in Exchange for Bills on His
S      Majesty's Treasury on the same terms as British Sterling Money.

S
T                          Commissariat Office,
E                      Sydney, 20th day of September, 1826.
R
L                   (Signed) W. Wemyss, Deputy Commissary-Genl.
I                  (Registered) William Lithgow, Asst. Commy.-Gen.,
N                                              Account Department
G                   (Approved) Ra. Darling.
```

The Minister, Huskisson, approved Darling's action in a despatch of January 17, 1828 (xiii, p. 725), enclosing a Treasury opinion (T. F. Lewis to Hay, *ibid.*, p. 726): ". . . such notes to be in no case in less sums than £5, and to be at all times exchangeable for bills upon this board at the same rate as British silver. This arrangement will prevent their being issued in excess, and will also probably render it unnecessary to resort at any time to the issue of dollars or other foreign coin . . .; and my Lords will take care to cause British silver money to be from time to time sent to New South Wales" (i.e. at times when the currency of Government notes indicated *prima facie* a shortage of internal currency).

[1] Reproduced in *Historical Records of Australia*, I, xi, pp. 637-38: "With a view of securing the circulation of such (British silver and copper) money in those colonies, . . . payment of British silver money to the amount of 4s. 4d. should be considered as equivalent to a Spanish dollar. . . ."

dollar was to be removed, after generations of use, from its customary role as British colonial currency, and British money substituted. His Government notes had supplemented the currency provided through loan to the Bank of New South Wales; and—the loan having been repaid and the notes withdrawn—John Dunmore Lang could express the relief of colonial business men in his conviction that it was "scarcely possible that any such change in the value of property, as was thus so unfortunately and so extensively experienced, (would) ever again occur in this country."[1]

But such prophecy was as ill-founded as Darling's report, in April 1828, that his arrangements for "improving the currency of the colony" had, so soon, "completely succeeded."[2]

For capital continued to pour into New South Wales, with the monied immigrants encouraged by Government, while the colony was being financially articulated; and the old bank and the new bank alike were not to be left out of a sharing of the profits of expansion. The two banks marched in step, and that a quick step, along the roads of colonial expansion. Richard Jones, president of the Bank of New South Wales, kept his ready money in the rival Bank of Australia, as did most of his fellow-directors; and John Macarthur and his fellow-directors of the Bank of Australia could solemnly assure the Governor, at the next crisis of the old bank's affairs, that it was of great advantage to have two banks in Sydney.[3] Like the Bank of Australia, the Bank of New South Wales had set itself, after general recovery in 1827 from the dislocation of business in 1826, to promoting a boom in land and stock. The Government loan to its board had no sooner been repaid than the bank

[1] *An Historical and Statistical Account of New South Wales*, by John Dunmore Lang, i, p. 346; London, 1834.
[2] Darling to Huskisson, April 10, 1828; xiv, p. 136.
[3] *Vide* xii, pp. 296 *et seq.*, and xiv, pp. 549 *et seq.*, for accounts of the early proceedings of the Bank of Australia. Similarly, Darling to Murray, December 29, 1828, and enclosures for details of the Bank of New South Wales's troubles in 1828, and the evidence of directors of both banks.

discarded the policy which Darling had imposed as a condition of loan—a strict limitation of discounts—and after rather more than a year's generous lending its current total of discounted bills was about £40,000; and the Bank of Australia's total, more than £60,000.[1]

This was in April 1828, after the second consecutive summer of intense drought.[2] The summer of 1828, too, turned out to be exceedingly dry. Meagre crops were harvested, many stock died, importation of breadstuffs had to be resorted to again. The banks were called upon to make heavy payments; in December the Bank of New South Wales approached Darling with a request for a loan of £15,000 to tide it over. "An almost universal state of insolvency threatens all classes," Richard Jones wrote[3] in the accustomed hyperbole of an age not used

[1] xiv, pp. 549 *et seq*. Bills amounting to £61,590 1s. 3d. had been discounted by the Bank of Australia.

[2] E.g. Sydney merchants had chartered four ships for Valparaiso and two for the Cape of Good Hope, to buy grain; wheat was at 15s. a bushel in Sydney in June 1828; in that month Darling suspended duties on imported breadstuffs (*vide* Darling to Huskisson, June 20, 1828, xiv, pp. 231–32; *Sydney Gazette*, June 12, June 19, 1828; *The Colony of New South Wales in 1828, passim*).

[3] President Bank of New South Wales to Darling, December 15, 1828; xiv, pp. 557 *et seq*.

Note that Chapter IV of Shann, *op. cit.*, comprises a substantially inaccurate account of "Governor Macquarie's Bank," especially p. 60: ". . . arose the rival Bank of Australia to which many leading officials and squatters adhered, such as ex-President J. T. Campbell, John Oxley and John McArthur. Their knowledge of the inner counsels of the older bank and perhaps its record of independence explain but hardly excuse the partisan line taken by Governor Darling against the Bank of New South Wales. The success of the old bank and the growth of the wool trade were attracting intending competitors from far and near. The promoters of a third bank in Sydney announced that their shareholding lists, in pointed reflection on the 'pure merinos' who founded the Bank of Australia, were to be open to every free colonist. They were persuaded, however, to coalesce with the Bank of New South Wales by the offer of additional shares in it.

"While the terms were under discussion, Darling 'discovered' a despatch (July 1823) forbidding his predecessor to renew the old bank's charter. A run set in. Darling would agree to advance money from the Treasury to ward off panic only on conditions amounting to the compulsory liquidation of the Bank of New South Wales. . . . Even so the damage to its credit seemed likely to be mortal, and a Government loan was accepted in the following year

to the operation of a free exchange economy. It was certainly true that drought and discounted optimism had placed the colony in a difficult situation. In April many of the chief landowners, including two Macarthurs (*vide (a) infra*) had addressed Darling asking for relief from due payments for land and rents, for now "events we neither foresaw nor could control have so disordered the manufacturing and commercial interests in Great Britain that our timber barely pays the expense of transport, and the value of our wool has sunk at least 50 per cent."[1] Darling agreed to extend the landowners' credit, but he was less amiably disposed towards the bank which he had assisted so recently. The representation of the shareholders' hardships is not without its comic interest. "In the letter of the president applying for assistance," Darling wrote, "it is stated that the dividends of last year (n.b. 1827–28) did not exceed half the amount of the previous year, which were at the rate of 35 per cent, and that the dividends of the present year would not be more than $12\frac{1}{2}$ per cent." (Actually, the 1825–26 dividend to June 30, 1826, "the period immediately proceeding our last embarrassment," was 35 per cent—which heightens the effect of this picture of the bank's participation in the woes of a stricken commerce.)

At any rate Darling advanced the required £15,000, but on condition that the bank undertake to close its doors within twelve months; in the meantime a Government nominee would sit on the board of directors.

on the drastic condition that the Bank be wound up within twelve months."
No reference is given to sources for this account except "*Sydney Gazette*, quoted in *View of Premises*, 1907."
Evidently the author has confused the bank's situation of May 1826, and its amelioration with the aid of a loan about which Darling had no qualms, with the bank's situation late in 1828, when a second loan was made with the conditions which Shann mentions. The voluminous correspondence in the records upon each of the three occasions of stress—in 1822, 1826, 1828—makes the course of events perfectly clear. There was no "partisan line" against the Bank of New South Wales, except in so far as the bank weakened its claim on Government goodwill by its policies.

[1] xiv, pp. 207–8.

IMPORTATION OF CAPITAL

But in fact the incessant feeding of the colony with capital from England soon restored the bank after this *malaise* as after the attack of 1826. It lost little time in repaying this second Government loan, nothing more was said about the undertaking to go into liquidation, and by 1830 the Colonial Treasurer was keeping public money (usually about £3,000) in the Bank of New South Wales, as in the Bank of Australia.[1] Both banks, it may be added, had at this stage been given a legal constitution, the Bank of Australia in 1827[2] and the Bank of New South Wales, which lost its limited liability, in 1828.[3] In 1832 the last vestiges of the dollar system were cleared away in New South Wales when an Act [4]authorized the payment in sterling of all fines, forfeitures, and penalties which under Brisbane's system had been legally due in Spanish dollars.

[1] *Cf.* Darling to Murray, September 21, 1830; xv, p. 73.
[2] By Act of Council, 8 Geo. IV, No. 4.   [3] 9 Geo. IV, No. 3.
[4] 2 Wm. IV, No. 6 (March 10, 1832).

Chapter 8

PAUPER EMIGRATION TO NEW SOUTH WALES
FROM 1831

(a) *Parliamentary Representation, 1832*
(b) *Condition of the Working Classes*
(c) *The New Poor Law, 1834*
(d) *Emigration*

THE triumvirate that had dug new channels for England's outward flow after the war had not long to do as one its task of transforming English policies and institutions to meet the new needs of an altered English society. The economic and social currents which Canning, Huskisson, and Peel directed were making now in the early 'thirties towards South America and Australia especially, though as yet North America received more British emigrants than Australia was organized to receive comfortably.

We saw that the three did much to recast and redirect British imperialism. But Canning died in August 1827, after four months as Prime Minister of England and five years in office as leader of the House of Commons, Secretary of State for Foreign Affairs, and, ultimately, Prime Minister. Peel, who had become Home Secretary in 1822, when Canning first led the Commons, withdrew from the Canning group, after five years—and as it fell out, within a few months of the about-to-be Prime Minister's death. It is of peculiar interest that Peel should have been a force in English politics during the quarter-century of national policy change 1822–1846, and always as a Tory. But he, of the three, completed much of the work of the Liberal Tories of the 'twenties: in the 'forties he would clinch their policy by sweeping away the remnants of the corn, tariff, and navigation laws which had protected an older England. Huskisson, unlike Peel, took office in Canning's shortlived Ministry; then, like Peel, in Goderich's Tory Ministry of 1827–28 (which never met Parliament); then in the Duke of Wellington's Ministry (1828–30), from which, however, he resigned in 1829. Next year he died as described (p. 291). Wellington himself fell that year, having lost Tory support by yielding to the new Liberalism's thrust for Catholic emancipation. This was an odd note seemingly on which to sound the knell of a Tory dominance which had lasted two-thirds of a century.

The achievements of the century's first Liberal Government (Lord Grey, 1830–34), and its successors in the 1830's, would be the Reform Act of 1832, the abolition of slavery in British possessions, the first effective Factory Act, municipal reform, and a new Poor Law.[1]

(a) Parliamentary Representation, 1832

We noted somewhat of the early abortive efforts to bring about parliamentary reform: in the late eighteenth century by liberal thinkers in various political allegiances; in the French Revolutionary period by middle class and working class associations; and then, after the war, by the advocacy of radicals in speech, pamphlet, and journal, and again by working class agitation. The machinery of the law ground all this opposition to powder which, however, would still manure the social soil, for in the seventeen or eighteen post-war years before the passage of the Representation of the People Act, 1832, motion after motion for an enquiry into the need for reform was put in the Commons. Thus the young Whig, Lord John Russell,

---

[1] Acts 2 & 3 Wm. IV, cap. 45 (1832), 3 & 4 Wm. IV, cap. 103 (1833), 4 & 5 Wm. IV, cap. 76 (1834) are the titles of the Reform, Factory and Poor Law Amendment Acts in that order. Municipal reform was accomplished under 3 & 4 Wm. IV, cap. 76, 77 (1833, Scotland), 5 & 6 Wm. IV, cap. 76 (1835, England and Wales), and 3 & 4 Vict., cap. 108 (1840, Ireland).

The *Edinburgh Review* contains in No. cxvii, July 1833 (Vol. 58, 1833–34), a good account of the first session of the reformed Parliament.

had moved in 1819 (the year of the Six Acts and the first steamboat) for such an enquiry. The Commons threw out his motion; but in debate on a similar motion by Lord John Russell in 1826 the Radical J. S. Hobhouse produced an enlightening analysis of the effect of some electoral abuses.[1] He said that voting on "great questions" in the Commons during 1821–22 showed that 57 members for open boroughs (of which there were 89 in England and Wales) voted consistently for the Government, but 107 voted consistently in Opposition. The members representing the 99 closed boroughs voted in very different groupings—151 for the Government, 12 against it. He found the composition of the House to be:

Type of Constituency	Number	Number of Members
English county	40	62
Welsh county or city	24	22
English and Welsh open city or borough	89	164
English and Welsh closed city or borough	99	163
Scottish county or borough	33	36
Irish county or borough	65	76
Totals	350	523

(There were 658 members in the House of Commons at this time; those listed were the regular attendants at sessions.) But Earl Grey himself, now Prime Minister and full of years, had as radical young Charles Grey of the 1790's given more striking evidence of the unrepresentative, managed nature of the Commons. Introducing his Representation of the People Bill in 1832, he would not be so forthright as when, in 1793, he presented to the House the petition of the Society of the Friends of the People.[2] This had set out that a majority of the 558 members (before Irish union) were nominees rather than

[1] *Annual Register*, 1826 (*History of Europe*, p. 98); vide Chapter 1 (b) *supra* for a general account of the political system and early attempts at reform.
[2] *Parliamentary History*, 1793, vol. xxx, col. 795.

elected persons: 154 influential persons returned 307 members of the House of Commons; six peers controlled 45 Commons seats.

It was a House similar in constitution to that which had been anathematized by Grey and Hobhouse, which in 1830 rejected Daniel O'Connell's Bill to establish biennial parliaments, vote by ballot, and universal suffrage; twelve members only voted with O'Connell for the Bill.[1] What was the England that the Commons did not represent? In the widening world of manufactures, cotton spinning, and weaving—"the great new raw industry of which everyone was talking"—counted already in 1830, 55,000 to 60,000 power looms, and three years later would count perhaps 100,000 power looms and 450,000 factory and handworkers.[2] Money wages in 1830, having fallen during the half-generation since the war, would remain at their low level for more than half a generation to come—until the mid-century period of expansion in a world enriched by the gold discoveries in California, Victoria, and New South Wales. But there were many who did not work in factories or in towns. "The man of the crowded countryside," resting on this low wage-basis of "comparative stability," was still "the typical Englishman," as Clapham points out; and he was being crowded out, to the worry of Government how to find a dumping ground for him (*vide* Chapter 7 (*a*) *supra*). The census of 1831 showed almost a million families still engaged in farming; they made, together with those working in subsidiary employments, perhaps half the English population.

But, rural or urban of domicile, agricultural or industrial of employment, the "manufacturing and labouring classes," the great majority of the English people, were destined to experience under Government whether Liberal or Tory of the next twenty years, no alleviation of their lot and often a deepening of their misery—excepting only their emigration. Anxious observers had dreaded since the year (1798) of Malthus and Edward Jenner a rising of the poor; they had used violence

[1] Halévy (*1815–30*), p. 282. [2] Clapham, *op. cit.*, i, p. 72.

to prevent it in the 1790's, the first years of the new century, 1811, 1817, 1819, and 1826 notably. So in the 1830's the Liberal supremacy in its turn would use parliament and the courts to stifle protest, and still in 1844 Friedrich Engels (Clapham says: the best informed observer of contemporary English society) would believe social revolution to be imminent.

Such is, barely, the background against which we may best scrutinize the movement of English policy, beginning with the reform struggle. The campaign opened with the return of a Liberal or Whig majority in 1830, after Wellington's fall, and the accession of Grey to office. As has been indicated, it was not a community levelled by the steamroller of an equal and general franchise that Grey sought nowadays, but rather the political recognition of classes which, already of economic significance, ought to be politically significant too. The Whigs' "problem was to satisfy the popular clamour by giving representation to the new industrial towns and by wiping out the most flagrant examples of rotten boroughs, without destroying the old system under which the aristocracy was assured of a prevailing voice in the government. The measure which they brought in was admirably adapted to this purpose."[1] We are told further, "There does not seem to have been any deep interest among the Whigs in genuine reform or in widespread extension of the franchise . . . but in the combined labour and middle class agitation the Whigs saw their opportunity."[2] The opportunity came to a point when the Tory majority returned at the ordinary general election of 1830 made its first business the dismissal of Wellington, who had conceded Catholic emancipation. Grey, with a Whig Cabinet, attained office. Promptly he brought down a Bill for reform of the parliamentary representation. As promptly, Parliament rejected it. (The specific clause on which the House of Commons was obdurate was that providing for a reduction of its membership from 658 to 596.) William IV granted Grey a dissolution; at the general election a Whig majority was returned; and the

[1] *Lords versus Commons*, by Emily Allyn, p. 17; New York, Century Press, 1931.   [2] Dietz, *op. cit.*, p. 473.

Reform Bill, offered again, passed the Commons but was rejected by the Lords, whose power over the Commons by control of so many of the Commons members was threatened by Grey's Bill. A third attempt, coupled with a threat to swamp the House of Lords with new creations, secured the passage of the Reform Act in 1832.

The Act marks an epoch, not perhaps of a struggle towards democracy so much as of the shifting of political emphasis from one propertied class to another. The borough franchise was extended to all occupiers paying £10 per annum rent; the county franchise to 60-year leaseholders and all copyholders paying £10 rent, and to short-term leaseholders and other tenants paying £50 rent. A redistribution of 143 seats was made, to give 22 large towns two members and 20 smaller towns one member each, and to give extra representation to the more populous counties and to Scotland (eight members more) and Ireland (five), the representation of counties in England being increased from 94 to 159 members. The 143 seats for distribution were made available by the disfranchisement of 56 closed boroughs having fewer than 2,000 inhabitants each but sending 111 members in all to Westminster; the reduction from two-member to one-member status of 30 boroughs with fewer than 4,000 inhabitants, and a reduction of the representation of one double borough (Weymouth and Melcombe Regis) which had had four members.

The principal effects of the Act were to iron out those inequalities of the traditional franchise by which poor county freeholders voted whereas rich leaseholders did not, and freeholders voted where copyholders (i.e. landowners with customary but not legal titles) did not; to make the borough franchise a simple qualification of small property (there had been four kinds of qualification before the Act); to increase the electorate by perhaps 455,000[1] persons though some were disfranchised under the new arrangements; to give more adequate representation to the new or more populous towns brought into

[1] This figure is given, without reference to its source, in *The Mechanism of the Modern State*, by J. A. R. Marriott, i, p. 481; Oxford, Clarendon

being chiefly by industrialization; and to terminate the corruption of public life incidental to the traffic in rotten boroughs. Pollard's expressions are nevertheless relevant. "Feudal traditions however," he says[1] of the situation after the Act was passed, "long clung to our franchise law, and with them the theory that it was the land, and not men, which should be represented in Parliament. The 'stake in the country,' which was used in the eighteenth century to defend the monopoly of political power by the landed aristocracy against the claims of mere wealth derived from banking or commerce, was employed in the nineteenth against the claims of intelligent poverty; and some contended that the number of a man's votes should be proportionate to his possessions."[2]

Press, 1927. Marriott writes, "The final and total result was the addition of some 455,000 electors to the roll—an addition which more than tripled the electorate." Marriott's figure may be incorrect. If the addition was 455,000, and more than tripled the electorate ("the electorate" being, presumably, the body of voters in England, Wales, Scotland, and Ireland), the pre-Reform Act electorate must have been about 228,000.

But O. F. Christie, also without giving an authority, states the pre-Reform Act electorate at about 160,000 (including fewer than 4,000 Scottish voters); he says the 1832 Act "added much less than half a million to the register" (*The Transition to Democracy, 1867–1914*, p. 1; London, Routledge, 1934).

C. Seymour gives (in *Electoral Reform in England and Wales*, p. 533; Newhaven, 1915) corrections of figures given by J. Lambert (in article, *The Nineteenth Century*, December 1899). Seymour's corrections are from parliamentary papers. He discounts pre-1832 electoral statistics as "marred by careless compilation or wilful misrepresentation." According to him the electorate, in *England and Wales only*, was 435,391 voters in 1831 and 652,771 in 1833.

Seymour and Lambert, thus, state an increase of the (England and Wales) electorate by about half the 1831 figure; Marriott states an increase of "the electorate" (presumably Great Britain) by about double the 1831 figure. The 1831 electorate, England and Wales only, according to the Seymour and Lambert sources, was almost double the number which Marriott suggests for *all* Britain. Halévy's figure for the total of electors after Reform, a few more than 800,000, is consistent with Seymour's figure for England and Wales only (Halévy, *op. cit.*, iii (*1831–40*), p. 45).

[1] *Op. cit.*, pp. 164–5.
[2] University graduates and occupiers for business purposes of premises in respect of which £10 is paid per annum still (1938) possess a second vote, though never in their home constituency.

Indeed the enfranchisement of 400,000 to 500,000 hitherto voteless persons, in this Great Britain and Ireland of more than 24,000,000 souls, was not a remarkably liberal feat. The Tory Prime Minister of 1785 had undertaken to do something comparable, for some of the nine millions of English, Scots, and Welsh who constituted the population then, when William Pitt was young, and Prime Minister. Pitt's Reform Bill,[1] defeated in the Commons on April 18, 1785, by 248 Tory and Whig votes to 174, had sought "to establish a rule by which the representation should change with the changes of the country," and, in this respect, too, setting Grey a model, to liquidate the evil of traffic in rotten boroughs. At that remote epoch, divided from the severe present by half a century and several wars, Pitt made three attempts at parliamentary reform, his effort culminating in the Bill of 1785, brought down when he was head of the Ministry and 26 years of age. His Bill anticipated most of the principles followed now, so long after, by his youth's contemporary who had outlived him. Pitt would have disfranchised 36 boroughs, to add to the representation of London and the counties, and disfranchised four more to enable the representation of certain large towns. London and the counties would have received 72 additional members, unrepresented towns, eight (this was prior to the great concentration of population in industrial towns which was made chiefly during and after the wars); 20 closed boroughs would have lost each a member to one or other of 20 open boroughs. One hundred seats, thus, would have been re-allotted (out of the contemporary Commons total of 558 seats, compared with Grey's re-allotment of 143 seats out of 658—Irish representation accounting for the increase of total membership). That is, Pitt would have redistributed 18 per cent of seats, Grey redistributed 22 per cent. Pitt's Bill had proposed, too, the extension of the franchise to copyholders (72,000 were to be enfranchised) and some householders, making in all an enlargement of the electorate by 99,000 voters. Pitt would have

[1] *Parliamentary History*, 1785, vol. xxv, cols. 432 *et seq.*

enfranchised an additional 1·1 per cent of the British population, Grey enfranchised 1·9 per cent.

Now, apart from its interest in political history the point of this comparison rests in the implication that the Whig or Liberal Lord Grey's legislation for parliamentary reform was not strikingly more "democratic," less partisan, less in the interest of specific classes of society having economic but not political power, than the Tory Pitt's draft of 1785. There is no reason to question the sincerity of Pitt's declaration that the motive of his proposals was the alteration of representation according to the alteration of population. Nor is there reason to question Grey's sincerity, for he made it clear in the House of Lords that his "Act to amend the representation of *the people* in England and Wales" was not designed for the advancement of representative democracy. In the debate in the Lords on his Bill he "met the objection that this was a dangerous addition to the power of the democracy, and a sacrifice of the agricultural interest," by pointing out that various of the towns to be enfranchised, "so far from being opposed to, were intimately connected with, the landed and agricultural interests. . . . The influence (of) large landed proprietors could not fail to make itself felt in the return of members, although the members so returned would naturally be looked up to as the guardians of the interests of the electors. . . . Let the question (of changed representation) be once satisfactorily set at rest and he was convinced that the legitimate interest of rank, property, and good conduct would be restored."[1]

After all, there was a difference only of judgment, not of attitude in matters essential, between the Liberal Prime Minister's argument and that of the crusted Tory sometime Lord Chancellor, Eldon. During the same debate Lord Eldon said,[2]

[1] *Annual Register*, 1832 (*History of Europe*, p. 103). *Cf.* Butler, *op. cit.*, pp. 26–27; Clapham, *op. cit.*, pp. 66, for the long-continued supremacy of agriculture in English economy.

[2] *Ibid.*, p. 136. Halévy gives a succinct judgment which may dispose of any notion that Grey or the Whig party was interested in working for the democratization of the British political system (*vide Histoire du peuple anglais*

"For forty years I have opposed all plans of reform, because I have seen no plan which in my opinion would improve the condition of the people." This was the judge who in a prosecution of radicals in the 1790's for sedition had made it a damning point that they sought "a representative Parliament." At sixty-eight years of age Grey thought not very differently from this; only he had the wit to see that a democratic clamour could be made the excuse for a reinforcement of the strength of the rising capitalist class in England. Five-sixths of the adult males of England would still lack a vote[1] after Grey's reform, and privilege would still be the basis of the Constitution. But now, by an abolition of the rotten borough system, the Lords' House would lose much of its control over the Commons; yet a Commons strengthened by capitalists who had not necessarily inherited their wealth, would worthily continue the British parliamentary tradition.

Speaking in the Lords on October 4, 1831, eight months before the Reform Bill went through, the Duke of Wellington made no bones about his own view:[2] "It is only by the influ-

au XIXe siècle, iii, de la crise de Reform Bill a l'avènement de Sir Robert Peel (*1830–41*), p. 10; Paris, Hachette, 1923). He says that Grey had long had in consideration a coalition with the ultra-Conservative Wellington, having held aloof when Lord Lansdowne and the Liberal *Edinburgh Review* group supported (1827) Canning's Tory-Liberalism; that since 1822 Grey had shown no interest in parliamentary reform; and that his advocacy in 1830–32 of a measure of reform was dictated by opportunism after the July Revolution in France.

Further, Halévy emphasizes (*ibid.*, p. 12) the class nature of Grey's first Ministry, in which, of a Cabinet of 14, 10 were members of the House of Lords. Of the four Commons in Cabinet, Lord Palmerston and Sir James Graham were great landed proprietors, and the leader of the House, Lord Althorp, was "*l'héritier présomptif de la grande famille de Spencer*" (He afterwards succeeded to the Spencer title and estates). Halévy says: "*Jamais ministère plus aristocratique n'avait gouverné le pays*"—than the Grey Liberal Administration.

[1] *Vide Encyclopaedia Britannica*, article *Parliament*, for an excellent summary of the Reform Act and its political background.

[2] *Parliamentary Debates*, 3rd series, 1831, vol. vii, col. 1,200.

For the events of the passage of the bill through the Lords, William IV's circular advising Opposition peers to absent themselves when the division on the bill was to be taken, etc., *vide* the good digest in *Annual Register*, 1832.

ence of property on the election of members of the House of Commons, and by the influence of the Crown and of this House, and of the influence of the property of the country upon its proceedings, that the great powers of such a body as the House of Commons can be exercised with discretion and safety." It seems from Grey's dissertation on the influence of property that he differed from his Tory predecessor as Prime Minister merely as to the manner in which that influence should be exercised, and by which class of propertied persons. When the Reform Bill had passed the House of Commons (March 23, 1832), the Lords (June 4), and had received the Royal Assent (June 7th), democracy donned no palms. Whigs now were Liberals, Tories were merely Conservatives, but hunger and oppression retained their ancient names. The Reform Bill made no vital change in English society, nor gave it any new direction, other than in reapportioning political power among sections of the propertied minority.

(b) *Condition of the Working Classes*

At any rate the still unrepresented mass of Englishmen were as restless and demonstrative, before long, under Grey's Liberalism as they had been under generations of Tory rulers. When the Tory Sir Robert Peel handed to the Liberal Lord Melbourne the keys of the Home Office, one servant of privilege addressed another. "(Trades unionism was) pointed out to me by Sir Robert Peel, in a conversation I had with him on the then state of the country," Lord Melbourne wrote in September 1831, "as the most formidable difficulty and danger with which we had to contend; and it struck me as well as the rest of His Majesty's servants in the same light."[1] "Trades unionism," a federation of workers in a number of industries and places—as distinct from "trade unionism," an organization of workers in a single industry in one place—was the menacing factor which Government had in view as the greatest potential

[1] *Cit. The History of Trade Unionism*, by Sidney and Beatrice Webb, p. 139; London, Longmans, 1920 edition.

evil: the mass organization of industrial and agricultural labourers. But before the Liberals brought thoroughly to bear on this movement the repressive machinery of State, they had to deal with the less complex situation of a revolt of the unorganized hungry. "On first taking office . . . in November 1830," Trevelyan writes,[1] "the Whigs had been faced with the last 'peasants' rising' in some of the southern counties, to obtain the wage of half a crown a day. The starving agricultural labourers rioted, but shed no blood, and destroyed little property; they were most cruelly punished by the panic-stricken Whigs, who allowed several of them to be hanged and four hundred and fifty of them to be transported to Australia." (The urgency of Goderich's reorientation of New South Wales development, to take "the unemployed British labourers"—a measure ordered almost immediately after the suppression of the riots—is readily understood in that circumstance. The sudden adjustment of Australia which he required, while his colleague, Lord Melbourne, was sending Peel's policemen on his errands to enrol more involuntary emigrants for the Australian convict ships, provides an example of the "interconnection of events" of which Professor Laski is apt to speak.)

But organized workers rather than bewildered rustics with empty bellies, were the bugbear of Whitehall. Experiment on the lines of trades unionism had been made in the two periods of depression preceding the 1830's. The Philanthropic Society and a Manchester trades union had sought, respectively in 1818–19 and 1826, to realize the One Big Union idea which became the goal of trade unionism through the nineteenth and early twentieth centuries. Those early organizations petered out, but in 1834 the trades union attempt was renewed on a large scale, chiefly at Robert Owen's instance. While Grey's

[1] *History of England*, by G. M. Trevelyan, footnote, p. 635; London, Longmans, 1929. *Cf.* Halévy (*1830–41*), p. 13. He writes, after a similar account of Melbourne's proceedings in 1830, "*Quelle singulière entrée de jeu pour un parti qui prétendait avoir l'attitude d'un parti populaire!*"

Poor Law Commission (*vide* (*c*) *infra*) was dragging out its length from 1834 to 1847, laying a relief basis which would serve during the rest of the century, discontents which had been no more than muffled by the repressions of the previous half century became loud once more as the quick, sure reasoning of hunger informed the working classes that Liberalism was concerned to save them from starvation in unemployment, rather than relieve them, in employment, by ensuring adequate wages and satisfactory working conditions. What would become stereotyped as "syndicalist" ideas moved support towards Owen's Grand National Consolidated Trades Union, which was founded in January 1834 as a federation of workingmen's clubs and trade lodges. Within a few weeks this One Big Union had a membership of half a million, including women and agricultural labourers. This was dangerous; and it was violent repression, and not Miss Martineau's arguments,[1] that prevented its growth. Why, workers in Derby had been attempting to conduct a mill of their own, in competition with the capitalist! "Until the last few years," Whig observers noted,[2] "unions among workmen had no other ostensible object than that which was the real one—the establishment or maintenance of a fixed rate of wages in a particular employment. Now the writers of those associations often assume a higher tone; they proclaim war against capitalists in general, and hold out the grand project of dividing profits among the class of producers which at present furnishes labour and

[1] *Cf.* e.g. *The Tendency of Strikes and Sticks to Produce Low Wages*, by Harriet Martineau, *passim*, London, 1834. The rapid disillusionment of working-class sections, early in the life of the reformed Commons, and their accompanying inclination towards extra-parliamentary rather than parliamentary action, were the situations which made a new role for Robert Owen (since the early post-war years he had lost public stature). Halévy writes (*1830–41*), p. 110, of his return to the stage: "*Il avait été en quelque sorte submergé par la grande vague démocratique qui, de 1830 à 1832, avait passé sur l'Angleterre. Maintenant les ouvriers revenaient, désenchantés de l'action politique, séduits de nouveau par l'idée de l'action sociale, . . . de l'action directe.*"

[2] *Edinburgh Review*, No. cxx, pp. 341–2; July 1834.

receives wages—a project which, of course, implies a complete social as well as political revolution." This was not laughable but it was ominous: the "socialism" that appeared before Marx.

Liberalism in power lost no time in indicating the method it would use in meeting this serious challenge to a new manufacturing interest only lately vested in great undertakings. In the winter of 1833 the "Derby turnouts" affected 1,500 workers who were locked out by their employers for refusing to dissociate themselves from their trade union. Next February the G.N.C.T.U. called upon its great membership for a levy of 1s. a member, for aid in Derby. But after four months' dispute the Derby employers carried their point, not without odium to the G.N.C.T.U. Early in March a strike of London gas stokers had been supported by Owen's organization, and a frantic publicity brought inimical eyes of gas-users to bear on the One Big Union. In the same month the conviction of the "Tolpuddle martyrs" gave unionism a serious setback and sounded the knell of the Grand National Consolidated Trades Union.

The Combination Laws had been repealed by the Tory Parliament in 1824, so that the attempt of six labourers of Tollpuddle, Dorset, to form a Friendly Society of Agricultural Labourers was not in itself an offence against the law. But by what the Webbs call "a scandalous perversion of the law" Lord Melbourne found it possible to move against the Dorchester labourers. They were prosecuted under a statute (37 George III, cap. 23) of 1797 against "seditious and illegal confederacies," which had been enacted in the course of the Pitt-Eldon legislative campaign against Liberals, during the war with Revolutionary France. For "administering unlawful oaths" to persons joining their little trade union these labourers (the constitution of whose society declared against violence) were sentenced on March 19, 1834, to seven years' transportation; and a month later Lord Howick (Lord Grey's son), one of the undersecretaries for the colonies, said in the House of Commons that they had sailed for Australia—an instance of expeditious savagery worthy of the Tories who had framed the Act which the Liberals executed.[1]

As the struggle became more intense between the unenfranchised working masses and the Liberals of whom they had hoped much, a Workingmen's Association, succeeding to the G.N.C.T.U. as the centre of proletarian agitation, petitioned the young Queen Victoria (1837) for social justice: "By many monstrous anomalies springing out of the constitution of society, the corruption of Government, and the defective education of mankind, we find the bulk of the nation toiling slaves from birth till death—thousands wanting food, or subsisting on the scantiest pittance."[2] This association had been organized "to seek by every legal means to place all classes of society in possession of equal political and social rights,"[3] and in the year of the petition to the Queen its leader, William Lovett, petitioned the House of Commons for a bill to provide (1) equal representation by equal electoral districts; (2) universal suffrage (including women); (3) annual Parliaments; (4) abolition of the property qualification for membership of the House of Commons; (5) vote by ballot; and (6) payment of members of the House of Commons. Most of these demands were translated into the constitutional practice of England, but only in the seventy years between 1858 and 1928.[4]

[1] For the Dorchester case *vide* Bland, Brown, and Tawney (*Select Documents*), pp. 638 *et seq.*, and the Webbs, *op. cit.*, pp. 135 *et seq.* A concise account of the case, with references to the full range of sources, is in *Injustice Within the Law*, by H. V. Evatt, *passim*; Sydney, Law Book Co., 1937. Mr. Justice Evatt gives in 130 pp., a complete digest of the means used by the Whig Government and magistrates in collaboration, to get a conviction which should be salutary in its effect on workers.

[2] *Cit. Select Documents*, p. 641.   [3] Dietz, *op. cit.*, p. 482.

[4] The Redistribution of Seats Act 1885 met some objections on the score of unequal representation, but there remained many serious anomalies even after the Representation of the People Act 1918.

Universal suffrage was not introduced in England until 1928.

Parliament's life is five years under the 1911 Parliament Act, but the Parliament that passed this Act extended its life until 1918

[*Footnote continued on opposite page.*

At this present (1837) Lord Melbourne's Liberal Ministry gave them short shrift. (Melbourne was Prime Minister, after Grey, in July to November 1834 and then from 1835 to 1841.) The six points became, less the claim for female suffrage, the People's Charter. But, already before the Commons had received Lovett's petition, the reception which such democratic proposals must get from the Liberals had been suggested by Joseph Hume's experience. (Hume sat in the House of Commons on the left wing of the Government party.) He said[1] in April 1834 that he had had "the greatest difficulty in prevailing upon the Ministers not to bring in a bill for putting down the trades unions."

But the working people's resentful front was less obvious, and popular pressure on Melbourne and Peel (Prime Minister from December 1834 to April 1835) was relaxed, during most of 1834–6, for the harvest was good in 1834 and 1835. Times were hard again, from 1837 when Victoria's reign began; and the National Charter Association, which took up the burden of the Workingmen's Associations, won considerable working-class support for Lovett's programme.[2] In the meantime, the experience of the first years of Liberalism in power had not encouraged those in work or those without work. But a trade union leader would recall in 1841 that self-help at least had

The property qualification for membership of the Commons was abolished in 1858.

The secret ballot was introduced by the Ballot Act 1872.

Payment of members was commenced when in 1911 the Asquith Liberal Government brought down in the Annual Appropriation Bill an item for the payment of £400 to each member of the House of Commons; a similar item has been included in each annual Appropriation Bill since.

The Australian Colonies (and the States of the Commonwealth of Australia) anticipated Britain in such reforms, making some of them generations before Britain. [1] *Cit.* Webbs, *op. cit.*, p. 142.

[2] The National Charter Convention of 1839 again petitioned Parliament to accept the Charter. Melbourne's Government had Chartist leaders arrested after riots. A militant section, the Physical Force Chartists, came into activity, and the National Charter Convention of 1842 was a prelude to the "Great Turnout," a general strike of northern textile workers against the new Poor Law and reduction of wages. (*et vide* Clapham, *op. cit.* i).

been forthcoming. "The . . . trades unions," G. J. Holyoake said[1] to unionists at Sheffield, on November 28, 1841, ". . . have generated a love of freedom, have knit together the victims of capital, when masters have forgotten honour and justice, and the world compassion and sympathy. When Government and religion were ranked with the oppressors, unions were the only barriers between the desolation of capital and machines, starvation and the poorhouse." Nor was understanding of the trades union movement confined to its leaders. "Whatever the real effect of trades unionism may be," the greatest organ of Liberal opinion held,[2] "it is quite impossible that while the liberal professions maintain among themselves a minimum rate of remuneration, and while all the landed proprietors in the country are combined in one great union against the consumer, with Parliamentary enactments at their back, any argument can be employed to convince the workmen that they act with injustice, in endeavouring to raise wages by the best means in their power."

It was in the textile districts, as we saw, that living conditions were most abominable and agitation loudest, in the post-war years from 1815. There, where the inventive genius of the eighteenth century was being exploited in great cotton manufactories, poverty was most hateful and a revolutionary spirit rife. Wages had fallen in every trade, but in the cotton industry more than others the steady fall from 1815 to 1830 had meant a disproportionate decline of living standards, for it was in the mill districts of Lancashire and Scotland that mechanization of industry was, still, performing its most painful dislocations of "technological unemployment." Factories had swallowed thousands as low wage workers, then spat them out into worse poverty as child and female labour was found especially profitable. As with the one-time cottage spinner, so now with the weaver. Early in the 1830's, considerably more than 200,000 men, women, and children worked in the cotton mills,

[1] *Cit. Trade Union Documents*, ed. W. Milne Bailey, p. 47; London, Bell, 1929.　　　　[2] *Ed. Rev.*, ccx, vol. 59.

supplying with machine yarn the looms of as many weavers. Nearly a quarter of a million of this great body of more than 400,000 cotton workers were women and girls. And now in their turn the remnant of handicraftsmen who had enjoyed a brief prosperity as mechanization increased the yarn output, were flung aside as the machine completed its assumption of the weaver's role. The power loom was discarding them. Where in 1820 there were 14,000 power looms, in 1833 there were 100,000. "Meanwhile," Clapham writes,[1] "the cotton hand-loom weavers, except those who worked on some specialty, were being crushed out with infinite misery, as the inquiries of 1834 and 1838–41 demonstrated, had demonstration been needed of such a crying national tragedy. The situation had been dangerous in the 'twenties, when Manchester weavers were said to be making, in a good year, 9s. a week and in a bad one 6s. 6d.—if at work."[2]

(c) *The New Poor Law*

Government accepted the situation that industrial towns were crowded, that living conditions in their poor quarters were disgusting, and that an increasing "reserve army of labour" must be kept alive. The Liberals used two principal methods of coping with this situation. One of them—the encouragement of the emigration of the poor which we found Lord Goderich erecting into a system—proved to be of great importance in assisting the development of the Australian

---

[1] *Op. cit.*, i, pp. 551–2, *cf.* Buer, *op. cit.*, p. 57: "Machinery did not finally replace handwork in fine muslins until the decade 1850–60. There was no power loom weaving for wool (as opposed to worsted) until 1839, and wool weaving was not a predominantly machine industry until the '60's."

[2] *Vide, op. cit.*, pp. 39–40, 536 especially, on the question of population concentration at and after this time, *et vide* Hammonds (*Town Labourer*), p. 110, for citation of a graphic picture of the cotton town of Bolton (Lancs) where the average earnings of a family of five were said to total 16s. 10d. a week; *Select Documents*, pp. 519–21, for evidence before the 1840 select committee on the health of towns; Allyn, *op. cit.*, p. 18, for the ravages of cholera in the crowded towns, even in 1831, when there were "50,000 victims."

colonies. The other method, a ministering on the basis of "the poor we have always with us," set itself to "rationalize"—to make as inexpensive as might be to the better off—the misery of the workless who could not, for this or that reason, be shipped away. Such people were costing those who paid the poor rates £6,000,000 or £7,000,000 a year. A new Poor Law (4 and 5 William IV, cap. 76, 1834) tried to put into effect the philosophy of *laissez faire* as it might fit the poor to suit the rich; i.e. the poor must work, if they could find a place between the multiplying machines; or emigrate; or, if they were able-bodied and adopted neither of these courses, starve. Dietz epitomizes the motive of the Liberals' Poor Law: "The new Poor Law of 1834 . . . rejected the old Tudor ideal of the well-ordered State; it renounced the assumption that society was responsible for the individual and ended the system of outdoor relief to workers whose wages were below certain standards."[1] But perhaps it will be found desirable for us to approach this question of poor relief and social responsibility, not from a moral height but on the level ground of expediency in general and cost in particular, as the makers of the Poor Law approached it.

The gravamen of the Act was the appointment of three Commissioners (of whom Sir George Nicholls was chairman) with power to group parishes (the old Poor Law units) for the better administration of relief. Each "Union," or group of parishes, would administer local relief through a Board of Guardians elected by ratepayers. Naturally, in a country still largely agricultural, the volume of poverty varied, in general terms, as the price of bread, and bread prices varied inversely according to the magnitude of the year's harvest. Sir George Nicholls's figures[2] for 1832–4–6 illustrate the working of the first element of this simple formula (see table opposite).

Now this reflected a serious position which though subject to such variations as the figures for those three years convey had not changed materially during the twenty

[1] *Op. cit.*, p. 481.   [2] *History of the English Poor Law*, ii, p. 466.

years which had passed since the peace settlement. Annual payments for poor relief from the rates had usually exceeded the annual payment on sinking fund account of the National Debt;[1] they could rise to an amount equivalent to about one-eighth of the entire national expenditure. Once since the war (in the year 1818) a sum exceeding £9,000,000 had been levied by poor-rating, and actual expenditure on poor relief, calculated per head of the whole population, had reached 13s. 3d. And the machine, which was undercutting workers and casting them on the rates, was gaining

	Population, England and Wales.	Average price of wheat per quarter.	Amount spent from poor rates.	Spent per head of population.
1832	14,105,600	63s. 4d.	£7,036,969	10s.
1834	14,372,000	51s. 11d.	£6,319,255	8s. 9½d.
1836	14,758,000	39s. 5d.	£4,717,630	6s. 4¾d.

ground every year. Not only was it pauperizing the handweavers of Lancashire by tens of thousands, and depriving fathers of their few pence of daily wages in order that their children might tend the machine for fewer pence; but it was making superfluous a proportion of farm labourers in the agricultural south of England; dismissing, too, the many hands of the old workshop-foundries, to recall but some of them to tend the steelworks' great furnaces. Nor was the population static. England, Wales, and Scotland together had gained 1,654,000 population between the first census (1801) and the second (1811); by 1821 another 1,795,000, by 1831 another 2,201,000, had been added to a population which then stood at 16,500,000 (Great Britain). And Ireland housed 7,750,000 more. The increase was most strongly marked in the industrial

[1] *Cf.* e.g. *Annual Register*, 1827 (*History of Europe*, p. 57) and other *Annual Registers* for budget figures, *cf.* Nicholls's figures for poor relief costs.

districts of north-western England, South Wales, and West Scotland.

The basic remedy (or palliative) was found not at home but abroad: 20,900 emigrants had sailed from England (including 485 for Australia) in 1825, in 1832 the total reached 103,140 (including 3,733 for Australia). Henceforward an increasing proportion of British paupers would seek a livelihood in Australia, whither in 1838, for example, 14,000 out of 33,000 emigrants sailed. But the movement of emigrants to the British colonies, including Australia, had as it were its Enabling Acts: measures of English domestic policy. Of these the 1834 Poor Law was among the chief.

With two main purposes the Commissioners began in 1834 to bring the Act into operation. Their purposes were to make the Poor Law administration nationally controllable, through the union system of larger units than the parish, and to secure, by direction of this improved mechanism, that the propertied classes that paid poor rates should not have to support ablebodied persons. Political economy found a neat formula for justification of this motive. "Relief to the ablebodied poor," the *Edinburgh Review*[1] considered, "can only be given (in) one of two ways—either gratuitously, or in exchange for labour. If the former alternative be assumed, is it not clear that the appropriation of any given sum in money must be a proportionate deduction from that fund which would otherwise be expended in employing labour?" It was clear; and the Commissioners went forward strong in the faith of the wage fund of which they were the champions. By the end of 1839 the improved machinery would have brought six-sevenths of the population under the Act.[2] By then, 13,691 of the 14,490 parishes of England were grouped in 583 unions. The boards of guardians of the unions comprised 20,865

[1] No. cxvii.
[2] Thomas Mackay's figures are used in this paragraph. He continued Nicholls's *History* in a vol. iii; London, King, 1899; *vide* pp. 274, 280 especially.

persons, of whom 4,198 sat *ex officio* and the balance were elected. So one object of the Act would be fairly attained within five years.

But that achievement of machinery was to have been preliminary to the second object, the effective use of the machinery. As to this, the historian of the Poor Law tells us that "no complete and classified list of the number of paupers appears to have been drawn up with a view of comparing the effect of the new system with the old"; but he reproduces an illuminating table from the Commissioners' fifth report. This surveyed eight counties in which the system was in force of unions, insistence on poorhouse occupancy on the part of paupers, and refusal of relief to the ablebodied. These eight (farming) counties had counted in the aggregate more than 300,000 paupers, of whom one-third were ablebodied: an appalling record for a small area of that agricultural south which the Secretary of State for War and the Colonies was in 1831–32 particularly anxious to clear of sturdy beggars. So when the new Poor Law machine had done its work, the total of paupers in the eight counties, who were on the union books in March 1839, was 170,000, only one-fifth of whom were ablebodied. Yet 1839 was a year of acute depression and widespread poverty. Now, in every one of the forty counties in which the 1834 Poor Law was operative by 1839, the ablebodied were (in theory at least) denied outdoor relief, but must enter the poorhouse or emigrate. And more than 150,000 emigrated in 1839–40. Still, the unions were at least saving from thieves' kitchens thousands of children "with whose weight the gallows (might have) groaned" had they been born in Pitt's day: at midsummer 1838 there were in 478 union workhouses 42,767 children under sixteen years. Clapham supplies[1] an admirable summary of the modifications which had to be made, during the years of poverty and hardship which followed, of the original intention of the Act. Outdoor relief to the ablebodied, he writes, was never quite dis-

[1] *Op. cit.*, i, pp. 580 *et seq.*

continued; "old habits, dread necessities, and easy compassion had beaten the Commissioners. . . . In the quarter ending Lady Day 1844, 231,000 people were relieved in the workhouses of England and 1,247,000 people outside them. For the corresponding quarter of 1848 the figures were 306,000 and 1,877,000." Such developments lie outside the scope of the present volume; but we are concerned to notice that the situation which the Imperial Government attempted to allay by building an elaborate system of assisted emigration to the Australian colonies—the situation of widespread poverty among the agricultural and industrial working classes of Britain—was a continuing situation, not a transient phenomenon. It would continue to promote a great emigration to developing Australia.

(d) Emigration

From the beginning of the 1820's to the beginning of the 1850's—from European peace to Australian gold—more than three million British were expatriated from the cold neighbourhood of the parish or the union to the warmer colonies which offered them work and bread. Of these, more than 222,000 sailed to Australasia. The new Poor Law, and the auxiliary arrangements which were made in the 'thirties in conjunction with it, brought about the despatch abroad of most of the millions; and Caroline Chisholm could say with force in 1844, "I have always been of opinion that poorhouses and Sunday collections for the poor had an injurious effect, and have looked to emigration as the national way of providing for the redundant population of Great Britain."[1] The Liberal Government looked likewise to emigration. But unlike Mrs. Chisholm it did not now consider that "to establish a well-fed peasantry" in the colonies would be "a Godlike undertaking." It would speed the workless to Australia or elsewhere, and provide some or all of the £15 or £20 required to land a pauper at Sydney Cove; but it no longer contemplated a peasantry

[1] *Cit. Caroline Chisholm*, by Margaret Swann, p. 27.

which might be made out of the waifs of the United Kingdom; there was more money in wool.

The traditional means of skimming off by transportation was by no means neglected in the 'thirties. The years 1833–41 would be years of continuous Liberal administration except for a few months of 1834–5; they were the period, also, of maximum transportation to New South Wales. From 1787 to 1841, more than 83,000 persons (12,000 of them were women) were transported to that colony; 27,000 of them were transported in 1833–41. That is, in about one-sixth part of the period of transportation to New South Wales—and that, the only portion of the period when Liberalism was in power— nearly one-third of transports were sent away. Many more sailed free than under restraint, it is true, during the nine Liberal years—more than 95,000 emigrants went then to Australasia—but we can never know how many of these free persons would have stayed at home, but for the pressure on them of the Liberal Poor Law. Well, there was room for shepherds and hutkeepers and shearers, in pastoral New South Wales.

Conclusion

A PASTORAL ECONOMY IN NEW SOUTH WALES FROM 1834

FROM John Wilson who adventured into the interior of New South Wales in 1798, and George Bass and Matthew Flinders who not long after traced the coastline, a succession of men surveyed the land, seas, and rivers of what would be Australia, the world's premier wool producer. Barrallier, Blaxland, Lawson, Throsby, Oxley, Cunningham, Hume, Hovell, and Sturt, the Hentys, Batman, and Fawkner, were pathfinders whose diverse excursions seem to have reached a common destination with Major Thomas Livingstone Mitchell, Surveyor-General of New South Wales, when he exclaimed, upon a view of "Australia Felix" (Victoria) in 1836, "A land so inviting, and still without inhabitants!"

Behind the explorers and surveyors the Imperial Government stood, sometimes directing, sometimes opposing their enterprise; but, of those enumerated, only the parties of the last three adventured without favour of Government. Similarly, the experiments of John Macarthur and others in sheep-breeding and grazing were sometimes encouraged—as by Camden and Bathurst—and sometimes deplored—as by Portland and Goderich. Then, the third *sine qua non* of an extensive pastoral use of Australia—the provision of capital—was in the 1820's facilitated by the Imperial Government, in the 1830's at once facilitated and deplored.

We have, seemingly, therefore, the situation that alike in its attitude towards exploration and survey, the provision of pastures, and the provision of finance, the Imperial authority kept two faces, while its colonial agent gyrated like a teetotum in the endeavour faithfully to mirror whichever face should be smiling at the moment. When we find that during King's term Whitehall has discouraged and encouraged pastoral enterprise; until late in Macquarie's term ignored it after the brief interest of *circa* 1804; acclaimed it during Brisbane's and fostered it during Darling's term; and then suddenly denounced it; during Bourke's term opposed it determinedly and then eyed it with passionless detachment—when we have acquainted ourselves with such apparent inconsistencies, we seem to perceive an eccentricity or irrationality in Britain's Principal Secretaries of State. After the irritable strictures of Goderich in 1831 upon graziers who "spread themselves over so great an extent of territory," Lord Glenelg, now in 1836 Secretary of State, writes urbanely, "The whole surface of the country exhibits a range of sheep walks which, though not naturally fertile, are yet, when occupied in large masses, of almost unrivalled value for the production of the finest description of wool. . . . The motives which are urging mankind to break through the restraints (of Government policy on unauthorized settlement) are too strong to be encountered with effect by ordinary means. All that remains for the Government in such circumstances is to assume the guidance and direction of enterprise which, though it cannot prevent or retard, it may yet conduct to happy results."

Now the changes of tone between Goderich or Glenelg, or Murray and Goderich, or between the Portland or Bathurst of one year and the Portland or Bathurst of the next, are not in fact indicative of unstable Government policy or of fickle ministers— just as the Macquarie of the post-war years did not "change," though his policy was different, from the Macquarie of the years before Waterloo. What happened, in any of these instances, was that ruling circumstances changed: the emphasis was shifted from one British view of the colony to another view, as British urgency demanded, while in New South Wales a rising local interest, distracted by no such diverse commitments, made undeviatingly towards its object. This seeming peculiarity—really an incident of the ancillary, colonial status which New South

Wales held *vis-à-vis* Britain—has been displayed, in many sections of the foregoing narrative, as the key to understanding of specific situations. Here it needs to be stressed at the moment of noticing the imminent pastoral transformation of Australia, for now the position was that the characteristic Australian economic development—the wool industry—was advanced far enough to cause British policy to drag in its train. Formerly, Australian economy had waited upon British convenience, at least whenever British control was effective; now, the colony had demonstrated conclusively that it had at command that "raw material of import to a manufacturing country as England is," for which Sir Joseph Banks had sighed a generation before.

The sequel was that British policy could no longer contemplate Australia at its imperial will, in terms merely of transportation, or capital investment, or pauper emigration—whichever seemed the most pressing momentary need—but had to heed this established local factor, the productive pastures of Australia. Lord Glenelg's quoted dissertation upon sheep walks is a philosopher's early acceptance of a change in the imperial weather. The change had originated on the Pacific coast of the Australian continent, where hundreds of thousands of sheep grazed.

The year, 1834, of John Macarthur's death was, it happened, the year of effective participation, on the part of English large capital, in Australian pastoral development. The advent from that time of adequate capital supplies made possible a great extension of settlement, the principal features of which were the squatting movement into the New South Wales interior, the migration of squatters from Van Diemen's Land to Port Phillip, and the overland drive of New South Wales squatters into Port Phillip. The boom which the application of capital from 1834 created was indeed the characteristic beginning of the pastoral stage of Australian society. A base was laid then for an Australian economy, and the seven years of the initial process would reveal many features of that economy as it would persist during the coming hundred years. Fifteen years after the commencement of the Australian wool export to England, or two years after the feeding by large English capital began in 1834, the old colony would have a clip of nearly four million pounds' weight of wool, and in 1842 the clip would be nearly ten million pounds.

When we have asked how this gigantic transformation was achieved—of the colony which immediately before the first wool export had packed a year's export surplus of all production into one little ship—we turn naturally for the answer to the histories of the five factors which introduced the pastoral stage. They were, as we have seen, large convict transportation, small capital export, and pauper emigration from Great Britain, and the vindication of New South Wales as a *milieu* suitable for sheepbreeding for fine wool, together with the mood of the English woollens manufacture for a new dependable source of supply. These several developments were brought to a head, and given orientation in terms of the two last-named, in an Act of the New South Wales Legislative Council in 1834.

The Forbes Act (5 William IV, No. 10) of that year was the expression in financial arrangements, of Macarthur's achievement on his runs. This was an "Act for removing doubts respecting the application to New South Wales of the laws and statutes of England relating to usury, and to limit and define the rate of interest which may be recovered when it hath not previously been agreed between the parties." It withheld from New South Wales the application of English limitation of interest rates. The Forbes Act fixed at eight per cent.—*where the contract did not specify otherwise*—the maximum rate of interest which might be recovered at law. In other words, the Act declared that in New South Wales any rate of interest acceptable to the borrower might be charged. The Act is the legislative base of the pastoral extension, and this is as much as to say that it is the economic constitution of Australia. The constitution would be modified from time to time—after the great gold-discoveries of the 1850's, for instance—but it would never be discarded though the Forbes Act and its supreme expression of *laissez faire* pass into oblivion: the Act attracted the capital which was needed to promote the establishment of Australia as a pastoral place.

The inspiration of this measure came from prospective English lenders as well as from New South Wales would-be borrowers, and it is of interest to find in the chief events of a dozen years' history of J. B. Montefiore, a pioneer in the application of English capital to wool-growing, illustration of the early felt effects of the influx of capital after the Forbes Act. Montefiore came to the colony before the end of the 1820's, highly recommended by the Treasury as an investor, and was given a large grant of land on the recommendation of the Colonial Office. Half a dozen years later Montefiore, now well established in the expanding colony, was among the sponsors of the bill which became the Forbes Act. "Capital once brought here can never be withdrawn," he argued before the Legislative Council sub-committee appointed in 1834 to investigate the question of interest rates, "and as the probability is that our exports will exceed our imports, the greater the introduction of capital . . . the greater will be the tendency to preserve the balance of trade. Pass the law to restrict the rate of interest, and you at once destroy the stamina of this colony." Instead, the Council passed a law which in effect removed restrictions on the rate of interest legally chargeable. Early in 1841 Montefiore Brothers, large promoters of the consequent boom in New South Wales, closed their doors in the crisis which ensued. A step corresponding to the Forbes Act policy had been taken in Van Diemen's Land four years earlier. There had been especial need for haste in the younger colony, separated from the New South Wales Government in December 1825 according to section 44 of the 1823 English Act 4 George IV, cap. 96. Van Diemen's Land had like New South Wales experienced economic crisis before 1826 was out, but a good island harvest in 1826 made it possible for producers there to export wheat to the mainland. The Lieutenant-Governor, Colonel George Arthur, complained more than once of the high rates of interest demanded for capital for producers, and the scarcity of capital forthcoming to sustain the declining seal and whale industries. But the colony was short of hands, at this interim of small transportation and the cessation of the flow of immigrant labourers, while New South Wales offered an avid market for island meat and wheat and while Van Diemen's Land pastoralists were mobilizing their resources to take advantage of the further favourable opportunity presented by the expanding wool trade. Somehow these several prospects must be realized: the cry went out for capital, capital at any price, and on April 24, 1830, the new Council of Van Diemen's Land concluded, in ten printed lines, "an Act to prevent doubts as to the application of the statutes of usury" (11 George IV, No. 6).

These important Acts of the Councils of the two Australian colonies soon attracted the English capital investment they invited. As with land, so with money, the meagre history of the convict era became suddenly, marking the era's close, a history of large operations. When the Forbes Act was passed the Bank of New South Wales (founded 1817) and the Bank of Australia (1826) were alone in the banking field. In 1834 the Commercial Banking Company of Sydney opened, and in 1835 the Chartered Bank of Australasia. The Union, Sydney and Port Phillip Banks opened for business in 1839, the year of an increase in the minimum price at which Crown lands might be sold. By 1843 the seven existing banks of deposit and issue—there was a savings bank at Sydney in addition—showed in their returns an aggregate paid up capital of £2,300,955. This compares with £685,527, aggregate at the end of 1838, and a pre-Forbes Act figure of only £84,321 of banking capital.

British capital and Australian economic need were in this way brought into an adjustment roughly satisfactory. We have seen how, of the other characteristic British expressions in Australia, that of emigration varied in kind and quantity from 1792 on, to follow after 1830 (in which year emigration from the British Isles to all destinations passed the 50,000 mark) a channel direct from the English workhouse to the Australian run. Emigration to Australia exceeded 12,000 in the four years 1831–4, a total considerably more than double that of any previous four-year period and equivalent to one-third more than the total for the decade 1821–30. And, if capital and free population exported from Great Britain were finding a satisfactory terminus in Australia at this time, the third main item of British export to the country—the convict—was in the four years 1831–4 sent in quantity exceeding slightly the total of free emigration, though as compared with the figures for 1821–30 the transportation figures for 1831–4 stood in a ratio of 13 : 17, whereas the emigration ratio 1831–4— 1821–30 was 12 : 9. The transportation channel from England to New South Wales carried a steady flow of about three thousand convicts yearly until it was closed in 1840, and the year, 1833, in which it carried its maximum volume (4,136 convicts) was the year in which the emigration channel carried its maximum volume to that date (4,093 emigrants).

The effect of this strange parallelism, of pauper and convict export, was seen dimly as in the long run incompatible with the best return on capital exported to Australia. The House of Commons in 1837 appointed a select committee accordingly, to discover a means of weaving these several threads into a saleable pattern. And the committee in the course of its report stated the position in a quite English way. ". . . The continuance of transportation to the Australian colonies would be inconsistent with the policy of encouraging emigration there, for transportation has a tendency to counteract the moral benefits of emigration, while, on the other hand, emigration tends to deprive transportation of its terrors. Your committee, however, cannot help doubting whether a sufficient supply of free labour will be obtained by the above-mentioned means (n.b. of emigration). For it appears to them, that while the minimum price for obtaining land is so low as 5s. an acre, a labourer can too quickly acquire land by the saving of his high wages, and too readily gratify the desire inherent in all men of independence. A labourer can therefore pass in too short a time from the condition of labourer to that of landowner. This fact was sufficiently proved by the papers laid before your committee. The want of labour is at this moment even greater than it was in 1831, when the existing regulations as to the disposal of land were adopted, notwithstanding the increase, as compared to former years, in the number of convicts and of free labourers who have gone out. This and the immense extent of land which has been sold clearly prove that the restriction on the facility of acquiring it, which was imposed by adopting the system of sale, has not been sufficient for its intended purpose. The price fixed upon land in 1831 appears merely to have been an experiment, and it probably would have been imprudent, by naming a higher price in the first instance, to increase the difficulty of introducing the change in the face of the prejudice which then prevailed against the whole system. If the existing system of transportation be discontinued, it would, in the opinion of your committee, be absolutely necessary to raise the minimum price of land at least to £1 an acre. . . ."

Wakefield's very good advice for the promotion of the colony in a manner to return dividends to England, ought, then, to be followed a little more faithfully—the reasoning was his, though the committee did not quote him. "Though your committee cannot consent to weigh the economical advantages of transportation against its moral evil," the enquirers had said hollowly, yet it must be considered whether prosperity and penalism were necessarily associated elements in the scheme for Australia.

Acting with accustomed promptitude on the committee's report, the imperial authority abolished in 1838 the system of assigning convicts, and by Order in Council of May 1840 discontinued convict transportation to New South Wales; and by order of August 1838 raised the minimum price at which Australian land might be sold, from 5s. to 12s. an acre. But the measures relating to landsale were irrelevant to the local issue inasmuch as the Wakefieldian theory of the concentration of settlement, after which they were fashioned, was inapplicable to the Australian pastoralists' need for wide lands. From 1833 successive Acts of Council sought to grapple with this problem. But the details of this and other contemporary policies during the transformation of Australia do not belong to the present narrative. It suffices to say that the Liberals of the 'thirties, slower than the Tories of the 'twenties to adapt their colonial policies to circumstance, fought like doctrinaires a war against the wool they needed, ceding an occasional armistice when Goderich or Glenelg closed Wakefield's now old-fashioned book. Such vaccilation is, however, very easily understood: New South Wales had been malleable stuff, without characteristic shape, until in the 1830's its sheepbreeders determined its form. New South Wales became Australia then, and enterprise travelled so fast from distant Sydney out to wastes still more remote, that Whitehall could scarcely recognize the land for which it legislated.

TABLE A

SOME ACTS OF PARLIAMENT, 1707–1834, RELATING TO TRANSPORTATION, TRADE, ETC.

Transportation, Prisons, etc.

TITLE	DATE	
6 Anne, c. 11	1707	Transportation of Irish beggars.
4 Geo. I, c. 2	1718	Transportation for felony.
6 Geo. I, c. 23	1720	Transportation for felony.
32 Geo. II, c. 28	1759	Gaol fees.
8 Geo. III, c. 15	1768	Transportation for felony.
14 Geo. III, c. 20	1774	Cleanliness and ventilation of prisons.
14 Geo. III, c. 59	1774	Gaol fees.
16 Geo. III, c. 43	1776	Hulks.
19 Geo. III, c. 74	1779	Penitentiaries.
24 Geo. III, c. 54	1784	Liquor in prisons.
24 Geo. III, c. 61	1784	Power to remit sentences of transportation.
27 Geo. III, c. 2	1787	Transportation to New South Wales.
28 Geo. III, c. 24	1788	Transportation to New South Wales.
30 Geo. III, c. 47	1790	Power of New South Wales Government to remit sentences.
34 Geo. III, c. 84	1794	Approving Bentham's Panopticon system.
43 Geo. III, c. 15	1803	Transportation.
55 Geo. III, c.146	1815	Transportation
56 Geo. III, c. 27	1816	Transportation.
3 Geo. IV, c. 84	1822	Reform of the penal code.
4 Geo. IV, c. 47	1823	Transportation.
4 Geo. IV, c. 64	1823	Reform of the penal code.
4 Geo. IV, c. 82	1823	Transportation.
4 Geo. IV, c. 96	1823	Transportation, Colonial Courts, etc.
5 Geo. IV, c. 19	1824	Reform of the penal code.
5 Geo. IV, c. 84	1824	Assignment of convicts.
6 Geo. IV, c. 69	1825	Re-transportation for colonial offenders.

Poor Relief, Labour Conditions, etc.

11 & 12 Geo. III, c. 30	1772	Workhouses in Ireland.
39 Geo. III, c. 81	1799	Trade union combination prohibited.
39 & 40 Geo. III, c.106	1800	Trade union combination prohibited.
42 Geo. III, c. 87	1802	First Factory Act.
5 Geo. IV. c. 95	1824	Repeal of the Combination Laws.
6 Geo. IV, c. 1	1825	Trade union offences.
4 & 5 Wm. IV, c. 76	1834	New Poor Law.

Civil Liberties

TITLE	DATE	
36 Geo. III, c. 7	1795	Treasonable practices.
36 Geo. III, c. 8	1795	Seditious meetings.
37 Geo. III, c. 23	1797	Seditious confederacies.
38 Geo. III, c. 36	1798	Habeas Corpus suspension.
39 Geo. III, c. 79	1799	Corresponding societies declared unlawful.
57 Geo. III, c. 3	1817	
57 Geo. III, c. 6	1817	Habeas Corpus suspension, seditious meetings, etc.
57 Geo. III, c. 7	1817	
57 Geo. III, c. 19	1817	
60 Geo. III, c. 1	1819	
60 Geo. III, c. 2	1819	
60 Geo. III, c. 4	1819	"The Six Acts"—seditious meetings, seditious libels, etc.
60 Geo. III, c. 6	1819	
60 Geo. III, c. 8	1819	
60 Geo. III, c. 9	1819	
7 & 8 Geo. IV, c. 37	1827	Corrupt practices at House of Commons elections.
10 Geo. IV, c. 1	1829	Suppressing Catholic Association in Ireland.
2 & 3 Wm. IV, c. 45	1832	First Reform Act.
3 & 4 Wm. IV, c. 103	1833	Abolition of Slavery in British possessions.

Trade and Tariffs

TITLE	DATE	
22 Geo. III, c. 82	1782	Burke's Act, committee for trade and foreign plantations.
36 Geo. III, c. 3	1795	Suspending corn duties.
39 Geo. III, c. 87	1799	Suspending corn duties.
43 Geo. III, c. 12	1802	Suspending corn duties.
44 Geo. III, c. 4	1803	Suspending corn duties.
44 Geo. III, c.109	1804	1804 Corn Law.
45 Geo. III, c. 26	1805	Suspending corn duties.
49 Geo. III, c. 23	1809	Suspending corn duties.
50 Geo. III, c. 19	1810	Suspending corn duties.
54 Geo. III, c. 69	1814	Removing restrictions on grain export.
55 Geo. III, c. 26	1815	1815 Corn Law.
59 Geo. III, c. 52	1819	Increasing wool duty (colonial wool).
5 Geo. IV, c. 86	1824	Charter of Australian Agricultural Company.
6 Geo. IV, c. 39	1825	Charter of Van Diemen's Land Company.
6 Geo. IV, c. 76	1825	Charter of Canada Company.
6 Geo. IV, c.114	1825	Huskisson's Reciprocity Act.
7 & 8 Geo. IV, c. 56	1827	Reducing Customs duties on many items.
7 & 8 Geo. IV, c. 62	1827	Suspending corn duties.

SOME ACTS OF PARLIAMENT, 1707–1834

Finance

TITLE	DATE	
44 Geo. III, c. 71	1804	Counterfeiting of Bank of England dollars.
56 Geo. III, c. 68	1816	Minting of gold; token silver coinage.
59 Geo. III, c.114	1819	Peel's Act; resumption of gold payments by Bank.
3 Geo. IV, c. 96	1822	Colonial accounts of England from 1823 required.
4 Geo. IV. c. 96	1823	(Section 8: Governor's taxing powers).
7 Geo. IV, c. 6	1826	Restricting note issue by country banks.
7 Geo. IV, c. 46	1826	Permitting joint stock banking.
9 Geo. IV, c. 83	1828	(Section xxi, etc., permitting colonial Legislative Council's wider financial powers).

TABLE B

SOME GOVERNMENT ORDERS AND ACTS OF COUNCIL, NEW SOUTH WALES AND VAN DIEMEN'S LAND, 1797–1834, RELATING TO CURRENCY, LAND, ETC.

Currency

INSTRUMENT	GOVERNOR	DATE	
Government Order	King	Oct. 1, 1800	Promissory note currency restriction
Government Order	King	Oct. 19, 1800	Valuation of various coins, in colony
Government Order	Macquarie	Feb. 5, 1814	Holey dollars
Government Order	Macquarie	July 8, 1815	Holey dollars
Government Order	Macquarie	Nov. 23, 1816	Promissory note currency restriction
Government Order	Brisbane	May 9, 1822	Rents and duties payable in Spanish dollars
Proclamation	Brisbane	July 25, 1822	Holey dollars
Proclamation	Brisbane	Nov. 15, 1822	Dumps
Government Order	Brisbane	Feb. 5, 1823	Salaries in Spanish dollars, Government accounts
Act of New South Wales Council (5 Geo. IV, No. 1)	Brisbane	1824	Spanish dollars legal tender
Act of New South Wales Council (7 Geo. IV, No. 3)	Darling	1826	Spanish Dollar Act Repeal Act
Act of Van Diemen's Land Council (7 Geo. IV, No. 3)	Arthur	1826	Spanish Dollar Act Repeal Act
Act of New South Wales Council (2 Wm. IV, No. 6)	Bourke	1832	Payments of fines, etc., in Sterling, *vice* Spanish Dollars

Land and Settlement

INSTRUMENT	DATE	GOVERNOR	
Government Order	Sept. 18, 1797	Hunter	Terms of settlement reminder
Government Order	May 5, 1798	Hunter	Assigned servants limited to 2 per officer
Government Order	Aug. 15, 1798	Hunter	Assigned servants limited to 2 per officer
Government Order	Oct. 1, 1800	King	Repeating Order of May 5, 1798
Government Order	Oct. 2, 1800	King	Assigned servants limitation
Government Order	Sept. 10, 1814	Macquarie	Conditions of assigned servants
Government Order	Sept. 7, 1816	Macquarie	Conditions of assigned servants
Act of New South Wales Council (7 Geo. IV, No. 5)	1826	Darling	Colonial penal settlements
Act of New South Wales Council (9 Geo. IV, Nos. 11, 12,	1827	Darling	Pounds and fencing
Act of New South Wales Council (10 Geo. IV, No. 6)	1829	Darling	Resumption of Crown Lands in permissive occupancy
Act of New South Wales Council (4 Wm. IV, No. 10)	1833	Bourke	Crown Lands
Act of New South Wales Council (5 Wm. IV, No. 12)	1834	Bourke	Crown Lands

Finance

Act of New South Wales Council (8 Geo. IV, No. 4)	1827	Darling	Bank of Australia Act
Act of New South Wales Council (9 Geo. IV, No. 3)	1828	Darling	Bank of New South Wales Act
Act of Van Diemen's Land Council (11 Geo. IV, No. 6)	1830	Arthur	Interest rate unrestricted
Act of New South Wales Council (5 Wm. IV, No. 10)	1834	Bourke	Interest rate unrestricted

BIBLIOGRAPHY

N.B.—The list of authorities and sources given below is intended merely as a guide to reading. The chief groups of sources used are given in the Author's Introduction, and more than 1,000 references included in footnotes to the text are intended to be guides to matters of detail. Here the object aimed at is an arrangement of reading by which the student may usefully study Anglo-Australian association at any period within the scope of the present treatment.

Chapters 1 and 2

THE GENESIS OF AUSTRALIAN SETTLEMENT
FIRST PHASE OF THE NEW SOUTH WALES PENAL SETTLEMENT

ÉLIE HALÉVY: *A History of the English People, 1815–1830*. London, 1926.

E. LIPSON: *The Economic History of England*, vol. iii. London, 1931.

J. HOLLAND ROSE: *The Revolutionary and Napoleonic Era, 1789–1815*. Cambridge, 1894.

J. H. CLAPHAM: *An Economic History of Modern Britain*, vol. i. Cambridge, 1926.

R. COUPLAND: *The American Revolution and the British Empire*. London, 1920.

H. E. EGERTON: *A Short History of British Colonial Policy, 1606–1909*. London, 1932 edition.

W. L. MATHIESON: *England in Transition, 1789–1832*. London, 1920.

EMILY ALLYN: *Lords v. Commons*. New York, 1931.

R. L. HILL: *Toryism and the People*. London, 1929.

D. G. BARNES: *A History of the English Corn Laws from 1660–1846*. London, 1930.

W. HASBACH: *The History of the English Agricultural Labourer*. London, 1909.

J. L. and BARBARA HAMMOND: *The Village Labourer, 1760–1832*. London, 1912

J. L. and B. HAMMOND: *The Town Labourer, 1760–1832*. London, 1925.

GEORGE NICHOLLS: *A History of the English Poor Law*, vols. i, ii. London, 1854.

THOMAS MACKAY: *A History of the English Poor Law*, vol. iii. London, 1899.

M. C. BUER: *Health, Wealth, and Population in the Early Days of the Industrial Revolution*. London, 1926.

W. S. THOMPSON: *Population Problems*. New York, 1935 edition.

BIBLIOGRAPHY

W. E. B. LLOYD: *A Hundred Years of Medicine.* London, 1936.

C. CREIGHTON: *A History of Epidemics in Britain (etc.),* vol. ii. Cambridge, 1894.

J. S. SWEENEY: *The Natural Increase of Mankind.* Baltimore, 1926.

A. M. CARR SAUNDERS: *The Population Problem.* Oxford, 1922.

COLEMAN PHILLIPSON: *Three Criminal Law Reformers: Beccaria, Bentham, Romilly.* London, 1923.

G. IVES: *A History of Penal Methods.* London, 1914.

ERNEST SCOTT: Chapters i–iii, *Cambridge History of the British Empire,* vol. vii, part i. Cambridge, 1933.

A. C. V. MELBOURNE: *Early Constitutional Development in Australia: New South Wales, 1788–1856,* chapters i, ii. Oxford, 1934.

G. B. BARTON: *History of New South Wales from the Records,* vol. i. Sydney, 1889.

A. BRITTON: *History of New South Wales from the Records,* vol. ii. Sydney, 1894.

A. E. BLAND, P. A. BROWN, and R. H. TAWNEY: *English Economic History: Select Documents.* London, 1914.

L. G. WICKHAM LEGG: *Select Documents illustrative of the History of the French Revolution,* vol. i. Oxford, 1905.

KENNETH N. BELL and W. P. MORELL: *Select Documents on British Colonial Policy, 1830–1860.* Oxford, 1928.

LORENZO SABINE: *Loyalists of the American Revolution.* Boston, 1864.

THOMAS BATEMAN: *Reports on the Diseases of London.* London, 1819.

JOHN HOWARD: *Account of the Principal Lazarettos in Europe.* London, 1791.

ROBERT OWEN: *The Life of Robert Owen, written by himself,* vols. i, ii. London, 1837.

DANIEL DEFOE: *Works,* Hazlitt's edition. London, 1843.

G. R. PORTER: *The Progress of the Nation in its various social and economical relations from the beginning of the nineteenth century.* London, 1851.

JEREMY BENTHAM: *History of the War between Jeremy Bentham and George III, by one of the belligerents (Works).* London, 1811.

WATKIN TENCH: *A Narrative of the Expedition to Botany Bay.* London, 1789.

WATKIN TENCH: *A Complete Account of the Settlement at Port Jackson.* London, 1793.

DAVID COLLINS: *An Account of the English Colony in New South Wales,* Collier's edition. London, 1910.

THOMAS BAYLY HOWELL: *State Trials,* vol. xxiii. 1794.

JOHN MACDONALD: *Reports of State Trials,* new series, vol. iii, 1831 to 1840. London, 1891.

BRITISH IMPERIALISM AND AUSTRALIA

FREDERICK WATSON: *Historical Records of Australia*, Series I, vol. i.

N.B.—Some histories of Australia which may be read after the records include:—

ARTHUR W. JOSE: *History of Australasia*. Sydney, 1899.

EDWARD JENKS: *A History of the Australasian Colonies*. Cambridge, 1912.

G. W. RUSDEN: *History of Australia*, vol. i. Melbourne, 1897.

EDWARD SHANN: *An Economic History of Australia*. Cambridge, 1930.

Chapter 3

AN ECONOMY OF MONOPOLY IN NEW SOUTH WALES FROM 1793

N.B.—The subject-matter of this chapter has remained almost uninvestigated. Some interesting interpretations and conclusions are, however, made in the following:—

EDWARD SHANN: *Economic History of Australia*, chapter ii.

S. H. ROBERTS: *History of Australian Land Settlement (1788–1920)*, chapter 1. Melbourne, 1924.

S. MACARTHUR ONSLOW: *Early Records of the Macarthurs of Camden*. Sydney, 1914.

These may be read in conjunction with the documents in *Historical Records of Australia*, Series I, vols. i to iv, and Series III, vols. i, ii, and with Collins's *op. cit.* and Britton's *op. cit.*

Chapters 4 and 5

THE DISTURBED ECONOMY OF POST-WAR ENGLAND
TRANSITION TO A FREE ECONOMY IN NEW SOUTH WALES, TO 1921

ÉLIE HALÉVY: *A History of the English People in 1815*. London, 1924.

A. F. FREMANTLE: *England in the Nineteenth Century* (first 2 vols). London, 1930, etc.

J. H. CLAPHAM: *Op. cit.*

H. R. EGERTON, *Op. cit.*

W. L. MATHIESON, *Op. cit.*

GEORGE NICHOLLS: *Op. cit.*

H. O. MEREDITH: *Outline of the Economic History of England*. London, 1908.

A. E. FEAVEARYEAR: *The Pound Sterling: A History of English Money*. Oxford, 1931.

W. A. CARROTHERS: *Emigration from the British Isles*, chapter iv. London, 1929.

ROBERT CHALMERS: *A History of Currency in the British Colonies*. London, 1893.

M. PHILLIPS: *A Colonial Autocracy*. London, 1909.

EDWARD SHANN: *Op cit.*, chapters iii–viii.

R. N. BILLIS and A. S. KENYON: *Pastures New*. Melbourne, 1930.

ERNEST SCOTT: *Cambridge History of the British Empire*, vii, i, chapters iv–v.

S. H. ROBERTS: *Cambridge History of the British Empire*, vii, i, chapter vii.

S. MACARTHUR ONSLOW: *Op. cit.*

GEORGE LEWIS: *Essays on the Administration of Great Britain from 1783 to 1830*. London, 1864.

JEREMY BENTHAM: *Catechism for Parliamentary Reform* (*Works*) London, 1864.

JAMES BONWICK: *Port Phillip Settlement*. London, 1883.

J. T. BIGGE: *Report on the State of the Colony of New South Wales* (*Miscellaneous Parliamentary Papers*).

J. T. BIGGE: *Report on Agriculture and Trade in New South Wales* (*Miscellaneous Parliamentary Papers*).

J. T. BIGGE: Evidence before, Van Diemen's Land: *Historical Records of Australia*, III, iii, pp. 215–508.

Historical Records of Australia, I, v–xi; III, ii–iv.

Edinburgh Review, Weekly Register, Gentleman's Magazine.

Chapters 6 and 7

THE POST-WAR EXPANSION OF ENGLAND, AND FURTHER COLONIZATION IN AUSTRALIA.

IMPORTATION OF CAPITAL INTO AUSTRALIA FROM CIRCA 1822.

N.B.—The subject matter of Chapter 7 is not elsewhere investigated. The English authorities for Chapter 6 include Halévy and Chalmers in list above.

M. PHILLIPS: *Op. cit.*

S. H. ROBERTS: *Cambridge History of the British Empire*, vii, i, chapter vii.

R. C. MILLS: *Colonization of Australia, 1829–1840*. London, 1914.

A. C. STAPLETON: *George Canning and His Times*. London, 1859.

T. R. MALTHUS: *Principles of Political Economy*. London, 1836 edition.

R. W. HORTON: *Inquiry into the Causes and Remedies of Pauperism*. London, 1830.

E. G. WAKEFIELD: *A Letter from Sydney* (1829), Everyman edition.
Historical Records of Australia, I, xi–xv; III, iv–vi.
Sydney Gazette, 1822–1831.
The Colony of New South Wales in 1828 (official).

On the *Further Colonization* section of Chapter 6, some useful material is in:
W. D. FORSYTH: *Governor Arthur's Convict System* (etc.). London, 1935.
J. S. BATTYE: *History of Western Australia.* Oxford, 1924.
JOHN WEST: *History of Tasmania.* Hobart, 1852.

Chapter 8

PAUPER EMIGRATION TO NEW SOUTH WALES FROM 1831.

EMILY ALLYN: *Op. cit.*
W. MILNE BAILEY: *Trade Union Documents.* London, 1929.
GEORGE NICHOLLS: *Op. cit.*, vol. ii.
CLAPHAM: *Op. cit.*
R. L. HILL: *Toryism and the People*, chapter v. London, 1929.
BLAND, BROWN, and TAWNEY: *Op. cit.*
ÉLIE HALÉVY: *Histoire du peuple anglais au XIXe siècle*, iii (*1830–1841*). Paris, 1923.
Encyclopaedia Britannica, article *Parliament*.
Parliamentary Debates, 3rd series.
Sessional Papers of the House of Lords (for 1837–38, Transportation Committee, Land and Emigration Commissioners' Reports).
Edinburgh Review, Gentleman's Magazine, Westminster Review.

INDEX

Addington Henry, Ministry of, and Port Phillip, 20, 132
Admiral Gambier, 198
Agriculture, revolution in English, 42–3, 152–60, 318–19; and British national policy, 247, *et vide Corn Laws*; beginnings of, in N.S.W., 13, 14, 82–91, 97; development of, in N.S.W. (from 1795), 99, 103, 106–8, 114, 119, 198; public, in N.S.W., 82, 85–6, 94, 96, 100, 103, 111, 112, 114, 295, 315, 317; in Tasmania, 277
Allan, David, 213 n
Althorp, Lord, 353 n
American Revolution, effects of, 30 *et seq.*
Ann, 129
Arkwright, Richard, 30, 53
Arndell, Thomas, on Phillip's settlers, 102 n
Arthur, Sir George, and V.D.L. Co., 281; population during Governorship of, 281–2
Ashley, Lord, 235 n
Assigned convicts, condition of, 207–8, 313–14
Assignment system (of convict labour), 49–71, 207, 223, 224, 241, 285, 302, 305, 316, 321, 375
l'Astrolabe, 272
Atlas, 130
Australian Agricultural Company, 280; purchase of wool from Macarthur, 193; chartered, 248, 267; constitution of, 295–6

Bacon, Francis, on transportation, 34
Balmain, William, 102, 109, 115, 119
Banking in England, 168–70, 211 n, 249, 250, *et vide Joint-stock banking*; in N.S.W., 211–12, 303, 325; 330 *et seq.*, 371–3

Bank of Australasia, 373
Bank of Australia, 333, 335, 337, 340, 341, 343, 373
Bank of England, history of, 168; suspension of payments by, 168; resumption of payments by, 182; loss of joint-stock banking monopoly of, 211 n, 249; establishment of branches of, 250
Bank of New South Wales, banknote of (1817), 188; early history of, 208, 211–12, 373; loans to, and vicissitudes of, in 1820's, 303, 330–43; notes of, in circulation (1821), 325; Act of, 343
Banks, Sir Joseph, Matra supported by, 38; on N.S.W., 147, 190–1; and Cowpastures grant, 195
Baring, Alexander, 181, 249
Baring, Frederick, 247 n, 322 n
Barnes, D. G., leading authority on Corn Laws, 22; on Corn Laws, 44, 153, 159
Barns, W., and North Australia, 268
Barrallier, Ensign Francis, explorations of, 199, 271, 368
Bass, George, explorations of, 271, 368
Bateman, Thomas, on health in England, 66
Bathurst, Earl, 214, 219–20, 248, 296–7, 304, 369
Bathurst Plains, 206
Batman, John, 272, 368
Baxter, A. McD., 310 n
Beauchamp, Lord, 37
Bellona, first Aust. immigrants in, 15, 68, 84, 95, 126–7
Bentham, Jeremy, law reformer, 8; *View of the Hard Labour Bill*, 76; *Catechism for Parliamentary Reform*, 172; and *Westminster Review* 251

Berlin decree, 51
Bigge, J. T., commission of, to Australia, 20, 214; and Tas. wool growing, 201; on effect of large transportation, 204–5; on truck wages, 207–8; reports of, 219 *et seq.*; on Macquarie, 220 *et seq.*, 224–5; on Macarthur, 222, 223 *n*; on employing convicts, 223; and Brisbane, 228–9
Blackstone, Judge, 70, 72
Blaxland, Gregory, 137, 199, 368
Blaxland, John, 137
Bligh, Captain William, deposition of, 7; reason for recall of, 17; number of convicts during Governorship of, 17; on immigrants, 137; currency measures of, 144, 210; on Macarthur, 197; proclaims N.S.W. in rebellion, 197; land grants by, 298 *n*
Blücher, Marshal, 157
Blue Mountains, crossing of, 198–9, 272
Boroughs, "closed," "rotten," 39–41, 348
Bourke, Sir Richard, 322, 324, 369
Bourne, Sturges, 181 *n*
Bowen, John, 275, 278
Bremer, Captain J. J. G., 269
Brisbane, Sir Thomas, instructions to, 16, 228; number of convicts arrived during Governorship of, 18, 297, 301; Treasury bills of, 214 *n*, 297; policy of, and Bigge, 228–9; land grants by, 299, 301, 304; and North Australia, 269; Governorship of, 296 *et seq.*; institution of land sale by, 300; Commissariat system of, 328 *n*, 331
Britannia, 150
Brodie, Walter, 82
Broughton, William, 82
Browne, James, 310
Buffalo, 113, 116, 196

Bullion committee, 169
Burdett, Sir Francis, 158, 244
Burke, Edmund, on gaol situation, 29, 36; as Parliamentarian, 42; on Corn Laws, 154

Calcutta, 131, 132, 134, 276
Campbell, J. T., 302 *n*, 341 *n*
Campbell, Robert, 118, 310, 312
Camden, Earl, 120 *n*, 193, 195
Canada, 131
Canada, 29, 33, 186, 262, 265, 293
Canada Company, 264, 267
Canals, 52
Canning, George, 186, 292 *n*.; on a closed borough, 40; and Corn Laws, 158, 247; foreign policy of, 185, 233 *et seq.*, 285 *et seq.*; and banking policy, 249; Prime Minister, 252, 290; and his colleagues, 234, 249, 263, 266, 290–2, 344–5; death of, 344
Capital Punishment, 70–71, 239 *n*, 240
Cartier, Jaques, 33
Cartwright, Major John, 54
Castlereagh, Viscount, 20, 158, 174, 175–7, 180–1, 184, 186
Chamber of Commerce (Sydney), 325, 333
Chartism, 358 *et seq.*
Child labour, 53, 161–3, 167, 246
Chisholm, Caroline, 46, 366
City of Edinburgh, 276
Coal mining (N.S.W.), 149–50, 248
Cobbett, William, 172, 180 *n*, 244, 258–9
Collins, Lieut.-Col. David, on Commissariat market monopoly, 100–101; and Port Phillip, 132–3, 271, 274; and Tasmania, 275 *et seq.*
Collins, William, and whaling, 276–277
Colonial Land and Emigration Commissioners, 254

Colonial revenue, 231-2, 299, 324
Colonies, organs for government of, 208 n, 296 n; currencies of, 144 n, 264, 295
Colonization, British, 29, 33, 67-8, 186-7, 234, 253 et seq.
Combination laws, 56-7, 243
Commercial Banking Co., 373
Commissariat (N.S.W.), rations issued by, 86-7, 89, 91, 96, 107, 113, 119, 120; fixed prices at, 91, 96, 100 n, 107, 114, 213, 295, 331; officers' monopoly at, 100-101, 104, 110; notes (1827), 338-339; separation of V.D.L. branch of, 282 n
Committee for trade and foreign plantations, 195, 208 n, 296 n
Commons, House of, *vide Parliament*
Continental system, 44, 247 n, 248
Congress of Vienna, 175-6
Convicts, number of, transported to, or arrived in, N.S.W., 17-18, 71, 78-9, 120, 121, 122, 127, 129, 202, 204, 216, 226, 297, 301, 316, 319, 367, 374; number of, transported to V.D.L., 278, 281, 319; pardons to, 121, 122, 221; Irish rebel, 129, 130; assignment of labour of, 207, 223-4, 241, 285, 302, 305, 316, 321; et vide Transportation
Cook, Captain James, 30
Cooper, Antony Ashley, *vide Lord Ashley*
Co-operative societies, 251
Co-operative trade union mill, 365
Corresponding societies, 54 et seq.
Coromandel, 131
Corn laws, 155-61, 173, 178, 237, 238, 246, 247
Cort, Henry, 30
Cotton industry, 30, 43, 52-3, 164-7, 360-1
Coulson, Samuel, 162
Countess of Harcourt, 269

Cox, William, 117
Crime, English, 53 n, 69 et seq., 239 et seq., English juvenile, 53 n
Criminal law, English, 69 et seq.
Crompton, Samuel, 30, 53
Cunningham, Allan, 368
Curr, Edward, 280
Currency, British, 182, 249; early, of N.S.W., 115, 140-6, 169, 196, 209, 211, 232, 295, 325 et seq.; early, of V.D.L., 281, 328 n, 338 n
Currency lads, 135, 138, 222, 311 n
Customs duties, etc., in England, 223, 238-9; in N.S.W., 231-2, 238 n

Dalrymple, Sir John, 51
Darling Downs, 200
Darling, Sir Ralph, instructions to, 229; number of convicts arrived during Governorship of, 316; and public farming, 315; Treasury bills of, 214 n, 297, 316; land grants by, 224, 230, 299, 305 et seq.; and New Zealand, 270-1; and Western Port, 272; general policy of, for N.S.W., 301, 317; land regulations by, 302 et seq., 320; and immigration, 305, 321; and the Bank of N.S.W., 335 et seq., 341 et seq.; note issue by, 338-9; recall of, 317
Davidson, Walter, 136, 280, 310
Debt, English public, 168, 169
Defoe, Daniel, on British mineral resources, 51; on population, 59-60
Dodd, Henry Edward, 82, 85
Dollar, Spanish, 141, 143, 146, 209, 232, 264, 281, 325 et seq.
Dollar Act, 281 n, 328 n, 329, 332 n, 338
Dorchester labourers, 180 n, 357-8
Doubleday, Thomas, 58
Dumaresq, Edward, 280
Dundas, Henry, 7, 14, 84

Dunkirk, 73
Dupin, Baron, 165
D'Urville, Dumont, 272
Dutch East India Co., 208

East India Co., 150, 209, 267, 268
East India Co. (Dutch), 208
Eden, William, 72
Eldon, Lord, 54, 55, 56, 174, 352–3
Elizabeth Farm, 117
Ellis, H., 322 n
Emancipees, 224–5, 227–9, 295; et vide Convicts, pardon to
Emu Plains, 317
Emigration, 68, 84, 94, 126–38, 173, 216–17, 241, 242, 252 et seq., 275, 305–6, 313, 319, 361 et seq.
Emigration Commission, 254, 321–322
Enclosure, 30, 45–7, 183
Engels, Friedrich, 244 n, 348
Estremina, 276
Exploration, vide Blue Mountains, Darling Downs, Port Phillip, Bass, Hovell, etc.

Factory Acts, 53, 161
Farmers (N.S.W.), 82–3, 85, 87, 89, 91, 93, 94, 97, 101, 106, 107, 119, 127, 197, 276
Farming, vide Agriculture
Farquhar, Sir Robert, 193
Fawkner, J. P., 368
Fencing Act, 312
Financial legislation, 170, 182, 232
First fleet, 29, 79–81, 83 n
Flanaghan, F., 307–8
Flax, cultivation of, in N.S.W., 148
Flinders, Captain Matthew, explorations of, 273, 368
Forbes, Sir Francis, 242 n
Forbes Act, 371–3
Fothergill, John, 76–7
Foveaux, Joseph, 113, 116, 192, 198
Fox, Charles James, 42
Freeman, Thomas, 82

French Revolution, effects of, 31 et seq.

Gambia, 29
Gaol fund, 231–2
George III, times of, 30; attack on life of, 57
George IV, 285, 286; attack on life of, 173–4
Gerrald, Joseph, 55 n
Glatton, 131, 134, 274
Glenelg, Lord, 369
Goderich, Viscount, Corn Law resolutions moved by, 158; emigration system of, 265, 321; Colonial Secretary of State, 266; Chancellor of the Exchequer, 263; and Wakefield, 266, 321; N.S.W. land regulations of, 318–20, 369; Prime Minister, 345
Gold Standard, 182, 249
Goulburn Plains, 200
Graham, Sir James, 353 n
G.N.C.T.U., 356–7
Grey (Charles), Earl, radical petition of, 39 n, 54, 346–7; Ministry of, 345 et seq.; Reform Bill of, 348 et seq.
Grenville, Lord, 14, 84, 87–8
Grose, Major Francis, 14, 79, 92 et seq., 121, 141

Halévy, Élie, leading authority on nineteenth-century England, 22; on Industrial Revolution, 164; on post-war emigration, 187–8; on effect of repeal of Combination Laws, 244–5; on English Socialists, 251; on Whigs and Democracy, 352 n

Hall, E. S., 311, 314
Hay, R. W., 322 n
Hazlitt, William, 251
Heath, Bridget, 135
Hentys, the, 368

INDEX

Hercules, 130
Hobart, Lord, 114, 122, 131, 134, 149
Hobhouse, J. S., 346
Hoddle, Robert, 314
Hodgskin, Thomas, 251
Hogan, Captain, 134
Hokianga, 270–1
Holy Alliance, 175–7, 184, 235
Holyoake, G. J., 360
Hope, 95
Horton, R. Wilmot, 254–8
Hospitals, condition of English, 64–5, 152 *n*
Housing (in England), 183
Hovell, Captain W. H., 271, 306 *n*, 368
Howard, John, and the hulks, 35; and English gaols, 72, 73; and Penitentiary Act, 77
Howick, Viscount, 322 *n*, 357–8
Hulks, 35, 71–3
Hume, Hamilton, expedition of, to Western Port, 271–2, 368; grant of land to, 306 *n*; other explorations of, 199
Hume, Joseph, on Corn Laws, 158; on trade union legislation, 244, 245, 359; attack of, on Darling's policy, 312 *n*
Hunter, Captain John, instructions to, 16; reason for recall of, 16, 103, 105; arrival of, in N.S.W., 98; Governorship of, 98, *et seq.*; reply to John Macarthur, 100; legislation of, 104–5; and public farming, 100, 110, 111
Huntsman, Benjamin, 30
Hurtado, —, 286
Huskisson, William, and wool duties, 223 *n*, 263; and Navigation Laws, 238, 253, 264, 292; tariff reforms by, 238–9, 247; and banking policy, 249; on Horton's proposal, 258; President, Board of Trade, 234, 239, 263; Colonial Secretary of State, 239, 305; and Western Australia, 283; and N.S.W. note issue, 339 *n*; Reciprocity Act of, 238, 253, 263, 264, 291–2; death of, 291
Hyams, Michael, 307–8

Immigration into Australia, 68, 84, 126–38, 216–17, 297, 305–6, 364
Immigrants, quality of early, 133–8
Industrial Revolution, effects of, 30–32, 59 *et seq.*, 164–6, 178–81
Inoculation, 259 *n*, 347
Inventions, 30, 52–3
Irish immigrants and England, 246, 253, 258; transports and N.S.W., 129–30; unemployed, 257
Iron manufacture in England, 30, 51; ore in N.S.W., 150

Jacobinism, 54, 177, 184, 234
Jamison, "Sir" John, 312
Janssen, Sir Stephen, 70 *n*, 71
Jenner, Edward, 347
John IV, 287
Johnson, Richard, 141
Johnston, George, 113, 116, 197, 198, 201
Joint-stock banking, 168, 249
Jones, Richard, 309, 312, 340, 341
Justinian, 87

Kent, Captain, 113
Kent, Duke of, 172, 181
Keynes, J. M., 244 *n*, 257 *n*
King, Captain P. G., instructions to, 16, 99; reason for recall of, 17, 122–3; and N.S.W. Corps officers 17, 102; on Macarthur, 102, 195; and public farming, 111–14; and officers' trading, 112, *et seq.*; legislation of, 115–16; contract of, with Robert Campbell, 118; land grants by, 119 *n*, 298 *n*; and Port Phillip, 273–4; Administration of, criticized, 123 *n*; and coal mining, 149, 200; successes of, 119, 120, 123 *n*, 124–5, 138

King, P. P., 269
Kitty, 141

Lady Barlow, 144
Lady Nelson, and coal trade, 149; and Western Port survey, 271; and Tasmanian settlement, 275; and N. Australian expedition, 269; and Norfolk I. transfer, 276
Laissez-faire, 251, 315
Land, system of grants of, 14, 88 n, 91, 119 n, 279 n, 297–301, 304, 319; grants of, N.S.W., 13–14, 88–91, 94, 95, 97, 119 n, 203, 217 n, 220–21, 224, 230, 298 n, 301, 305–11; grants of, Tas., 277, 278, 281; grants of, W.A., 284; system of sale of, tender, 300 et seq.; system of sale of, by auction, 318–20, 375
Lang, Dr. J. D., 131 n, 323, 336 n, 340
Lansdowne, Lord, 353 n
Law, John, 268
Lawson, Thomas, Blue Mountains expedition of, 199, 368
Liberty Plains, 84, 127
Lister, William, 64
Lithgow, W., 302 n, 339 n
Liverpool, Lord, 166 n, 177, 209, 246
Liverpool Plains, 200
Lockyer, Major, 283
London Workingmen's Association, 358
Lord Lieut., 277
Lords, House of, vide Parliament
Lovett, William, 358

Macarthur, Elizabeth, 107–8, 109 n
Macarthur family, 189 n, 294, 311
Macarthur, Hannibal, 312
Macarthur, James, 225, 311
Macarthur, John, dispute of, with Bligh, 7; and sheep-breeding, 18–19, 120, 136, 139, 147, 148, 188, 189 et seq., 202, 222–3, 293, 368; first land grant to, 95, 117 n; inspector of public works, 96; King on, 102; and rum traffic, 102; on condition of colony, 108–9; Duke of Portland on, 117; and Elizabeth Farm, 117; duel of, with Paterson, 117; arrest of (1801), 117; sent to England (1801), 192, (1809), 198; and N.S.W. Corps rebellion, 197; settlers' and Bligh's opinions of, 197; in exile, 198; and Macquarie, 200 et seq., 218, 219; and Tas. wool growing, 202; Bigge's opinion of, 222, 223 n; political outlook of, 225; landholdings of, 119, 195; return of, to Sydney (1805), 117 n, 125, 136; James Macarthur's opinion of, 225; praises Darling, 312; director, Bank of Australia, 340, 341 n; Colonial Secretary, 197; death of, 370
Macdonald, A., 37
Machine wrecking, 172
Mackintosh, Sir James, 184, 240
Macquarie, Lachlan, instructions to, 16; reason for recall of, 17–18; number of convicts arrived during Governorship of, 17, 18, 202, 297; and immigrants, 137–8, 217, 297; appointment of, 198; and extension of settlement, 198–200; and Macarthur, 200 et seq.; and wool growing, 201, 202; achievements of, 202 et seq., 214 et seq., 227 et seq., 293, 296–7, 369; land grants by, 203, 217 n, 222, 298 n; and public works, 203, 205, 206, 212, 225, 329; and colonial finance, 142, 208, 209 et seq., 231–2, 329; assignment regulations of, 207; and "emancipations," 221, 225; Bigge's opinion of, 224–5; departure of, for England, 296; and Government livestock, 315 n

INDEX

Malthus, Thomas Robert, 181 n, on population, 58-61, 64, 157, 256; on Corn Law policy, 158; Cobbett on, 259; Owen on, 64; on emigration, 256
Manufactures, growth of British, 160-7, 247, 360-1
Margarot, Maurice, 55 n, 109 n
Marsden, Samuel, 102, 118, 220
Marx, Karl, 77, 244, 357
Mary Anne, 128 n
Marylebone, parish emigration schemes, 258
Matra, James Maria, 38
McQueen, Col. T. P., 283
Melbourne, Lord, 235 n, 354 et seq.
Merino Sheep and Wool, 192 et seq., 201-2, 222, 277-78, 280, 309
Millbank penitentiary, 77
Minerva, 142
Minimum wage, Bill for a, 59 n, 153
Minorca, 131
Mitchell, Major T. L., 314, 368
Montefiore, J. B., 309-10, 372
Montfort, Denys de, 35
Mountgarrett, Jacob, 275
Muir, Thomas, 54, 55 n
Murdoch, Peter, 280
Murray, Sir George, 283, 315
Murray, Lieut., 274

Napoleon I, continental system of, 44, 247 n, 248; Berlin decree of, 51; First Consul, Emperor, 155; sent to Elba, 157, 175; and the 100 Days, 175
National Charter Association, 359
Navigation laws, 238, 292
Newgate gaol, 36
New South Wales, population of, *vide Population*; exploration and settlement of, *vide Settlement* and under names of explorers; trade of, 270-1, 307, 314-15, et *vide Wool*; wool growing in, *vide Wool*; land granted in, *vide* under names of Governors; currency of, *vide Currency*
N.S.W. Act (1823), 232, 241
N.S.W. Corps, officers of, 92, 101, 105, 115-18, 193, 196; Administration (1792-95), 90-8, 105, 106 (1808-9), 196-8
New Zealand, 262, Sydney trade with, 270-1
N.Z. Company, 267, 270
Nicholls, Sir George, 362
Nile, 131
Norfolk Island, penal settlement of, 86, 87, 89, 113; evacuation of farmers from, 275-6; N.S.W. penal settlement at, 317
North Australia settlements, 269-70
Northumberland, Duke of, 201
Nowlan, Timothy, 280

Oastler, Richard, 235 n
Ocean, 131, 132, 275
O'Connell, Daniel, 347
O'Connor, Roderic, 280
O'Neil, Peter, 129
Orphan fund, 231-2
Owen, Robert, on social causes of crime, 50; on Malthus, 64, 66; evidence of, before 1816 committee, 912; *Essays* of, 162, 163; labour colonies plan of, 171-2, 181; and co-operative movement, 251-2; and trade unionism, 355-7

Paine, Tom, 55 n
Palmer, John, 81, 116, 197, 198, 278 n
Palmer, Thomas, 55
Palmerston, Lord, 353 n
Panopticon system, 76
Park, Mungo, 191
Parliament, constitution of, before 1832, 39-43, 345-6; reform of, advocated, 41-2, 54, 179-80, 346 et seq., 358
Parnell, Sir Henry, 156, 157

Pasteur, Louis, 64
Paterson, William, 97, 98, 113, 116, 117, 198, 201
Pedro of Brazil, 287
Peel River Estate flock, 193
Peel, Sir Robert, jun., and Joseph Swann, 180 n; 1819 Act of, 182; circular of, for emigrants, 216–17; Home Secretary, 234; cousin of Thomas Peel, 263; reform of criminal law by, 239–41; and Acts for N.S.W., 241, 264; and transportation, 241 n; on Horton's proposal, 258; and John Wild, 241 n; and banking policy, 249; and Canning, 234, 264, 290–1; succeeded by Lord Melbourne, 354; opinion of, on trade unionism, 354; Prime Minister, 359
Peel, Sir Robert, sen., 161
Peel, Thomas, and W.A., 262–3, 283–4
Peel's Act, 182
Penal code of England, 70 et seq., 238–42
Permissive occupancy, 302, 310
Perseus, 131
Peterloo, 179
Petitions, on the Corn Laws, 157, 160–1; of N.S.W. farmers, 106, 107
Philanthropic Society, 355
Phillip, Captain Arthur, 7; instructions to, 13, 38, 79, 82, 148; number of convicts arrived during Governorship of, 17, 78; landing of, at Sydney, 29; Governorship of, 78 et seq.; land grants by, 85, 88, 89, 97, 103; and public farming, 82, 83, 85, 86, 89, 111; on currency, 141
Pitt, William, 7; Prime Minister, 29; on parliamentary corruption, 41; Reform Bills of, 41–2, 181 n, 351, 352; and wartime reform movements, 54, 56, 181; and committee on corn, 153; policies of, 153 et seq.; death of, 155
Place, Francis, 244
Police fund, 231–2
Poor Law (1834), 356, 361–7
Poor relief, English methods of, 47 et seq., 153, 356, 361–7; cost of, 50, 173, 243; Robert Owen's plan of, 171–3, 181
Population, theories of, 58 et seq.; of U.K., 30, 363; circumstances of increase of, 59 et seq., 256; of N.S.W., 38 n, 80, 86, 87, 94, 119, 120, 138, 202–3, 206, 216, 221–2, 299; of N.S.W., native-born, 135, 138; of Tasmania, 275, 277
Porpoise, 143, 145, 149, 276
Portland, Duke of, 100, 101, 105, 117, 369
Port Macquarie, 317
Port Phillip, 132–3, 200, 267, 271–2, 274
Port Phillip Bank, 373
Pounds Act, 312
Power loom, 53, 166, 361
Prisons, condition of English, 36, 71–3, 76–7
Property wage, 143, 207–8
Public debt, 168, 169
Public expenditure, U.K., 168; N.S.W., 213, 214 n, 297, 301, 316
Public health, 61–7, 151–2
Public works, N.S.W., 203, 205, 206, 295
Punishment, English methods of, 70 et seq.; N.S.W. methods of, 70 n, 241, 317

Quit-rents, 299, 303, 321

Ratcliffe, William, 52
Raffles, Sir T. S., 268
Raine, Thomas, 272
Reciprocity Act, 238, 253, 264, 291–2

INDEX

Reeves, John, 54, 55
Reform Bills of Grey, 348 et seq.; of O'Connell, 347; of Pitt, 41-2, 181 n, 351-2; of Russell, 179-80, 346
Reilly, Alexander, 135, 278
Ricardo, David, 169, 240, 244 n
Rice, cultivation of, N.S.W., 149
Rice, Spring, 265
Richmond, Lord, 322 n
Robbins, Charles, 271
Robinson ("Prosperity") Frederick, vide Goderich
Romilly, Sir Samuel, 70
Ross, Major, 86
Rounds system, 50
Rowley, Capt. William, 118
Royal Admiral, 143, 145, 241 n
Royal Marines (in N.S.W.), 29, 82, 84, 88, 92, 127, 191
Rum trade (in N.S.W.), 95, 96, 101, 102, 110, 111, 112, 115, 231
Russell, Lord John, 177, 179, 180, 346

Sadler, Michael Thomas, 58, 235 n
Samarang, 209
Scarlett, Sir James, 181 n, 259, 290
Schenley, E. W. H., 283
Scottish Martyrs, 54, 55 n, 84 n, 109 n
Settlement, extension of N.S.W., 86, 89, 95, 97, 99, 103, 131, 132, 149, 199, 200, 230
Shaftesbury, Earl of, vide Ashley
Sheep, importation of, by Macarthur, 191, 192, 193; Foveaux-Macarthur transaction in, 192 n; breeding of, by Macarthur, vide Macarthur, John; number of, in N.S.W., 193, 195, 196, 197, 222, 224; in Tasmania, 201, 277; breeds of, 191-93, 201; et vide Merino Sheep and Wool
Sheffield, Lord, 34, 158
Singapore, purchase of, 268
Sirius, 81, 86

Six Acts, 180-1
Skirving, William, 55 n
Slavery in British colonies, 284-5
Sligo, Marquis of, 310
Smith, Adam, 34, 56 n
Smith, Sydney, 181
Socialism (English), 251
Sorell, William, 202 n, 213 n, 281
South Australia, 263
Spanish dollar, vide Dollar, Spanish
Speenhamland system, 47-50, 54, 153
Stirling Castle, 323
Stirling, Capt. James, 270, 283, 284
Sturt, Capt. Charles, 368
Success, 269
Sufficient price, 261-2
Supply, 86, 87
Swann, Joseph, 180 n
Swan River Settlement, 262, 282-284
Sydney Bank, 373
Sydney Chamber of Commerce, 325, 333
Sydney, Lord, 29

Tamar, 269, 270
Tasmania, separation of from N.S.W., 241, 372; wool growing in, 201-2, 277-78, 280; settlement of 273-82; immigration into, 275, 279; land granted in, 277, 278, 281; currency of, 281, 328 n, 338 n; population of, 275, 277; 1830 Act in, 372-3
Taxation, in England, 1815, 169
Tench, Capt. Watkin, 127
Thompson, William, 251
Thomson, Poulett, 235 n
Throsby, Charles, explorations of, 199, 368
Thynne, 109
Tickets of occupation, 302
Tolpuddle Martyrs, 180 n, 357-8
Tooke, Horne, 54
Tooke, William, 181